GED

Vocabulary
3000

OFFICIAL Test Prep

Contents

Introduction

Welcome to **GED Vocabulary 3000!** This product is a vocabulary builder designed to help you increase your vocabulary and earn a higher score on the exam. The words in these lists have been selected from a group of high frequency words that have appeared on previous exams.

This audiobook contains 3000 vocabulary words grouped into blocks of 100 words. These words are grouped into three levels: easy, medium, and hard. Each word is spelled out, and defined. Additionally, to better help you understand the word, several synonyms and antonyms are provided, as well as a sentence exemplifying how the word is used. For example, for the word "essential," you will first see the spelling of the word. Next, you will see the definition, "a quality or part needed to make something what it is." This is followed by the synonyms, "crucial" and "fundamental" and the antonyms, "inessential" and "unnecessary." Finally, you will see an example sentence: "good food is essential to a healthy lifestyle."

It is best to study these words in groups of 100 at time, so as not to overwhelm yourself with too many words at once. As you study, be sure to take frequent breaks. Additionally, as you study and become more familiar with the words in a section, begin to challenge yourself.

Don't forget that learning new words takes time and dedication. However, with a little help from this book, you will be on your way to learning more vocabulary and earning a higher score on the exam.

Vocabulary

Easy Words Exercise - 1

1. AFFAIR - *[spell]*- A F F A I R
    Definition: a private matter
    Synonym:
    Antonym:
    Sentence: He decided that his affairs were none of his mother's business.

2. REALIST- *[spell]*- R E A L I S T
    Definition: person interested in what is real rather than what is imaginary or theoretical
    Synonym: pragmatist
    Antonym:
    Sentence: He considered himself too much of a realist to entertain such fanciful ideas.

3. INSULTING - *[spell]*- I N S U L T I N G
    Definition: something that is said scornfully, rudely, or offensively
    Synonym: abusive, derogatory
    Antonym: complimentary, kind
    Sentence: His comments were insulting to her character.

4. OBSESSIVE- *[spell]*- O B S E S S I V E
    Definition: having to do with or causing to be obsessed (keep the attention of to an unreasonable or unhealthy extent)
    Synonym: compulsive
    Antonym:
    Sentence: His attitude toward her was somewhat obsessive.

5. SLEIGH - *[spell]*- S L E I G H
    Definition: carriage or cart used on ice and snow
    Synonym:
    Antonym:
    Sentence: A horse drove the sleigh through the snow.

6. IMMORAL - *[spell]*- I M M O R A L
    Definition: wrong or wicked
    Synonym: evil, degenerate
    Antonym: ethical, honest
    Sentence: The politician's immoral actions caused him to lose his office.

7.   REINFORCEMENT- *[spell]-* R E I N F O R C E M E N T
     Definition: act of strengthening with new force or materials
     Synonym: support, brace
     Antonym:
     Sentence: The beam added reinforcement to the ceiling of the building.

8.   COLLISION - *[spell]-* C O L L I S I O N
     Definition: a violent rushing against
     Synonym: concussion, impact
     Antonym:
     Sentence: The collision of the cars damaged both vehicles.

9.   SUBSTITUTE - *[spell]-* S U B S T I T U T E
     Definition: a person or thing serving in another's place
     Synonym: alternative, backup
     Antonym:
     Sentence: Cramming is a poor substitute for dedicated and rigorous study.

10. ABSENTEE- *[spell]-* A B S E N T E E
     Definition: a person who is not present
     Synonym:
     Antonym:
     Sentence: Absentees from the meeting were sent information packets to
     fill them in on what they missed.

11. SEGMENTAL - *[spell]-* S E G M E N T A L
     Definition: composed of pieces or separated parts
     Synonym: divided, fragmented
     Antonym:
     Sentence: An ant has a segmental body.

12. COMPARATIVE - *[spell]-* C O M P A R A T I V E
     Definition: measured by examining similarities and differences
     Synonym: correlative, relative
     Antonym: unqualified, absolute
     Sentence: She did a comparative study of American and British literature.

13. ALLOTMENT - *[spell]-* A L L O T M E N T
     Definition: division into parts or shares
     Synonym: allocation, allowance
     Antonym: whole
     Sentence: Everyone at the party was given an allotment of the cake.

14. INKLING - *[spell]-* I N K L I N G
     Definition: a vague notion
     Synonym: idea, clue

Antonym:
Sentence: She had an inkling that her boyfriend would propose to her over the weekend.

15. SESSION - *[spell]*- S E S S I O N
Definition: a sitting or meeting of a court, counsel, legislature, etc.
Synonym: gathering, conference
Antonym:
Sentence: The conference was made up of several different sessions on different topics.

16. CONFECTION - *[spell]*- C O N F E C T I O N
Definition: piece of candy or something sweet
Synonym: dessert, pastry
Antonym:
Sentence: She made a delicate confection of chocolate and coconut.

17. EXPERIMENT - *[spell]*- E X P E R I M E N T
Definition: trying something in order to find out about it
Synonym: test, trial
Antonym:
Sentence: He created an experiment to find out if he did indeed have a rodent problem.

18. INDIVIDUAL - *[spell]*- I N D I V I D U A L
Definition: a person
Synonym: entity, being
Antonym:
Sentence: He is certainly a unique individual.

19. COLLECTIBLE - *[spell]*- C O L L E C T I B L E
Definition: an object considered suitable for a collection
Synonym:
Antonym:
Sentence: The toys that come in children's meals at McDonald's are considered to be collectibles by some.

20. ARCTIC - *[spell]*- A R C T I C
Definition: extremely cold
Synonym: frigid, glacial
Antonym: warm, tropic
Sentence: She strongly disliked the arctic feel of winter.

21. TANGLE - *[spell]*- T A N G L E
Definition: to twist and twine together in a tangled mass
Synonym: twisted, knotted

Antonym:
Sentence: She brushed her hair because it had become tangled.

22. SCORE - *[spell]*- S C O R E
Definition: the record of points made in a game, contest, or test
Synonym: count, record
Antonym:
Sentence: The score of the game was completely unpredictable.

23. REBELLIOUS- *[spell]*- R E B E L L I O U S
Definition: defying authority
Synonym: disobedient, unmanageable
Antonym: obedient, compliant
Sentence: The teenager seemed to be going through a rebellious stage.

24. SPARE - *[spell]*- S P A R E
Definition: show mercy to
Synonym: forgive, pardon
Antonym:
Sentence: The general spared the life of the enemy soldiers.

25. FRECKLED - *[spell]*- F R E C K L E D
Definition: marked with light brown spots on the skin
Synonym: mottled, speckled
Antonym:
Sentence: The boy's face and shoulders were freckled from the sun.

26. ABDUCTOR- *[spell]*-A B D U C T O R
Definition: a person who steals someone
Synonym: kidnapper, hijacker
Antonym:
Sentence: The abductor agreed to return the stolen child in return for a ransom.

27. MYTHOLOGY - *[spell]*- M Y T H O L O G Y
Definition: group of myths relating to a particular country or person
Synonym: lore, fables
Antonym:
Sentence: Many students study Greek and Roman mythology in school.

28. REVAMP- *[spell]*- R E V A M P
Definition: to patch up or repair
Synonym: repair, overhaul
Antonym:
Sentence: She decided she needed to revamp her office.

29. EXCELLENCY - *[spell]*- E X C E L L E N C Y
Definition: unusually good quality
Synonym: greatness, merit
Antonym: deficiency, inferiority
Sentence: Her Excellency in the field of science gained her much recognition.

30. RUBBERNECK - *[spell]*- R U B B E R N E C K
Definition: person who stares and gapes, especially as a tourist
Synonym:
Antonym:
Sentence: The man got into an accident when he was rubbernecking while driving.

31. ROMANCE - *[spell]*- R O M A N C E
Definition: a love story
Synonym:
Antonym:
Sentence: She enjoyed reading a romance on some occasions.

32. ARROGANCE - *[spell]*- A R R O G A N C E
Definition: excessive pride
Synonym: haughtiness, egotism
Antonym: humility, modesty
Sentence: His arrogance was disliked by many.

33. PREFERMENT- *[spell]*- P R E F E R M E N T
Definition: advancement or promotion
Synonym: improvement, upgrading
Antonym: downgrade, regression
Sentence: He was given preferment after working for fifteen years for the company.

34. BYSTANDER - *[spell]*- B Y S T A N D E R
Definition: a person who looks on but does not take part
Synonym: onlooker, spectator
Antonym: participant, player
Sentence: The bystanders at the game offered support by cheering the team on.

35. RECEIVABLE- *[spell]*- R E C E I V A B L E
Definition: fit for acceptance
Synonym: acceptable, collectible
Antonym: unacceptable
Sentence: The flowers she ordered were not receivable, so she sent them back.

36. UNDERWAY - *[spell]*- U N D E R W A Y
   Definition: going on or in progress
   Synonym: ongoing, afoot
   Antonym:
   Sentence: Only a few days after getting engaged, her wedding plans were well underway.

37. DISGUSTING - *[spell]*- D I S G U S T I N G
   Definition: unpleasant
   Synonym: abominable, distasteful
   Antonym: agreeable, delightful
   Sentence: Though he found it disgusting, the husband told his new wife the meal she cooked was delicious.

38. MINDFUL - *[spell]*- M I N D F U L
   Definition: aware
   Synonym: heedful, thoughtful
   Antonym: careless, heedless
   Sentence: The mother advised her children to always be mindful of other people's feelings.

39. IMPATIENCE - *[spell]*- I M P A T I E N C E
   Definition: uneasiness and eagerness
   Synonym: excitement, restlessness
   Antonym: calmness, patience
   Sentence: Her impatience to see the doctor was obvious because she kept pacing the room.

40. SAPPY - *[spell]*- S A P P Y
   Definition: silly or foolish
   Synonym: mushy, maudlin
   Antonym: realistic, serious
   Sentence: She thought the popular movie was incredibly sappy.

41. INCREMENTAL - *[spell]*- I N C R E M E N T A L
   Definition: having to do with or becoming greater, especially in a regular series
   Synonym: accumulative, additional
   Antonym:
   Sentence: Over the years, he experienced an incremental pay increase.

42. PAMPER- *[spell]*- P A M P E R
   Definition: indulge too much
   Synonym: spoil, coddle
   Antonym: deny, withhold
   Sentence: The mother was guilty of pampering her child.

43. INTERVIEW - *[spell]* - I N T E R V I E W
Definition: a meeting to talk over something in particular
Synonym: conference, conversation
Antonym:
Sentence: He had an interview with a top accounting firm.

44. PAMPHLET- *[spell]* - P A M P H L E T
Definition: booklet in paper covers
Synonym: brochure, booklet
Antonym:
Sentence: He passed out pamphlets about his new business.

45. PROFESSION- *[spell]* - P R O F E S S I O N
Definition: occupation requiring special education or training
Synonym: career, occupation
Antonym: avocation, hobby
Sentence: He wanted to go into a profession in the field of science.

46. OVERTHROW- *[spell]* - O V E R T H R O W
Definition: take away the power of
Synonym: dethrone, depose
Antonym:
Sentence: The people decided to overthrow the king.

47. PEACHY- *[spell]* - P E A C H Y
Definition: fine or wonderful
Synonym: dandy, excellent
Antonym:
Sentence: He went to work that day thinking everything was peachy.

48. PERFECTIONIST- *[spell]* - P E R F E C T I O N I S T
Definition: a person who is not content with anything that is not perfect
Synonym: idealist, stickler
Antonym:
Sentence: She was a perfectionist when it came to her artwork.

49. ADMINISTRATION - *[spell]* - A D M I N I S T R A T I O N
Definition: managing business affairs
Synonym: authority, control
Antonym:
Sentence: The administration of the company was known for its innovation.

50. SUPERVISION - *[spell]* - S U P E R V I S I O N
Definition: management or direction
Synonym: guidance, administration

Antonym:
Sentence: Under the supervision of her parents, the child completed her homework.

51. TRANSLATION - *[spell]*- T R A N S L A T I O N
Definition: a being changed from one language to another
Synonym:
Antonym:
Sentence: She provided a translation to her friend who didn't speak Spanish.

52. RESTRAINT- *[spell]*- R E S T R A I N T
Definition: a holding back or hindering from action or motion
Synonym: control, restriction
Antonym: disinhibition
Sentence: Though usually she went overboard, she managed to show great restraint in her cooking of Thanksgiving dinner.

53. OVEREMPHASIZE- *[spell]*- O V E R E M P H A S I Z E
Definition: give too much force or stress to
Synonym: exaggerate, magnify
Antonym: lessen, ignore
Sentence: The CEO of the company overemphasized the importance of the marketing campaign.

54. SQUEEGEE- *[spell]*- S Q U E E G E E
Definition: tool used for removing water from windows after washing
Synonym:
Antonym:
Sentence: He used a squeegee to wash the windows of his car.

55. WHIMSY - *[spell]*- W H I M S Y
Definition: playful or fanciful notions
Synonym: caprice
Antonym:
Sentence: On a whimsy, she decided to paint her living room purple.

56. MISHAP - *[spell]*- M I S H A P
Definition: an unlikely accident
Synonym: misfortune, disaster
Antonym: blessing, boon
Sentence: The mishap caused a major setback in their plans.

57. VETO - *[spell]*- V E T O
Definition: the power of a president, governor, etc. to reject bills
Synonym: ban, deny

Antonym: allow, permit
Sentence: The president vetoed the new legislation.

58. EXAGGERATE - *[spell]*- E X A G G E R A T E
Definition: make greater than it is
Synonym: amplify, emphasize
Antonym: understate
Sentence: He had a tendency to exaggerate the severity of the situation.

59. MEMORIZE - *[spell]*- M E M O R I Z E
Definition: commit to memory
Synonym: learn, remember
Antonym: forget
Sentence: She tried to memorize the names of all the people she met that evening.

60. REBOUND- *[spell]*- R E B O U N D
Definition: to spring back
Synonym: recoil, ricochet
Antonym:
Sentence: The boy played a game with himself by rebounding a ball off a wall in the garage.

61. BARGE - *[spell]*- B A R G E
Definition: push oneself rudely
Synonym: push, plow
Antonym:
Sentence: It is usually considered rude to barge into a room without knocking first.

62. MUZZLE - *[spell]*- M U Z Z L E
Definition: compel to keep silent about something
Synonym:
Antonym:
Sentence: He tried to muzzle her about his secret.

63. PREDETERMINE- *[spell]*- P R E D E T E R M I N E
Definition: decide beforehand
Synonym: predestine
Antonym:
Sentence: The parents had practically predetermined where their son would go for college.

64. TRANCE - *[spell]*- T R A N C E
Definition: state of limited consciousness somewhat like sleep, such as in hypnosis

Synonym: coma, stupor
Antonym:
Sentence: Staring off into space, she looked to be in a trance.

65. SATE - *[spell]*- S A T E
Definition: to satisfy fully
Synonym: gratify, satiate
Antonym:
Sentence: Only a delicious home cooked meal could sate him.

66. TEXTURAL - *[spell]*- T E X T U R A L
Definition: having to do with texture (the arrangement of threads in a woven fabric)
Synonym:
Antonym:
Sentence: The child had an aversion to strange textural quality of the food.

67. ABORT- *[spell]*- A B O R T
Definition: to fail to develop completely
Synonym: terminate, interrupt
Antonym: continue, start
Sentence: The police force was ordered to abort their mission after it was deemed too dangerous.

68. ZINGER - *[spell]*- Z I N G E R
Definition: a quick or witty retort
Synonym: wisecrack, quip
Antonym:
Sentence: He replied with a zinger to her question.

69. BLOSSOM - *[spell]*- B L O S S O M
Definition: to flower or develop
Synonym: bloom, flourish
Antonym: barren, decline
Sentence: The flower began to blossom early in the spring.

70. BLOAT - *[spell]*- B L O A T
Definition: to swell up
Synonym: swell, inflate
Antonym: shrink, deflate
Sentence: Her stomach was bloated because she ate too much.

71. PROPORTIONAL- *[spell]*- P R O P O R T I O N A L
Definition: in the proper or corresponding size or extent
Synonym: coordinating, equivalent

Antonym: disproportionate

Sentence: The amount of food she put on the plate was not proportional to the size of the plate.

72. UNDERTAKE - *[spell]*- U N D E R T A K E
Definition: to attempt or try
Synonym: initiate, engage
Antonym: cease, finish
Sentence: He was reluctant to undertake any more projects at work because he was so busy.

73. DIMINUTIVE - *[spell]*- D I M I N U T I V E
Definition: very small
Synonym: tiny, minute
Antonym: large, behemoth
Sentence: Because she was so diminutive in stature, she had trouble reaching high places.

74. PREDICAMENT- *[spell]*- P R E D I C A M E N T
Definition: an unpleasant, difficult, or dangerous situation
Synonym: crisis, dilemma
Antonym:
Sentence: He found himself in quite a predicament when he double-booked himself.

75. ALARMIST - *[spell]*- A L A R M I S T
Definition: someone who is easily worried needlessly
Synonym: pessimist
Antonym: optimist
Sentence: Being a parent made her an alarmist when it came to her daughter's health.

76. BASHFUL - *[spell]*- B A S H F U L
Definition: uneasy in unfamiliar situations
Synonym: sheepish, timid
Antonym: bold, aggressive
Sentence: The young child avoided social situations because he was bashful.

77. NORMALCY - *[spell]*- N O R M A L C Y
Definition: the usual standard
Synonym: regular, ordinary
Antonym: extraordinary, unusual
Sentence: After the crisis, the country was glad to return to normalcy.

78. SHATTER - *[spell]*- S H A T T E R
    Definition: to break into pieces
    Synonym: burst, fracture
    Antonym: construct, complete
    Sentence: The plate shattered when she dropped it on the floor.

79. CONTROVERSIAL - *[spell]*- C O N T R O V E R S I A L
    Definition: having to do with conflict arising from differences of opinion
    Synonym: contentious, questionable
    Antonym: safe, uncontroversial
    Sentence: The new law was controversial.

80. TAPESTRY - *[spell]*- T A P E S T R Y
    Definition: fabric with pictures or designs woven in it
    Synonym:
    Antonym:
    Sentence: The ancient tapestry depicted a battle.

81. HOODLUM - *[spell]*- H O O D L U M
    Definition: criminal or gangster
    Synonym: ruffian, delinquent
    Antonym:
    Sentence: He had unfairly acquired a reputation as a hoodlum, simply because of the car he drove.

82. TENANT - *[spell]*- T E N A N T
    Definition: a person paying rent for the temporary use of the land or buildings of another person
    Synonym: dweller, renter
    Antonym:
    Sentence: Her neighbor was the newest tenant in the apartment complex.

83. IRK - *[spell]*- I R K
    Definition: cause to feel disgusted
    Synonym: annoy, bother
    Antonym: please, delight
    Sentence: The brother was irked by his sister's games.

84. OCCURRENCE- *[spell]*- O C C U R R E N C E
    Definition: an event or happening
    Synonym: incident, happening
    Antonym:
    Sentence: A solar eclipse is a rare occurrence.

85. DUPLICATE - *[spell]*- D U P L I C AT E
    Definition: exactly like something else

Synonym: reproduction, copy
Antonym: original
Sentence: The document was a duplicate of the original.

86. DROWSY - *[spell]-* D R O W S Y
Definition: half asleep
Synonym: sleepy, dozy
Antonym: alert, awake
Sentence: Feeling drowsy, he curled up on the couch to take a nap.

87. BACKFIRE - *[spell]-* B A C K F I R E
Definition: to bring a result which is opposite of what was expected
Synonym: fail, flop
Antonym: achieve, succeed
Sentence: He had to come up with an alternative when his plan backfired.

88. SLOBBER - *[spell]-* S L O B B E R
Definition: to drool
Synonym: dribble, froth
Antonym:
Sentence: The dog's slobber dripped from his mouth to the floor.

89. PURVEY - *[spell]-* P U R V E Y
Definition: to supply food or provisions
Synonym: provide, furnish
Antonym:
Sentence: The helicopter was able to purvey supplies to the stranded soldiers.

90. MIGRAINE - *[spell]-* M I G R A I N E
Definition: a severe headache
Synonym:
Antonym:
Sentence: Her migraine was so severe that she had to go to the hospital.

91. SPLATTER- *[spell]-* S P L A T T E R
Definition: to splash
Synonym: splash, squirt
Antonym:
Sentence: He panicked when he accidentally splattered paint on his new carpet.

92. DAFT- *[spell]-* D A F T
Definition: foolish
Synonym: silly, absurd

Antonym: serious
Sentence: Her antics made her seem daft.

93. EXCRUCIATING - *[spell]*- E X C R U C I A T I N G
Definition: causing great suffering
Synonym: painful, agonizing
Antonym: easy, light
Sentence: The pain from her broken arm was excruciating.

94. PILGRIM- *[spell]*- P I L G R I M
Definition: a person who makes a journey to some sacred place
Synonym:
Antonym:
Sentence: Each year at this time, thousands of pilgrims make the trip to Mecca.

95. SUMMATION - *[spell]*- S U M M A T I O N
Definition: process of finding the sum or total
Synonym:
Antonym:
Sentence: A summation of spending revealed that the company was under its established budget.

96. CATCHING - *[spell]*- C A T C H I N G
Definition: likely to spread from one person to another
Synonym: infectious, communicable
Antonym:
Sentence: Some emotions, like enthusiasm, are catching.

97. PREDECEASE- *[spell]*- P R E D E C E A S E
Definition: die before someone
Synonym:
Antonym:
Sentence: She was predeceased by her husband by only a matter of months.

98. SATCHEL - *[spell]*- S A T C H E L
Definition: a small bag for carrying clothes, books, etc.
Synonym: backpack, knapsack
Antonym:
Sentence: The student carried his books in a satchel.

99. PUNCTUALITY- *[spell]*- P U N C T U A L I T Y
Definition: being on time
Synonym: promptness

Antonym: lateness, tardiness
Sentence: She insisted on punctuality for all of her employees.

100.   RELATIVITY- *[spell]*- R E L A T I V I T Y
        Definition: a being related or compared to each other
        Synonym:
        Antonym:
        Sentence: Once he mastered Einstein's theory of relativity, his grades in
        Physics improved.

Easy Words Exercise - 2

101. SERGEANT - *[spell]*- S E R G E A N T
Definition: a military officer ranking above a corporal
Synonym:
Antonym:
Sentence: Now a sergeant in the military, he aspired to move up the ranks.

102. COMRADE - *[spell]*- C O M R A D E
Definition: companion or friend
Synonym: colleague, crony
Antonym: enemy, foe
Sentence: The two men had been friends since their days as comrades in the military.

103. UNDERSCORE - *[spell]*- U N D E R S C O R E
Definition: to emphasize
Synonym: accentuate, highlight
Antonym:
Sentence: The speaker underscored the importance of his message by repeating it several times.

104. SECONDARY - *[spell]*- S E C O N D A R Y
Definition: next after the first in order, place, time, importance, etc.
Synonym: subordinate, unimportant
Antonym: primary, significant
Sentence: His secondary reason for attending the conference was to see his old boss.

105. COMMONSENSICAL - *[spell]*- C O M M O N S E N S I C A L
Definition: showing practicality
Synonym: sensible, levelheaded
Antonym: impractical, foolish
Sentence: He always thought in the most commonsensical way.

106. HUFFY - *[spell]*- H U F F Y
Definition: easily offended
Synonym: crabby, disgruntled
Antonym: cheerful, happy
Sentence: Her huffy attitude was due to a rough day at work.

107. BIRTHRIGHT - *[spell]*- B I R T H R I G H T
Definition: rights or privileges that a person receives at birth
Synonym: legacy, inheritance
Antonym:
Sentence: Her birthright entitled her to inherit all of the estate.

108. LUMPISH - *[spell]*- L U M P I S H
Definition: heavy and clumsy
Synonym: awkward, cumbersome
Antonym:
Sentence: The lumpish box was difficult to carry up the stairs.

109. PITIFUL- *[spell]*- P I T I F U L
Definition: deserving feelings of sorrow from another for suffering or distress
Synonym: pitiable, pathetic
Antonym:
Sentence: The child's cries were pitiful when she broke her arm.

110. PATERNAL- *[spell]*- P A T E R N A L
Definition: of or like a father
Synonym:
Antonym:
Sentence: After the death of his father, his uncle became the paternal figure in his life.

111. TRILOGY - *[spell]*- T R I L O G Y
Definition: group of three plays, operas, novels, etc. which form a related series
Synonym:
Antonym:
Sentence: The author wrote a trilogy that followed the lives of several characters.

112. AVAILABILITY - *[spell]*- A V A I L A B I L I T Y
Definition: being capable of use
Synonym: vacant, accessible
Antonym: occupied, limited
Sentence: Because of his limited availability, appointments with the doctor had to be made months in advance.

113. BYLINE - *[spell]*- B Y L I N E
Definition: the line at the beginning of a written work that states the name of the writer
Synonym:

Antonym:
Sentence: She chose to use a pseudonym as her byline.

114. TINGE - *[spell]*- T I N G E
Definition: color slightly
Synonym: hue, tint
Antonym:
Sentence: The camellias are tinged with red around the edges of their petals.

115. F O X Y - *[spell]*- F O X Y
Definition: sly or crafty
Synonym: artful, cunning
Antonym: guileless
Sentence: Her foxy plan is what ultimately earned her a promotion.

116. SHAGGY - *[spell]*- S H A G G Y
Definition: covered with a thick, mass of hair, wool, etc.
Synonym: hairy, furry
Antonym: bare, shaven
Sentence: The shaggy dog was in desperate need of a grooming.

117. CONSCIENCE - *[spell]*- C O N S C I E N C E
Definition: sense of what is right and wrong
Synonym: morals, principles
Antonym:
Sentence: He wanted to ignore his neighbors' fighting, but his conscience insisted he call the police.

118. INCOME - *[spell]*- I N C O M E
Definition: money that comes from property, business, work, etc.
Synonym: wage, salary
Antonym: debt, expense
Sentence: Though he didn't have a grand income, it was enough to get by.

119. MOSAIC - *[spell]*- M O S A I C
Definition: decoration made of small pieces of stone, glass, etc. laid out to form a picture
Synonym: collage, montage
Antonym:
Sentence: The backsplash in the kitchen was a colorful mosaic.

120. TECHNIQUE - *[spell]*- T E C H N I Q U E
Definition: skill of a composing artist, such as a musician, painter, etc.
Synonym: style, method

Antonym:
Sentence: The artist had a unique technique for painting animals.

121. REARRANGE- *[spell]*- R E A R R A N G E
Definition: to put in a new or different order
Synonym: reorganize, readjust
Antonym:
Sentence: The child rearranged all of the books on her bookshelf.

122. BREAKAGE - *[spell]*- B R E A K A G E
Definition: a place where something has come apart into pieces
Synonym: crack, gap
Antonym:
Sentence: Because of extensive breakage, the vase could not be repaired.

123. PARALYTIC- *[spell]*- P A R A L Y T I C
Definition: have a condition in which one loses the power of motion or
sensation in a part of the body
Synonym: paralyzed, debilitated
Antonym: able-bodied, sound
Sentence: He became a paralytic after the accident.

124. JEALOUSY - *[spell]*- J E A L O U SY
Definition: dislike or fear of rivals
Synonym: grudge, resentment
Antonym:
Sentence: She had a clear jealousy of her boyfriend's ex.

125. ACCOMPLISHED- *[spell]*- A C C O M P L I S H E D
Definition: an expert
Synonym: skilled, adept
Antonym: amateur
Sentence: After studying dance for only a year, the girl was quite
accomplished.

126. OVERKILL- *[spell]*- O V E R K I L L
Definition an excess of what is actually necessary
Synonym: excessive, extravagant
Antonym: moderate
Sentence: His smashing his old laptop when he got a new one was
overkill.

127. PETITION- *[spell]*- P E T I T I O N
Definition: a formal request to a superior
Synonym: appeal, plea

Antonym:
Sentence: The teacher began a petition to get rid of standardized tests.

128. BANDITRY - *[spell]*- B A N D I T R Y
Definition: robbery
Synonym: thievery, burglary
Antonym:
Sentence: The man turned to a life of banditry in order to stay alive.

129. INNOCENCE - *[spell]*- I N N O C E N C E
Definition: freedom from sin, wrong, or guilt
Synonym: blamelessness, guiltlessness
Antonym: experience, corruption
Sentence: Her innocence in the crime was obvious to the jury.

130. TREMENDOUS - *[spell]*- T R E M E N D O U S
Definition: very severe
Synonym: astounding, overwhelming
Antonym:
Sentence: After suffering a tremendous blow to the head, she was knocked unconscious.

131. TRUANT - *[spell]*- T R U A N T
Definition: child who stays away from school without permission.
Synonym:
Antonym:
Sentence: His last year of high school, he was mostly truant, having missed more days than he attended.

132. UNLEASH - *[spell]*- U N L E A S H
Definition: to abandon control of
Synonym: release, discharge
Antonym: capture, cage
Sentence: The dragon unleashed his fury on the unsuspecting town.

133. BIOGRAPHICAL - *[spell]*- B I O G R A P H I C A L
Definition: having to do with a person's life
Synonym:
Antonym:
Sentence: He wrote a biographical sketch that was published in the magazine.

134. CHARACTERISTIC - *[spell]*- C H A R A C T E R I S T I C
Definition: distinguishing from others
Synonym: distinctive, idiosyncrasy

Antonym: atypical, uncharacteristic
Sentence: He accepted his award with characteristic modesty.

135. BANISH - *[spell]*- B A N I S H
Definition: to drive away
Synonym: exile, expel
Antonym: welcome, invite
Sentence: After breaking the rules, he was banished from the council.

136. NIBBLE - *[spell]*- N I B B L E
Definition: eat at with quick, small bites
Synonym: munch, nosh
Antonym: gobble, devour
Sentence: He nibbled on a sandwich before going to the meeting.

137. DEMORALIZE - *[spell]*- D E M O R A L I Z E
Definition: corrupt the morals of
Synonym: deprave, corrupt
Antonym: elevate, improve
Sentence: The court case proved the lawyer had been demoralized by greed.

138. DISSATISFACTORY - *[spell]*- D I S S A T I S F A C T O R Y
Definition: causing discontent
Synonym: deficient, disappointing
Antonym: satisfactory, pleasing
Sentence: She found the work of the contractor she hired to be dissatisfactory.

139. SLIPPERY - *[spell]*- S L I P P E R Y
Definition: causing or likely to cause sliding
Synonym: slick, greasy
Antonym: dry, secure
Sentence: The freezing rain made the sidewalk slippery.

140. BLOCKISH - *[spell]*- B L O C K I S H
Definition: very dull or stupid
Synonym: doltish, cloddish
Antonym: genius, brilliant
Sentence: Everyone thought him quite blockish, but he was actually quite smart.

141. INNARDS - *[spell]*- I N N A R D S
Definition: the internal organs of the body
Synonym: insides, guts
Antonym:

Sentence: Before cooking the turkey for Thanksgiving, she had to remove the innards.

142. IMPROPER- *[spell]*- I M P R O P E R
Definition: not in accordance with accepted standards
Synonym: incorrect, inadvisable
Antonym: acceptable, appropriate
Sentence: The child's behavior at the restaurant was completely improper.

143. MISEMPLOY - *[spell]*- M I S E M P L O Y
Definition: use wrongly or improperly
Synonym: abuse, misuse
Antonym: cherish, commend
Sentence: The man misemployed the tools.

144. LICENSE - *[spell]*- L I C E N S E
Definition: permission given by law to do something such as marry, carry on business, etc.
Synonym: certificate, authorization
Antonym: ban, prohibition
Sentence: In order to open a restaurant, she had to acquire a license.

145. LITERALLY - *[spell]*- L I T E R A L L Y
Definition: without exaggeration
Synonym: exactly, completely
Antonym: figuratively
Sentence: The area literally received a foot of snow over the weekend.

146. THOROUGHFARE - *[spell]*- T H O R O U G H F A R E
Definition: passage, road, or street open at both ends
Synonym: lane, boulevard
Antonym:
Sentence: He passed through the thoroughfare to get to the market.

147. ALIGNMENT - *[spell]*- A L I G N M E N T
Definition: bringing into a line
Synonym: arrangement, calibration
Antonym:
Sentence: Sometimes, it is necessary to adjust the alignment of the wheels on your car.

148. WARBLE - *[spell]*- W A R B L E
Definition: to sing or whistle with melodic embellishments
Synonym: sing, chirp
Antonym:
Sentence: The bird warbled outside the window.

149. INGREDIENT - *[spell]*- I N G R E D I E N T
Definition: one of the parts of a mixture or combination
Synonym: element, factor
Antonym:
Sentence: The secret ingredients in the recipe were the spices.

150. TRANSFERABLE - *[spell]*- T R A N S F E R A B L E
Definition: capable of being conveyed from one person or place to another
Synonym: interchangeable, movable
Antonym: stationary, fixed
Sentence: Upon his death, the man's fortune was transferable to his daughters.

151. BURGLARIZE - *[spell]*- B U R G L A R I Z E
Definition: to break into a building in order to steal
Synonym: rob, steal
Antonym:
Sentence: Everyone was surprised when the building was burglarized overnight.

152. SEWER - *[spell]*- S E W E R
Definition: an underground pipe or channel for carrying off waste, water, or refuse
Synonym: drain, gutter
Antonym:
Sentence: The road was closed when a sewer line broke.

153. CONFINE - *[spell]*- C O N F I N E
Definition: keep within limits
Synonym: restrict, hinder
Antonym: liberate, release
Sentence: He was confined within the jail cell until his sentence could be determined.

154. MEMOIR - *[spell]*- M E M O I R
Definition: biography
Synonym: autobiography
Antonym:
Sentence: The author wrote a memoir about her interesting life.

155. UNDESIRABLE - *[spell]*- U N D E S I R A B L E
Definition: objectionable
Synonym: unsatisfactory, abominable
Antonym: acceptable, desirable

Sentence: Though undesirable, the weather by no means spoiled their jaunt in the park.

156. HUMPY - *[spell]*- H U M P Y
Definition: full of rounded lumps that stick out
Synonym: lumpy
Antonym: smooth
Sentence: The humpy texture of the furniture she bought caused her to return it.

157. TAWNY - *[spell]*- T A W N Y
Definition: brownish-yellow
Synonym: bronze, brown
Antonym:
Sentence: The dog was a tawny color with black spots.

158. REPLICA- *[spell]*- R E P L I C A
Definition: a copy, duplicate, or reproduction
Synonym: likeness, imitation
Antonym: original
Sentence: The museum featured a replica of some well known historical documents.

159. SPLINTER- *[spell]*- S P L I N T E R
Definition: a thin, sharp piece of bone, wood, glass, etc.
Synonym: sliver, chip
Antonym:
Sentence: After walking barefoot across the porch, he got a splinter in his heel.

160. COEXIST - *[spell]*- C O E X I S T
Definition: exist together at the same time
Synonym: synchronize, coincide
Antonym:
Sentence: The two groups were able to coexist peacefully.

161. HEADSTONE - *[spell]*- H E A D S T O N E
Definition: stone set at the head of a grave
Synonym: tombstone, marker
Antonym:
Sentence: The old headstone was so weathered that you could barely read it.

162. SLANG - *[spell]*- S L A N G
Definition: words, phrases, not usually used in formal conversation or writing

Synonym: jargon, vernacular
Antonym:
Sentence: The teenagers were fond of using the latest slang.

163. RARITY- *[spell]*- R A R I T Y
Definition: something seldom seen or found
Synonym: scarcity, oddity
Antonym:
Sentence: That kind of harmonious relationship between siblings is often a rarity.

164. GOBBLE - *[spell]*- G O B B LE
Definition: eat fast and greedily
Synonym: devour, gorge
Antonym: nibble
Sentence: The hungry child gobbled up her lunch.

165. HERBAL - *[spell]*- H E R B A L
Definition: having to do with or consisting of herbs
Synonym:
Antonym:
Sentence: She drank herbal tea to soothe her sore throat.

166. OMEN- *[spell]*- O M E N
Definition: a sign of what is to happen
Synonym: warning, portent
Antonym:
Sentence: He took his bad dreams as an omen.

167. MISTAKEN - *[spell]*- M I S T A K E N
Definition: wrong in opinion
Synonym: erroneous, inaccurate
Antonym: correct, accurate
Sentence: She was mistaken in her opinion of him.

168. EXPLANATORY - *[spell]*- E X P L A N A T O R Y
Definition: serving to explain
Synonym: informative, illuminative
Antonym:
Sentence: His explanatory remarks help to clarify the issue.

169. PARENTHOOD- *[spell]*- P A R E N T H O O D
Definition: condition of being a parent
Synonym: motherhood, fatherhood
Antonym:
Sentence: His new parenthood made him a good deal more responsible.

170. IGNITION - *[spell]*- I G N I T I O N
Definition: a setting on fire
Synonym: explosion, detonation
Antonym:
Sentence: After the ignition of the firewood, the house was warm and cozy.

171. INFLUENTIAL - *[spell]*- I N F L U E N T I A L
Definition: having power over others
Synonym: powerful, persuasive
Antonym: ineffective, unimportant
Sentence: Parents are typically very influential on their children.

172. RETREAT- *[spell]*- R E T R E A T
Definition: to go back or withdraw
Synonym: evacuation, departure
Antonym: advance
Sentence: The army retreated when they realized they were defeated.

173. ANNUAL - *[spell]*- A N N U A L
Definition: happening once a year
Synonym: yearly
Antonym:
Sentence: Customers waited outside the store to be let in for the huge annual sale.

174. TRADEMARK - *[spell]*- T R A D E M A RK
Definition: a mark, picture, name, word, or symbol used to identify and distinguish a product or merchandise
Synonym: logo, symbol
Antonym:
Sentence: The image was a trademark of the company.

175. PLUCKY- *[spell]*- P L U C K Y
Definition: having or showing courage
Synonym: spunky, spirited
Antonym: afraid, cowardly
Sentence: The child was plucky even in the face of danger.

176. UNSUSPECTED - *[spell]*- U N S U S P E C T E D
Definition: free from suspicion
Synonym: accepted, uncontested
Antonym: disputed, suspected
Sentence: He was unsuspected in the crime.

177. TYRANT - *[spell]*- T Y R A N T
Definition: a person who uses power cruelly or unjustly
Synonym: oppressor, despot
Antonym:
Sentence: Tired of the tyrant's restrictive laws, the people overthrew him.

178. CIRCUMSTANCE - *[spell]*- C I R C U M S T A N C E
Definition: conditions that accompany an act or event
Synonym: cause, factor
Antonym:
Sentence: The circumstances surrounding their marriage were rather unusual.

179. CIVILIZATION - *[spell]*- C I V I L I Z A T I O N
Definition: people or cultures who have reached advanced stages of development
Synonym: development, advancement
Antonym: barbarism, primitiveness
Sentence: The civilization was a result of hundreds of years of development.

180. BELOVED - *[spell]*- B E L O V E D
Definition: very dearly loved
Synonym: cherished, dear
Antonym: loathed, hated
Sentence: He married her because she was truly his beloved.

181. HANDOUT - *[spell]*- H A N D O U T
Definition: portion of food, clothing, or money given out
Synonym: contribution, donation
Antonym:
Sentence: The homeless woman went to the shelter, hoping for a handout.

182. PLEASURABLE- *[spell]*- P L E A S U R A B L E
Definition: pleasant
Synonym: nice, enjoyable
Antonym: irritating, annoying
Sentence: She found the music of the orchestra to be quite pleasurable.

183. SCORNFUL - *[spell]*- S C O R N F U L
Definition: showing contempt
Synonym: sneering, disdainful
Antonym: gracious, respectful
Sentence: The mother's scornful look clearly showed her disapproval.

184. JUDGMENTAL - *[spell]*- J U D G M E N T A L
Definition: having to do with forming an opinion about something
Synonym: subjective, discretionary
Antonym:
Sentence: She had a tendency to be very judgmental about people's actions.

185. PETTY- *[spell]*- P E T T Y
Definition: have little importance or value
Synonym: unimportance, trivial
Antonym: major, important
Sentence: She held the grudge for a rather petty reason.

186. UTMOST - *[spell]*- U T M O S T
Definition: of the greatest quality, degree, etc.
Synonym: extreme, maximum
Antonym:
Sentence: Bravery is of the utmost importance for a soldier.

187. TRAGEDY - *[spell]*- T R A G E D Y
Definition: a serious play having an unhappy or disastrous ending
Synonym:
Antonym:
Sentence: The play was a tragedy and left the audience crying.

188. UMPIRE - *[spell]*- U M P I R E
Definition: person who rules on the plays in a game
Synonym: referee, judge
Antonym:
Sentence: The umpire's call at the baseball game caused an uproar in the stadium.

189. TRUMP - *[spell]*- T R U M P
Definition: to surpass
Synonym: advantage, outmaneuver
Antonym:
Sentence: He was able to trump her hand in the card game.

190. POMMEL- *[spell]*- P O M M E L
Definition: a rounded knob on the hilt of a sword or dagger
Synonym:
Antonym:
Sentence: The warrior grabbed the pommel of his sword, preparing to draw it if necessary.

191. INESTIMABLE - *[spell]-* I N E S T I M A B L E
Definition: not capable of being calculated or guessed at
Synonym: invaluable, priceless
Antonym:
Sentence: The family heirloom, though nothing extravagant, was inestimable in her eyes.

192. SWAGGER - *[spell]-* S W A G G E R
Definition: to walk with a bold, rude, or superior air
Synonym: strut, prance
Antonym:
Sentence: His swagger after receiving the promotion was obvious.

193. R I F L E - *[spell]-* R I F L E
Definition: to search and rob
Synonym: ransack, burgle
Antonym:
Sentence: The thief rifled through the man's belongings before taking a phone and a wallet.

194. AGENDA - *[spell]-* A G E N D A
Definition: a routine of things that needs to be accomplished
Synonym: schedule, program
Antonym:
Sentence: Students were advised to keep a daily agenda with their assignments.

195. EXTINGUISH - *[spell]-* E X T I N G U I S H
Definition: to cause to cease burning
Synonym: quench, smother
Antonym: kindle, ignite
Sentence: They weary campers extinguished the fire and went to bed.

196. OVERSHADOW- *[spell]-* O V E R S H A D O W
Definition: be more important than
Synonym: dominate, eclipse
Antonym:
Sentence: The terrible storm overshadowed the good news.

197. LAGOON - *[spell]-* L A G O O N
Definition: pond or lake connected to a larger body of water
Synonym: pond, pool
Antonym:
Sentence: The children went swimming in the lagoon.

198. STUMP - *[spell]*- S T U M P
   Definition: to make unable to do, answer, etc.
   Synonym: confuse, bewilder
   Antonym:
   Sentence: The student was stumped by the teacher's questions.

199. DELETION - *[spell]*- D E L E T I O N
   Definition: act of taking something out
   Synonym: cancellation, expunction
   Antonym: insertion, inclusion
   Sentence: The author made several deletions while editing his book.

200. FASTENER - *[spell]*- F A S T E N E R
   Definition: something that ties, locks or holds together a door, garment, etc.
   Synonym: latch, buckle
   Antonym:
   Sentence: The buttons on her blouse served as fasteners.

Easy Words Exercise - 3

201. STOUTHEARTED - *[spell]*- S T O U T H E A R T E D
      Definition: brave
      Synonym: adventurous, brave
      Antonym: cowardly, afraid
      Sentence: The soldier was stouthearted even in the midst of battle.

202. RECOGNIZABLE - *[spell]*- R E C O G N I Z A B L E
      Definition: that can be made aware of as already known
      Synonym: discernible, apparent
      Antonym: ambiguous, imperceptible
      Sentence: His face was easily recognizable in the crowd.

203. DOSAGE - *[spell]*- D O S A G E
      Definition: amount of medicine to be given or taken at a time
      Synonym: measure, quantity
      Antonym:
      Sentence: The doctor prescribed a small dosage of the medication.

204. BASIS - *[spell]*- B A S I S
      Definition: the fundamental principle
      Synonym: foundation, support
      Antonym: top, peak
      Sentence: Correct grammar is the basis of good writing.

205. GULF - *[spell]*- G U L F
      Definition: a large bay
      Synonym: inlet, basin
      Antonym:
      Sentence: Many different types of wildlife made their home in the gulf.

206. ENTRUST - *[spell]*- E N T R U S T
      Definition: give the care of
      Synonym: assign, allocate
      Antonym: keep, hold
      Sentence: She entrusted him with her darkest secrets.

207. TIMID - *[spell]*- T I M I D
      Definition: easily frightened

Synonym: shy, demure
Antonym: brave, bold
Sentence: Though she was a timid person, it didn't stop her from trying new things.

208. STAGNANT - *[spell]*- S T A G N A N T
Definition: not running or flowing
Synonym: motionless, dormant
Antonym: activity, energetic
Sentence: The pool of water was completely stagnant.

209. PANICKY - *[spell]*- P AN I C K Y
Definition: caused by a sudden outbreak of alarm
Synonym: anxious, nervous
Antonym: calm, comforted
Sentence: The absence of her father made the child panicky.

210. INHUMANE - *[spell]*- I N H U M A N E
Definition: lacking in kindness or mercy
Synonym: barbaric, brutal
Antonym: humane, kind
Sentence: It is inhumane to keep pets locked up all day in a cage outdoors.

211. MISGUIDANCE - *[spell]*- M I S G U I D AN C E
Definition: misdirection
Synonym:
Antonym:
Sentence: He fell prey to the misguidance of his friends.

212. DUNGEON - *[spell]*- D U N G E O N
Definition: a dark underground room where prisoners are kept
Synonym: prison
Antonym:
Sentence: The prisoners were taken immediately to the dungeon.

213. UNKINDLY - *[spell]*- U N K I N D LY
Definition: harsh or unfavorable
Synonym:
Antonym:
Sentence: I have never been treated so unkindly in my life.

214. EXCITABILITY - *[spell]*- E X C I T A B I L I T Y
Definition: the quality of being easily stirred up emotionally
Synonym:
Antonym:

Sentence: The child's excitability was due to her anticipation of the vacation.

215. DREARY - *[spell]*- D R E A R Y
Definition: without cheer
Synonym: bleak, colorless
Antonym: cheerful, bright
Sentence: She looked out the window to see a dreary September sky.

216. UNPREDICTABLE - *[spell]*- U N P R E D I C T A B L E
Definition: uncertain
Synonym: fickle, unreliable
Antonym: certain, definite
Sentence: The weather is often unpredictable.

217. GODLESS - *[spell]*- G O D L E S S
Definition: not believing in God
Synonym:
Antonym:
Sentence: He lived a godless life until he met his wife and she convinced him to convert.

218. STRAGGLE - *[spell]*- S T R A G G L E
Definition: to wander in a scattered fashion
Synonym: dawdle, wander
Antonym:
Sentence: The child straggled behind his classmates.

219. SCREWY - *[spell]*- S C R E W Y
Definition: very odd or peculiar
Synonym: eccentric, abnormal
Antonym: normal, regular
Sentence: Something seemed screwy about their relationships.

220. ASTRONOMY - *[spell]*- A S T R O N O M Y
Definition: a science that deals with the sun, stars, moon, etc.
Synonym:
Antonym:
Sentence: Because she loved to study outer space, she decided to study astronomy in college.

221. EXTERMINATION - *[spell]*- E X T E R M I N A T I O N
Definition: complete destruction
Synonym: annihilation, eradication
Antonym:

Sentence: The man saw to the extermination of the rodents infesting his house.

222. MAXIMIZE - *[spell]*- M A X I M I Z E
Definition: increase or magnify to the highest possible amount
Synonym: boost, inflate
Antonym: minimize, diminish
Sentence: He searched for bargains in order to maximize his spending power.

223. CHARMED - *[spell]*- C H A R M E D
Definition: protected as by a magic spell
Synonym: enchanted, fortunate
Antonym: unfortunate
Sentence: He seemed to live a charmed life, with every possible wish coming true.

224. SNUGGLE - *[spell]*- S N U G G L E
Definition: lie or press near for warmth or comfort
Synonym: cuddle, nestle
Antonym: separate, release
Sentence: The puppy snuggled up to its mother for warmth.

225. HAZE - *[spell]*- H A Z E
Definition: small amount of mist, smoke, dust, etc.
Synonym: cloud, fog
Antonym:
Sentence: The early morning haze made the commute to work difficult.

226. RADIOLOGY - *[spell]*- R A D I O L O G Y
Definition: Science dealing with x-rays for medical diagnosis or treatment
Synonym:
Antonym:
Sentence: The nurse decided to shift her career path by studying radiology.

227. MISINTERPRET - *[spell]*- M I S I N T E R P R E T
Definition: to explain wrongly
Synonym: misread, misunderstand
Antonym:
Sentence: It was too easy to misinterpret his words.

228. DISINTEGRATION - *[spell]*- D I S I N T E G R A T I O N
Definition: a breaking up
Synonym: fragmentation, decentralization
Antonym:

Sentence: After the disintegration of government, the country was launched into chaos.

229. SCENERY - *[spell]*- S C E N E R Y
Definition: the general appearance of a place
Synonym: surroundings, furnishings
Antonym:
Sentence: She took a drive along the mountains to enjoy the scenery.

230. STRATEGIC - *[spell]*- S T R A T E G I C
Definition: of strategy (skillful planning and management)
Synonym: crucial, important
Antonym: inessential, insignificant
Sentence: The general made a strategic plan to win the battle.

231. HEAP - *[spell]*- H E A P
Definition: pile of many things thrown or lying together in a confused way
Synonym: stack, jumble
Antonym:
Sentence: She had a heap of books on the floor of her room.

232. DREADFUL - *[spell]*- D R E A D F U L
Definition: causing great fear
Synonym: frightening, horrible
Antonym: innocuous, inoffensive
Sentence: He caught a dreadful cold after being in the rain all afternoon.

233. MIDTERM - *[spell]*- M I D T E R M
Definition: the middle of a school or office term
Synonym:
Antonym:
Sentence: Students had to take a midterm exam in January.

234. RETORT - *[spell]*- R E T O R T
Definition: reply quickly or sharply
Synonym: quip, rejoinder
Antonym:
Sentence: She was always ready with a witty retort.

235. HEADMASTER - *[spell]*- H E A D M A S T E R
Definition: person in charge of a school, especially a private school
Synonym: principal, administrator
Antonym:
Sentence: The headmaster of the school had very high expectations for his students.

236. GIGGLE - *[spell]*- G I G G L E
Definition: laugh in a silly or undignified way
Synonym: chuckle, snicker
Antonym:
Sentence: The girls giggled as they watched the boys walk by.

237. CENTERPIECE - *[spell]*- C E N T E R P I E CE
Definition: the focal feature or outstanding point
Synonym: climax, highlight
Antonym:
Sentence: The centerpiece of the conference was the keynote speaker.

238. INFLAMMATION - *[spell]*- I N F L A M M A T I O N
Definition: a diseased condition of some part of the body, marked by redness and swelling
Synonym: redness, swelling
Antonym:
Sentence: The inflammation of his wrist was due to a broken bone.

239. SANITIZE - *[spell]*- S A N I T I Z E
Definition: to make so as to prevent disease
Synonym: decontaminate, disinfect
Antonym:
Sentence: Be sure to sanitize the countertops in the kitchen after cutting food.

240. RESPONSIBILITY - *[spell]*- R E S P O N S I B I L I T Y
Definition: being obliged or expected to account for something
Synonym: duty, accountability
Antonym:
Sentence: Children should learn responsibility at a young age.

241. INSTALLATION - *[spell]*- I N S T A L L A T I O N
Definition: a being put in place for use
Synonym: establishment, accession
Antonym: removal
Sentence: She was completely happy with the installation of her new entertainment center.

242. ANTISOCIAL - *[spell]*- A N T I S O C I A L
Definition: opposed to associating with other people
Synonym: introverted, aloof
Antonym: sociable, outgoing
Sentence: Feeling antisocial, she decided not to go to the party.

243. BROTHERHOOD - *[spell]*- B R O T H E R H O O D
Definition: a group of men with some common aim, belief, or profession
Synonym: fraternity, kinship
Antonym:
Sentence: The men, all of the same faith, formed a brotherhood.

244. DISTINCTION - *[spell]*- D I S T I N C T I O N
Definition: a distinguishing from others
Synonym: differentiation, feature
Antonym:
Sentence: A distinction of the author's books was his writing style.

245. ZANY - *[spell]*- Z A N Y
Definition: comical in a ludicrous or whimsical way
Synonym: crazy, kooky
Antonym:
Sentence: The novel was a zany interpretation of recent political events.

246. MAJORITY - *[spell]*- M A J O R I T Y
Definition: the largest number
Synonym: most, bulk
Antonym:
Sentence: The majority of his life was spent serving others.

247. BLABBERMOUTH - *[spell]*- B L A B B E R M O U T H
Definition: a person who talks too much and without good judgment
Synonym: gossip, chatterbox
Antonym:
Sentence: Because she was such a blabbermouth, no one trusted her with their secrets.

248. ENTHRONE - *[spell]*- E N T H R O NE
Definition: set in high authority
Synonym: crown, inaugurate
Antonym: dethrone
Sentence: As soon as the new king was enthroned, peace began to come to the kingdom.

249. TAILGATE - *[spell]*- T A I L G A T E
Definition: board at the back of a truck that can be let down or removed when loading or unloading
Synonym:
Antonym:
Sentence: At the drive-in theater, the couple put down the tailgate and sat on it to watch the movie.

250. BINDING - *[spell]*- B I N D I N G
Definition: anything that holds together by promise or obligation
Synonym: irrevocable, mandatory
Antonym: optional, inessential
Sentence: The student signed a binding contract, asserting that they would attend the college.

251. SHAMELESS - *[spell]*- S H A M E L E S S
Definition: without any feeling of having done something wrong or improper
Synonym: corrupt, indecent
Antonym: decent, moral
Sentence: She was shameless when it came to speaking her mind.

252. CONTAMINANT - *[spell]*- C O N T A M I N A N T
Definition: something that makes impure by contact
Synonym: pollutant, impurity
Antonym: purifier
Sentence: A contaminant was found in the water supply of the city.

253. THORNY - *[spell]*- T H O R N Y
Definition: full of spines
Synonym: sharp, prickly
Antonym: smooth, even
Sentence: The thorny plant was difficult to pull up.

254. PROFITABLE - *[spell]*- P R O F I T A B L E
Definition: yielding a financial gain
Synonym: lucrative, gainful
Antonym: unprofitable
Sentence: The business venture proved to be quite profitable.

255. TRANQUIL - *[spell]*- T R A N Q U I L
Definition: calm and peaceful
Synonym: temperate, serene
Antonym: hectic, chaotic
Sentence: He visited the tranquil lake once a year for some relaxation.

256. FORMERLY - *[spell]*- F O R M E R LY
Definition: at an earlier time
Synonym: previously, once
Antonym: later, afterwards
Sentence: She had formerly disliked him, but her opinion changed over time.

257. UNANSWERABLE - *[spell]*- U N A N S W E R A B L E
Definition: that cannot be disproved
Synonym: conclusive, compelling
Antonym: ambiguous, disputable
Sentence: His theory proved to be utterly unanswerable.

258. HOGWASH - *[spell]*- H O G W A S H
Definition: worthless stuff
Synonym: nonsense, absurdity
Antonym:
Sentence: His story was full of hogwash.

259. DEPORTATION - *[spell]*- D E P O R T A T I O N
Definition: removal from a country
Synonym: expulsion, eviction
Antonym:
Sentence: Many illegal immigrants were faced with deportation because of the new law.

260. BARRIER - *[spell]*- B A R R I E R
Definition: something that is in the way
Synonym: hurdle, obstacle
Antonym: opening
Sentence: The wall around the property created a barrier that he had to surmount.

261. TEMPLATE - *[spell]*- T E M P L A T E
Definition: a pattern or mold from which something is formed
Synonym: pattern, arrangement
Antonym:
Sentence: She used a template to sew the blanket.

262. REDUPLICATE - *[spell]*- R E D U P L I C A T E
Definition: to double or repeat
Synonym: copy, imitate
Antonym:
Sentence: She had to reduplicate the recipe to have enough food for her guests.

263. CANVAS - *[spell]*- C A N V A S
Definition: a strong cloth
Synonym: tarp
Antonym:
Sentence: The workers spread a canvas out in the backyard on which to do their work.

264. SPLENDID - *[spell]* - S P L E N D I D
Definition: magnificent or gorgeous
Synonym: beautiful, dazzling
Antonym: ordinary, dull
Sentence: The sun created a splendid array of color on the stained glass window.

265. SERENE - *[spell]* - S E R E N E
Definition: peaceful or calm
Synonym: undisturbed, tranquil
Antonym: agitated, turbulent
Sentence: She enjoyed the serene atmosphere at the lake house.

266. COMPRESSED - *[spell]* - C O M P R E S S E D
Definition: squeezed together
Synonym: crammed, constricted
Antonym: enlarged, expanded
Sentence: The clothes were compressed into a storage container.

267. UNEVENTFUL - *[spell]* - U N E V E N T F U L
Definition: without important or striking occurrences
Synonym: dull, tedious
Antonym: exciting, interesting
Sentence: Though the food at the party was great, it was ultimately uneventful.

268. AFFECTATION - *[spell]* - A F F E C T A T I O N
Definition: behavior designed to impress others
Synonym: pretense, artificiality
Antonym: genuineness
Sentence: His affectations soon began to annoy everyone in the office.

269. ABSURD—[spell]—A B S U R D
Definition: clearly not true or logical
Synonym: ridiculous
Antonym: reasonable, sensible
Sentence: Though he knew his nightmare was completely absurd, he still felt afraid.

270. TYPICAL - *[spell]* - T Y P I CA L
Definition: being representative
Synonym: usual, conventional
Antonym: abnormal, eccentric
Sentence: His behavior at the social gathering was typical for him.

271. SCRIPT - *[spell]*- S C R I P T
Definition: written letters
Synonym:
Antonym:
Sentence: We asked Helen to address the invitations because of her beautiful script.

272. REFERRAL - *[spell]*- R E F E R R A L
Definition: the act of directing a person somewhere for information or something required
Synonym:
Antonym:
Sentence: She was given a referral from her general doctor for a dermatologist.

273. SELDOM - *[spell]*- S E L D O M
Definition: not often
Synonym: infrequently, occasionally
Antonym: often, frequently
Sentence: She seldom discussed her personal life at work.

274. COMPENSATION - *[spell]*- C O M P E N S A T I O N
Definition: something given as an equivalent
Synonym: earnings, coverage
Antonym: loss, penalty
Sentence: He was given compensation for being injured on the job.

275. SPECIES - *[spell]*- S P E C I E S
Definition: group of related organisms
Synonym: class, variety
Antonym:
Sentence: There are many different species of bear.

276. SHRILL - *[spell]*- S H R I L L
Definition: having a high pitch
Synonym: sharp, discordant
Antonym:
Sentence: The mother got her children's attention by scolding them in a shrill voice.

277. FACELESS - *[spell]*- F A C E L E S S
Definition: lacking individual characteristics
Synonym: forgettable, nameless
Antonym:
Sentence: She was just a faceless individual in the crowd.

278. COATING - *[spell]*- C O A T I N G
Definition: layer covering a surface
Synonym: blanket, veneer
Antonym:
Sentence: He gave the walls a new coating of paint.

279. READINESS - *[spell]*- R E A D I N E S S
Definition: being prepared for action or use at once
Synonym: preparedness
Antonym: inability, unpreparedness
Sentence: Students had to take a test to determine their readiness for the workplace.

280. BLOOMING - *[spell]*- B L O O M I N G
Definition: flourishing
Synonym: budding, blossoming
Antonym: barren, declining
Sentence: She was a blooming woman in her early twenties.

281. DEPENDABLE - *[spell]*- D E P E N D A B L E
Definition: trustworthy
Synonym: loyal, reliable
Antonym: unreliable, untrustworthy
Sentence: Their friendship was strong because they knew each other to be dependable.

282. ATTEST - *[spell]*- A T T E S T
Definition: give proof or evidence
Synonym: authenticate, substantiate
Antonym: contradict, oppose
Sentence: He could attest to the fact that she didn't do her job very well.

283. LOGO - *[spell]*- L O G O
Definition: symbol, name or trademark
Synonym: emblem, symbol
Antonym:
Sentence: The company logo used a flashy font and a bright image.

284. MANIAC - *[spell]*- M A N I A C
Definition: an insane person
Synonym: psycho, lunatic
Antonym:
Sentence: She acted like a maniac after her recent breakup.

285. INCONSEQUENT - *[spell]*- I N C O N S E Q U E N T
Definition: not logical

Synonym: inconsiderable, minor
Antonym: logical, pertinent
Sentence: His assumptions about her character were inconsequent.

286. HAUL - *[spell]*- H A U L
Definition: pull or drag with force
Synonym: tote, tow
Antonym:
Sentence: He hauled the firewood into his house from his yard.

287. CHAMBER - *[spell]*- C H A M B E R
Definition: a room in a house
Synonym: bedroom, cell
Antonym:
Sentence: She took most of her meetings in a chamber at the back of the home.

288. TEXTUAL - *[spell]*- T E X T U A L
Definition: of or having to do with the main body of reading matter in a book
Synonym:
Antonym:
Sentence: Literature students were encouraged to use textual evidence in their final papers.

289. INDICATION - *[spell]*- I N D I C A T I O N
Definition: thing that points out
Synonym: intimation, inkling
Antonym:
Sentence: There was no indication beforehand that an earthquake would happen.

290. CORRUPTION - *[spell]*- C O R R U P T I O N
Definition: bribery or dishonesty
Synonym: fraud, crime
Antonym:
Sentence: The company was failing largely due to internal corruption.

291. OUTPOURING - *[spell]*- O U T P O U R I N G
Definition: anything that is flowing out of
Synonym: flood, outburst
Antonym:
Sentence: In her song, the singer had an outpouring of emotion.

292. FRAGMENTARY - *[spell]*- F R A G M E N T A R Y
Definition: made up of broken pieces

Synonym: disconnected, scattered
Antonym: whole, complete
Sentence: The fragmentary nature of the story confused her.

293. SEEMING - *[spell]*- S E E M I N G
Definition: apparent or appearing to be
Synonym: apparent, professed
Antonym: real, true
Sentence: His seeming kindness was all a ploy to get attention.

294. COMPANIONABLE - *[spell]*- C O M P A N I O N A B L E
Definition: pleasant to be with
Synonym: amicable, friendly
Antonym: disagreeable, unfriendly
Sentence: His companionable nature made him an ideal person to travel with.

295. AGITATION - *[spell]*- A G I T A T I O N
Definition: violent shaking or moving
Synonym: churning, rocking
Antonym: steady, calm
Sentence: Washing machines clean your clothes, in part, by using agitation.

296. BEARABLE - *[spell]*- B E A R A B L E
Definition: something that can be borne
Synonym: endurable, manageable
Antonym: intolerable, unendurable
Sentence: His hardship was bearable because of the support of his closest friends.

297. UNDENIABLE - *[spell]*- U N D E N I A BLE
Definition: that cannot be disputed
Synonym: evident, definite
Antonym: disputable, doubtful
Sentence: Her great contribution to the company was undeniable.

298. ENTHUSIASTIC - *[spell]*- E N T H U S I A S T I C
Definition: full of eager interest
Synonym: ardent, avid
Antonym: apathetic, disinterested
Sentence: Her enthusiastic attitude is the reason why she was hired.

299. SAGA - *[spell]*- S A G A
Definition: a long narrative story
Synonym: chronicle, epic

Antonym:

Sentence: The saga told the story of a hero's adventures.

300.   STARVATION - *[spell]*- S T A R V A T I O N

Definition: suffering from extreme hunger

Synonym: famine, deprivation

Antonym:

Sentence: The children of the family suffered from starvation.

Easy Words Exercise - 4

301. COMMENTARY - *[spell]*- C O M M E N T A R Y
Definition: series of notes explaining parts of a book
Synonym: explanation, narration
Antonym:
Sentence: The commentary in the margins of the book was very helpful.

302. NIMBLE - *[spell]*- N I M B L E
Definition: active and sure-footed
Synonym: agile, deft
Antonym: clumsy, bungling
Sentence: The gymnast was impressively nimble.

303. HEALTHFUL - *[spell]*- H E A L T H F U L
Definition: giving well being
Synonym: wholesome
Antonym: unhealthy
Sentence: She made a conscious effort to eat only healthful foods.

304. CALLIGRAPHY - *[spell]*- C A L L I G R A P H Y
Definition: handwriting
Synonym: script
Antonym:
Sentence: She took a class in calligraphy to learn more about the art of writing.

305. ACCEPTABILITY- *[spell]*- A C C E P T A B I L I T Y
Definition: a quality that is agreeable
Synonym: welcome, respectable
Antonym: inadequate, insufficient
Sentence: The employer was searching for more than acceptability in his candidatesâ€"he wanted them to be extraordinary.

306. WRETCHED - *[spell]*- W R E T C H E D
Definition: very unfortunate or miserable
Synonym: pathetic, depressed
Antonym:
Sentence: He was in a wretched state after his dog died.

307. NONEXISTENT - *[spell]*- N O N E X I S T E N T
Definition: not being
Synonym: tenuous, vacant
Antonym: present, actual
Sentence: Her motivation was practically nonexistent.

308. FRAGILE - *[spell]*- F R A G I L E
Definition: easily broken or damaged
Synonym: delicate, feeble
Antonym: strong, sturdy
Sentence: She had to be careful when shipping the fragile ornaments.

309. SITUATE - *[spell]*- S I T U A T E
Definition: to place or locate
Synonym: settle, place
Antonym: unsettle, disarrange
Sentence: At the park, the mother situated herself so she could see her children.

310. ANCESTOR - *[spell]*- A N C E S T O R
Definition: a person from whom someone is descended
Synonym: forefather, forebear
Antonym: descendant
Sentence: Curious about her origins, she decided to research her ancestors.

311. SLIVER - *[spell]*- S L I V E R
Definition: a long, thin piece that has been split or broken off of something
Synonym: slice, fragment
Antonym:
Sentence: She cut a small sliver of the pie for herself.

312. RUSTLE - *[spell]*- R U S T L E
Definition: a light, soft sound of things gently rubbing together
Synonym: swish, whisper
Antonym:
Sentence: The leaves rustled outside of her window.

313. INSTANTLY - *[spell]*- I N S T A N T L Y
Definition: at once
Synonym: immediately, instantaneously
Antonym:
Sentence: She felt the chill instantly when she stepped outside.

314. PHILOSOPHY- *[spell]*- P H I L O S O P H Y
Definition: study of the truth or principles underlying all knowledge
Synonym:
Antonym:
Sentence: He has considered majoring in philosophy, but worries he won't be able to find a job.

315. SCRAPE - *[spell]*- S C R A P E
Definition: rub with something sharp or rough
Synonym: grind, chafe
Antonym:
Sentence: The branch of the tree scraped against the window.

316. RABBLE- *[spell]*- R A B B L E
Definition: a disorderly, boisterous crowd
Synonym: mob
Antonym:
Sentence: The rabble cheered to see the corrupt official arrested.

317. CHAPERONE - *[spell]*- C H A P E R O N E
Definition: an older person who is in charge of overseeing younger people or children
Synonym: escort, guardian
Antonym:
Sentence: There were at least a dozen chaperones at the school dance.

318. SACRIFICE - *[spell]*- S A C R I F I C E
Definition: act of offering to a god
Synonym: offering
Antonym:
Sentence: The people made a sacrifice to the gods in hopes for a fruitful harvest.

319. REACTANT- *[spell]*- R E A C T A N T
Definition: an element or compound that enters into a chemical reaction
Synonym:
Antonym:
Sentence: The chemist had to carefully measure the reactants in his formula.

320. YOWL - *[spell]*- Y O W L
Definition: to utter a long cry
Synonym: bawl, bay
Antonym:
Sentence: The cat began to yowl at the cupboard for food.

321. HESITANCE - *[spell]* - H E S I T A N C E
Definition: tendency to fail to act promptly
Synonym: disinclination, aversion
Antonym: inclination, eagerness
Sentence: His hesitance in proposing to his girlfriend was due to worries his parents wouldn't approve.

322. NEGLECTFUL - *[spell]* - N E G L E C T F U L
Definition: careless or negligent
Synonym: careless, negligent
Antonym: attentive, caring
Sentence: The child was taken away from the neglectful parents.

323. INDEPENDENCE - *[spell]* - I N D E P E N D E N C E
Definition: condition of being free from control, influence, support, etc.
Synonym: freedom, liberty
Antonym: dependence, servitude
Sentence: The state finally achieved independence and established its own government.

324. ASHAMED - *[spell]* - A S H A M E D
Definition: feeling disturbed or uncomfortable from doing something wrong or improper
Synonym: embarrassed, regretful
Antonym: proud, confident
Sentence: He was ashamed to admit he had been part of the conspiracy.

325. CHAMPIONSHIP - *[spell]* - C H A M P I O N S H I P
Definition: occupying first place
Synonym: winner
Antonym: loser
Sentence: They became the championship team after winning every game that season.

326. NARRATION - *[spell]* - N A R R A T I O N
Definition: act of telling
Synonym:
Antonym:
Sentence: The narration told the story of a great hero.

327. AMAZEMENT - *[spell]* - A M A Z E M E N T
Definition: great surprise
Synonym: astonishment, bewilderment
Antonym: indifference
Sentence: The brilliance of his writing left her in amazement.

328. VENGEFUL - *[spell]*- V E N G E F U L
Definition: seeking payback
Synonym: retaliating, vindictive
Antonym:
Sentence: He felt vengeful about the great wrong his friend did to him.

329. SILO - *[spell]*- S I L O
Definition: an airtight building in which fodder for livestock is stored
Synonym: storehouse, granary
Antonym:
Sentence: The farmer stored grain in the silo on his property.

330. PRESIDENCY- *[spell]*- P R E S I D E N C Y
Definition: the chief office of the company, corporation, society, etc.
Synonym:
Antonym:
Sentence: The Senator decided, after much debate, to make a bid for the presidency.

331. QUAVER- *[spell]*- Q U A V E R
Definition: to shake tremulously
Synonym: tremble, quiver
Antonym:
Sentence: The child quavered at the thought of going back to school after summer break.

332. AUTHENTICATE - *[spell]*- A U T H E N T I C A T E
Definition: to establish the genuineness of
Synonym: verify, substantiate
Antonym:
Sentence: He was unable to authenticate her story, so he didn't believe her.

333. INAPPARENT - *[spell]*- I N A P P A R E N T
Definition: not noticeable
Synonym: invisible, imperceptible
Antonym: detectable, obvious
Sentence: The flaws of the artwork were inapparent to everyone except the artist.

334. SUGGESTIVE - *[spell]*- S U G G E S T I V E
Definition: tending to suggest ideas, acts, or feelings
Synonym: signifying, symbolic
Antonym:
Sentence: Her comments were suggestive of displeasure when it came of her job.

335. PERSONABLE- *[spell]*- P E R S O N A B L E
Definition: having a pleasing appearance or personality
Synonym: likable, pleasant
Antonym: abrasive, unlikable
Sentence: Because he was so personable, he made an excellent salesperson.

336. REVENGEFUL- *[spell]*- R E V E N G E F U L
Definition: feeling or showing a strong desire to get even for a wrong
Synonym: vindictive, spiteful
Antonym:
Sentence: He felt revengeful over the death of his father.

337. SUPERB - *[spell]*- S U P E R B
Definition: grand and stately
Synonym: admirable, excellent
Antonym: poor, unremarkable
Sentence: At the restaurant, the couple had a superb steak.

338. ELDERLY - *[spell]*- E L D E R L Y
Definition: somewhat old
Synonym: aged, venerable
Antonym: young
Sentence: Though somewhat elderly, he did not consider himself old enough to retire.

339. TOPPLE - *[spell]*- T O P P L E
Definition: to fall forward
Synonym: collapse, falter
Antonym: hold, steady
Sentence: The tower of cupcakes toppled over onto the floor.

340. ABUNDANCE- *[spell]*- A B U N D A N C E
Definition: a great quantity
Synonym: plenty, bounty
Antonym: scarcity, deficiency
Sentence: Because there was an abundance of cake after the party, many guests took some home with them.

341. ASHORE - *[spell]*- A S H O R E
Definition: to land
Synonym: aground, beached
Antonym: asea
Sentence: A rescue team was brought in when a live whale washed ashore.

342. SCALY - *[spell]-* S C A L Y
Definition: covered with scales (overlapping plates forming the outer covering on fishes and reptiles)
Synonym:
Antonym:
Sentence: The skin of the fish had a scaly texture.

343. HEADING - *[spell]-* H E A D I N G
Definition: something written or printed at the top of a page
Synonym: title, caption
Antonym:
Sentence: The heading on her dissertation included her name and the title of her paper.

344. INSANITY - *[spell]-* I N S A N I T Y
Definition: state of mental unsoundness
Synonym: madness, craziness
Antonym: sanity, soundness
Sentence: Her insanity was only a fabrication of the people around her.

345. ADDITIVE- *[spell]-* A D D I T I V E
Definition: a substance that is added to another substance (such as food) in order to preserve it
Synonym: preservative
Antonym:
Sentence: Most foods you buy in the grocery store have additives of some kind.

346. LURCH - *[spell]-* L U R C H
Definition: a sudden leaning or rolling to one side
Synonym: careen, falter
Antonym: steady, straighten
Sentence: The car lurched as it hit the speed bump.

347. UNCOMMON - *[spell]-* U N C O M M O N
Definition: rare or unusual
Synonym: infrequent, extraordinary
Antonym: common, usual
Sentence: It was not uncommon for her to make extravagant meals on Sunday.

348. RUDIMENT- *[spell]-* R U D I M E N T
Definition: part to be learned first
Synonym: fundamental, foundation
Antonym:
Sentence: The rudiments of math are addition and subtraction.

349. INFINITE - *[spell]*- I N F I N I T E
Definition: without limits or bounds
Synonym: limitless, immeasurable
Antonym: finite, measurable
Sentence: He seemed to have an infinite amount of money at his disposal.

350. BOLT- *[spell]*- B O L T
Definition: sudden start or rush
Synonym: bound, dart
Antonym:
Sentence: She was running late for her meeting, so she bolted down the hall.

351. ENLARGEMENT - *[spell]*- E N L A R G E M E N T
Definition: a making of something bigger or larger
Synonym: augmentation, growth
Antonym: compression, contraction
Sentence: He had an enlargement of the photo made to hang above the mantle.

352. HOCUS - *[spell]*- H O C U S
Definition: play a trick on
Synonym: hoax, cheat
Antonym:
Sentence: The magician was able to hocus the audience into believing he actually pulled a rabbit out of a hat.

353. ILLUSION - *[spell]*- I L L U S I O N
Definition: appearance or feeling that misleads because it is not real
Synonym: delusion, hallucination
Antonym: fact, reality
Sentence: She saw right through the illusion of security he offered her.

354. LAUGHABLE - *[spell]*- L A U G H A B L E
Definition: something that is amusing and causes one to laugh
Synonym: comical, absurd
Antonym:
Sentence: His actions, though intended to be serious, were laughable.

355. FAITHFUL - *[spell]*- F A I T H F U L
Definition: worthy of trust
Synonym: loyal, reliable
Antonym: disloyal, faithless
Sentence: He knew he could count on her as his faithful friend.

356. ALLOWANCE - *[spell]*- A L L O W A N C E
Definition: a sum granted to meet expenses
Synonym: allotment, allocation
Antonym: whole
Sentence: Each month, the company granted its employees an allowance for rent.

357. SHORTAGE - *[spell]*- S H O R T A G E
Definition: too small an amount
Synonym: deficiency, dearth
Antonym: abundance, plenty
Sentence: There was no shortage of books in the library.

358. COWARDICE - *[spell]*- C O W A R D I C E
Definition: lack of courage
Synonym: fearfulness, timidity
Antonym: bravery, courage
Sentence: His cowardice caused him to miss a once in a lifetime opportunity

359. BIAS - *[spell]*- B I A S
Definition: tendency to favor one side too much
Synonym: prejudice, favoritism
Antonym: equality, balance
Sentence: The mother tried hard never to show bias toward either of her children.

360. SPIDERY- *[spell]*- S P I D E R Y
Definition: long and thin like a spider's legs
Synonym:
Antonym:
Sentence: The teenage girl was spidery with her long arms and legs.

361. FODDER - *[spell]*- F O D D E R
Definition: food for livestock like cattle
Synonym:
Antonym:
Sentence: The farmer bought a load of fodder for his cattle.

362. ABBEY- *[spell]*- A B B E Y
Definition: a monastery or convent, in which monks and nuns live
Synonym: convent, nunnery
Antonym:
Sentence: Seeking shelter, the homeless man made his way to the abbey.

363. DESERVEDLY - *[spell]*- D E S E R V E D L Y
Definition: justly
Synonym: justifiably, appropriately
Antonym: unfairly, undeservedly
Sentence: The child deservedly received punishment for his disrespectful language.

364. PAWN- *[spell]*- P A W N
Definition: an unimportant person or thing used by someone to gain some advantage
Synonym:
Antonym:
Sentence: He was merely a pawn in her grand plan.

365. MIGRANT - *[spell]*- M I G R A N T
Definition: moving from place to place
Synonym: nomadic, transient
Antonym: stationary
Sentence: He lived a migrant lifestyle because of his job.

366. OBITUARY- *[spell]*- O B I T U A R Y
Definition: notice of death
Synonym:
Antonym:
Sentence: He saw a name he recognized in the obituaries.

367. LATITUDE - *[spell]*- L A T I T U D E
Definition: distance north or south on the equator measured by degrees
Synonym:
Antonym:
Sentence: States with a higher latitude typically have a colder climate.

368. GLANCE - *[spell]*- G L A N C E
Definition: quick look directed at someone or something
Synonym: glimpse, peek
Antonym: stare
Sentence: She stole a glance at the boy across the room.

369. UNKEMPT - *[spell]*- U N K E M P T
Definition: not properly cared for
Synonym: shaggy, scruffy
Antonym: clean, kempt
Sentence: The child looked unkempt in her raggedly clothes.

370. INFERNAL - *[spell]*- I N F E R NAL
Definition: hateful or shocking

Synonym: accursed, confounded
Antonym: heavenly, otherworldly
Sentence: He couldn't stand the infernal racket coming from the apartment below him.

371. GROUCHY - *[spell]*- G R O U C H Y
Definition: tending to grumble
Synonym: complaining, irritable
Antonym: agreeable, affable
Sentence: She was always grouchy when she became hungry.

372. CANOPY - *[spell]*- C A N O P Y
Definition: a covering over a bed, entrance, doorway, etc.
Synonym: awning
Antonym:
Sentence: The little girl had a canopy that hung over her bed.

373. DISPATCH - *[spell]*- D I S P A T C H
Definition: send off to some place for a particular reason
Synonym:
Antonym:
Sentence: She dispatched her son to carry a message to his father.

374. SALTY - *[spell]*- S A L T Y
Definition: terse and witty
Synonym: sharp, lively
Antonym:
Sentence: When his words insulted her, she embarrassed him with her salty reply.

375. OCEANIC- *[spell]*- O C E A N I C
Definition: having to do with an ocean (great body of water)
Synonym: aquatic, maritime
Antonym:
Sentence: In college he took a class in oceanic sciences.

376. TREATISE - *[spell]*- T R E A T I S E
Definition: a formal book or writing dealing with some subject
Synonym: essay
Antonym:
Sentence: The author wrote a treatise on theology.

377. REFRESHMENT- *[spell]*- R E F R E S H M E N T
Definition: something that provides with new energy
Synonym: food, drink
Antonym:

Sentence: Refreshments were available for purchase at the concession stand.

378. FORGETFUL - *[spell]*- F O R G E T F U L
Definition: apt to fail to remember
Synonym: absentminded
Antonym: mindful
Sentence: She kept a detailed agenda in her planner because she was so forgetful.

379. MASSIVE - *[spell]*- M A S S I V E
Definition: very bulky and heavy
Synonym: large, enormous
Antonym: small, miniscule
Sentence: The new sofa looked massive in her living room.

380. ATTACHMENT - *[spell]*- A T T A C H M E N T
Definition: a connection
Synonym: bond, connector
Antonym: separation
Sentence: Because of his attachment to her, he had a hard time leaving her.

381. LEAKAGE - *[spell]*- L E A K A G E
Definition: a hole or crack not meant to be there that lets something in or out
Synonym: leak, outpouring
Antonym:
Sentence: There seemed to be a leakage from some container in the refrigerator.

382. FRACTION - *[spell]*- F R A C T I O N
Definition: a very small part
Synonym: fragment, portion
Antonym: whole, entirety
Sentence: The furniture store sold the sofa at a fraction of the cost of its competitor.

383. FAMILIARIZE - *[spell]*- F A M I L I A R I Z E
Definition: make well-acquainted with something
Synonym: acquaint, enlighten
Antonym:
Sentence: Before starting her new job, she had to familiarize herself with company procedures.

384. FRETFUL - *[spell]*- F R E T F U L
Definition: apt to be peevish, unhappy or worried
Synonym: irritable, restless
Antonym:
Sentence: He was fretful about his job.

385. ABANDON- *[spell]*- A B A N D O N
Definition: to give up entirely
Synonym: disregard, unrestraint
Antonym: restraint, control
Sentence: On a whim of reckless abandon, the young couple decided to run away and start a new life.

386. GUTSY - *[spell]*- G U T S Y
Definition: full of courage
Synonym: bold, brave
Antonym: afraid, cowardly
Sentence: Feeling gutsy, he decided to go skydiving.

387. MERCIFUL - *[spell]*- M E R C I F U L
Definition: having feeling or showing more kindness than justice requires
Synonym: gracious, forgiving
Antonym: vengeful, cruel
Sentence: The judge was known to be merciful.

388. RUFFIAN - *[spell]*- R U F F I A N
Definition: a rough, brutal, or cruel person
Synonym: hoodlum, delinquent
Antonym:
Sentence: There was a wanted poster showing the face of the ruffian.

389. TODDLE - *[spell]*- T O D D L E
Definition: to walk with short, unsteady steps, as a baby does
Synonym: totter, waddle
Antonym:
Sentence: The child toddled excitedly across the room.

390. PERSUASION- *[spell]*- P E R S U A S I O N
Definition: a winning over in order to do or to believe
Synonym: convincing, influencing
Antonym: ineffectuality
Sentence: His persuasion made her see things his way.

391. DUMPY - *[spell]*- D U M P Y
Definition: short and fat
Synonym: chubby, chunky

Antonym:
Sentence: The dog was somewhat dumpy in its old age.

392. FRIGID - *[spell]*- F R I G I D
Definition: very cold
Synonym: freezing, frosty
Antonym: warm, hot
Sentence: Her frigid attitude toward him was due to her anger.

393. HUMONGOUS - *[spell]*- H U M O N G O U S
Definition: extraordinarily large
Synonym: giant, gargantuan
Antonym: tiny, miniscule
Sentence: He brought home a humongous watermelon for dessert.

394. INSIGHTFUL - *[spell]*- I N S I G H T F U L
Definition: having or showing understanding or wisdom
Synonym: astute, sharp
Antonym:
Sentence: The child made several insightful observations about the problem.

395. SAINT - *[spell]*- S A I N T
Definition: a very holy person
Synonym:
Antonym:
Sentence: He was considered a saint by the Catholic Church.

396. SPUTTER- *[spell]*- S P U T T E R
Definition: to make spitting and popping noises
Synonym: stammer, stumble
Antonym:
Sentence: He knew something was wrong when the car began to sputter.

397. IMPURE - *[spell]*- I M P U R E
Definition: not pure
Synonym: unclean, dirty
Antonym: clean pure
Sentence: Because the water was impure, it was not fit for drinking.

398. INVINCIBLE - *[spell]*- I N V I N C I B L E
Definition: unable to be conquered
Synonym: indestructible, indomitable
Antonym: beatable, breakable
Sentence: After his victory in the race, he felt invincible.

399. TIMEWORN - *[spell]*- T I M E W O R N
      Definition: worn by long existence or use
      Synonym:
      Antonym:
      Sentence: The old building, though in good shape, looked timeworn.

400. BUMPER - *[spell]*- B U M P E R
      Definition: a device that protects against damage from pushing or striking
      Synonym: cushion, buffer
      Antonym:
      Sentence: His car's bumper was dented after being rear-ended by a truck.

Easy Words Exercise - 5

401. RECLINE - *[spell]*- R E C L I N E
Definition: to lean back
Synonym: repose, lounge
Antonym:
Sentence: After a long day of work, she reclined on the sofa and watched TV.

402. STABILITY - *[spell]*- S T A B I L I T Y
Definition: the strength to stand or endure
Synonym: strength, support
Antonym: uncertainty, weakness
Sentence: He was relieved by the stability of his job.

403. ABOUND - *[spell]*- A B O U N D
Definition: to be many
Synonym: proliferate
Antonym: scarce, few
Sentence: The shop at the corner abounded with interesting knick-knacks.

404. MINORITY - *[spell]*- M I N O R I T Y
Definition: smaller party or group opposed to a majority
Synonym:
Antonym: majority
Sentence: At the social gathering, men were a minority.

405. REVERIE - *[spell]*- R E V E R I E
Definition: dreamy thoughts
Synonym: contemplation, daydreams
Antonym:
Sentence: He was too lost in his reverie to realize that the kitchen sink had overflowed.

406. PROBLEMATIC - *[spell]*- P R O B L E M A T I C
Definition: having the nature of a matter of doubt or difficulty
Synonym: troubling, difficult
Antonym: incontestable, unquestionable
Sentence: She found the lack of ethics in her friends to be highly problematic.

407. FUTURISTIC - *[spell]*- F U T U R I S T I C
Definition: of or relating to the future
Synonym:
Antonym:
Sentence: The idea of self-driving cars may seem futuristic, but this may actually not be all that far off.

408. PRIDEFUL - *[spell]*- P R I D E F U L
Definition: thinking well of oneself
Synonym: arrogant, conceited
Antonym: humble, modest
-Sentence: She was quite prideful when it came to her musical abilities.

409. NAVIGATION - *[spell]*- N A V I G A T I O N
Definition: act or process of managing a ship or aircraft
Synonym:
Antonym:
Sentence: In order to be a pilot, you need to be good at navigation.

410. FORMALITY - *[spell]*- F O R M A L I T Y
Definition: procedure required by custom or rule but has little true value
Synonym: convention
Antonym:
Sentence: The second round of interviews is really just a formality.

411. TANKARD - *[spell]*- T A N K A R D
Definition: a large drinking mug with a handle and a hinged cover
Synonym: mug, stein
Antonym:
Sentence: He drank the beer from a tankard.

412. QUAKE - *[spell]*- Q U A K E
Definition: shake or tremble from cold, anger, etc.
Synonym: shiver, quiver
Antonym:
Sentence: The dog began to quake with fear upon seeing its master.

413. INSEPARABLE - *[spell]*- I N S E P A R A B L E
Definition: not able to be pulled apart
Synonym: indivisible, conjoined
Antonym: separable, dividable
Sentence: The siblings were practically inseparable, doing everything together.

414. PLUNGER - *[spell]*- P L U N G E R
Definition: person or thing that throws something with force into a liquid

Synonym:
Antonym:
Sentence: A plunger was used to unclog the sink.

415. POCKMARK - *[spell]*- P O C K M A R K
Definition: mark or pit on the skin
Synonym: blemish, flaw
Antonym:
Sentence: She used makeup to cover up the pockmarks on her skin.

416. CHOOSY - *[spell]*- C H O O S Y
Definition: fussy
Synonym: selective, finicky
Antonym: undemanding, open
Sentence: She was very choosy about the kinds of food she ate.

417. OODLES - *[spell]*- O O D L E S
Definition: large or unlimited in quantity
Synonym: abundance, masses
Antonym:
Sentence: The child had collected oodles of action figures.

418. OUTERMOST - *[spell]*- O U T E R M O S T
Definition: farthest out
Synonym: distant, fringe
Antonym: closest, nearest
Sentence: The man advised them to pick the apples on the outermost branches of the tree.

419. FLAIL - *[spell]*- F L A I L
Definition: to strike with or as if with a flail
Synonym: batter, hit
Antonym:
Sentence: He began to flail the wall in his anger.

420. DAMPER - *[spell]*- D A M P E R
Definition: a person or thing that discourages
Synonym: hindrance, restraint
Antonym: encouragement
Sentence: The rain put a damper on their picnic.

421. REMARKABLE - *[spell]*- R E M A R K A B L E
Definition: worthy of notice
Synonym: noteworthy, extraordinary
Antonym: average, commonplace

Sentence: Her grades in school were remarkable considering the circumstances.

422.   MAKESHIFT - *[spell]*- M A K E S H I F T
Definition: something used for a time instead of the right thing
Synonym:
Antonym:
Sentence: While camping, they made a makeshift tent out of two blankets.

423.   AFTERMATH - *[spell]*- A F T E R M A T H
Definition: result of something, especially something bad
Synonym: consequence, outcome
Antonym: origin, source
Sentence: The people were faced with great destruction in the aftermath of the storm.

424.   AMPLE - *[spell]*- A M P L E
Definition: more than enough
Synonym: abundant, bountiful
Antonym: lacking, meager
Sentence: After the harvest, the farmer had an ample amount of corn.

425.   SERENADE - *[spell]*- S E R E N A D E
Definition: music played or sung outdoors at night, especially by a lover under a sweetheart's window
Synonym: song
Antonym:
Sentence: Outside her window, her boyfriend serenaded her.

426.   COMPREHENSIBLE - *[spell]*- C O M P R E H E N S I B L E
Definition: easily understandable
Synonym: coherent, intelligible
Antonym: ambiguous, obscure
Sentence: The instructional materials were comprehensible.

427.   RAKISH - *[spell]*- R A K I S H
Definition: immoral or dissolute
Synonym: raffish, depraved
Antonym:
Sentence: His rakish behavior ultimately led to his downfall.

428.   DILEMMA - *[spell]*- D I L E M M A
Definition: a situation that requires a decision between two difficult choices
Synonym: quandary, conundrum
Antonym:

Sentence: He found himself in a dilemma over whether to accept the new job or keep his old one.

429. REVELATION - *[spell]*- R E V E L A T I O N
Definition: act of making known
Synonym: announcement, discovery
Antonym: concealment, cover-up
Sentence: After years of knowing her, he made the revelation that he was adopted.

430. UNSETTLED - *[spell]*- U N S E T T L E D
Definition: not determined or decided
Synonym: perturbed, restless
Antonym: calm, firm
Sentence: She felt unsettled as soon as she walked in the old house.

431. MIGRATION - *[spell]*- M I G R A T I O N
Definition: a moving from one place to another
Synonym: flight, journey
Antonym:
Sentence: The family was in a constant state of migration.

432. POSTMARK - *[spell]*- P O S T M A R K
Definition: an official mark stamped on mail to record the place and date of mailing
Synonym:
Antonym:
Sentence: The letter was postmarked over a week ago.

433. CHEERLESS - *[spell]*- C H E E R L E S S
Definition: without joy or comfort
Synonym: gloomy, dreary
Antonym: cheerful, uplifting
Sentence: Because the room was utterly cheerless, he decided to redecorate.

434. MECHANICAL - *[spell]*- M E C H A N I C A L
Definition: having to do with a machine or machinery
Synonym: automated
Antonym: manual
Sentence: He was an expert in all things mechanical.

435. SCIENTIFIC - *[spell]*- S C I E N T I F I C
Definition: using the facts and laws of science (knowledge observed by facts and truths)
Synonym:

Antonym:
Sentence: He was recognized for his groundbreaking scientific research.

436. SQUEAKY - *[spell]*- S Q U E A K Y
Definition: making short, sharp, shrill sounds
Synonym:
Antonym:
Sentence: The squeaky door alerted her to the fact that someone had come home.

437. MORTALITY - *[spell]*- M O R T A L I T Y
Definition: condition of being sure to die sometime
Synonym: fatality,
Antonym: immortality
Sentence: The old man finally came to terms with his mortality.

438. ROOMY - *[spell]*- R O O M Y
Definition: having plenty of space
Synonym: spacious, commodious
Antonym:
Sentence: The SUV he bought was roomy inside.

439. BISTRO - *[spell]*- B I S T R O
Definition: a small wine shop and restaurant
Synonym:
Antonym:
Sentence: He had dinner and wine at the small French bistro down the street.

440. ADJOIN - *[spell]*- A D J O I N
Definition: to be next to and/or in contact with
Synonym: connect, abut
Antonym: disconnect, divide
Sentence: The library adjoins the government offices downtown.

441. CLERGY - *[spell]*- C L E R G Y
Definition: a person who is ordained for religious work
Synonym: ministry
Antonym:
Sentence: All the clergy of the church gathered together to make some important decisions.

442. SPUNKY - *[spell]*- S P U N K Y
Definition: courageous or plucky
Synonym: fearless, spirited
Antonym: halfhearted

Sentence: Her spunky attitude in the face of adversity won her the respect of her peers.

443. PARTICIPANT - *[spell]*- P A R T I C I P A N T
Definition: person who shares or participates
Synonym: actor, player
Antonym: spectator
Sentence: All participants in the race were given a free t-shirt.

444. PHENOMENAL - *[spell]*- P H E N O M E N A L
Definition: extraordinary or remarkable
Synonym: exceptional, superior
Antonym: unremarkable, unexceptional
Sentence: His athletic abilities were phenomenal.

445. ODDITY - *[spell]*- O D D I T Y
Definition: strangeness or peculiarity
Synonym: abnormality, irregularity
Antonym:
Sentence: Because of his appearance, he was viewed as something of an oddity.

446. ARRANGEMENT - *[spell]*- A R R A N G E M E N T
Definition: being put in proper order
Synonym: preparation
Antonym: disorder, disagreement
Sentence: She found the arrangement of flowers quite satisfactory.

447. COLOSSAL - *[spell]*- C O L O S S A L
Definition: of huge size
Synonym: gigantic, vast
Antonym: small, miniscule
Sentence: He was taken aback by the colossal size of their home.

448. BREATHABLE - *[spell]*- B R E A T H A B L E
Definition: fit or able to draw in air
Synonym:
Antonym:
Sentence: The fabric of the shirt was quite breathable, making it suitable for exercise.

449. DETHRONE - *[spell]*- D E T H R O NE
Definition: remove from power
Synonym: oust, dismiss
Antonym: enthrone, crown
Sentence: The king was dethroned after he lost the war.

450. TUTORIAL - *[spell]*- T U T O R I A L
Definition: of or having to do with a private teacher
Synonym: lesson
Antonym:
Sentence: The teacher created several tutorials for students to review at home.

451. MATRON - *[spell]*- M A T R O N
Definition: wife or widow, especially one mature in age
Synonym:
Antonym:
Sentence: The matron constantly had advice for the younger women in her life.

452. RAFFISH - *[spell]*- R A F F I S H
Definition: showy and cheap
Synonym: tawdry, rakish
Antonym:
Sentence: Some of the older neighborhoods in the city have a tattered, raffish charm.

453. ORDEAL - *[spell]*- O R D E A L
Definition: a severe test or experience
Synonym: affliction, torment
Antonym:
Sentence: What was supposed to be just a short test turned out to be a huge ordeal.

454. SLUDGE - *[spell]*- S L U D G E
Definition: soft mud or mire
Synonym: muck, sediment
Antonym:
Sentence: The melting snow formed sludge in her front yard.

455. ENERGIZE - *[spell]*- E N E R G I Z E
Definition: give vigor to
Synonym: animate, invigorate
Antonym: deaden, dampen
Sentence: She was energized by her short nap.

456. IDENTIFICATION - *[spell]*- I D E N T I F I C A T I O N
Definition: a being recognized as a particular person or thing
Synonym: recognition
Antonym:
Sentence: The celebrity was annoyed by her identification by fans while she was on vacation.

457. HURRAH - *[spell]*- H U R R A H
Definition: shout of joy or approval
Synonym: cheer
Antonym:
Sentence: Everyone let out a hurrah when the man walked into the surprise party.

458. RECOVERY - *[spell]*- R E C O V E R Y
Definition: the act of becoming healthy again after an illness or injury
Synonym: convalescence
Antonym:
Sentence: She had a long recovery period after her injury.

459. HUMIDITY - *[spell]*- H U M I D I TY
Definition: a being moist or damp
Synonym: dankness, dampness
Antonym: aridity, dryness
Sentence: The humidity in the air was almost too much to handle on the hot summer day.

460. BALANCED - *[spell]*- B A L A N C E D
Definition: having equality in weight, force or effect
Synonym: equitable
Antonym: biased, partial
Sentence: He knew that his time needed to be balanced between work and pleasure.

461. ACREAGE - *[spell]*- A C R E A G E
Definition: number of acres (unit of measuring land)
Synonym: expanse, property
Antonym:
Sentence: When he purchased the farm, he acquired substantial acreage.

462. SPOILAGE - *[spell]*- S P O I L A G E
Definition: act of damaging, injuring, or going bad
Synonym: ruination, decay
Antonym: ripening, development
Sentence: A spoilage of the groceries in her fridge occurred when she lost power for several days.

463. REFINISH - *[spell]*- R E F I N I SH
Definition: to give a new coating
Synonym: redecorate, clad
Antonym: roughen
Sentence: She refinished the antique furniture to be used on her home.

464. MARATHON - *[spell]*- M A R A T H O N
Definition: a race on foot
Synonym:
Antonym:
Sentence: His goal was to run his first marathon before he turned thirty.

465. CANCELLATION - *[spell]*- C A N C E L L A TI O N
Definition: the act of putting something to an end or withdrawing
Synonym: annulment, abandonment
Antonym: continuation
Sentence: She submitted the form to request a cancellation of her magazine subscription.

466. INFIRMITY - *[spell]*- I N F I R M I T Y
Definition: sickness
Synonym: weakness, affliction
Antonym: robustness, good health
Sentence: His infirmity was due to a virus he caught while he was overseas.

467. PLIABLE - *[spell]*- P L I A B L E
Definition: easily bent
Synonym: bendable, flexible
Antonym: rigid, inflexible
Sentence: The pliable clay was shaped into the form of a dog.

468. NAUSEA - *[spell]*- N A U S E A
Definition: the feeling a person is about to vomit
Synonym:
Antonym:
Sentence: She felt some nausea after riding the roller coaster.

469. LABORATORY - *[spell]*- L A B O R A T O R Y
Definition: place where scientific work is done
Synonym: lab
Antonym:
Sentence: The scientist got to work in his laboratory.

470. NIGGLING - *[spell]*- N I G G L I N G
Definition: trifling or mean
Synonym: finicky, fussing
Antonym:
Sentence: She was offended by his niggling comments.

471. SERUM - *[spell]*- S E R U M
Definition: a liquid used to cure or prevent disease

Synonym:
Antonym:
Sentence: The serum was the cure for the poison.

472. CONDITIONAL - *[spell]*- C O N D I T I O N A L
Definition: depending on something
Synonym: limited, provisional
Antonym: unconditional
Sentence: Their going to the concert was conditional upon their other plans that weekend.

473. ADRIFT - *[spell]*- A D R I F T
Definition: floating without being guided in a direction
Synonym: afloat, unanchored
Antonym: anchored
Sentence: The unmanned boat was found adrift at sea.

474. NAB - *[spell]*- N A B
Definition: catch or seize suddenly
Synonym: capture, snatch
Antonym: liberate, free
Sentence: He wanted to nab the item before it sold out.

475. TOURISM - *[spell]*- T O U R I S M
Definition: traveling for pleasure
Synonym:
Antonym:
Sentence: Tourism was the main industry of the state.

476. QUAINT - *[spell]*- Q U A I N T
Definition: strange, old-fashioned, or odd in a pleasing or amusing way
Synonym: charming, attractive
Antonym:
Sentence: The old house, though it needed repairs, was quaint.

477. NOMINATION - *[spell]*- N O M I N A T I O N
Definition: a naming a candidate for office
Synonym: selection, designation
Antonym:
Sentence: He was surprised to receive the nomination for president.

478. DIVISIVE - *[spell]*- D I V I S I V E
Definition: tending to cause division or disagreement
Synonym: dissenting, disruptive
Antonym:

Sentence: His opinions were divisive in nature, causing disagreements among his friends.

479. IMMENSITY - *[spell]* - I M M E N S I T Y
Definition: very great size or extent
Synonym: enormity, vastness
Antonym: insignificance, smallness
Sentence: She felt overwhelmed by the immensity of the project.

480. GRENADE - *[spell]* - G R E N A D E
Definition: a small bomb typically thrown by hand
Synonym: bomb, explosive
Antonym:
Sentence: The soldier carried a grenade in his backpack for emergencies.

481. MISMANAGE - *[spell]* - M I S M A N A G E
Definition: to manage badly
Synonym: mishandle, blunder
Antonym:
Sentence: The president of the company was often accused of mismanaging financial accounts.

482. NOOK - *[spell]* - N O O K
Definition: a cozy little corner
Synonym: alcove, niche
Antonym:
Sentence: There was a nook in the house where she always liked to read.

483. BELLE - *[spell]* - B E L L E
Definition: beautiful woman or girl
Synonym: coquette, beauty
Antonym: eyesore
Sentence: She was known as the belle of the town.

484. NAMESAKE - *[spell]* - N A M E S A K E
Definition: one named after another
Synonym:
Antonym:
Sentence: He was the namesake of his father.

485. MISCHANCE - *[spell]* - M I S C H A N C E
Definition: bad luck
Synonym: misfortune, accident
Antonym: fortunate, lucky
Sentence: It was purely mischance that caused the accident.

486. FOREWORD - *[spell]*- F O R E W O R D
    Definition: a brief introduction or preface to a book
    Synonym: preface, prologue
    Antonym: epilogue, conclusion
    Sentence: In the foreword of the book, the author discussed what inspired him to write it.

487. IMMEASURABLE - *[spell]*- I M M E A S U R A B L E
    Definition: too vast to be measured
    Synonym: boundless, immense
    Antonym: limited, finite
    Sentence: His enthusiasm seemed to be immeasurable.

488. ENGAGEMENT - *[spell]*- E N G A G E M E N T
    Definition: appointment to be made to meet someone at a certain time
    Synonym:
    Antonym:
    Sentence: He refused her invitation for lunch because he had a prior engagement.

489. PUBLICITY - *[spell]*- P U B L I C I T Y
    Definition: public notice
    Synonym: attention, exposure
    Antonym:
    Sentence: The company received much publicity from the promotional ads in the paper.

490. RETROACTIVE - *[spell]*- R E T R O A C T I V E
    Definition: having an effect on what is past
    Synonym:
    Antonym:
    Sentence: The tax credit was, unfortunately, not retroactive.

491. DAMSEL - *[spell]*- D A M S E L
    Definition: a young girl who is not married
    Synonym: maiden, miss
    Antonym:
    Sentence: The young man offered the damsel his coat since it was raining.

492. LEARNED - *[spell]*- L E A R N E D
    Definition: having, showing or requiring much knowledge
    Synonym: scholarly, educated
    Antonym: uneducated, ignorant
    Sentence: He was learned in the ways of healing.

493. SMART - *[spell]*- S M A R T
Definition: to feel sharp pain
Synonym: hurt, ache
Antonym:
Sentence: The paper cut on her finger began to smart.

494. COLONIZE - *[spell]*- C O L O N I Z E
Definition: establish a settlement of people sent from their own country to settle a new land
Synonym: conquer, settle
Antonym:
Sentence: Great Britain sent citizens overseas to colonize the Americas.

495. HOSPITALIZATION - *[spell]*- H O S P I T A L I Z A T I O N
Definition: act of being put in a hospital for medical treatment
Synonym:
Antonym:
Sentence: A brief period of hospitalization made him realize he needed to take better care of himself.

496. MARKEDLY - *[spell]*- M A R K E D L Y
Definition: noticeably
Synonym: distinctly
Antonym: unremarkably, indistinctly
Sentence: The new hotel was markedly better than the old one.

497. DISRUPTIVE - *[spell]*- D I S R U P T I V E
Definition: causing a destruction in the continuity of something
Synonym: troublesome, rowdy
Antonym: disciplined, settled
Sentence: The child's outburst was quite disruptive to the rest of the class.

498. INFECTIOUS - *[spell]*- I N F E C T I O U S
Definition: spread by infection (disease caused by introduction of disease-producing microorganisms in the tissues of people, animals, etc.)
Synonym: contagious, spreading
Antonym:
Sentence: The nation was gripped by an outbreak of an infectious disease.

499. SCRAWNY - *[spell]*- S C R A W N Y
Definition: lean or thin
Synonym: skinny, lanky
Antonym: fat, heavy
Sentence: The woman tried to fatten the scrawny cat by giving it table scraps.

500.   PERSPIRE - *[spell]*- P E R S P I R E
        Definition: to sweat
        Synonym:
        Antonym:
        Sentence: Because of the high temperature, he began to perspire.

Easy Words Exercise - 6

501. ASTROLOGY - *[spell]*- A S T R O L O G Y
Definition: the study of the stars to foretell the future
Synonym: horoscope
Antonym:
Sentence: Interested in what the future might hold, she sought to learn more about astrology.

502. LADLE - *[spell]*- L A D L E
Definition: a large, cup-shaped spoon for dipping out liquids
Synonym: scoop
Antonym:
Sentence: She used a ladle to serve the soup.

503. AUTHORIZATION - *[spell]*- A U T H O R I Z A T I O N
Definition: act or process of giving the power or right
Synonym: endorsement, sanction
Antonym:
Sentence: Giving his official authorization of the project allowed her to begin more quickly.

504. BARGAIN - *[spell]*- B A R G A I N
Definition: something that can be bought cheap
Synonym: deal, discount
Antonym: rip-off
Sentence: She bought the purse for quite a bargain.

505. INNOVATION - *[spell]*- I N N O V A T I O N
Definition: change made in the established way of doing things
Synonym: novelty, modernization
Antonym: custom, tradition
Sentence: Recent innovations in science have produced some interesting inventions.

506. FABULOUS - *[spell]*- F A B U L O U S
Definition: amazing
Synonym: astonishing, astounding
Antonym: commonplace, boring
Sentence: She found the boutique downtown to be completely fabulous.

507. STRETCHER - *[spell]*- S T R E T C H E R
Definition: a kind of carrier, usually a canvas on a frame, used for carrying the wounded or sick
Synonym: litter, pallet
Antonym:
Sentence: At the hospital, the patient was taken to the ER on a stretcher.

508. TROPICAL - *[spell]*- T R O P I C A L
Definition: hot and humid
Synonym: warm, lush
Antonym:
Sentence: Tired of so much snow, he decided to move somewhere more tropical.

509. CLASSIFY - *[spell]*- C L A S S I F Y
Definition: to arrange into groups
Synonym: arrange, organize
Antonym: disorganize
Sentence: In order to better classify all the files, he spread them all out onto the desk.

510. OVERTURN - *[spell]*- O V E R T U R N
Definition: to turn upside down
Synonym: capsize, topple
Antonym: approve, keep
Sentence: Her world was overturned by one phone call.

511. PHARMACY - *[spell]*- P H A R M A C Y
Definition: place where drugs and medicines are prepared or sold
Synonym: drugstore, apothecary
Antonym:
Sentence: She went to the pharmacy to purchase cold medicine.

512. INFREQUENT - *[spell]*- I N F R E Q U E N T
Definition: occurring seldom or far apart
Synonym: seldom, rare
Antonym: often, regular
Sentence: He was an infrequent visitor to his mother.

513. MISUSAGE - *[spell]*- M I S U S A G E
Definition: wrong or improper usage
Synonym: misapplication, misuse
Antonym:
Sentence: The misusage of the tool could cause injury.

514. CENTURY - *[spell]*- C E N T U R Y
Definition: a period of 100 years
Synonym:
Antonym:
Sentence: Each century in human history has been vastly different from the last.

515. SHOWERY - *[spell]*- S H O W E R Y
Definition: a short fall of rain
Synonym: rainy, sodden
Antonym: arid, clear
Sentence: The weather forecast promised a showery day.

516. MANUSCRIPT - *[spell]*- M A N U S C R I P T
Definition: book or paper written by hand or on a computer
Synonym:
Antonym:
Sentence: The author sent his manuscript off to the publisher.

517. OVERSTATE - *[spell]*- O V E R S T A T E
Definition: to say too strongly
Synonym: exaggerate, amplify
Antonym: downplay, simplify
Sentence: He had a tendency to overstate the problem.

518. SUSPENSION - *[spell]*- S U S P E N S I O N
Definition: a being held in place a while
Synonym: interruption, freeze
Antonym: continuation, persistence
Sentence: As a result of her actions, she was given a suspension for her duties at work.

519. YONDER - *[spell]*- Y O N D E R
Definition: being over there
Synonym: away, beyond
Antonym:
Sentence: He told his son to fetch the shovel over yonder.

520. TASTEFUL - *[spell]*- T A S T E F U L
Definition: refined
Synonym: classy, elegant
Antonym: crude, rough
Sentence: She was always tasteful when it came to her clothing.

521. SNOOZE - *[spell]*- S N O O Z E
Definition: to take a nap or doze

Synonym: doze, slumber
Antonym: awakening, consciousness
Sentence: Lying in the hammock in the warm sun, he soon began to snooze.

522. BESTRIDE - *[spell]*- B E S T R I D E
Definition: to sit on or stand over
Synonym: straddle
Antonym:
Sentence: In order to ride, you must sit bestride the horse.

523. WHITTLE - *[spell]*- W H I T T L E
Definition: to cut or trim
Synonym: reduce, diminish
Antonym:
Sentence: He whittled a piece of wood into the shape of a bird.

524. GRAVE - *[spell]*- G R A V E
Definition: serious
Synonym: heavy, weighty
Antonym: frivolous, insignificant
Sentence: Everyone was quiet because of the grave circumstances they faced.

525. BENEFICIAL - *[spell]*- B E N E F I C I A L
Definition: producing good
Synonym: favorable, helpful
Antonym: disadvantageous, harmful
Sentence: She left the seminar with many beneficial ideas about how to improve her business.

526. AMUSEMENT - *[spell]*- A M U S E M E N T
Definition: condition of feeling happy or entertained
Synonym: happiness, delight
Antonym: boredom
Sentence: She experienced great amusement at the magic show.

527. ALIGHT - *[spell]*- A L I G H T
Definition: to get out or down from
Synonym: descend, disembark
Antonym: mount, climb
Sentence: Arriving back home, he alighted from his horse's back.

528. FILTH - *[spell]*- F I L T H
Definition: very dirty conditions
Synonym: foulness, dirt

Antonym: cleanliness
Sentence: She couldn't stand to be in the filth of his apartment.

529. SHERIFF - *[spell]*- S H E R I F F
Definition: the most important law-enforcing officer of a county
Synonym: officer, constable
Antonym:
Sentence: The sheriff was well known throughout the county.

530. CORRESPONDENT - *[spell]*- C O R R E S P O N D E N T
Definition: a person who communicates by writing letters
Synonym:
Antonym:
Sentence: Her pen pal was an attentive correspondent, writing letters once a week.

531. DISASTROUS - *[spell]*- D I S A S T R O U S
Definition: bringing suffering and loss
Synonym: catastrophic, cataclysmic
Antonym: fortunate, favorable
Sentence: The effects of the tornado were disastrous.

532. CHEAPEN - *[spell]*- C H E A P E N
Definition: cause to be thought little of
Synonym: demean, degrade
Antonym: elevate, exalt
Sentence: Her actions cheapened her reputation as a reliable source of information.

533. MISBEHAVIOR - *[spell]*- M I S B E H A V I O R
Definition: bad behavior
Synonym: impropriety, misconduct
Antonym:
Sentence: The child was punished for his misbehavior.

534. RECKLESS - *[spell]*- R E C K L E S S
Definition: lacking in caution or prudence
Synonym: foolhardy, thoughtless
Antonym: careful, attentive
Sentence: Her reckless behavior while behind the wheel almost cost her life.

535. MISCHIEVOUS - *[spell]*- M I S C H I E V O U S
Definition: causing acts that create harm or trouble, often unintentionally
Synonym: troublesome, wicked

Antonym: behaved, orderly
Sentence: The child was known for his mischievous nature.

536. BROADSIDE - *[spell]*- B R O A D S I D E
      Definition: direct into the side
      Synonym: sidelong
      Antonym:
      Sentence: The car ran directly into the broadside of the bus.

537. DISTINGUISHED - *[spell]*- D I S T I N G U I S H E D
      Definition: well-known because of a quality or achievement
      Synonym: esteemed, august
      Antonym: flighty, undignified
      Sentence: A distinguished doctor won the award at the conference.

538. SIDEKICK - *[spell]*- S I D E K I C K
      Definition: partner or close friend
      Synonym: companion, accomplice
      Antonym:
      Sentence: The hero's sidekick managed to save the day.

539. MILLIONAIRE - *[spell]*- M I L L I O N A I R E
      Definition: person whose wealth amounts to a million or more dollars
      Synonym:
      Antonym:
      Sentence: He became a millionaire through hard work.

540. PRESERVATIVE - *[spell]*- P R E S E R V A T I V E
      Definition: a substance that will prevent decay or injury
      Synonym:
      Antonym:
      Sentence: Many foods on the market contain preservatives.

541. TRIFLING - *[spell]*- T R I F L I N G
      Definition: having little value or importance
      Synonym: insignificant, worthless
      Antonym: important
      Sentence: She viewed all of her son's girlfriends as trifling and shallow.

542. FLOWERY - *[spell]*- F L O W E R Y
      Definition: containing many fine words and fanciful expressions
      Synonym: grandiloquent, purple
      Antonym: plain, simple
      Sentence: His flowery letter did not impress her.

543. HORRIFIC - *[spell]*- H O R R I F I C
      Definition: causing horror

Synonym: horrendous, abominable
Antonym:
Sentence: She was never the same after she witnessed the horrific event.

544. PASSIONATE - *[spell]* - P A S S I O N A T E
Definition: having or showing strong feelings
Synonym: ardent, desirous
Antonym: frigid
Sentence: She was passionate about her teaching career.

545. CAPTIVATION - *[spell]* - C A P T I V A T I ON
Definition: being held captive by beauty or interest
Synonym: charm, fascination
Antonym: disinterest, boredom
Sentence: She had the audience in complete captivation.

546. ARGUMENTATIVE - *[spell]* - A R G U M E N T A T I V E
Definition: fond of verbal disagreement
Synonym: combative, quarrelsome
Antonym: agreeable, compromising
Sentence: Because of his argumentative nature, many people avoided him.

547. GIFTED - *[spell]* - G I F T E D
Definition: having natural ability or special talent
Synonym: accomplished, brilliant
Antonym:
Sentence: The parents found their child was very gifted at all things musical.

548. OBJECTION - *[spell]* - O B J E C T I O N
Definition: something said or written against something else
Synonym: argument, disagreement
Antonym: acceptance, agreement
Sentence: She had an objection to the news article.

549. PASSIVE - *[spell]* - P A S S I V E
Definition: not resisting
Synonym: resigned, yielding
Antonym: resistant, unyielding
Sentence: She was typically very passive about making decisions.

550. GRUNGY - *[spell]* - G R U N G Y
Definition: very dirty or run-down
Synonym: filthy, dilapidated
Antonym: clean, neat

Sentence: Despite her child's protest, the mother threw out his grungy sweatpants.

551. INABILITY - *[spell]*- I N A B I L I T Y
Definition: lack of power or means
Synonym: impotence, weakness
Antonym: capacity, ability
Sentence: The teacher's inability to control her class was problematic.

552. BORDERLINE - *[spell]*- B O R D E R L I N E
Definition: on the border or boundary
Synonym: marginal
Antonym: innermost
Sentence: His grade was on the borderline of passing.

553. DISABILITY - *[spell]*- D I S A B I L I T Y
Definition: lack of ability or power
Synonym: handicap, impairment
Antonym: advantage, benefit
Sentence: The car accident left him with a severe disability that inhibited his walking.

554. BEAUTEOUS - *[spell]*- B E A U T E O U S
Definition: very pretty to see or hear
Synonym: attractive, comely
Antonym: hideous, ugly
Sentence: Her beauteous face was admired by all.

555. THISTLE - *[spell]*- T H I S T L E
Definition: any of various composite plants with prickly stalks and leaves
Synonym: barb, bramble
Antonym:
Sentence: The man worked hard to get the thistles out of his front lawn.

556. UPSTAGE - *[spell]*- U P S T A G E
Definition: to draw attention away from
Synonym: overshadow
Antonym:
Sentence: The boy attempted to upstage his brother's recital by throwing a fit.

557. EXPECTANCY - *[spell]*- E X P E C T A N C Y
Definition: something that is thought to probably happen
Synonym: anticipation, prospect
Antonym:
Sentence: The weatherman's expectancy of a storm proved right.

558. MIDWIFE - *[spell]*- M I D W I F E
Definition: person who helps women in childbirth
Synonym:
Antonym:
Sentence: The woman hired a midwife to help her with the birth of her child.

559. HOLLOW - *[spell]*- H O L L O W
Definition: having nothing, only air inside
Synonym: empty, void
Antonym: full
Sentence: The hollow space below the stairs was used for storage.

560. REAPPEARANCE - *[spell]*- R E A P P E A R A N C E
Definition: to appear again
Synonym: recurrence, repetition
Antonym:
Sentence: His sudden reappearance in his hometown was due to his recent divorce.

561. BALLAD - *[spell]*- B A L L A D
Definition: a poem or song that tells a story
Synonym:
Antonym:
Sentence: There are many famous ballads in the English language.

562. SLIGHT - *[spell]*- S L I G H T
Definition: to treat as if not very important
Synonym: affront, insult
Antonym: honor, respect
Sentence: He slighted his intern by sending her to get coffee instead of putting her to work.

563. GIGANTIC - *[spell]*- G I G A N T I C
Definition: huge
Synonym: enormous, colossal
Antonym: miniscule, tiny
Sentence: The house was gigantic compared to her one bedroom apartment.

564. GADGET - *[spell]*- G A D G E T
Definition: a small mechanical device
Synonym: device, gizmo
Antonym:
Sentence: The gadget was designed to make life in the kitchen easier by incorporating a can opener, corkscrew and bottle opener all in one.

565. PRECONDITION - *[spell]*- P R E C O N D I T I O N
Definition: prerequisite
Synonym: qualification, requirement
Antonym: optional, nonessential
Sentence: Field experience was a precondition for the job.

566. SLITHERY - *[spell]*- S L I T H E R Y
Definition: slippery or crawly
Synonym:
Antonym:
Sentence: The slithery creature crept across the floor.

567. SARCASTIC - *[spell]*- S A R C A S T I C
Definition: using ironical or cutting taunts or remarks
Synonym: saucy, mocking
Antonym:
Sentence: Her sarcastic remarks, though funny, were also bitter.

568. TOOTHY - *[spell]*- T O O T H Y
Definition: showing many teeth
Synonym:
Antonym:
Sentence: The child gave a toothy grin when he opened his presents.

569. IMPOLITE - *[spell]*- I M P O L I T E
Definition: having or showing bad manners
Synonym: boorish, disrespectful
Antonym: mannerly, polite
Sentence: His remarks were considered impolite by some.

570. S O L O I S T - *[spell]*- S O L O I S T
Definition: a person who performs alone
Synonym:
Antonym:
Sentence: The soloist in the orchestra was clearly very talented.

571. OBESITY - *[spell]*- O B E S I T Y
Definition: being extremely overweight
Synonym: overweight, fatness
Antonym: trim, skinny
Sentence: Obesity is a big problem in America.

572. REPRESSION - *[spell]*- R E P R E S S I O N
Definition: act of preventing from acting
Synonym: constraint, suppression
Antonym: unconstraint, openness

Sentence: The repression of the people eventually resulted in discontent and, finally, rebellion.

573. INVITATION - *[spell]*- I N V I T AT I O N
Definition: a polite request to come some place or do something
Synonym: summons, petition
Antonym:
Sentence: He was given an invitation to his niece's graduation.

574. TALENTED - *[spell]*- T A L E N T E D
Definition: having natural ability
Synonym: proficient, accomplished
Antonym: clumsy, incompetent
Sentence: He was talented in all the arts: drama, singing, and visual.

575. DOWNFALL - *[spell]*- D O W N F A L L
Definition: coming to ruin
Synonym: collapse, deterioration
Antonym: ascent, upswing
Sentence: The downfall of the empire was due to corruption in the government.

576. LOGICAL - *[spell]*- L O G I C A L
Definition: having to do with the principles of reasoning and inference
Synonym: probable, reasonable
Antonym: illogical, improbable
Sentence: His story was a logical explanation for his absence.

577. MALFUNCTION - *[spell]*- M A L F U N C T I O N
Definition: an improper working
Synonym: failure, bug
Antonym: working, flawless
Sentence: An engineer had to be called in when the computer began to malfunction.

578. DEFECTIVE - *[spell]*- D E F E C T I V E
Definition: not perfect or complete
Synonym: faulty, deficient
Antonym: adequate, sufficient
Sentence: She returned the kitchen appliance to the store because she found it defective.

579. INESCAPABLE - *[spell]*- I N E S C A P A B L E
Definition: that cannot be escaped or avoided
Synonym: unavoidable, inevitable

Antonym: escapable, avoidable
Sentence: The meeting was inescapable.

580. EXPIRATION - *[spell]*- E X P I R A T I O N
Definition: coming to an end
Synonym: termination, cessation
Antonym: beginning, commencement
Sentence: The expiration date on the milk carton was over a week old.

581. SCOOTER - *[spell]*- S C O O T E R
Definition: a child's vehicle consisting of a footboard, two wheels, and an upright handlebar
Synonym:
Antonym:
Sentence: The child used his scooter in the cul-de-sac.

582. SLAVERY - *[spell]*- S L A V E R Y
Definition: condition of being a slave
Synonym: bondage, captivity
Antonym: freedom, liberty
Sentence: She spent most of her life in slavery before being freed.

583. DISADVANTAGEOUS - *[spell]*- D I S A D V A N T A G E O U S
Definition: unfavorable
Synonym: adverse, injurious
Antonym: favorable, advantageous
Sentence: The rain was disadvantageous to the team during the football game.

584. JAUNT - *[spell]*- J A U N T
Definition: a short journey or excursion, especially for pleasure
Synonym: excursion, trek
Antonym:
Sentence: He went for a jaunt through the park.

585. SMUGGLE - *[spell]*- S M U G G L E
Definition: import or export secretly or illegally
Synonym:
Antonym:
Sentence: The men were arrested for trying to smuggle weapons across the border.

586. RAVEL - *[spell]*- R A V E L
Definition: to fray out
Synonym: loosen, disentangle

Antonym: twist, wind
Sentence: The hem of her dress began to ravel.

587. REGRETFUL - *[spell]*- R E G R E T F U L
Definition: expressing a feeling of being sorry
Synonym: sorrowful, apologetic
Antonym:
Sentence: She immediately felt regretful about her harsh words to her fiancÃ©.

588. HARVEST - *[spell]*- H A R V E S T
Definition: reaping and gathering food crops
Synonym: crops
Antonym:
Sentence: Despite the drought, this year's harvest was impressive.

589. FOAMY - *[spell]*- F O A M Y
Definition: covered with a bubbly substance
Synonym: frothy
Antonym:
Sentence: The dessert was foamy in consistency.

590. SQUEAMISH - *[spell]*- S Q U E A M I S H
Definition: easily shocked by anything not proper
Synonym: prudish, modest
Antonym:
Sentence: She was always squeamish when it came to gossip.

591. SLAPHAPPY - *[spell]*- S L A P H A P P Y
Definition: foolish or giddy, but in an agreeable way
Synonym: dazed, bewildered
Antonym:
Sentence: After going all night without sleep, my children were a little slaphappy in the morning.

592. INFERTILE - *[spell]*- I N F E R T I L E
Definition: barren, incapable of reproduction
Synonym: sterile, impotent
Antonym: productive, fertile
Sentence: After years of trying to have children without success, the couple assumed they were infertile.

593. DEPARTURE - *[spell]*- D E P A R T U R E
Definition: the act of going away
Synonym: escape, exit

Antonym: arrival, coming
Sentence: They celebrated his departure to his new job with a party.

594. FRENZIED - *[spell]*- F R E N Z I E D
Definition: greatly excited
Synonym: frantic, agitated
Antonym: balanced, calm
Sentence: She found herself frenzied over the arrival of her guest.

595. IDIOTIC - *[spell]*- I D I O T I C
Definition: very stupid or foolish
Synonym: foolish, silly
Antonym: sensible, smart
Sentence: Her idiotic actions got her in trouble at work.

596. LYRICAL - *[spell]*- L Y R I C A L
Definition: having the characteristics of a lyric (short poem expressing emotion)
Synonym: musical, expressive
Antonym:
Sentence: The lyrical quality of her voice enthralled many people.

597. HOSTESS - *[spell]*- H O S T E S S
Definition: a woman who receives another person as a guest
Synonym:
Antonym:
Sentence: She was an excellent hostess, serving her guests all sorts of food and wine.

598. INTEGRATE - *[spell]*- I N T E G R A T E
Definition: make into a whole
Synonym: combine, assimilate
Antonym: disconnect, divide
Sentence: She tried very hard to integrate her mother's ideas into her wedding.

599. SCRAMBLE - *[spell]*- S C R A M B L E
Definition: to make one's way by climbing, crawling, etc.
Synonym: struggle, rush
Antonym:
Sentence: The hiker scrambled up the side of the mountain.

600. SOFT-SPOKEN - *[spell]*- S O F T - S P O K E N
Definition: talking with a quiet voice
Synonym: quiet, gentle
Antonym:

Sentence: A soft-spoken individual, everyone had to listen closely to hear the guest speaker.

Easy Words Exercise - 7

601. SERMON - *[spell]*- S E R M O N
Definition: a public talk on religion or something connected with religion
Synonym: lecture, lesson
Antonym:
Sentence: The minister gave a moving sermon about love.

602. CONCUSSIVE - *[spell]*- C O N C U S S I V E
Definition: having an injury to the brain caused by a physical blow or fall
Synonym:
Antonym:
Sentence: Though he had no outward wounds, he was injured by the concussive force of the crash.

603. SLIMY - *[spell]*- S L I M Y
Definition: covered with soft, sticky mud or something like it
Synonym: gooey, muddy
Antonym:
Sentence: The slimy food turned out to be jelly.

604. SNOWBALL - *[spell]*- S N O W B A L L
Definition: a ball made of snow pressed together
Synonym: escalate, intensify
Antonym: decrease, lessen
Sentence: Her one health problem soon began to snowball and caused a myriad of other problems.

605. OVERCAST- *[spell]*- O V E R C A S T
Definition: cloudy or dark
Synonym: gloomy, dreary
Antonym: clear, bright
Sentence: It was a dreary, overcast day.

606. HOMEY - *[spell]*- H O M E Y
Definition: homelike
Synonym: comfortable, cozy
Antonym: uncomfortable
Sentence: The hotel room was quite homey.

607. FRAILTY - *[spell]*- F R A I L T Y
Definition: a fault due to weakness, especially of moral character
Synonym: foible, shortcoming
Antonym: merit, virtue
Sentence: A tendency to break his marriage vows was the president's only frailty.

608. PREARRANGE- *[spell]*- P R E A R R A N G E
Definition: arrange beforehand
Synonym:
Antonym:
Sentence: He made sure to prearrange reservations at the restaurant for his anniversary.

609. VOYAGE - *[spell]*- V O Y A G E
Definition: a journey or travel by water
Synonym: travel, excursion
Antonym:
Sentence: The man set out on a voyage overseas.

610. REPTILE- *[spell]*- R E P T I L E
Definition: a cold-blooded animal such as a lizard or snake
Synonym:
Antonym:
Sentence: Snakes and lizards are reptiles.

611. HYPERACTIVE - *[spell]*- H Y P E R A C T I V E
Definition: overactive
Synonym: excitable, wild
Antonym: calm
Sentence: The child was always hyperactive after having a lot of sugar.

612. JAGGED - *[spell]*- J A G G E D
Definition: with sharp points sticking out
Synonym: uneven, rugged
Antonym: smooth, even
Sentence: The broken glass had a jagged edge.

613. SIDLE - *[spell]*- S I D L E
Definition: to move sideways
Synonym: edge, tilt
Antonym:
Sentence: He sidled up to his co-worker at the meeting in order to ask a question.

614. OVERHANG- *[spell]*- O V E R H A N G
Definition: to project over
Synonym: extend, protrude
Antonym: recede, recess
Sentence: There was a slight overhang from the roof at the back of the house.

615. ASSORTED - *[spell]*- A S S O R T E D
Definition: selected to be of different kinds
Synonym: various, sundry
Antonym: similar, unvaried
Sentence: She bought a box of assorted donuts to take to breakfast.

616. PEACEABLE- *[spell]*- P E A C E A B L E
Definition: liking or keeping peace (freedom from strife or war)
Synonym: friendly, amiable
Antonym: belligerent, unfriendly
Sentence: The treaty was aimed at creating a peaceable relationship between the countries.

617. ATMOSPHERE - *[spell]*- A T M O S P H E R E
Definition: the character or mood of one's environment
Synonym:
Antonym:
Sentence: The atmosphere of the room during the wedding was one of joy.

618. BLUBBER - *[spell]*- B L U B B E R
Definition: to cry loudly
Synonym: weep, sob
Antonym: laugh, smile
Sentence: She began to blubber after receiving the bad news.

619. STUBBY - *[spell]*- S T U B B Y
Definition: short and thick
Synonym: fat, heavyset
Antonym: lanky, long
Sentence: The old dachshund had short, stubby legs.

620. SCRAPBOOK - *[spell]*- S C R A P B O O K
Definition: book in which pictures or clippings are pasted and kept
Synonym:
Antonym:
Sentence: She kept a scrapbook of all her travels.

621. TAXATION - *[spell]*- T A X A T I O N
Definition: act or system of taxing (money paid by people for the support of the government)
Synonym:
Antonym:
Sentence: The taxation enacted by the county was very high.

622. FEATHERY - *[spell]*- F E A T H E R Y
Definition: like feathers, soft
Synonym: plumed, downy
Antonym:
Sentence: She sank into the feathery mattress and fell right asleep.

623. DEMOLITION - *[spell]*- D E M O L I T I O N
Definition: destruction
Synonym: annihilation, extermination
Antonym: construction, raising
Sentence: The demolition of the building took place after it was condemned.

624. CAPABILITY - *[spell]*- C A P A B I L I TY
Definition: ability to learn to do
Synonym: capacity, competence
Antonym: impotence, inability
Sentence: He had the capability of learning new words quickly.

625. PROTECTIVE- *[spell]*- P R O T E C T I V E
Definition: defensive
Synonym: safeguarding, sheltering
Antonym: assault, attack
Sentence: The mother duck was quite protective of her babies.

626. TOWERING - *[spell]*- T O W E R I N G
Definition: very high
Synonym: colossal, gigantic
Antonym: common, insignificant
Sentence: The child built a towering structure from blocks.

627. SHADOWY - *[spell]*- S H A D O W Y
Definition: having much shadow or shade
Synonym: dark, hazy
Antonym: clear, bright
Sentence: The shadowy hallway was frightening to the child.

628. CONGRATULATORY - *[spell]*- C O N G R A T U L A T O R Y
Definition: expressing pleasure at another person's happiness

Synonym: celebratory, complimentary
Antonym: deprecate
Sentence: He sent her a congratulatory email in light of her promotion.

629. FRAGRANCE - *[spell]*- F R A G R A N C E
Definition: a sweet smell
Synonym: aroma, perfume
Antonym:
Sentence: The fragrance of baking bread was unmistakable.

630. NOSH - *[spell]*- N O S H
Definition: eat between meals
Synonym: munch, snack
Antonym:
Sentence: He kept a lot of snacks in his desk to nosh on throughout the day.

631. FUNCTIONAL - *[spell]*- F U N C T I O N A L
Definition: having or carrying out a particular purpose
Synonym: operational, functioning
Antonym: nonfunctional, nonoperational
Sentence: The car, though functional, was nothing extravagant.

632. HARMLESS - *[spell]*- H A R M L E S S
Definition: causing no pain, loss, injury, etc.
Synonym: benign, innocuous
Antonym: harmful, dangerous
Sentence: She thought the snake was poisonous, but it turned out to be harmless.

633. DISCRIMINATE - *[spell]*- D I S C R I M I N A T E
Definition: make or see a difference
Synonym: distinguish, discern
Antonym:
Sentence: He was able to discriminate between the two similar types of cheese.

634. SKIMPY - *[spell]*- S K I M P Y
Definition: not enough
Synonym: sparse, inadequate
Antonym: plenty, ample
Sentence: She thought the servings at the restaurant were skimpy.

635. INHABITED - *[spell]*- I N H A B I T E D
Definition: lived in
Synonym: occupied

Antonym:
Sentence: The house did not look like it had been inhabited for a long time.

636. SHEEPISH - *[spell]*- S H E E P I S H
Definition: awkwardly bashful or embarrassed
Synonym: timid, abashed
Antonym: bold, aggressive
Sentence: He smiled sheepishly when he asked her out.

637. COOPERATIVE - *[spell]*- C O O P E R A T I V E
Definition: wanting to work with others
Synonym: collegial, symbiotic
Antonym: uncooperative, unilateral
Sentence: His cooperative nature made him a good leader.

638. ORNAMENTAL- *[spell]*- O R N A M E N T A L
Definition: having to do with something decorative
Synonym: decorative
Antonym: functional, utilitarian
Sentence: She has a large brass doorknocker on her front door, but it's largely ornamental.

639. GARGLE - *[spell]*- G A R G L E
Definition: wash or rinse the throat with liquid
Synonym:
Antonym:
Sentence: She gargled with mouthwash before bed.

640. MISFORTUNE - *[spell]*- M I S F O R T U N E
Definition: bad or adverse fortune
Synonym: adversity, mischance
Antonym: luck, fortune
Sentence: It was a misfortune that he died so young.

641. DISPLEASURE - *[spell]*- D I S P L E A S U R E
Definition: the feeling of being offended or annoyed
Synonym: disapproval, dissatisfaction
Antonym: approval, pleasure
Sentence: He felt great displeasure when he heard the scandalous news.

642. BAGGAGE - *[spell]*- B A G G A G E
Definition: burden of beliefs, ideas, or experience
Synonym:
Antonym:

Sentence: He felt that his experiences in life had created quite a lot of emotional baggage.

643. CAPTIVITY - *[spell]*- C A P T I V I T Y
Definition: condition of being in prison
Synonym: bondage, confinement
Antonym: freedom, liberation
Sentence: The animals at the zoo had lived in captivity their entire lives.

644. EVERLASTING - *[spell]*- E V E R L A S T I N G
Definition: lasting forever
Synonym: eternal, immortal
Antonym: brief, fleeting
Sentence: He vowed his everlasting love to his fiancÃ©.

645. ENDURING - *[spell]*- E N D U R I N G
Definition: lasting
Synonym: permanent, abiding
Antonym:
Sentence: The snow was enduring, lasting for over a week before it melted.

646. ENFOLD - *[spell]*- E N F O L D
Definition: wrap up
Synonym: clutch, cover
Antonym:
Sentence: Feeling cold, he enfolded himself in a warm fleece blanket.

647. OVERCOME- *[spell]*- O V E R C O M E
Definition: to win victory over
Synonym: beat, defeat
Antonym:
Sentence: He was able to overcome his fears with great effort.

648. QUARRELSOME- *[spell]*- Q U A R R E L S O M E
Definition: too ready to fight or dispute
Synonym: argumentative, disagreeable
Antonym: affable, agreeable
Sentence: He had a quarrelsome nature.

649. NETWORK - *[spell]*- N E T W O R K
Definition: a group of people/things connected so they can work together
Synonym: organization, structure
Antonym:
Sentence: A network of businesses worked together to keep prices low.

650. BITTER - *[spell]*- B I T T E R
Definition: having a sharp, unpleasant taste
Synonym: harsh, sour
Antonym: sweet
Sentence: The cheese had a bitter taste that she did not find appealing.

651. DISPOSABLE - *[spell]*- D I S P O S A B L E
Definition: something that can be gotten rid of
Synonym: expendable
Antonym:
Sentence: Considering the leftovers disposable, she threw them in the garbage.

652. PUNISHABLE- *[spell]*- P U N I S H A B L E
Definition: liable to cause pain, loss, or discomfort for some wrong or offense
Synonym: penalize
Antonym: pardonable, excusable
Sentence: Stealing is an offense that is punishable by law.

653. BARRETTE - *[spell]*- B A R R E T T E
Definition: a pin with a clasp worn by women in their hair
Synonym: fastener, pin
Antonym:
Sentence: The little girl loved to wear barrettes in her hair.

654. FROTHY - *[spell]*- F R O T H Y
Definition: foamy
Synonym: bubbling, fizzing
Antonym: flat
Sentence: A cappuccino is a frothy beverage.

655. IMPRESSIVE - *[spell]*- I M P R E S S I V E
Definition: able to have a strong effect on the mind or feelings
Synonym: powerful, influential
Antonym: inconsequential, insignificant
Sentence: His view of the Grand Canyon from where he stood was impressive.

656. MARINA - *[spell]*- M A R I N A
Definition: dock where supplies are available for boats
Synonym:
Antonym:
Sentence: The fisherman went to the marina to buy bait for his journey.

657. GUISE - *[spell]*- G U I S E
Definition: style of dress
Synonym: garb, appearance
Antonym:
Sentence: The celebrity traveled in the guise of just an average person.

658. REVERSIBLE- *[spell]*- R E V E R S I B L E
Definition: that can be made opposite
Synonym:
Antonym:
Sentence: Her reversible comforter was floral on one side and pink on the other.

659. POPULARITY- *[spell]*- P O P U L A R I T Y
Definition: fact or condition of being liked or admired by most people
Synonym: recognition, acclaim
Antonym: unpopularity, dislike
Sentence: His popularity as a performer was due, in part, to his charisma.

660. OATH - *[spell]*- O A T H
Definition: a solemn promise
Synonym: vow, pledge
Antonym:
Sentence: He made an oath to help the girl find her mother.

661. OVERSEE- *[spell]*- O V E R S E E
Definition: to look after
Synonym: manage, supervise
Antonym:
Sentence: It was his job to oversee the task.

662. CAVITY - *[spell]*- C A V I T Y
Definition: a hollow place
Synonym: hole, crater
Antonym: bulge, protuberance
Sentence: There was only a cavity where a fencepost used to be.

663. DINGHY - *[spell]*- D I N G H Y
Definition: a small rowboat
Synonym:
Antonym:
Sentence: They fled the sinking cruise ship in a dinghy.

664. SILENCER - *[spell]*- S I L E N C E R
Definition: person or thing that creates an absence of all sound
Synonym: muffler

Antonym:
Sentence: The silencer on the gun ensured that the shots would not be heard.

665.   HASSLE - *[spell]*- H A S S L E
Definition: struggle or contest
Synonym: bother, harass
Antonym:
Sentence: She found making dinner a hassle because she was so tired.

666.   TRUCE - *[spell]*- T R U C E
Definition: temporary peace
Synonym: amnesty, armistice
Antonym: war, fighting
Sentence: The two fighting countries finally agreed on a truce.

667.   GLINT - *[spell]*- G L I N T
Definition: gleam or flash of light
Synonym: glimmer, twinkle
Antonym:
Sentence: She saw a glint of something on the carpet and knew it was the ring she'd lost.

668.   FASHIONABLE - *[spell]*- F A S H I O N A B L E
Definition: following the latest in the prevailing trends in clothing
Synonym: chic, trendy
Antonym: old-fashioned, outdated
Sentence: Always fashionable, she was the talk of the office.

669.   SPITEFUL- *[spell]*- S P I T E F U L
Definition: eager to annoy or irritate
Synonym: vindictive, hateful
Antonym: friendly, lovable
Sentence: The spiteful dog chewed up all of its owner's shoes when he was left for the day.

670.   POPULATION- *[spell]*- P O P U L A T I O N
Definition: people of a city or a country
Synonym:
Antonym:
Sentence: The county had a very diverse population.

671.   REFERABLE- *[spell]*- R E F E R A B L E
Definition: that can be turned to for information or help
Synonym:
Antonym:

Sentence: The thesaurus is a book that is referable when you are in need of a word.

672. SNIFFY - *[spell]*- S N I F F Y
Definition: inkling to draw air through the nose as if in contempt or scorn
Synonym: haughty, arrogant
Antonym: humble, modest
Sentence: She was very sniffy when it came to the suggestions of her friends.

673. FIXEDLY - *[spell]*- F I X E D L Y
Definition: without change
Synonym: intently, attentively
Antonym:
Sentence: She stared fixedly at the people across the street.

674. ABLAZE- *[spell]*- A B L A Z E
Definition: on fire
Synonym: burning, fiery
Antonym: dim, cold
Sentence: With the logs ablaze in the fireplace, the house felt cozy and warm.

675. TRADITIONAL - *[spell]*- T R A D I T I O N A L
Definition: having to do with the handing down of beliefs, opinions, customs, etc.
Synonym: conventional, classic
Antonym:
Sentence: The couple decided to have a very traditional wedding.

676. INCONCLUSIVE - *[spell]*- I N C O N C L U S I V E
Definition: not convincing
Synonym: ambiguous, unclear
Antonym: certain, conclusive
Sentence: The results of the test were inconclusive.

677. SCENIC - *[spell]*- S C E N I C
Definition: of or having to do with natural scenery
Synonym: picturesque, breathtaking
Antonym:
Sentence: On his way to work, he drove through downtown to take the scenic route.

678. OINTMENT- *[spell]*- O I N T M E N T
Definition: a substance often containing medicine used on the skin to heal or soothe

Synonym: balm
Antonym:
Sentence: He put ointment on the burn.

679.   UNWRITTEN - *[spell]*- U N W R I T T E N
Definition: understood or customary but not expressed in writing
Synonym: accepted, tacit
Antonym: explained, explicated
Sentence: The lawyer was always sure to follow the unwritten rules of ethics.

680.   DERAIL - *[spell]*- D E R A I L
Definition: to run off the tracks, as with a train
Synonym:
Antonym:
Sentence: When the train derailed, the result was catastrophic.

681.   VACATE - *[spell]*- V A C A T E
Definition: to give up occupancy of
Synonym: leave, abandon
Antonym: occupy, remain
Sentence: They had to temporarily vacate their home when they found it was infested with termites.

682.   SCAVENGE - *[spell]*- S C A V E N G E
Definition: to search through waste, junk, etc., for something that can be saved or used
Synonym:
Antonym:
Sentence: The bird scavenged about the yard for worms.

683.   JABBER- *[spell]*- J A B B E R
Definition: to talk or speak rapidly and indistinctly
Synonym: babble, blather
Antonym: quiet, silence
Sentence: The girl jabbered on excitedly about her soccer game.

684.   BLISTER - *[spell]*- B L I S T E R
Definition: to attack with sharp words
Synonym:
Antonym:
Sentence: His blistering words were incredibly hurtful.

685.   CEASELESS - *[spell]*- C E A S E L E S S
Definition: going all the time
Synonym: incessant, continual

Antonym: ending, ceasing
Sentence: The music played on a ceaseless loop.

686. GUTLESS - *[spell]*- G U T L E S S
Definition: lacking courage
Synonym: timid, feeble
Antonym: bold, brave
Sentence: He resolved not to be gutless and, as a result, asked her out.

687. UNIMAGINABLE - *[spell]*- U N I M A G I N A B L E
Definition: that cannot be conceived
Synonym: unbelievable, fantastic
Antonym: believable, common
Sentence: The death of her father was unimaginable.

688. BARCODE - *[spell]*- B A R C O D E
Definition: a series of vertical lines with spaces between which can be read by a machine
Synonym:
Antonym:
Sentence: In most stores, they use barcodes to check prices and ring up customers.

689. FOOTING - *[spell]*- F O O T I N G
Definition: basis of understanding
Synonym: foundation, basis
Antonym:
Sentence: She had a strong footing in math and science.

690. DELIBERATION - *[spell]*- D E L I B E R A T I O N
Definition: careful thought
Synonym: consideration, debate
Antonym: disregard
Sentence: After great deliberation, the jury came to a verdict.

691. TAMBOURINE - *[spell]*- T A M B O U R I N E
Definition: a small shallow drum with jingling metal discs
Synonym:
Antonym:
Sentence: She played the tambourine and the drums in the band.

692. PEEK- *[spell]*- P E E K
Definition: to look quickly and slyly
Synonym: peep, glimpse
Antonym: ignore, overlook

Sentence: The child peeked around the corner at the guests who had come into the house.

693. SHRUBBERY - *[spell]*- S H R U B B E R Y
Definition: small tree-like plants collected into a mass
Synonym: shrubs, bushes
Antonym:
Sentence: He planted shrubbery just beside his front porch.

694. PLAYWRIGHT- *[spell]*- P L A Y W R I G H T
Definition: writer of plays
Synonym: author, writer
Antonym:
Sentence: The playwright penned many famous plays.

695. TWIDDLE - *[spell]*- T W I D D L E
Definition: twirl or play with idly
Synonym: fidget, fiddle
Antonym:
Sentence: Nervous about her date, the girl twiddled with her hair.

696. QUIRK- *[spell]*- Q U I R K
Definition: a peculiar or strange way of acting
Synonym: oddity, peculiarity
Antonym;
Sentence: One of her quirks was her insistence on using a coupon to buy everything.

697. SATISFACTORY - *[spell]*- S A T I S F A C T O R Y
Definition: good enough to meet or fulfill demands or desires
Synonym: tolerable, decent
Antonym: inadequate, insufficient
Sentence: The student, though not exceptional, did satisfactory work.

698. THRASHER - *[spell]*- T H R A S H E R
Definition: person who beats
Synonym:
Antonym:
Sentence: The dog was known as a thrasher because of his forcefully wagging tail.

699. INOPERABLE - *[spell]*- I N O P E R A B L E
Definition: incurable
Synonym: deadly, fatal
Antonym: curable, treatable
Sentence: She found out that she had an inoperable tumor.

700.   SCALD - *[spell]*- S C A L D
        Definition: burn with hot liquid or steam
        Synonym:
        Antonym:
        Sentence: She accidentally scalded herself with the boiling water.

Easy Words Exercise - 8

701.   DISTRAUGHT - *[spell]*- D I S T R A U G H T
        Definition: in a state of mental confusion
        Synonym: upset, agitated
        Antonym: composed, collected
        Sentence: She found herself feeling distraught over the amount of work she had to get done.

702.   OVERJOYED - *[spell]*- O V E R J O Y E D
        Definition: very happy
        Synonym: delighted, elated
        Antonym: depressed, sorrowful
        Sentence: She was overjoyed to be reunited with her son after 15 years.

703.   COMBATANT - *[spell]*- C O M B A T A N T
        Definition: one who fights in a war
        Synonym: attacker, antagonist
        Antonym:
        Sentence: Germany was one of the major combatants in World War II.

704.   INEXPENSIVE - *[spell]*- I N E X P E N S I V E
        Definition: not costing much money
        Synonym: cheap, economical
        Antonym: expensive, pricey
        Sentence: She was surprised to find that the designer shoes were actually quite inexpensive.

705.   DIGESTIVE - *[spell]*- D I G E S T I V E
        Definition: of or for the breaking down of food in the stomach
        Synonym:
        Antonym:
        Sentence: The doctor determined the patient had some serious digestive issues.

706.   CLIMAX - *[spell]*- C L I M A X
        Definition: the highest point of interest
        Synonym: capstone, turning point
        Antonym: bottom, anticlimax
        Sentence: He kept us spellbound as his story neared its climax.

707. AWAKENING - *[spell]*- A W A K E N I NG
Definition: a waking up
Synonym: arousing, stimulating
Antonym: sleeping, resting
Sentence: After an abrupt awakening, he could not fall back asleep.

708. SCALLOP - *[spell]*- S C A L L O P
Definition: a series of curves on the edge of a dress, etc.
Synonym:
Antonym:
Sentence: The hem of her dress was scalloped.

709. QUARTERLY - *[spell]*- Q U A R T E R L Y
Definition: happening or done four times a year
Synonym:
Antonym:
Sentence: He was responsible for generating quarterly reports of the company's profits.

710. DEPARTED - *[spell]*- D E P A R T E D
Definition: a dead person
Synonym: decedent, corpse
Antonym:
Sentence: At the funeral of the recently departed man, there was much weeping.

711. BESTREWN - *[spell]*- B E S T R E W N
Definition: scattered around
Synonym: dispersed, disseminated
Antonym: gathered, collected
Sentence: The playing cards were bestrewn about the table.

712. SMUDGE - *[spell]*- S M U D G E
Definition: a dirty mark or stain
Synonym: blot, blemish
Antonym:
Sentence: The charcoal the artist was using left dark smudges on her fingers.

713. THUNDERSTRUCK - *[spell]*- T H U N D E R S T R U C K
Definition: astonished
Synonym: amazed, aghast
Antonym:
Sentence: She was thunderstruck to learn that she was adopted.

714. COCKEYED - *[spell]*- C O C K E Y E D
Definition: tilted or twisted to one side
Synonym: awry, crooked
Antonym: level, straight
Sentence: He is suspicious of strangers, and views them with a cockeyed expression.

715. INTERPRETATION - *[spell]*- I N T E R P R E T AT I O N
Definition: an explaining the meaning of
Synonym: understanding, analysis
Antonym:
Sentence: Her interpretation of the poem was a bit far-fetched.

716. BLAZE - *[spell]*- B L A Z E
Definition: a bright flame or fire
Synonym: flame, burn
Antonym:
Sentence: The blaze soon consumed the house, burning it down in its entirety.

717. BLEAK - *[spell]*- B L E A K
Definition: depressing
Synonym: cheerless, desolate
Antonym: cheerful, bright
Sentence: Having just lost his job, he had a pretty bleak outlook for the future.

718. INACCURACY - *[spell]*- I N A C C U R A C Y
Definition: error or mistake
Synonym: blunder, defect
Antonym: accuracy, correctness
Sentence: The medical test's inaccuracy led her to believe she had a serious disease when, in fact, she did not.

719. SENATE - *[spell]*- S E N A T E
Definition: a governing or lawmaking assembly
Synonym: parliament, council
Antonym:
Sentence: After a long campaign, he was elected to serve in the Senate.

720. COMPETITIVE - *[spell]*- C O M P E T I T I V E
Definition: having to do with a contest
Synonym: aggressive, ambitious
Antonym:
Sentence: His competitive nature compelled him to try and win every game.

721. SLEAZY - *[spell]*- S L E A Z Y
Definition: disreputable
Synonym: sordid, tacky
Antonym: fine, reputable
Sentence: She tried to ignore the sleazy headlines she saw on the gossip magazines.

722. OVERREACH - *[spell]*- O V E R R E A C H
Definition: to get the better of by cunning
Synonym: overdo, overextend
Antonym:
Sentence: Through cleverness, he was able to overreach his boss's objections.

723. EVENTFUL - *[spell]*- E V E N T F U L
Definition: full of important happenings
Synonym: exciting, memorable
Antonym: dull, uneventful
Sentence: He was looking for a quiet, restful evening but it turned out to be quite eventful instead.

724. OVERACHIEVE - *[spell]*- O V E R A C H I E V E
Definition: to perform better than expected
Synonym:
Antonym:
Sentence: Although no one expected it, he overachieved on the test.

725. HERBIVOROUS - *[spell]*- H E R B I V O R O U S
Definition: feeding on grass or other plants
Synonym:
Antonym:
Sentence: Horses are herbivorous creatures.

726. ACCUSATORY - *[spell]*- A C C U S A T O R Y
Definition: having a charge of doing something wrong
Synonym: allegation, complaint
Antonym:
Sentence: She asked in an accusatory tone if he had stolen her book.

727. NIGHTMARE - *[spell]*- N I G H T M A R E
Definition: very distressing dream
Synonym:
Antonym:
Sentence: She often had nightmares about her worst fears.

728. SEAWARD - *[spell]*- S E A W A R D
Definition: toward the sea (large body of water)
Synonym:
Antonym:
Sentence: The man headed seaward in order to catch a boat.

729. COMMONALITY - *[spell]*- C O M M O N A L I T Y
Definition: a common quality
Synonym: synonymous, similar
Antonym: dissimilar
Sentence: A commonality between the two of them is their stubborn nature.

730. THWART - *[spell]*- T H W A R T
Definition: to prevent from doing something
Synonym: obstruct, hinder
Antonym: facilitate
Sentence: She attempted to thwart her boss's plans of promoting her because she didn't want the job.

731. UNAVOIDABLE - *[spell]*- U N A V O I D A B L E
Definition: that cannot be avoided
Synonym: inevitable, certain
Antonym: escapable, avoidable
Sentence: He decided to tell her the truth because it was simply unavoidable.

732. PENALTY - *[spell]*- P E N A L T Y
Definition: punishment imposed by law
Synonym: punishment, damages
Antonym:
Sentence: He had to pay a penalty for his mistakes on his taxes.

733. YAMMER - *[spell]*- Y A M M E R
Definition: to complain
Synonym: moan, whine
Antonym:
Sentence: The child had a tendency to yammer on about everything.

734. TWINE - *[spell]*- T W I N E
Definition: a strong thread or string made of two or more strands twisted together
Synonym: yarn, coil
Antonym:
Sentence: The chef used the twine to bind up the stuffed chicken breasts.

735.   AFFECTIONATE - *[spell]*- A F F E C T I O N A TE
Definition: showing love
Synonym: tender, caring
Antonym: aloof, unfeeling
Sentence: The two siblings were extremely affectionate toward each other.

736.   OBSCENITY - *[spell]*- O B S C E N I TY
Definition: the quality of offending decency
Synonym: indecency, profanity
Antonym: decency, pleasantry
Sentence: His words were an obscenity not appropriate to a work environment.

737.   TOLERANCE - *[spell]*- T O L E R A N C E
Definition: a willingness to endure the beliefs and actions of which one does not approve
Synonym: fortitude, patience
Antonym: weakness, disapproval
Sentence: The teacher had remarkable tolerance when it came to her talkative class.

738.   TRACT - *[spell]*- T R A C T
Definition: stretch of land, water, etc.
Synonym: area, lot
Antonym:
Sentence: He purchased the tract of land from his brother.

739.   FIDGETY - *[spell]*- F I D G E T Y
Definition: restless
Synonym: jittery, uneasy
Antonym: calm, composed
Sentence: Feeling fidgety, he got up and paced the room.

740.   RELIANCE - *[spell]*- R E L I A N C E
Definition: trust or dependence
Synonym: dependence
Antonym: self-reliance, self-sufficiency
Sentence: The child's reliance on her mother was unsettling considering her age.

741.   FLURRY - *[spell]*- F L U R R Y
Definition: a sudden commotion
Synonym: outbreak, turmoil
Antonym: peace, calm
Sentence: The fire alarm ringing in the building caused a flurry of motion.

742. SENSUAL - *[spell]*- S E N S U A L
Definition: of or having to do with the bodily senses rather than the mind or soul
Synonym: sensuous, tactile
Antonym:
Sentence: She found listening to the band's music to be a sensual experience.

743. COMPLICATION - *[spell]*- C O M P L I C A T I O N
Definition: confused state of affairs
Synonym: complexity, confusion
Antonym: health, wellness
Sentence: A complication arose in their vacation plans when a hurricane hit, causing their flight to be cancelled.

744. HOBO - *[spell]*- H O B O
Definition: a person who wanders about and lives by begging or doing odd jobs
Synonym: tramp, wanderer
Antonym:
Sentence: The hobo lived beneath the city bridge.

745. EXCESSIVE - *[spell]*- E X C E S S I V E
Definition: too much
Synonym: exorbitant, inordinate
Antonym: modest, moderate
Sentence: The number of apples she purchased to make a pie turned out to be quite excessive.

746. REGARDLESS - *[spell]*- R E G A R D L E S S
Definition: with no heed
Synonym: heedless
Antonym:
Sentence: He decided that, regardless of the snow on the roads, he needed to go to the store.

747. NAMELY - *[spell]*- N A M E L Y
Definition: that is to say
Synonym:
Antonym:
Sentence: He asked if she was going to the party, namely so he could ask her to go with him.

748. PRECURSORY - *[spell]*- P R E C U R S O R Y
Definition: indicative of something to follow
Synonym: foregoer, harbinger

Antonym:
Sentence: The cold temperatures were precursory of the snow.

749. FORCIBLE - *[spell]-* F O R C I B L E
Definition: made or done using force
Synonym:
Antonym:
Sentence: The police entered the house in quite a forcible manner.

750. AVENGE - *[spell]-* A V E N G E
Definition: to take revenge
Synonym: vindicate, redress
Antonym:
Sentence: He decided that, no matter what, he would avenge his father's death.

751. PERSISTENCE - *[spell]-* P E R S I S T E N C E
Definition: the act of continuing on firmly
Synonym: tenacity, perseverance
Antonym: irresolution, idleness
Sentence: His persistence eventually landed him the promotion he wanted.

752. TRITE - *[spell]-* T R I T E
Definition: worn out by use
Synonym: commonplace, clichÃ©
Antonym: original, unique
Sentence: The author was known for use of trite phrases in an unexpected way.

753. VOCAL - *[spell]-* V O C A L
Definition: inclined to talk freely
Synonym: outspoken, articulate
Antonym: quiet, silent
Sentence: She was always vocal about her opinions.

754. SLURP - *[spell]-* S L U R P
Definition: to eat or drink with a noisy gurgling sound
Synonym:
Antonym:
Sentence: She slurped up the last of the milk in her cereal bowl.

755. LEGENDARY - *[spell]-* L E G E N D A R Y
Definition: celebrated or described by legend (story coming from the past)
Synonym: fabled, mythical

Antonym:
Sentence: He was somewhat legendary as a high school athlete in his hometown.

756. TRUDGE - *[spell]*- T R U D G E
Definition: to go on foot
Synonym: shuffle, plod
Antonym:
Sentence: The tired joggers trudged down the pathway to home.

757. AMNESIA - *[spell]*- A M N E S I A
Definition: partial or entire loss of memory due to brain injury
Synonym: forgetfulness
Antonym:
Sentence: For months, she suffered from amnesia, unable to even remember her family.

758. KINK - *[spell]*- K I N K
Definition: a twist or curl in a thread or rope
Synonym: bend, crinkle
Antonym: straighten,
Sentence: He wondered why water wouldn't go through the hoseâ€"then he discovered it had a kink in it.

759. PICTORIAL - *[spell]*- P I C T O R I A L
Definition: having to do with pictures
Synonym: illustrative, graphic
Antonym:
Sentence: She was inspired to take a trip after buying a pictorial guide to Ireland.

760. TUSSLE - *[spell]*- T U S S L E
Definition: to struggle or wrestle
Synonym: scuffle, skirmish
Antonym:
Sentence: The boys tussled in the backyard in good-natured play.

761. OVERHAUL - *[spell]*- O V E R H A U L
Definition: examine thoroughly so as to make any changes or repairs as needed
Synonym: restore, reconstruct
Antonym: fall short
Sentence: The old house was going to get a complete overhaul.

762. STORYBOARD - *[spell]*- S T O R Y B O A R D
Definition: a set of panels with sketches showing the sequences of events

for a motion picture, program, or commercial
Synonym: picture, sketch
Antonym:
Sentence: The director created a storyboard of the scene to discuss with his writers.

763. CARDIAC - *[spell]*- C A R D I A C
Definition: having to do with the heart
Synonym:
Antonym:
Sentence: The woman went to the doctor and found she had several cardiac problems.

764. OBLONG - *[spell]*- O B L O N G
Definition: longer than broad
Synonym: oval, elliptical
Antonym:
Sentence: The table was oblong in shape.

765. TERRORIZE - *[spell]*- T E R R O R I Z E
Definition: to fill with great fear
Synonym: bully, intimidate
Antonym:
Sentence: The boy enjoyed terrorizing his younger siblings.

766. FASCINATE - *[spell]*- F A S C I N A T E
Definition: attract very strongly
Synonym: enchant, captivate
Antonym: repulse, bore
Sentence: He was fascinated by her overwhelming beauty and charm.

767. OCCASIONAL - *[spell]*- O C C A S I O N A L
Definition: happening only once in a while
Synonym: sporadic, intermittent
Antonym: regular, frequent
Sentence: She ate fairly healthfully, except for an occasional splurge on sweets.

768. MASTERY - *[spell]*- M A S T E R Y
Definition: rule or control
Synonym: command, leadership
Antonym:
Sentence: The teacher had mastery over her classroom.

769. TRUSS - *[spell]*- T R U S S
Definition: to tie or fasten

Synonym:
Antonym:
Sentence: The little boy was just learning to truss his shoes.

770. UNFOUNDED - *[spell]*- U N F O U N D E D
Definition: without reason or basis
Synonym: baseless, unjustified
Antonym: justified, substantiated
Sentence: It turned out that his accusation was completely unfounded.

771. OVERSHOOT - *[spell]*- O V E R S H O O T
Definition: to aim over, higher than, or beyond
Synonym: overreach
Antonym:
Sentence: He managed to overshoot his goal for the marathon.

772. ASSESS - *[spell]*- A S S E S S
Definition: estimate of value
Synonym: appraise, estimate
Antonym:
Sentence: In order to assess his weight loss, he charted his progress.

773. LUNACY - *[spell]*- L U N A C Y
Definition: insanity
Synonym: madness, mania
Antonym: sanity
Sentence: Her alleged lunacy was eventually disproven.

774. ARITHMETIC - *[spell]*- A R I T H ME T I C
Definition: art or practice of making calculations with numbers
Synonym: computation, mathematics
Antonym:
Sentence: Arithmetic was his favorite subject in school.

775. AUTOGRAPH - *[spell]*- A U T O G R A P H
Definition: a person's signature
Synonym: signature
Antonym:
Sentence: The little boy asked the celebrity for his autograph.

776. RESTRICTIVE - *[spell]*- R E S T R I C T I V E
Definition: confining
Synonym: opposed, prohibitive
Antonym: allowing
Sentence: The tight dress she wore was rather restrictive of her movements.

777. ABBREVIATION - *[spell]*- A B B R E V I A T I O N
Definition: part of a word or phrase that stands for the whole
Synonym: compression, shortening
Antonym: extension, lengthening
Sentence: The abbreviation FBI stands for Federal Bureau of
Investigation.

778. TEMPTATION - *[spell]*- T E M P T A T I O N
Definition: a being made to try or do something by an offer of pleasure or
reward
Synonym: lure, attraction
Antonym:
Sentence: She ignored the temptation of the cookies in her cupboard.

779. CALCULATING - *[spell]*- C A L C U L A T I N G
Definition: scheming and selfish
Synonym: wily, shrewd
Antonym: artless, naÃ¯ve
Sentence: Few people trusted him because he seemed to be so calculating.

780. FUMBLE - *[spell]*- F U M B L E
Definition: feel or grope about clumsily
Synonym: botch, bumble
Antonym:
Sentence: The football player lost the game by fumbling the ball.

781. DETERIORATE - *[spell]*- D E T E R I O R A T E
Definition: become lower in quality or value
Synonym: depreciate, degrade
Antonym: elevate, improve
Sentence: As his health began to deteriorate, he visited the doctor more
frequently.

782. PARLIAMENT - *[spell]*- P A R L I A M E N T
Definition: council or congress that is the highest lawmaking body in
some countries
Synonym: congress
Antonym:
Sentence: Britain's Parliament makes many important decisions every
day.

783. FRISKY - *[spell]*- F R I S K Y
Definition: playful
Synonym: jumpy, lively
Antonym: calm, lifeless
Sentence: The kitten was frisky when it was let out of its cage.

784. FORTRESS - *[spell]*- F O R T R E S S
Definition: a large fortified place or building
Synonym: citadel, garrison
Antonym:
Sentence: The child liked to imagine his tent of sheets as a powerful fortress.

785. MISTRESS - *[spell]*- M I S T R E S S
Definition: woman who is at the head of the household
Synonym:
Antonym:
Sentence: As mistress of the household, she took care of many duties.

786. CHANGEABILITY - *[spell]*- C H A N G E A B I L I T Y
Definition: a quality that can be altered
Synonym: fickleness, malleability
Antonym: stability, decisiveness
Sentence: Because of the changeability of her nature, her actions were hard to predict.

787. OPTIMAL - *[spell]*- O P T I M A L
Definition: most favorable
Synonym: ideal , best
Antonym: worst
Sentence: The student studied hard in order to obtain optimal results on the test.

788. PERKY - *[spell]*- P E R K Y
Definition: cheerful or brisk
Synonym: optimistic, bubbly
Antonym: glum, gloomy
Sentence: He could tell she was in a good mood from her perky attitude.

789. GULCH - *[spell]*- G U L C H
Definition: a deep, narrow ravine with steep sides
Synonym:
Antonym:
Sentence: A small stream flowed through the gulch.

790. BOUNDARY - *[spell]*- B O U N D A R Y
Definition: a limiting line or thing
Synonym: border, confine
Antonym: center, interior
Sentence: When he reached the boundary of the city, he saw a sign.

791.   LOATHE - *[spell]*- L O A T H E
       Definition: feeling strong dislike and disgust for
       Synonym: abhor, hate
       Antonym: love, adore
       Sentence: He loathed going outside in the cold rain.

792.   OOMPH - *[spell]*- O O M P H
       Definition: energy or vitality
       Synonym: stamina, potency
       Antonym: idleness, laziness
       Sentence: Their cheering at the sideline gave him the extra oomph to
       finish the race.

793.   BRAWL - *[spell]*- B R A W L
       Definition: a noisy quarrel
       Synonym: altercation, argument
       Antonym: agreement, peace
       Sentence: When a brawl broke out, the police had to break it up.

794.   MANAGE - *[spell]*- M A N A G E
       Definition: guide or handle with skill or authority
       Synonym: administer, handle
       Antonym:
       Sentence: He was tasked with managing the long-term project.

795.   INACCESSIBILITY - *[spell]*- I N A C C E S S I B I L I T Y
       Definition: being hard to get at, reach, or enter
       Synonym:
       Antonym: accessibility
       Sentence: The inaccessibility of the park caused him to go home.

796.   FICTIONALIZE - *[spell]*- F I C T I O N A L I Z E
       Definition: give an imaginary or made up form to
       Synonym:
       Antonym:
       Sentence: The author fictionalized his life story instead of telling it in a
       memoir.

797.   DEMOTION - *[spell]*- D E M O T I O N
       Definition: act of reducing in rank
       Synonym: downgrade
       Antonym: promotion
       Sentence: When he constantly kept showing up late to his job, his boss
       had no choice but to serve him a demotion.

798. DESTRUCTIBLE - *[spell]*- D E S T R U C T I B L E
Definition: capable of being ruined
Synonym: perishable
Antonym: invincible
Sentence: Due to its destructible nature, he could not ship the gift.

799. JUMBLE - *[spell]*- J U M B L E
Definition: to mix or confuse
Synonym: tangled, cluttered
Antonym: sorted, arranged
Sentence: After finding out the terrible news, her thoughts were all jumbled.

800. UNFORESEEN - *[spell]*- U N F O R E S E E N
Definition: not known beforehand
Synonym: unexpected, surprising
Antonym: expected, predicted
Sentence: Due to unforeseen circumstances, the party had to be cancelled

Easy Words Exercise - 9

801. SEMISWEET - *[spell]-* S E M I S W E E T
Definition: moderately sweet
Synonym:
Antonym:
Sentence: She put semi sweet chocolate chips in the cookies.

802. COMPETENCE - *[spell]-* C O M P E T E N C E
Definition: ability to do something
Synonym: capability, expertise
Antonym: incompetence, inability
Sentence: His competence ensured that he would complete a quality project on time.

803. TURNKEY - *[spell]-* T U R N K E Y
Definition: person in charge of the keys of a prison, jail, etc.
Synonym: guard, warden
Antonym:
Sentence: The sergeant in the police force was assigned the job of turnkey for the evening.

804. TIMBER - *[spell]-* T I M B E R
Definition: wood used for building, making furniture, etc.
Synonym:
Antonym:
Sentence: The land was used primarily for its timber.

805. RAMBLE- *[spell]-* R A M B L E
Definition: to wander about in talking or writing
Synonym: meander, wander
Antonym:
Sentence: Her grandfather had a tendency to ramble when he told stories about his youth.

806. FAILURE - *[spell]-* F A I L U R E
Definition: being unable to do or become what is wanted or expected
Synonym: defeat, deficiency
Antonym: success, accomplishment
Sentence: She did not let failure slow her down.

807. ANIMATION - *[spell]*- A N I M A T I ON
Definition: liveliness
Synonym: spirit, vivacity
Antonym: calmness, dullness
Sentence: Her animation clearly was due to her happiness.

808. ARCHAIC- *[spell]*- A R C H A I C
Definition: out of date
Synonym: antiquated, primitive
Antonym: contemporary, current
Sentence: The teacher's archaic way of speaking made it difficult for him to relate to his students.

809. HEROICS - *[spell]*- H E R O I C S
Definition: word or actions that seem grand or noble but are only for effect
Synonym: bravado
Antonym:
Sentence: For all his heroics, he was quite a coward.

810. BLACKOUT - *[spell]*- B L A C K O U T
Definition: a temporary failure of memory
Synonym:
Antonym:
Sentence: After he was knocked out in the car accident, he experienced a blackout.

811. BLAMELESS - *[spell]*- B L A M E L E S S
Definition: free from fault
Synonym: faultless, innocent
Antonym: guilty, culpable
Sentence: The jury determined that he was blameless for his crime.

812. SNIVEL - *[spell]*- S N I V E L
Definition: to cry with sniffling or whimpering
Synonym: complain, groan
Antonym:
Sentence: The little girl sniveled after being punished for hitting her brother.

813. SCRAWL - *[spell]*- S C R A W L
Definition: poor or careless handwriting
Synonym: scribble
Antonym:
Sentence: He scrawled his signature on the bottom of the document.

814. PARTICLE- *[spell]*- P A R T I C L E
Definition: a very little bit
Synonym: piece, fleck
Antonym:
Sentence: Particles of dust floated through the air.

815. LIMITLESS - *[spell]*- L I M I T L E S S
Definition: boundless
Synonym: endless, immeasurable
Antonym: finite
Sentence: His potential in sports seemed to be limitless.

816. EXHAUSTION - *[spell]*- E X H A U S T I O N
Definition: extreme fatigue
Synonym: weariness, fatigue
Antonym: vigor, rejuvenation
Sentence: She felt complete exhaustion after her intense workout.

817. GLOOMY - *[spell]*- G L O O M Y
Definition: full of deep shadows and darkness
Synonym: bleak, dismal
Antonym: bright, cheerful
Sentence: Even though the sky looked gloomy, she decided to go camping anyway.

818. PERMANENCY- *[spell]*- P E R M A N E N C Y
Definition: state of being intended to last
Synonym: indestructible, perpetuation
Antonym: transience
Sentence: The permanency of the old building was proven when it withstood the hurricane.

819. HEARTFELT - *[spell]*- H E A R T F E L T
Definition: with deep feeling
Synonym: sincere, genuine
Antonym: apathetic, cold
Sentence: His heartfelt apology won her over.

820. PREMATURE- *[spell]*- P R E M A T U R E
Definition: before the proper time
Synonym: early
Antonym:
Sentence: The baby was kept in intensive care for several weeks because it was premature.

821. IMPRINT - *[spell]*- I M P R I N T
Definition: mark made by pressure
Synonym: impression, stamp
Antonym:
Sentence: His hand left an imprint on the glass.

822. BEWITCH - *[spell]*- B E W I T C H
Definition: to put under a spell
Synonym: beguile, enrapture
Antonym: disenchant, disgust
Sentence: She found that to bewitch him was entirely too easy.

823. CLAMMY - *[spell]*- C L A M M Y
Definition: cold or damp
Synonym: sweaty, moist
Antonym: dry, arid
Sentence: Whenever she was nervous, her hands began to feel clammy.

824. PERIODICALLY- *[spell]*- P E R I O D I C A L L Y
Definition: at regular intervals
Synonym: intermittent, occasionally
Antonym: constant
Sentence: The mother would periodically go check on her sleeping infant.

825. MOTTO - *[spell]*- M O T T O
Definition: brief sentence adopted as a rule of conduct
Synonym: slogan, maxim
Antonym:
Sentence: Her motto in life was "never give up."

826. DESCRIPTIVE - *[spell]*- D E S C R I P T I V E
Definition: the act of giving pictures with words
Synonym: detailed, vivid
Antonym:
Sentence: The descriptive language of the poem made it memorable.

827. KEEPSAKE - *[spell]*- K E E P S A K E
Definition: thing kept in memory of the giver
Synonym: remembrance, memento
Antonym:
Sentence: He brought all of his children a keepsake back from his business trip to France.

828. CLOSURE - *[spell]*- C L O S U R E
Definition: the end
Synonym: finish, conclusion

Antonym: beginning, commencement
Sentence: At the closure of the meeting, he congratulated everyone on their success.

829. LIFESTYLE - *[spell]*- L I F E S T Y L E
Definition: a person or group's characteristic manner of living
Synonym: behavior, conduct
Antonym:
Sentence: She was used to living a lavish lifestyle.

830. INSINCERITY - *[spell]*- I N S I N C E RI T Y
Definition: lack of honesty
Synonym: falsity, deceitfulness
Antonym: honesty, truthfulness
Sentence: Though he thanked her, his insincerity was obvious.

831. HARSH - *[spell]*- H A R S H
Definition: unpleasant to the touch, ear, or sight
Synonym: severe, sharp
Antonym: pleasant, mild
Sentence: She found his tone of voice too harsh for her liking.

832. DISCONTENTED - *[spell]*- D I S C O N T E N T E D
Definition: not happy
Synonym: unsatisfied, displeased
Antonym: content, satisfied
Sentence: Discontented with her decision to go to the party, she returned home instead.

833. ADVISABLE - *[spell]*- A D V I S A B L E
Definition: to be recommended
Synonym: sensible, suitable
Antonym: imprudent, inappropriate
Sentence: Going outside in this terrible storm is certainly not advisable.

834. SIMULATION - *[spell]*- S I M U L A T I O N
Definition: imitation of something anticipated or something likely to appear in testing
Synonym: imitation, reproduction
Antonym:
Sentence: The students in the driver's education classroom had to take a driving simulation.

835. SINKAGE - *[spell]*- S I N K A G E
Definition: act or process of going or falling down
Synonym: depression, descent

Antonym:
Sentence: The sinkage of the tree into the swamp happened very quickly.

836. ICICLE - *[spell]*- I C I C L E
Definition: a pointed, hanging stick of ice formed by the freezing of dripping water
Synonym:
Antonym:
Sentence: After the winter storm, icicles hung from all the trees.

837. WITCHERY - *[spell]*- W I T C H E RY
Definition: magic
Synonym:
Antonym:
Sentence: He couldn't help but fall prey to her witchery.

838. HUMORLESS - *[spell]*- H U M O R L E S S
Definition: without anything funny or amusing
Synonym: stuffy
Antonym:
Sentence: The holiday party at the office was completely humorless.

839. SEVERALLY - *[spell]*- S E V E R A L L Y
Definition: separately
Synonym: individually, independently
Antonym: together, united
Sentence: She decided that, severally, she and her friends would attend the party.

840. CONFIDENCE - *[spell]*- C O N F I D E N C E
Definition: firm belief or trust
Synonym: faith, assurance
Antonym: doubt, hesitation
Sentence: He had the utmost confidence in her.

841. PHONY- *[spell]*- P H O N Y
Definition: not genuine
Synonym: counterfeit, fake
Antonym: real, genuine
Sentence: Her excuses about being late to work seemed phony.

842. INSECURITY - *[spell]*- I N S E C U R I T Y
Definition: not free of danger or risk
Synonym: vulnerability, uncertainty
Antonym: security, safety
Sentence: She felt some insecurity about her financial future.

843. ABNORMALITY- *[spell]*-A B N O R M A L I T Y
Definition: a feature, act or occurrence that is not normal
Synonym: deformity, irregularity
Antonym: regularity, conformity
Sentence: After discovering the garment had a slight abnormality, she returned it to the store.

844. MUTANT - *[spell]*- M U T A N T
Definition: organism produced by an alteration
Synonym: deformity, deviant
Antonym:
Sentence: The experiment resulted in a mutant creature.

845. POVERTY- *[spell]*- P O V E R T Y
Definition: condition of being poor
Synonym: destitution
Antonym: wealth, riches
Sentence: The family was in a state of poverty after both parents lost their jobs.

846. REPELLENT- *[spell]*- R E P E L L E N T
Definition: disagreeable or distasteful
Synonym: revolting, offensive
Antonym: attractive, appealing
Sentence: He found her taste in music to be repellent.

847. DELEGATE - *[spell]*- D E L E G A T E
Definition: a person given authority to act for others
Synonym: representative, envoy
Antonym:
Sentence: The people elected delegates to represent them in the government.

848. MAJESTIC - *[spell]*- M A J E S T I C
Definition: of or having royal dignity
Synonym: impressive, splendid
Antonym: lowly, humble
Sentence: The colorful parrot was majestic in its beauty.

849. OCCUPATION- *[spell]*- O C C U P A T I O N
Definition: business, employment, or trade
Synonym: job, career
Antonym: pastime, recreation
Sentence: I've always felt that you should choose an occupation that makes you happy.

850. HOSTAGE - *[spell]*- H O S T A G E
Definition: person held by an enemy as a pledge that certain promises will be carried out
Synonym: prisoner, captive
Antonym:
Sentence: She was held hostage until her parents paid the ransom.

851. RESEMBLANCE- *[spell]*- R E S E M B L A N C E
Definition: similar appearance
Synonym: likeness, similarity
Antonym: dissimilarity
Sentence: She had a strong resemblance to her mother.

852. ANTLERED- *[spell]*- A N T L E R E D
Definition: having horns on top of the head
Synonym: horned
Antonym:
Sentence: Deer are antlered creatures.

853. BANNER - *[spell]*- B A N N E R
Definition: flag
Synonym: emblem, pennant
Antonym:
Sentence: The banner showed the family crest.

854. JOCKEY - *[spell]*- J O C K E Y
Definition: maneuver so as to get the advantage
Synonym: maneuver, navigate
Antonym:
Sentence: The man tried to jockey for the new managerial position.

855. ALLY - *[spell]*- A L L Y
Definition: a person, nation or group that is united for some cause
Synonym: associate, colleague
Antonym: enemy, opponent
Sentence: She found her friend to be a much-needed ally.

856. SEAM - *[spell]*- S E A M
Definition: line formed by sewing together two pieces of cloth, canvas, leather, etc.
Synonym:
Antonym:
Sentence: The seam of her pants began to split, so she had to re-sew them.

857. GRAFFITI - *[spell]*- G R A F F I T I
Definition: drawings or writing scratched or drawn onto a wall or other

surface
Synonym:
Antonym:
Sentence: Several teenagers were charged with vandalism for graffiti on the building.

858. INEFFICIENT - *[spell]*- I N E F F I C I E N T
Definition: not able to produce an effect without waste of time or energy
Synonym: wasteful, ineffective
Antonym: capable, able
Sentence: The time used for the class was inefficient.

859. THOUGHTLESS - *[spell]*- T H O U G H T L E S S
Definition: without thinking or ideas
Synonym: inconsiderate, impolite
Antonym: thoughtful
Sentence: Her thoughtless actions greatly hurt her boyfriend's feelings.

860. INDECISIVE - *[spell]*- I N D E C I S I V E
Definition: having the habit of hesitation or putting off decisions
Synonym: hesitant, uncertain
Antonym: certain, decisive
Sentence: They were so indecisive they could hardly make small decisions.

861. HIVE - *[spell]*- H I V E
Definition: a busy, swarming place full of people or animals
Synonym:
Antonym:
Sentence: The train station was a hive of activity during the holiday.

862. RUDDY - *[spell]*- R U D D Y
Definition: red or reddish
Synonym: rubicund
Antonym:
Sentence: Her ruddy cheeks showed her embarrassment.

863. HOPELESS - *[spell]*- H O P E L E S S
Definition: feeling or having no hope (feeling that one's desires will not happen)
Synonym: despairing,
Antonym: hopeful, optimistic
Sentence: The situation felt hopeless because he could not think of a solution.

864. ASSASSIN - *[spell]*- A S S A S S I N
Definition: a person who kills someone well known by a secret attack
Synonym: murderer, slayer
Antonym: victim, fatality
Sentence: The assassin was hired to kill the well-known politician.

865. SUFFIX - *[spell]*- S U F F I X
Definition: an addition made at the end of a word to form another word of different meaning or function
Synonym:
Antonym:
Sentence: Often, a word can be changed by adding a suffix.

866. FUDDLE - *[spell]*- F U D D L E
Definition: confuse or muddle
Synonym: bemuse, befuddle
Antonym:
Sentence: Her mind was fuddled when she couldn't figure out the math problem.

867. SCAMP - *[spell]*- S C A M P
Definition: an unprincipled person
Synonym: rascal, rogue
Antonym:
Sentence: He was known by everyone as the office scamp.

868. NURSERY - *[spell]*- N U R S E R Y
Definition: room set apart for the use and care of babies
Synonym:
Antonym:
Sentence: The new parents painted the nursery of their baby daughter.

869. PETTISH- *[spell]*- P E T T I S H
Definition: peevish, cross
Synonym: angry, cantankerous
Antonym: cheerful
Sentence: She felt pettish after having a bad day.

870. HEAVYSET - *[spell]*- H E A V Y S E T
Definition: built heavily
Synonym: broad, stocky
Antonym: narrow, thin
Sentence: For most of his life he had been a heavyset individual.

871. EXCEPTIONAL - *[spell]*- E X C E P T I O N A L
Definition: out of the ordinary

Synonym: unusual, extraordinary
Antonym: commonplace, familiar
Sentence: The dinner she made was exceptional.

872. DASHING - *[spell]*- D A S H I N G
Definition: stylish
Synonym: dapper, debonair
Antonym: unstylish
Sentence: He looked quite dashing in his suit and tie.

873. SWIMMINGLY - *[spell]*- S W I M M I N G L Y
Definition: with great ease or success
Synonym: smoothly, effortlessly
Antonym:
Sentence: The student thought his project was going along swimmingly well.

874. BLOUSE - *[spell]*- B L O U S E
Definition: a loose-fitting garment that covers the top of the body
Synonym: shirt
Antonym:
Sentence: She put on a dressy blouse and pants for her interview.

875. GLARING - *[spell]*- G L A R I N G
Definition: very easily seen
Synonym: conspicuous, obvious
Antonym: inconspicuous
Sentence: The accountant had made a glaring error.

876. BACHELOR - *[spell]*- B A C H E L O R
Definition: a man who is not married
Synonym: single
Antonym:
Sentence: He preferred to remain a bachelor, so he didn't date many women.

877. BALM - *[spell]*- B A L M
Definition: an oily substance used to heal
Synonym: ointment, lotion
Antonym:
Sentence: She used a balm to help heal the injuries from her burns.

878. POSSIBILITY- *[spell]*- P O S S I B I L I T Y
Definition: something that can happen
Synonym: prospect, eventuality

Antonym: actuality, certainty
Sentence: There was a possibility of thunderstorms over the weekend.

879.   RELATION- *[spell]*- R E L A T I O N
       Definition: act of telling
       Synonym:
       Antonym:
       Sentence: His relation of the story was not nearly as funny as his wife's.

880.   FREQUENCY - *[spell]*- F R E Q U E N C Y
       Definition: rate of occurrence
       Synonym: recurrence, regularity
       Antonym: infrequency, irregularity
       Sentence: The frequency of snow increased during February.

881.   BOTHERSOME - *[spell]*- B O T H E R S O ME
       Definition: causing worry or fuss
       Synonym: troublesome, annoying
       Antonym: helpful, convenient
       Sentence: Though his actions were bothersome, she tried not to worry too much about it.

882.   BLOCKAGE - *[spell]*- B L O C K A G E
       Definition: the state of being obstructed by something
       Synonym: hindrance, stoppage
       Antonym:
       Sentence: The blockage in his arteries caused a heart attack because blood flow was limited.

883.   GLADSOME - *[spell]*- G L A D S O M E
       Definition: glad
       Synonym: joyful, cheerful
       Antonym: dour, morose
       Sentence: There is gladsome news from the front lines; the war is over!

884.   REVULSION - *[spell]*- R E V U L S I O N
       Definition: a sudden, violent change or reaction, especially of disgust
       Synonym: repulsion, loathing
       Antonym: antipathy, displeasure
       Sentence: Her revulsion at the violent movie made her turn it off.

885.   DWARFISH - *[spell]*- D W A R F I S H
       Definition: much smaller than usual
       Synonym: short, diminutive
       Antonym: giant, gargantuan

Sentence: Dwarfish in stature, she had to have much of her furniture modified to suit her.

886. SHAKY - *[spell]*- S H A K Y
Definition: shaking
Synonym: trembling, jittery
Antonym: secure, steady
Sentence: Her fear caused her hands to be shaky.

887. CONSEQUENT - *[spell]*- C O N S E Q U E N T
Definition: following as a result
Synonym: ensuing, subsequent
Antonym:
Sentence: His long illness and consequent absence was devastating to his work.

888. BLOODLINE - *[spell]*- B L O O D L I N E
Definition: series of ancestors in a family
Synonym: genealogy, lineage
Antonym:
Sentence: His bloodline could be traced back to a series of kings and queens.

889. RAVISHING- *[spell]*- R A V I S H I N G
Definition: unusually attractive, pleasing, or striking
Synonym: beautiful, gorgeous
Antonym: homely, ugly
Sentence: He thought his date looked ravishing in her red dress.

890. TWINGE - *[spell]*- T W I N G E
Definition: a sudden sharp pain
Synonym: pang, spasm
Antonym:
Sentence: He felt a twinge of guilt at having to miss his friend's birthday party.

891. SHTICK - *[spell]*- S H T I C K
Definition: a comedy act
Synonym:
Antonym:
Sentence: The comedian was known from his somewhat controversial shtick.

892. TEEMING - *[spell]*- T E E M I N G
Definition: alive
Synonym: abundant, full

Antonym:
Sentence: At noon, the restaurant was teeming with customers.

893. CHILDISH - *[spell]*- C H I L D I S H
Definition: like a young boy or girl
Synonym: immature, naÃ¯ve
Antonym: mature, wise
Sentence: Though he looked older than his age, he still acted childish.

894. VISITANT - *[spell]*- V I S I T A N T
Definition: a guest
Synonym: visitor, company
Antonym: host
Sentence: The woman was eager to please her visitants.

895. ALERT - *[spell]*- A L E R T
Definition: watchful
Synonym: vigilant, attentive
Antonym: careless, inattentive
Sentence: The teacher was alert for signs of cheating during the test.

896. SNOOTY - *[spell]*- S N O O T Y
Definition: snobbish or conceited
Synonym: haughty, arrogant
Antonym: friendly, humble
Sentence: Her snooty attitude toward people of lower social standing was very unappealing.

897. AFFAIR - *[spell]*- A F F A I R
Definition: a private matter
Synonym:
Antonym:
Sentence: He decided that his affairs were none of his mother's business.

898. REALIST- *[spell]*- R E A L I S T
Definition: person interested in what is real rather than what is imaginary or theoretical
Synonym: pragmatist
Antonym:
Sentence: He considered himself too much of a realist to entertain such fanciful ideas.

899. INSULTING - *[spell]*- I N S U L T I N G
Definition: something that is said scornfully, rudely, or offensively
Synonym: abusive, derogatory

Antonym: complimentary, kind
Sentence: His comments were insulting to her character.

900.   OBSESSIVE- *[spell]*- O B S E S S I V E
Definition: having to do with or causing to be obsessed (keep the attention of to an unreasonable or unhealthy extent)
Synonym: compulsive
Antonym:
Sentence: His attitude toward her was somewhat obsessive.

Easy Words Exercise - 10

901. RAFFLE- *[spell]*- R A F F L E
Definition: sale in which many people each pay a small sum for a chance to win a prize
Synonym:
Antonym:
Sentence: There was a raffle at the door of the party.

902. POSTSCRIPT- *[spell]*- P O S T S C R I P T
Definition: addition to a letter, written after the author's name has been signed
Synonym:
Antonym:
Sentence: In the postscript of his email, the husband mentioned he would be home in two days.

903. RADIANCE- *[spell]*- R A D I A N C E
Definition: vivid brightness
Synonym: emanation, glow
Antonym: dimness, dullness
Sentence: We could tell she was in love with him because there was a radiance about her when she was with him.

904. ARTIFACT - *[spell]*- A R T I F A C T
Definition: anything made by humans in the past
Synonym: relic
Antonym:
Sentence: Many artifacts were found at the archeological site.

905. DABBLE - *[spell]*-D A B B L E
Definition: to do something in a slight way
Synonym: tinker, trifle
Antonym:
Sentence: In her free time, she liked to dabble in painting.

906. SUMMARIZE - *[spell]*- S U M M A R I Z E
Definition: to make a brief statement about the main points of
Synonym: rehash, outline

Antonym:
Sentence: The politician summarized his plan at the end of his speech.

907. AVALANCHE - *[spell]*- A V A L A N C H E
Definition: a large mass of snow that descends from a mountain into a valley
Synonym: landslide
Antonym:
Sentence: An avalanche ravaged the village at the base of the mountain.

908. INFANCY - *[spell]*- I N F A N C Y
Definition: condition of being a baby
Synonym: babyhood, childhood
Antonym: old age
Sentence: Children show great development in their infancy.

909. FINALE - *[spell]*- F I N A L E
Definition: the last part, end
Synonym: conclusion, cessation
Antonym: beginning, opening
Sentence: The finale of the TV show was surprising to all of its fans.

910. HONESTY - *[spell]*- H O N E S T Y
Definition: having a nature that is honest (not lying)
Synonym: sincerity
Antonym: dishonesty, falseness
Sentence: He was known for his honesty in all things.

911. INCIDENT - *[spell]*- I N C I D E N T
Definition: an individual occurrence or event
Synonym: occurrence, event
Antonym:
Sentence: The firefighters were unsure what incident had caused the fire.

912. NUMBING - *[spell]*- N U M B I N G
Definition: that causes unfeeling
Synonym: paralyzed, anesthetize
Antonym: animate, enliven
Sentence: He was given a numbing medicine at the dentist office.

913. APPRENTICE - *[spell]*- A P P R E N T I C E
Definition: a person who is learning a trade or an art
Synonym: pupil, neophyte
Antonym: expert, professional
Sentence: As an apprentice in painting, he had to learn many basic skills.

914. SITUATION - *[spell]*- S I T U A T I O N
Definition: combination of circumstances
Synonym: condition, position
Antonym:
Sentence: She found herself in quite a difficult situation at work.

915. FLASHY - *[spell]*- F L A S H Y
Definition: showy
Synonym: gaudy, tawdry
Antonym: modest, plain
Sentence: Her flashy clothing was clearly designed to get attention.

916. RELUCTANCY- *[spell]*- R E L U C T A N C Y
Definition: a feeling of showing unwillingness
Synonym: hesitancy, faltering
Antonym:
Sentence: I can recommend him wholeheartedly, without reluctancy.

917. FREEDOM - *[spell]*- F R E E D O M
Definition: condition of being not under another's control
Synonym: independence, liberty
Antonym: servitude, slavery
Sentence: He valued his freedom more than anything.

918. AGGRESSOR - *[spell]*- A G G R E S S O R
Definition: someone that begins an attack or quarrel
Synonym: assailant, invader
Antonym: victim
Sentence: Because she was seen as an aggressor, she had very few friends.

919. DESTINE - *[spell]*- D E S T I N E
Definition: cause by fate
Synonym: predetermined, fated
Antonym:
Sentence: He seemed destined for greatness.

920. MANEUVER - *[spell]*- M A N E U V E R
Definition: to manipulate or move with skill
Synonym: scheme, position
Antonym:
Sentence: He maneuvered himself into his boss's good graces.

921. GENIUS - *[spell]*- G E N I U S
Definition: very great natural power of the mind
Synonym: acumen, brilliance

Antonym: ignorance, ineptitude
Sentence: His genius allowed him to excel as a scientist.

922. DEVOUR - *[spell]*- D E V O U R
Definition: to eat hungrily
Synonym: ingest, gobble
Antonym:
Sentence: The child devoured his dinner in a matter of minutes.

923. THROTTLE - *[spell]*- T H R O T T L E
Definition: lever, pedal, etc. working as a valve that regulates the flow of gas, steam, etc.
Synonym:
Antonym:
Sentence: He used the throttle to fire up the engine of the train.

924. TOTTER - *[spell]*- T O T T E R
Definition: stand or walk with shaky, unsteady steps
Synonym: teeter, lurch
Antonym:
Sentence: The baby calf tottered across the field.

925. INCUBATE - *[spell]*- I N C U B A T E
Definition: maintain the proper temperature for eggs in order for them to hatch
Synonym:
Antonym:
Sentence: The chicken eggs had to be incubated in order to hatch.

926. FAMISHED - *[spell]*- F A M I S H E D
Definition: very hungry
Synonym: starving, ravenous
Antonym: full, sated
Sentence: The boys were famished after playing an intense game of football.

927. MINDLESS - *[spell]*- M I N D L E S S
Definition: without intelligence
Synonym: thoughtless, senseless
Antonym: reasonable, sensible
Sentence: The student found the work to be mindless.

928. ARCHAEOLOGY - *[spell]*- A R C H A E O L O G Y
Definition: the study of people, customs and life in ancient times
Synonym:

Antonym:
Sentence: He went to college in order to study archaeology.

929.   ENGRAVE - *[spell]*- E N G R A V E
Definition: cut deeply in
Synonym: carve, chisel
Antonym:
Sentence: She had her husband's name engraved on her wedding band.

930.   DISBAND - *[spell]*- D I S B A N D
Definition: to break up as an organization
Synonym: disperse, dissolve
Antonym: assemble, unite
Sentence: The committee was disbanded when it did not accomplish its goals.

931.   PRICKLY- *[spell]*- P R I C K L Y
Definition: sharp points or thorns
Synonym: thorny, nettlesome
Antonym: smooth, even
Sentence: The texture of his chin was quite prickly after he didn't shave for two days.

932.   BANGLE - *[spell]*- B A N G LE
Definition: a small ornament hanging from a bracelet
Synonym:
Antonym:
Sentence: The girl loved to wear bangle bracelets.

933.   PORTRAYAL- *[spell]*- P O R T R A Y A L
Definition: making a likeness by words or drawing
Synonym: depiction, portraiture
Antonym:
Sentence: The movie's portrayal of the politician was quite unflattering.

934.   SPLURGE- *[spell]*- S P L U R G E
Definition: to indulge in a costly luxury
Synonym: binge, extravagance
Antonym:
Sentence: He decided that, after a hard day's work, he would splurge on an expensive meal from his favorite restaurant.

935.   ELABORATION - *[spell]*- E L A B O R A T I O N
Definition: the act of giving great detail
Synonym: illustration, discussion
Antonym:

Sentence: Her elaboration about her wedding plans enthralled her bridesmaids.

936. MARINADE - *[spell]*- M A R I N A D E
Definition: a special vinegar, wine, combination of spices, etc. used for soaking meat before being cooked
Synonym:
Antonym:
Sentence: The chef put the meat into a delicious marinade before cooking it.

937. FOREBODING - *[spell]*- F O R E B O D I N G
Definition: to have an inward prediction of
Synonym: premonition, apprehension
Antonym:
Sentence: The dark clouds overhead filled me with a sense of foreboding.

938. SEARCHING - *[spell]*- S E A R C H I N G
Definition: examining carefully
Synonym: inquiring, probing
Antonym:
Sentence: Her searching gaze seemed to try to determine the truth of his story.

939. COMMERCIAL - *[spell]*- C O M M E R C I A L
Definition: made to be sold for profit
Synonym: corporate, marketable
Antonym: noncommercial
Sentence: The product was manufactured for commercial purposes.

940. HUNCHBACK - *[spell]*- H U N C H B A C K
Definition: a person whose back has a hump on it
Synonym:
Antonym:
Sentence: He had become a hunchback due to a back injury.

941. TRIPOD - *[spell]*- T R I P O D
Definition: three-legged support system for a camera
Synonym: stand, mount
Antonym:
Sentence: The photographer used a tripod to take shots at the park.

942. EXPANSION - *[spell]*- E X P A N S I ON
Definition: a making larger
Synonym: increase, proliferation
Antonym: compression, diminishment

Sentence: They decided the house needed an expansion, including a bedroom and a bathroom.

943. FLESHLY - *[spell]*- F L E S H L Y
Definition: worldly
Synonym: bodily, corporeal
Antonym: non temporal
Sentence: The priest seemed to be overly concerned with fleshly occupations.

944. PERMISSIBLE- *[spell]*- P E R M I S S I B L E
Definition: allowable
Synonym: admissible, allowable
Antonym: forbidden, prohibited
Sentence: The parents decided it was permissible for their daughter to go to the party.

945. VALID - *[spell]*- V A L I D
Definition: sound or well-founded
Synonym: accurate, authentic
Antonym:
Sentence: He made many valid points in his argument.

946. SIDESHOW - *[spell]*- S I D E S H O W
Definition: a small show in connection with a larger one
Synonym:
Antonym:
Sentence: A sideshow at the circus contained an impressive petting zoo.

947. TERMINATE - *[spell]*- T E R M I N A T E
Definition: to bring to an end
Synonym: stop, finish
Antonym: begin, encourage
Sentence: The employer decided to terminate the contract of two of his staff members.

948. TRIUMPHANT - *[spell]*- T R I U M P H A N T
Definition: victorious or successful
Synonym: celebratory, glorious
Antonym:
Sentence: She felt triumphant when she came in third place during the race.

949. REPLETION- *[spell]*- R E P L E T I O N
Definition: a being abundantly supplied
Synonym: satiation, gratification

Antonym: lack, need

Sentence: The repletion of food in the pantry looked like it would last forever.

950. MYSTICAL - *[spell]*- M Y S T I C A L
Definition: having some secret meaning
Synonym: magical, supernatural
Antonym: obvious, apparent
Sentence: The artwork had a mystical quality.

951. Y A C H T - *[spell]*- Y A C H T
Definition: a boat used for private cruising
Synonym: boat, cruiser
Antonym:
Sentence: The man purchased a yacht to entertain himself on weekends.

952. EXPRESSIBLE - *[spell]*- E X P R E S S I B L E
Definition: that can be put into words
Synonym:
Antonym:
Sentence: Her fears were so intense as to barely be expressible.

953. PATRIOTIC- *[spell]*- P A T R I O T I C
Definition: loving one's country
Synonym: nationalistic
Antonym: unpatriotic
Sentence: Wanting to be patriotic, he hung his country's flag from his home.

954. TEMPORARY - *[spell]*- T E M P O R A R Y
Definition: lasting for a short time only
Synonym: interim, momentary
Antonym: enduring, lasting
Sentence: She decided she would take the temporary job until she could find something permanent.

955. SUMMIT - *[spell]*- S U M M I T
Definition: the highest point
Synonym: peak, pinnacle
Antonym: base, bottom
Sentence: The hikers climbed to the summit of the mountain.

956. ARTISTRY - *[spell]*- A R T I S T R Y
Definition: artistic qualities or workmanship
Synonym: finesse, proficiency

Antonym: ineptness, inability
Sentence: Because of the artistry of his work, he was soon promoted.

957. ABILITY- *[spell]*- A B I L I T Y
Definition: the state of being able to do something
Synonym: capability, capacity
Antonym: inability, ignorance
Sentence: She had an incredible ability to turn ordinary objects into art.

958. MOURNFUL - *[spell]*- M O U R N F U L
Definition: full of grief or sadness
Synonym: melancholy, despairing
Antonym: happy, joyful
Sentence: The mournful poem made her sad.

959. BULLETIN - *[spell]*- B U L L E T I N
Definition: a short statement of recent events for the information of the public
Synonym: announcement, dispatch
Antonym:
Sentence: A bulletin was issued about the recent wildfire raging through the state.

960. BANQUET - *[spell]*- B A N Q U E T
Definition: a large meal with many courses
Synonym: feast
Antonym:
Sentence: There was a large banquet to honor the new president of the company.

961. THEATRICAL - *[spell]*- T H E A T R I C A L
Definition: of or having to do with the theater or something dramatic
Synonym: exaggerated, melodramatic
Antonym:
Sentence: Her presentation before her classmates was a bit theatrical.

962. RUSTIC - *[spell]*- R U S T I C
Definition: belonging to or suitable for the country
Synonym: country, rural
Antonym: sophisticated, cultured
Sentence: She wanted to buy a rustic home in a rural area.

963. RESENTMENT- *[spell]*- R E S E N T M E N T
Definition: the feeling that one has of being injured or insulted
Synonym: grievance, grudge
Antonym:

Sentence: He felt resentment toward his mother when she didn't let him
go on the school trip.

964. ALLIANCE - *[spell]*- A L L I A N C E
Definition: a union formed by mutual agreement
Synonym: bond, coalition
Antonym: disagreement
Sentence: The two forces formed an alliance when they realized it would
help them win.

965. DISORIENT - *[spell]*- D I S O R I E N T
Definition: cause to lose one's bearings
Synonym: confuse
Antonym:
Sentence: He felt disoriented after spinning in circles.

966. MISPRONOUNCE - *[spell]*- M I S P R O N O U N C E
Definition: pronounce incorrectly
Synonym: garbled, slurred
Antonym: enunciate
Sentence: The teacher mispronounced the student's name.

967. MISLEAD - *[spell]*- M I S L E A D
Definition: cause to go in the wrong direction
Synonym: deceive, misinform
Antonym:
Sentence: It was easy to be misled by the advertisement.

968. ELEGANCE - *[spell]*- E L E G A N C E
Definition: refined grace
Synonym: taste, refinement
Antonym: crudeness, coarseness
Sentence: She had an elegance of taste that made her beautiful and
fashionable.

969. ACIDITY- *[spell]*- A C I D I T Y
Definition: like an acid in quality
Synonym: acridness, acerbity
Antonym:
Sentence: She knew there had to be an enormous amount of vinegar in the
recipe from the acidity she tasted.

970. SKEWER - *[spell]*- S K E W E R
Definition: pierce as if with a skewer (long pin of metal or wood)
Synonym: jab, pin

Antonym:
Sentence: He skewered the meat and cooked it on the grill.

971. NICKNAME - *[spell]*- N I C K N A M E
Definition: name added to a person's real name
Synonym: epithet
Antonym:
Sentence: She was given a nickname by her new boyfriend.

972. MILEAGE - *[spell]*- M I L E A G E
Definition: distance covered or traveled
Synonym:
Antonym:
Sentence: The mileage they covered in their journey that day was impressive.

973. OCTAGONAL- *[spell]*- O C T A G O N A L
Definition: a shape with eight angles and eight sides
Synonym:
Antonym:
Sentence: The table was octagonal in shape.

974. MANAGEMENT - *[spell]*- M A N A G E M E N T
Definition: a handling or controlling
Synonym: administration, authority
Antonym:
Sentence: She aspired to move into management within the company.

975. NEARSIGHTED - *[spell]*- N E A R S I G H T E D
Definition: seeing distinctly at a short distance only
Synonym: shortsighted
Antonym:
Sentence: Because she was nearsighted, she was never looking toward the future.

976. SHAPELESS - *[spell]*- S H A P E L E S S
Definition: without a definite form
Synonym: formless, nebulous
Antonym: formed, shapely
Sentence: The shadow on the wall was shapeless and mysterious.

977. CONTINUATION - *[spell]*- C O N T I N U A T I O N
Definition: act of going on without stopping
Synonym: continuity, perpetuation
Antonym: cessation, termination
Sentence: The second volume offered a continuation of the first.

978. EVAPORATE - *[spell]*- E V A P O R A T E
Definition: vanish, disappear
Synonym: dissipate, fade
Antonym: appear, materialize
Sentence: When the rumors began to evaporate, he finally felt more secure.

979. SHADY - *[spell]*- S H A D Y
Definition: in the shade
Synonym: shadowy, cloudy
Antonym: clear, bright
Sentence: He sat in the shady spot beneath the tree.

980. CONNECTIVE - *[spell]*- C O N N E C T I V E
Definition: anything that joins one thing to another
Synonym: conjoining, juncture
Antonym:
Sentence: In the accident, he damaged the connective tissue between joints in his arm.

981. ALTERNATE- *[spell]*- A L T E R N A T E
Definition: to take turns
Synonym:
Antonym:
Sentence: Because their mother insisted they share, the children decided to alternate playing the video game.

982. DEVELOPMENTAL - *[spell]*- D E V E L O P M E N T A L
Definition: having to do with changing over time
Synonym: evolving, formative
Antonym:
Sentence: The project was still in developmental stages.

983. GULL - *[spell]*- G U L L
Definition: deceive or cheat
Synonym: bamboozle, dupe
Antonym:
Sentence: The swindler was able to gull the man into giving him the money he wanted.

984. NOTIFICATION - *[spell]*- N O T I F I C A T I O N
Definition: a making known
Synonym: proclamation, alert
Antonym:
Sentence: She was sent a notification of her bill in the mail.

985. VEGETATION - *[spell]* - V E G E T A T I O N
Definition: plant life
Synonym: flora, greenery
Antonym:
Sentence: Vegetation in the area was plentiful.

986. ANNOYANCE - *[spell]* - A N N O Y A N C E
Definition: a feeling of being caused uneasiness, especially by repeated acts
Synonym: displeasure, exasperation
Antonym: satisfaction, happiness
Sentence: Her little brother was such an annoyance that the girl finally locked herself in her room to get away from him.

987. ALPHABETICAL - *[spell]* - A L P H A B E T I C A L
Definition: arranged in order of the letters of the alphabet
Synonym:
Antonym:
Sentence: The students' names on the rosters were in alphabetical order.

988. HILARITY - *[spell]* - H I L A R I T Y
Definition: great merriment
Synonym: laughter, mirth
Antonym:
Sentence: The hilarity of the situation made everyone laugh.

989. INFRINGE - *[spell]* - I N F R I N G E
Definition: act contrary to or violate (a law, obligation, right, etc.)
Synonym: breach, violate
Antonym: observe, comply
Sentence: He felt his rights had been infringed upon by the new law.

990. SPLASH - *[spell]* - S P L A S H
Definition: cause water, mud, etc. to fly about
Synonym: splatter, squirt
Antonym: dry, dehydrate
Sentence: Her pants were covered in mud after she splashed through a puddle.

991. FATALITY - *[spell]* - F A T A L I T Y
Definition: death that results from a disaster or accident
Synonym: casualty
Antonym:
Sentence: There were three fatalities as a result of the car accident.

992. BOUTIQUE - *[spell]*- B O U T I Q U E
Definition: a small shop that specializes in stylish clothes
Synonym: store
Antonym:
Sentence: The girl loved to shop for unique clothes at the boutiques downtown.

993. PROSPERITY- *[spell]*- P R O S P E R I T Y
Definition: a condition of good fortune or success
Synonym:
Antonym:
Sentence: He experienced unexpected prosperity when he won the lottery.

994. MINISCULE - *[spell]*- M I N I S C U L E
Definition: very small
Synonym: tiny, little
Antonym: giant, big
Sentence: The project required a miniscule effort.

995. INCONSISTENCY - *[spell]*- I N C O N S I S T E N C Y
Definition: lacking in agreement or harmony
Synonym: discrepancy, disparity
Antonym: agreement, accord
Sentence: The students were well aware of the inconsistency of the teacher's enforcement of the rules.

996. HUMORIST - *[spell]*- H U M O R I S T
Definition: a person who's writing is full of funny or amusing qualities
Synonym: satirist, comedian
Antonym:
Sentence: The humorist was known for his sarcasm in his writing.

997. DOTING - *[spell]*- D O T I N G
Definition: foolishly fond
Synonym: adoring, affectionate
Antonym: negligent, unaffectionate
Sentence: His doting attitude toward his daughter caused her to be spoiled.

998. ASOCIAL - *[spell]*- A S O C I A L
Definition: reluctant to associate with other people
Synonym: antisocial, introverted
Antonym: sociable
Sentence: Because he was typically asocial, he did not like going to parties.

999. RIVET - *[spell]*- R I V E T
Definition: to fasten with a small bolt
Synonym: fasten
Antonym:
Sentence: The two pieces of metal were riveted together.

1000. HASTY - *[spell]*- H A S T Y
Definition: done or made in a hurry
Synonym: hurried, rapid
Antonym: careful, cautious
Sentence: His hasty remarks were considered offensive by some.

Medium Words Exercise - 1

1001. TOTALIZE - *[spell]*- T O T A L I Z E
Definition: a making whole
Synonym: complete, add
Antonym: estimate, subtract
Sentence: The author totalized the book by adding an epilogue.

1002. CABOOSE - *[spell]*- C A B O O S E
Definition: the last car on a train
Synonym:
Antonym:
Sentence: The caboose of the train held the quarters in which the crew slept and rested.

1003. TABOO - *[spell]*- T A B O O
Definition: forbidden by custom or tradition
Synonym: banned, forbidden
Antonym: allowable, permissible
Sentence: It is usually considered taboo to hug a complete stranger.

1004. RECURVE - *[spell]*- R E C U R V E
Definition: to bend back
Synonym:
Antonym:
Sentence: At the end of the woods, the path recurved back toward the park.

1005. REMAINDER - *[spell]*- R E M A I N D E R
Definition: the part left over
Synonym: balance, residue
Antonym:
Sentence: She used the remainder of the fabric to make a doll for her daughter.

1006. SERIAL - *[spell]*- S E R I A L
Definition: a story published, broadcast or televised one part at a time
Synonym:
Antonym:
Sentence: The book was originally published as a serial.

1007. SWANKY - *[spell]* - S W A N K Y
Definition: stylish or dashing
Synonym: smart, classy
Antonym: inferior, trashy
Sentence: The couple decided that, for their honeymoon, they wanted to stay in a swanky hotel.

1008. BAFFLING - *[spell]* - B A F F L I N G
Definition: puzzling
Synonym: bewildering, confusing
Antonym: comprehensible, fathomable
Sentence: The answer to the math problem was baffling to her.

1009. DUMBFOUND - *[spell]* - D U M B F O U ND
Definition: to amaze and make unable to speak
Synonym: bewilder, confuse
Antonym:
Sentence: She was dumbfounded by the math problem.

1010. IMMOVABLE - *[spell]* - I M M O V A B L E
Definition: unable to be moved
Synonym: fixed, stubborn
Antonym: flexible, mobile
Sentence: He was immovable in his views on the issue.

1011. ACKNOWLEDGMENT - *[spell]* - A C K N O W L E D G M E N T
Definition: something done or given to show someone has received a favor or service.
Synonym: affirmation, concession
Antonym: denial, dissent
Sentence: As an acknowledgement of the fact that she had done her chores, the father gave his daughter her weekly allowance.

1012. THWACK - *[spell]* - T H W A C K
Definition: to strike vigorously with a stick or something flat
Synonym: whack, blow
Antonym:
Sentence: During the storm, the branches of the trees thwacked against the window.

1013. RUBBISH - *[spell]* - R U B B I SH
Definition: worthless or useless stuff
Synonym: trash, junk
Antonym:
Sentence: She decided to clear all of the rubbish out of her office.

1014. TABLOID - *[spell]*- T A B L O I D
Definition: a newspaper, especially one that has sensational headlines
Synonym:
Antonym:
Sentence: The tabloid published sensational headlines about popular celebrities.

1015. KINGDOM - *[spell]*- K I N G D O M
Definition: nation that is governed by a king or a queen
Synonym: country, dynasty
Antonym:
Sentence: During the king's reign, there was prosperity throughout the kingdom.

1016. POLYGON - *[spell]*- P O L Y G O N
Definition: a shape with three or more sides and angles
Synonym:
Antonym:
Sentence: The building was in the shape of a polygon.

1017. FADDISH - *[spell]*- F A D D I S H
Definition: inclined to follow trends
Synonym: trendy
Antonym:
Sentence: The teenager was always faddish in her sense of fashion.

1018. HEIGHTEN - *[spell]*- H E I G H T E N
Definition: make or become more intense
Synonym: intensify, enhance
Antonym: diminish, reduce
Sentence: The suspense of the movie was heightened by the star's superb acting.

1019. OVERLAP - *[spell]*- O V E R L A P
Definition: cover and extend beyond
Synonym: overhang, overlay
Antonym:
Sentence: The responsibilities of the two jobs overlapped one another.

1020. CINEMATIC - *[spell]*- C I N E M A T I C
Definition: having to do with a motion picture
Synonym:
Antonym:
Sentence: He was an expert in all things cinematic.

1021. MYSTERIOUS - *[spell]*- M Y S T E R I O U S
Definition: hard to explain or understand
Synonym: enigmatic
Antonym: obvious, apparent
Sentence: There was something mysterious about him.

1022. MEMBERSHIP - *[spell]*- M E M B E R S H I P
Definition: fact or state of being a person, animal or thing belonging to a group
Synonym:
Antonym:
Sentence: She cancelled her membership to the gym because it cost too much.

1023. SPINDLE - *[spell]*- S P I N D L E
Definition: the rod or pin used in spinning to twist, wind or hold thread
Synonym:
Antonym:
Sentence: The seamstress put a new spool of thread on the spindle.

1024. LANDFALL - *[spell]*- L A N D F A L L
Definition: a sighting or reaching of land
Synonym:
Antonym:
Sentence: At dawn, the ship finally made landfall.

1025. ANGST - *[spell]*- A N G S T
Definition: anxiety
Synonym: dread, apprehension
Antonym: calmness
Sentence: Teenagers are sometimes stereotyped as constantly experiencing great angst.

1026. LETHAL - *[spell]*- L E T H A L
Definition: deadly
Synonym: mortal, fatal
Antonym: beneficial, harmless
Sentence: Scuba diving without the proper equipment could be lethal.

1027. FINALIZE - *[spell]*- F I N A L I Z E
Definition: to make conclusive
Synonym: complete, wrap up
Antonym: begin, introduce
Sentence: The couple had only to finalize their paperwork before they could bring their adopted daughter home.

1028. APOLITICAL - *[spell]*- A P O L I T I C A L
Definition: not concerned with politics
Synonym:
Antonym:
Sentence: Frustrated with government, he identified himself as apolitical.

1029. SCREECHY - *[spell]*- S C R E E C HY
Definition: crying out sharply in a high voice
Synonym: shriek, scream
Antonym:
Sentence: The screechy sound coming from the car suggested something was broken.

1030. SCRIBE - *[spell]*- S C R I B E
Definition: person who copies manuscripts
Synonym:
Antonym:
Sentence: The scribe copied a few pages before retiring for the evening.

1031. KNAPSACK - *[spell]*- K N A P S A C K
Definition: a bag with two shoulder straps
Synonym: satchel, backpack
Antonym:
Sentence: She filled her knapsack with snacks for the journey.

1032. CLARITY - *[spell]*- C L A R I T Y
Definition: clearness
Synonym: lucidity, clearness
Antonym: cloudiness, obscurity
Sentence: Her clarity on the issue left no room for doubt.

1033. GLOROIUS - *[spell]*- G L O R I O US
Definition: magnificent
Synonym: splendid, notable
Antonym: unimpressive
Sentence: His view of the mountains from his home was glorious.

1034. NEEDLESS - *[spell]*- N E E D L E S S
Definition: not needed
Synonym: pointless, unnecessary
Antonym: reasonable, necessary
Sentence: Needless to say she was excited about the party.

1035. GRACEFUL - *[spell]*- G R A C E F U L
Definition: having or showing beauty in form or movement
Synonym: agile, elegant

Antonym: awkward, clumsy
Sentence: Everything about the ballerina's movements was graceful.

1036. TREASURY - *[spell]*- T R E A S U R Y
Definition: building, room, or other place where money or valuables are kept for security
Synonym: coffer, bank
Antonym:
Sentence: All of the state's money was stored in the treasury.

1037. NOISELESS - *[spell]*- N O I S E L E S S
Definition: making little sound
Synonym: quiet, silent
Antonym: loud, noisy
Sentence: She let out a noiseless sob.

1038. RIVALRY - *[spell]*- R I V A L R Y
Definition: the act of competing for the same goal
Synonym: competition, antagonism
Antonym:
Sentence: The two siblings had a rivalry since their youth.

1039. FLOUNDER - *[spell]*- F L O U N D E R
Definition: struggling awkwardly without making progress
Synonym: stumble, blunder
Antonym:
Sentence: She floundered for words that would truly express her sympathy.

1040. ULTRAMODERN - *[spell]*- U L T R A M O D E R N
Definition: having, or characterized by, the latest, most current style, technique, etc.
Synonym: advanced, current
Antonym:
Sentence: When it came to fashion, she was always ultramodern.

1041. ACTUALITY - *[spell]*- A C T U A L I T Y
Definition: something that is real
Synonym: factuality, reality
Antonym: unreality
Sentence: He thought he had lost his keys; in actuality, he had just misplaced them.

1042. DANDY - *[spell]*- D A N D Y
Definition: a man who is overly concerned with his looks
Synonym: fop, pretty boy

Antonym:
Sentence: She considered her boyfriend a dandy because he was always looking at himself in the mirror.

1043. QUASH - *[spell]*- Q U A S H
Definition: to put down completely
Synonym: cancel, nullify
Antonym:
Sentence: Her dreams of being a pro-athlete were quashed by the injury.

1044. ABOARD - *[spell]*- A B O A R D
Definition: in or on a ship, bus, train, or airplane
Synonym: embarked, loaded
Antonym: disembark, dismount
Sentence: After all students were aboard the school bus, the driver started the engine.

1045. ABSORBENT - *[spell]*- A B S O R B E N T
Definition: able to take in liquid
Synonym: porous, spongy
Antonym: impermeable
Sentence: That particular brand of paper towel is known for being extremely absorbent.

1046. SIGNIFICANT - *[spell]*- S I G N I F I C A N T
Definition: full of meaning or importance
Synonym: meaningful, compelling
Antonym: unimportant, trivial
Sentence: Though disconcerting, her dream was surely not significant in any way.

1047. SHARD - *[spell]*- S H A R D
Definition: a broken piece or fragment
Synonym: remnant, bit
Antonym:
Sentence: A week after breaking a glass on the counter, she kept finding shards around the kitchen.

1048. CONTOUR - *[spell]*- C O N T O U R
Definition: outline of a figure
Synonym: delineation, silhouette
Antonym:
Sentence: In the darkness, we could barely see the contours of the landscape.

1049. MATURITY - *[spell]*- M A T U R I T Y
Definition: full development
Synonym: adulthood
Antonym: youth, immaturity
Sentence: The child was to inherit his father's fortune when he reached maturity.

1050. SAVAGE - *[spell]*- S A V A G E
Definition: not civilized
Synonym: untamed, barbaric
Antonym: civilized, tame
Sentence: The pioneers viewed the natives of the land as savage.

1051. REPLACEMENT - *[spell]*- R E P L A C E M E N T
Definition: a taking the place of
Synonym: substitute
Antonym:
Sentence: The father sought to find a replacement toy for her daughter after she lost it.

1052. RAGGEDY - *[spell]*- R A G G E D Y
Definition: worn or torn into rags
Synonym: tattered, battered
Antonym: pristine, unused
Sentence: The child refused to give up her raggedy stuffed animal.

1053. SIZABLE - *[spell]*- S I Z A B L E
Definition: fairly large
Synonym: considerable, ample
Antonym: little, small
Sentence: The girl inherited a sizable fortune from her parents.

1054. ACCESSORY - *[spell]*- A C C E S S O R Y
Definition: a lesser part or addition
Synonym: component, extra
Antonym: principal, primary
Sentence: She viewed him as merely an accessory to her plan.

1055. DAINTY - *[spell]*- D A I N T Y
Definition: small and pretty
Synonym: delicate
Antonym:
Sentence: The little girl, dressed all in pink with a bow in her hair, was quite dainty.

1056. D E S O L A T I O N - *[spell]*- D E S O L A T I O N
Definition: ruined and deserted
Synonym: devastation, bareness
Antonym: construction, development
Sentence: The desolation of the city after the war was vast.

1057. PEACEFUL - *[spell]*- P E A C E F U L
Definition: full of peace (freedom from strife or war)
Synonym: friendly, serene
Antonym: agitated, turbulent
Sentence: After the war, the country entered into a peaceful period.

1058. HEROINE - *[spell]*- H E R O I N E
Definition: woman or girl admired for her bravery, good deeds, or other noble qualities
Synonym:
Antonym:
Sentence: She was considered a heroine in the community for her brave actions.

1059. DISGRACEFUL - *[spell]*- D I S G R A C E F U L
Definition: causing the loss of honor or respect
Synonym: shameful, dishonorable
Antonym: honorable, respectable
Sentence: His disgraceful actions caused his parents to disown him.

1060. SENIORITY - *[spell]*- S E N I O R I T Y
Definition: priority or precedence
Synonym: precedence, ranking
Antonym: disadvantage, inferiority
Sentence: Because he had seniority, he was the first pick for promotion.

1061. COMPLEMENT - *[spell]*- C O M P L E M E N T
Definition: something that completes or makes perfect
Synonym: accompaniment, balance
Antonym:
Sentence: The wine was the perfect complement to dinner.

1062. SERIOUS - *[spell]*- S E R I O U S
Definition: showing deep thought or purpose
Synonym: somber, humorless
Antonym: flippant, trivial
Sentence: She was serious about quitting her job to be a writer.

1063. COMPUTATION - *[spell]*- C O M P U T A T I O N
Definition: the act of calculating

Synonym: calculation, figuring
Antonym: conjecture, estimation
Sentence: According to his computation, they needed to budget a hundred dollars for the expense.

1064. INSERTION - *[spell]*- I N S E R T I O N
Definition: act of putting in
Synonym: injection
Antonym:
Sentence: After the insertion of the thermometer into the turkey, it was easy to see it was not fully cooked.

1065. WHIRLWIND - *[spell]*- W H I R L W I N D
Definition: to move or travel quickly
Synonym: rapid, rush
Antonym: slow, deliberate
Sentence: They took a whirlwind tour of Europe.

1066. TRAMPLE - *[spell]*- T R A M P L E
Definition: to tread heavily on
Synonym: crush, flatten
Antonym:
Sentence: She tried not to trample on her new puppy that always seemed to be under her feet.

1067. PLANTATION - *[spell]*- P L A N T A T I O N
Definition: a large farm or estate
Synonym:
Antonym:
Sentence: The novel took place on a Southern plantation in the 1800s.

1068. JUMBO - *[spell]*- J U M B O
Definition: very big
Synonym: gigantic, colossal
Antonym: small, miniscule
Sentence: He made dinner using several jumbo steaks.

1069. REEVALUATE - *[spell]*- R E E V A L U A T E
Definition: make a new estimation of value
Synonym: reconsider, reassess
Antonym:
Sentence: She had to reevaluate her choice of restaurant when they walked in the door and saw it was overly crowded.

1070. ENTIRETY - *[spell]*- E N T I R E T Y
Definition: wholeness

Synonym: completeness, absoluteness
Antonym: fraction, part
Sentence: She would not give up until she had run the race in its entirety.

1071. PLASTICITY - *[spell]*- P L A S T I C I T Y
Definition: make or become plastic
Synonym: malleability
Antonym: rigidity
Sentence: I prefer to work with another brand of clay because it has a greater plasticity.

1072. KINDLINESS - *[spell]*- K I N D L I N E S S
Definition: a feeling of doing good rather than harm
Synonym: benevolence, charity
Antonym: cruelty, harshness
Sentence: His kindliness was exhibited when he offered his lunch to the homeless man.

1073. SIGHTSEEING - *[spell]*- S I G H T S E E I N G
Definition: going around to see objects or places of interest
Synonym: tourism, traveling
Antonym:
Sentence: They went to Europe primarily to go sightseeing.

1074. MYTHICAL - *[spell]*- M Y T H I C A L
Definition: like a myth (traditional story, often involving supernatural beings)
Synonym: fabled, legendary
Antonym:
Sentence: She took a class in mythical studies.

1075. IMPROVEMENT - *[spell]*- I M P R O V E M E N T
Definition: a making better
Synonym: advance, development
Antonym: decline, deterioration
Sentence: After much studying, her grades saw great improvement.

1076. SEPARATION - *[spell]*- S E P A R A T I O N
Definition: act of dividing or taking apart
Synonym: division, estrangement
Antonym:
Sentence: The United States government has a separation of church and state.

1077. COMPONENT - *[spell]*- C O M P O N E N T
Definition: one of the parts that make up a whole

Synonym: element, factor
Antonym: whole
Sentence: An important component of higher math is the ability to do basic calculations.

1078. HANDFUL - *[spell]*- H A N D F U L
Definition: person or thing that is hard to manage
Synonym:
Antonym:
Sentence: Their two-year-old child was quite a handful.

1079. TESTIMONIAL - *[spell]*- T E S T I M O N I A L
Definition: certificate of character, conduct, qualifications, value etc.
Synonym: tribute, homage
Antonym: concealment, condemnation
Sentence: At the trial, he gave his testimonial about the accused.

1080. ARCHITECTURE - *[spell]*- A R C H I T E C T U R E
Definition: the science of planning and designing buildings
Synonym: construction, engineering
Antonym:
Sentence: She wanted to study architecture in school.

1081. EMERGENCY - *[spell]*- E M E R G E N C Y
Definition: a sudden need for immediate action
Synonym: crisis, exigency
Antonym:
Sentence: The ambulance whizzing down the road suggested an emergency up ahead.

1082. LAYOVER - *[spell]*- L A Y O V E R
Definition: a stopping for a time in a place
Synonym: hiatus, stopover
Antonym:
Sentence: He had a three-hour layover between flights at the airport.

1083. COCKY - *[spell]*- C O C K Y
Definition: conceited
Synonym: arrogant, brash
Antonym: humble, meek
Sentence: His cocky attitude annoyed his coworkers and made him unpopular.

1084. COCOON - *[spell]*- C O C O O N
Definition: a protective covering spun by insects while they are in the larvae stage

Synonym: encasing, envelopment
Antonym:
Sentence: Caterpillars place themselves in a cocoon before they become butterflies.

1085. SCALP - *[spell]*- S C A L P
Definition: to buy and sell to make small quick profits
Synonym:
Antonym:
Sentence: Outside the concert hall, many people tried to scalp tickets.

1086. RAUNCHY - *[spell]*- R A U N C H Y
Definition: vulgar or obscene
Synonym: lewd, filthy
Antonym:
Sentence: The mother would not let her child see the PG-13 movie because of a few raunchy scenes.

1087. SATELLITE - *[spell]*- S A T E L L I T E
Definition: a subservient follower
Synonym: lackey
Antonym:
Sentence: Ukraine is a former Soviet satellite.

1088. FABLE - *[spell]*- F A B L E
Definition: short story made up to teach a lesson
Synonym: fairytale, parable
Antonym:
Sentence: Many fables contain animals as characters and teach morals about love or family.

1089. HINGE - *[spell]*- H I N G E
Definition: to depend on
Synonym: revolve, pivot
Antonym:
Sentence: His promotion hinged upon his performance on his current project.

1090. PRESERVER - *[spell]*- P R E S E R V E R
Definition: person or thing that saves and protects from danger
Synonym:
Antonym:
Sentence: The drowning man was able to latch onto a life preserver and float to safety.

1091. HARPOON - *[spell]* - H A R P O O N
Definition: a barbed spear with a rope tied to it, usually for catching and killing whales
Synonym: spear, weapon
Antonym:
Sentence: The sailors attacked the sea monster with harpoons.

1092. ABSORPTION - *[spell]* - A B S O R P T I O N
Definition: the process of holding liquid
Synonym: intake, retention
Antonym:
Sentence: His absorption of difficult mathematics was astounding.

1093. STUBBORN - *[spell]* - S T U B B O R N
Definition: fixed in purpose or opinion
Synonym: unyielding, obstinate
Antonym: flexible, irresolute
Sentence: Even as an infant, the child was stubborn.

1094. BEFALL - *[spell]* - B E F A L L
Definition: happen to
Synonym: ensue, transpire
Antonym:
Sentence: She hoped that nothing would befall her during the long expedition.

1095. NOVEL - *[spell]* - N O V E L
Definition: of a new kind or nature
Synonym: original, unusual
Antonym: common, familiar
Sentence: His invention was a novel idea.

1096. HARMLESS - *[spell]* - H A R M L E S S
Definition: not capable of causing pain, loss or damage
Synonym: gentle, benign
Antonym: vicious, harmful
Sentence: Though the dog had a ferocious bark, she was really quite harmless.

1097. ANTSY - *[spell]* - A N T S Y
Definition: restless
Synonym: fidgety, impatient
Antonym: calm, relaxed
Sentence: Feeling antsy about the results, she paced the room.

1098. THIEVERY - *[spell]*- T H I E V E R Y
Definition: the act of stealing
Synonym:
Antonym:
Sentence: He was sent to jail for his thievery.

1099. INEXPLICABLE - *[spell]*- I N E X P L I C A B L E
Definition: that cannot be explained, understood or accounted for
Synonym: baffling, incomprehensible
Antonym: fathomable, comprehensible
Sentence: His insistence on going to the park despite the rain was inexplicable.

1100. SHUDDERY - *[spell]*- S H U D D E R Y
Definition: characterized by or causing trembling
Synonym:
Antonym:
Sentence: The frightening scene in the movie left the girl shuddery.

Medium Words Exercise - 2

1101. MICROSCOPIC - *[spell]*- M I C R O S C O P I C
Definition: so small as to be invisible without a microscope
Synonym: tiny, miniscule
Antonym: giant, huge
Sentence: The bacteria was microscopic.

1102. ENDANGERED - *[spell]*- E N D A N G E R E D
Definition: liable to become extinct
Synonym: threatened
Antonym:
Sentence: The panda bear, because of its small population, is considered endangered.

1103. RETRIEVE - *[spell]*- R E T R I E V E
Definition: to get again or recover
Synonym: fetch, recapture
Antonym: release, relinquish
Sentence: He managed to retrieve the cooler that fell off his boat into the ocean.

1104. BETRAYAL - *[spell]*- B E T R A Y A L
Definition: the act of being disloyal to a friend, leader, or cause
Synonym: deception, treason
Antonym: devotion, faithfulness
Sentence: His betrayal caused her to lose all faith in him.

1105. SPECIALTY - *[spell]*- S P E C I A L T Y
Definition: a special study, line of work, profession, etc.
Synonym:
Antonym:
Sentence: Her specialty as a chef was making pastries.

1106. GRADUATION - *[spell]*- G R A D U A T I O N
Definition: a finishing of studies at school or university
Synonym:
Antonym:
Sentence: The boy was happy his grandparents were able to come to his graduation.

1107. SOLAR - *[spell]* - S O L A R
Definition: of the sun
Synonym:
Antonym:
Sentence: The solar panels were used to create power for the home.

1108. ENTERTAINER - *[spell]* - E N T E R T A I N E R
Definition: a person who keeps others pleasantly interested
Synonym:
Antonym:
Sentence: As a musician, he considered himself a great entertainer.

1109. SLUMBER - *[spell]* - S L U M B E R
Definition: to sleep lightly or doze
Synonym: drowse, nap
Antonym: wakefulness
Sentence: After nearly an hour of crying, the child drifted off into a restless slumber.

1110. PERCENTAGE - *[spell]* - P E R C E N T A G E
Definition: rate or proportion of each hundred
Synonym: proportion, ratio
Antonym: whole, entirety
Sentence: She was given a percentage of all sales she made.

1111. KNOWLEDGEABLE - *[spell]* - K N O W L E D G E A B L E
Definition: well-informed
Synonym: experience, smart
Antonym: foolish, unwise
Sentence: Though he was knowledgeable about many things, he knew nothing about raising a child.

1112. FLAMMABILITY - *[spell]* - F L A M M A B I L I T Y
Definition: quality of being easily set fire
Synonym: combustible
Antonym:
Sentence: The material had a high flammability.

1113. FEISTY - *[spell]* - F E I S T Y
Definition: full of lively spirit
Synonym: exuberant, spirited
Antonym: fearful, timid
Sentence: Her feisty nature sometimes got her in trouble.

1114. SILKEN - *[spell]* - S I L K E N
Definition: made of or like silk (fine, soft fiber)

Synonym: satiny, sleek
Antonym: rough, jagged
Sentence: She wore a decorative silken robe.

1115. GIMMICK - *[spell]*- G I M M I C K
Definition: hidden or tricky condition
Synonym: artifice, ruse
Antonym:
Sentence: The advertisement for a free gift turned out to be just a gimmick.

1116. OFFSET - *[spell]*- O F F S E T
Definition: make up for
Synonym: compensate, counterbalance
Antonym:
Sentence: He tried to offset his laziness over the weekend by working extra hours during the week.

1117. AILMENT - *[spell]*- A I L M E N T
Definition: a disorder of the body or mind
Synonym: illness, sickness
Antonym: health
Sentence: Her only ailment was her sometimes stiff joints.

1118. QUESTIONNAIRE - *[spell]*- Q U E S T I O N N A I R E
Definition: a written or printed list of questions used to gather information
Synonym:
Antonym:
Sentence: He had to answer a questionnaire when he signed up for the dating site.

1119. ABOMINABLE - *[spell]*- A B O M I N A B L E
Definition: causing hatred or disgust
Synonym: unpleasant, disagreeable
Antonym: attractive, respectable
Sentence: Finding the content of the book to be abominable, the critic wrote and published a harsh review.

1120. REFEREE - *[spell]*- R E F E R E E
Definition: a judge of play in certain games or sports
Synonym:
Antonym:
Sentence: The referee upset the crowd during the baseball game when he called an "out."

1121. REVOLVE - *[spell]*- R E V O L V E
Definition: move in a circle
Synonym: turn, spin
Antonym:
Sentence: The Earth revolves around the sun.

1122. ASSAULT - *[spell]*- A S S A U L T
Definition: a sudden attack made with blows or weapons
Synonym: onslaught, charge
Antonym:
Sentence: The assault was successful in beating back the enemy.

1123. EDIBILITY - *[spell]*- E D I B I L I T Y
Definition: fitness for eating
Synonym:
Antonym:
Sentence: He was uncertain of the edibility of the week-old leftovers in his fridge.

1124. VILLAIN - *[spell]*- V I L L A I N
Definition: a very wicked person
Synonym: criminal, scoundrel
Antonym: hero, savior
Sentence: The villain in the movie was one the audiences loved to hate.

1125. INSISTENCE - *[spell]*- I N S I S T E N C E
Definition: act of continuing to make a firm demand or statement
Synonym: persistence, demand
Antonym:
Sentence: She finally gave in to his insistence that she call her father.

1126. SNUFFLE - *[spell]*- S N U F F L E
Definition: breathe noisily through the nose
Synonym: sniffle
Antonym:
Sentence: She snuffled at the thought of having to go outside in the rain.

1127. NAUGHTY - *[spell]*- N A U G H T Y
Definition: not obedient
Synonym: misbehaved, mischievous
Antonym: obedient, controlled
Sentence: The child was being naughty so she was punished.

1128. REPRESENTATION - *[spell]*- R E P R E S E N T A T I O N
Definition: act of standing for or being a sign or symbol of
Synonym: likeness, portrayal

Antonym:
Sentence: The sculpture was meant to be a symbolic representation of their struggle for independence.

1129. ATTENDANT - *[spell]-* A T T E N D A N T
Definition: a person who waits on another
Synonym: assistant, servant
Antonym:
Sentence: The attendant brought him whatever he needed.

1130. NARRATIVE - *[spell]-* N A R R A T I V E
Definition: a story or account
Synonym: tale, recounting
Antonym:
Sentence: Everyone in the room listened to his narrative with interest.

1131. ENTWINE - *[spell]-* E N T W I N E
Definition: become twisted or woven together
Synonym: enmesh, entangle
Antonym: disentangle
Sentence: The necklaces in her jewelry box had become entwined and were not easily separated.

1132. FEVERISH - *[spell]-* F E V E R I S H
Definition: having a condition in which the body temperature is higher than normal
Synonym: febrile
Antonym:
Sentence: The mother took her child to the doctor because he was feverish.

1133. UNBEATABLE - *[spell]-* U N B E A T A B L E
Definition: that cannot be defeated
Synonym: invincible, unsurpassable
Antonym: beatable
Sentence: When it came to strategy games, he was unbeatable.

1134. HEADLINE - *[spell]-* H E A D L I N E
Definition: word printed at the top of a newspaper telling what it is about
Synonym: title
Antonym:
Sentence: The headline of the paper told of the recent natural disaster in Europe.

1135. DISLOCATE - *[spell]-* D I S L O C A T E
Definition: pull out of joint

Synonym:
Antonym:
Sentence: She took several days off work because she dislocated her shoulder.

1136. SEIZE - *[spell]*- S E I Z E
Definition: to take hold of suddenly
Synonym: grab, snatch
Antonym:
Sentence: The tyrant attempted to seize control of the government.

1137. COMPASSIONATE - *[spell]*- C O M P A S S I O N A T E
Definition: wanting to relieve someone else's suffering
Synonym: sympathetic, kind
Antonym: inhumane, malevolent
Sentence: Mother Teresa was known for her compassionate nature.

1138. ENCLOSURE - *[spell]*- E N C L O S U R E
Definition: a place that is shut in on all sides
Synonym: cage, pen
Antonym:
Sentence: He made an enclosure in the backyard for his puppies to play in.

1139. SLOGAN - *[spell]*- S L O G A N
Definition: a word or phrase used by a business, club, political party, etc.
Synonym: motto, jingle
Antonym:
Sentence: The company's slogan was catchy so that everyone remembered it.

1140. FUNDAMENTAL - *[spell]*- F U N D A M E N T A L
Definition: essential or basic
Synonym: central, elementary
Antonym: unnecessary
Sentence: The fundamentals of English are grammar and reading.

1141. CARRIAGE - *[spell]*- C A R R I A G E
Definition: a manner of holding the head and body
Synonym:
Antonym:
Sentence: She had the carriage of a princess or a queen.

1142. NUGGET - *[spell]*- N U G G E T
Definition: a valuable lump
Synonym:

Antonym:
Sentence: She offered him a few nuggets of wisdom.

1143. STRETCHABILITY - *[spell]*- S T R E T C H A B I L I T Y
Definition: ability to draw out or extend
Synonym:
Antonym:
Sentence: Because she was so economical, she was also able to determine the stretchability of her groceries.

1144. MELODRAMATIC - *[spell]*- M E L O D R A M A T I C
Definition: sensational and exaggerated
Synonym: histrionic, overwrought
Antonym: subdued
Sentence: She had a tendency to be melodramatic about pretty much everything.

1145. RUGGED - *[spell]*- R U G G E D
Definition: covered with rough edges
Synonym: jagged, rocky
Antonym:
Sentence: The rugged terrain was dangerous except to experienced hikers.

1146. KNUCKLE - *[spell]*- K N U C K L E
Definition: joint in a finger
Synonym:
Antonym:
Sentence: His knuckles were sore from where he had punched the wall in anger.

1147. LIBERALITY - *[spell]*- L I B E R A L I T Y
Definition: generosity
Synonym: benevolence, charity
Antonym: selfishness
Sentence: His liberality with his money was known by everyone.

1148. SLEEPLESS - *[spell]*- S L E E P L E S S
Definition: without sleep
Synonym: insomniac, wakeful
Antonym: asleep, dozing
Sentence: She spent many sleepless nights tossing and turning and worrying about the issue.

1149. ENFORCEMENT - *[spell]*- E N F O R C E M E N T
Definition: the act of forcing obedience to
Synonym: administration, execution

Antonym:
Sentence: The judge was famous for his clear-cut enforcement of the law.

1150. INEXPERIENCE - *[spell]*- I N E X P E R I E N C E
Definition: lack of practice or skill
Synonym:
Antonym:
Sentence: Her inexperience in dating made her feel a little embarrassed on her blind date.

1151. DISTRESSFUL - *[spell]*- D I S T R E S S F U L
Definition: causing great pain or sorrow
Synonym: disquieting, disruptive
Antonym:
Sentence: After the distressful experience, she read a book to relax.

1152. EMBARRASSMENT - *[spell]*- E M B A R R A S S M E N T
Definition: act of making uneasy and ashamed
Synonym: chagrin, abashment
Antonym:
Sentence: Much to his embarrassment, his mother showed his baby pictures to his new girlfriend.

1153. ANXIETY - *[spell]*- A N X I E T Y
Definition: uneasy over thoughts or fears
Synonym: angst, apprehension
Antonym: collectedness, calmness
Sentence: She experienced anxiety every time she had to board a plane.

1154. CHAOS - *[spell]*- C H A O S
Definition: great confusion
Synonym: anarchy, disarray
Antonym: harmony, order
Sentence: The country was launched into chaos after the assassination of the president.

1155. OVERRATE - *[spell]*- O V E R R A T E
Definition: estimate too highly
Synonym: exaggerate, magnify
Antonym: underrate, undervalue
Sentence: In my opinion, the show is overrated.

1156. IGNORANCE - *[spell]*- I G N O R A N C E
Definition: lack of knowledge
Synonym: unintelligence, inexperience
Antonym: understanding, competence

Sentence: Her ignorance about other cultures caused her to seem like a bigot.

1157. KNOBBY - *[spell]*- K N O B B Y
Definition: covered with rounded lumps
Synonym: lumpy, bumpy
Antonym: smooth, even
Sentence: The bark of the tree was knobby.

1158. BERET - *[spell]*- B E R E T
Definition: a cap with no visor
Synonym:
Antonym:
Sentence: She wore a beret that matched her scarf.

1159. INVENTION - *[spell]*- I N V E N T I O N
Definition: the original making up of something
Synonym: design, creation
Antonym:
Sentence: The invention of the light bulb revolutionized life as we know it.

1160. HARNESS - *[spell]*- H A R N E S S
Definition: a combination of leather straps, bands and other pieces used to hitch a horse or other animal to a carriage, wagon, etc.
Synonym:
Antonym:
Sentence: The farmer prepared the horse by putting on its harness.

1161. BELIEVABLE - *[spell]*- B E L I E V A B L E
Definition: able to be accepted as true
Synonym: conceivable, credible
Antonym: implausible, improbable
Sentence: Though she didn't want to, she found his excuse believable.

1162. FAVORABLE - *[spell]*- F A V O R A B L E
Definition: showing approval
Synonym: agreeable, supportive
Antonym: disagreeable, unfavorable
Sentence: She was glad to hear his favorable response to her question.

1163. DEEM - *[spell]*- D E E M
Definition: to come to form an opinion
Synonym: think, believe
Antonym:

Sentence: Though he was talented, she did not deem him the best singer she'd ever heard.

1164. PLATFORM - *[spell]*- P L A T F O R M
Definition: a raised, level surface
Synonym: stage, stand
Antonym:
Sentence: The speaker stood on a platform to give his address.

1165. ROGUE - *[spell]*- R O G U E
Definition: a dishonest or unprincipled person
Synonym: crook, rascal
Antonym:
Sentence: Known as a rogue; no one trusted him.

1166. DAPPER - *[spell]*- D A P P E R
Definition: neat and trim
Synonym: stylish, sharp
Antonym: slovenly, disheveled
Sentence: Dressed in a new outfit, she went to the party feeling dapper.

1167. ROUSING - *[spell]*- R O U S I N G
Definition: stirring or vigorous
Synonym: stimulating, refreshing
Antonym: unexciting
Sentence: The story of his leaving home was rousing to his audience.

1168. SNITCH - *[spell]*- S N I T C H
Definition: an informer
Synonym: tattletale, double-crosser
Antonym:
Sentence: A search began to find the snitch who told the government about the dishonest practices within the business.

1169. ANNOUNCEMENT - *[spell]*- A N N O U N C E M E N T
Definition: the act of giving formal or public notice
Synonym: disclosure, notice
Antonym:
Sentence: The couple made an announcement about their engagement.

1170. HOMESTEAD - *[spell]*- H O M E S T E A D
Definition: house with its buildings and grounds
Synonym: abode, dwelling
Antonym:
Sentence: The homestead sat on several acres of land.

1171. RESERVATION - *[spell]*- R E S E R V A T I O N
Definition: something not expressed
Synonym: skepticism, doubt
Antonym:
Sentence: She didn't mention it, but she had reservations about her blind date.

1172. DICTATION - *[spell]*- D I C T A T I O N
Definition: act of reading words while another person writes them down
Synonym: transcription
Antonym:
Sentence: After he had finished his dictation of the letter to his secretary, he moved on to other business.

1173. APPAREL - *[spell]*- A P P A R E L
Definition: clothing
Synonym: dress, garment
Antonym:
Sentence: One of her greatest pleasures in life was to buy fashionable apparel.

1174. ORIGIN - *[spell]*- O R I G I N
Definition: thing from which anything comes
Synonym: source, beginning
Antonym: ending, result
Sentence: The origin of the problem was unclear.

1175. INAPPROPRIATE - *[spell]*- I N A P P R O P R I A T E
Definition: unsuitable
Synonym: improper, wrong
Antonym: appropriate, proper
Sentence: The man made several inappropriate remarks in his speech.

1176. FATED - *[spell]*- F A T E D
Definition: destined to happen
Synonym: inevitable, predestined
Antonym:
Sentence: Their meeting seemed fated to happen.

1177. PREACHY - *[spell]*- P R E A C H Y
Definition: inclined to give earnest advice, especially in a meddling or tiresome way
Synonym:
Antonym:
Sentence: He intended to be helpful, but his advice came across as preachy.

1178. DOMAIN - *[spell]*- D O M A I N
Definition: territory under the control of one ruler
Synonym: realm, territory
Antonym:
Sentence: The king ruled his domain fairly and justly.

1179. AGGRAVATE - *[spell]*- A G G R A V A T E
Definition: to make something more of a burden
Synonym: exacerbate, irritate
Antonym: appease, mollify
Sentence: If you tell a lie, it will only aggravate the guilt you feel.

1180. OUTRAGE - *[spell]*- O U T R A G E
Definition: showing great offense
Synonym: offend, incense
Antonym: delight, pleasure
Sentence: The politician's outrage at the new policy was obvious.

1181. COARSEN - *[spell]*- C O A R S E N
Definition: to make or become made up of large parts
Synonym: clump, roughen
Antonym: fine, thin
Sentence: The texture of the carpet had become coarsened over the years.

1182. SCRAP - *[spell]*- S C R A P
Definition: a small piece
Synonym: leftover, fragment
Antonym:
Sentence: She fed her dog several scraps from dinner.

1183. MEASURABILITY - *[spell]*- M E A S U R A B I L I T Y
Definition: quality or condition of being able to find out the exact size or quality
Synonym:
Antonym:
Sentence: The measurability of the product's value was important to him.

1184. REESTABLISH - *[spell]*- R E E S T A B L I S H
Definition: to establish again or restore
Synonym: renew, restore
Antonym:
Sentence: Though the king tried to reestablish himself after a brief exile, his efforts failed.

1185. MEMORIALIZE - *[spell]*- M E M O R I A L I Z E
Definition: to preserve the memory of

Synonym: commemorate
Antonym:
Sentence: The great leader was memorialized in the song.

1186. ARTERY - *[spell]*- A R T E R Y
Definition: any of the vessels that carry blood from the heart to different parts of the body
Synonym: vessel
Antonym:
Sentence: He had to be taken to the hospital after the wound severed an artery.

1187. THROATY - *[spell]*- T H R O A T Y
Definition: sound produced in the front of the neck
Synonym: hoarse, gruff
Antonym: soft, smooth
Sentence: She gave a throaty laugh at his joke.

1188. SNATCH - *[spell]*- S N A T C H
Definition: to take hold of or seize suddenly
Synonym: grab
Antonym:
Sentence: The little boy snatched the toy from his sister's hands.

1189. REASSEMBLE - *[spell]*- R E A S S E M B L E
Definition: to come or bring together again
Synonym: restore, reconstruct
Antonym: demolish, destroy
Sentence: After taking apart his watch to replace the battery, he had to reassemble it.

1190. HANDICRAFT - *[spell]*- H A N D I C R A F T
Definition: trade or art requiring skill with the hands
Synonym:
Antonym:
Sentence: The market sold various decorative handicrafts.

1191. BLACKMAIL - *[spell]*- B L A C K M A I L
Definition: an attempt to get money from another person by threats
Synonym: extortion
Antonym:
Sentence: She attempted to blackmail him by threatening to reveal his darkest secrets.

1192. SIDESPLITTING - *[spell]*- S I D E S P L I T T I N G
Definition: extremely funny

Synonym: hilarious, entertaining
Antonym:
Sentence: The comedian's routine was sidesplitting.

1193. REPRODUCTION - *[spell]*- R E P R O D U C T I O N
Definition: a being made or created again
Synonym: copy, imitation
Antonym: original
Sentence: The museum housed a reproduction of the famous painting.

1194. LIMITATION - *[spell]*- L I M I T A T I O N
Definition: having bounds
Synonym: restriction, bound
Antonym: limitless, boundless
Sentence: Though his handicap caused some physical limitations, he did not let it hold him back.

1195. MOTIVATION - *[spell]*- M O T I V A T I O N
Definition: act or process of furnishing with an incentive
Synonym: stimulus, instigation
Antonym: disincentive
Sentence: He lacked motivation in getting the project done.

1196. TRICKERY - *[spell]*- T R I C K E R Y
Definition: use of deception
Synonym: fraud, chicanery
Antonym:
Sentence: The child used trickery to get his way.

1197. CLASSICAL - *[spell]*- C L A S S I C A L
Definition: having to do with a work of art that serves as a standard of excellence
Synonym: canonical
Antonym:
Sentence: Shakespeare's works are considered classical.

1198. FIZZLE - *[spell]*- F I Z Z L E
Definition: fail or end in failure
Synonym: wane, die
Antonym:
Sentence: His enthusiasm began to fizzle when he realized he had much work he had to do.

1199. RANDOMIZE - *[spell]*- R A N D O M I Z E
Definition: to put, take, or perform without definite method or purpose
Synonym:

Antonym:

Sentence: The teacher randomized the order of the student's seating arrangement.

1200.   AMBUSH - *[spell]*- A M B U S H

Definition: a surprise attack

Synonym: trap

Antonym:

Sentence: The soldiers formulated a plan to ambush their enemies.

Medium Words Exercise - 3

1201. TRAVAIL - *[spell]*- T R A V A I L
Definition: to toil or labor
Synonym: struggle, tribulation
Antonym:
Sentence: After much travail, the artist completed the sculpture.

1202. EVALUATION - *[spell]*- E V A L U A T I O N
Definition: a finding out of the value of
Synonym: judgment, appraisal
Antonym:
Sentence: Employees had to undergo yearly evaluations.

1203. ADVENTURESOME - *[spell]*- A D V E N T U R E S O M E
Definition: bold and daring
Synonym: courageous, audacious
Antonym: cowardly, fearful
Sentence: Feeling adventuresome, the young boy set out to explore the woods.

1204. INSPECTION - *[spell]*- I N S P E C T I O N
Definition: an examination of something
Synonym: investigation, research
Antonym: neglect, ignorance
Sentence: After an inspection of the injury, it wasn't so bad after all.

1205. CARCASS - *[spell]*- C A R C A S S
Definition: a dead animal
Synonym: corpse, remains
Antonym:
Sentence: She swerved to avoid hitting the carcass in the road.

1206. EMPLOYMENT - *[spell]*- E M P L O Y M E N T
Definition: work
Synonym: job, career
Antonym: unemployment, joblessness
Sentence: She searched the want ads, hoping to find employment.

1207. AUDITORY - *[spell]*- A U D I T O R Y
Definition: having to do with hearing
Synonym: acoustic, aural
Antonym:
Sentence: Her auditory nerves were damaged, affecting her sense of hearing for life.

1208. OPTIONAL - *[spell]*- O P T I O N A L
Definition: left to one's own choice
Synonym: elective, discretional
Antonym: compulsory, force
Sentence: Her boss said the project was optional.

1209. HAUNTED - *[spell]*- H A U N T E D
Definition: visited by ghosts
Synonym:
Antonym:
Sentence: The old house was considered haunted by everyone in the neighborhood.

1210. DISAVOW - *[spell]*- D I S A V O W
Definition: to deny that one knows about or is responsible for something
Synonym: refute, contradict
Antonym: acknowledge, admit
Sentence: He could no longer disavow the company's plan to fire some of his staff.

1211. CLUNKER - *[spell]*- C L U N K E R
Definition: something worthless
Synonym: junk, trash
Antonym: treasure
Sentence: He was glad when he could finally exchange that old clunker for a newer car.

1212. JUGGLE - *[spell]*- J U G G L E
Definition: to catch, hold, or balance in a risky, perilous, or precarious way
Synonym: shuffle, manipulate
Antonym:
Sentence: Between her children's activities, her job, and making dinner, the mother had to juggle many different activities.

1213. MARITAL - *[spell]*- M A R I T A L
Definition: having to do with marriage
Synonym: nuptial

Antonym:
Sentence: The couple decided to write their own marital vows.

1214. REFLECTIVE - *[spell]*- R E F L E C T I V E
Definition: that gives back a likeness or image of
Synonym:
Antonym:
Sentence: The reflective surface of the lake showed the surrounding forest.

1215. DEMOUNT - *[spell]*- D E M O U N T
Definition: remove from a higher position
Synonym: dismount
Antonym:
Sentence: The soldiers failed to recognize the general until he had demounted his horse.

1216. SLOPE - *[spell]*- S L O P E
Definition: to go up or down at an angle
Synonym: tilt, slant
Antonym:
Sentence: The steep slope of the hill made it difficult to climb.

1217. DOLT - *[spell]*- D O L T
Definition: a dull or stupid person
Synonym: blockhead, fool
Antonym: brain, genius
Sentence: His behavior earned him a reputation as a dolt.

1218. CLATTER - *[spell]*- C L A T T E R
Definition: a loud, confused noise
Synonym: racket, clangor
Antonym: peace, quiet
Sentence: She could tell from the clatter in the kitchen that he was attempting to make breakfast.

1219. BUNDLED - *[spell]*- B U N D L E D
Definition: a number of things wrapped together
Synonym: packaged, tied
Antonym:
Sentence: The company offered packages that bundled several services into one price.

1220. GRATITUDE - *[spell]*- G R A T I T U D E
Definition: kindly feeling because of a favor received
Synonym: appreciation, gratefulness

Antonym: ingratitude, ungratefulness
Sentence: She felt immense gratitude toward him for saving her life.

1221. OBSERVE - *[spell]*- O B S E R V E
Definition: to see and note
Synonym: notice, monitor
Antonym: overlook, ignore
Sentence: He sat quietly on his porch to observe the birds in the tree.

1222. FINANCE - *[spell]*- F I N A N C E
Definition: money or funds
Synonym: banking, investment
Antonym:
Sentence: Helen was never good with money, so we were all shocked that she chose a career in finance.

1223. REFINE - *[spell]*- R E F I N E
Definition: to free from impurities
Synonym: perfect, polish
Antonym: dirty, corrupt
Sentence: Oil has to be refined before it can be used.

1224. PERSEVERANCE - *[spell]*- P E R S E V E R A N C E
Definition: sticking to a purpose or an aim
Synonym: tenacity, steadfastness
Antonym:
Sentence: His perseverance in job-hunting eventually paid off.

1225. CHERISH - *[spell]*- C H E R I S H
Definition: to hold dear
Synonym: admire, adore
Antonym: despise, loathe
Sentence: The parents cherished their newborn child.

1226. MOISTURIZE - *[spell]*- M O I S T U R I Z E
Definition: adding or restoring wetness to
Synonym: dampen, saturate
Antonym: dry, arid
Sentence: She found it important to moisturize her dry skin.

1227. TERRIFIC - *[spell]*- T E R R I F I C
Definition: extremely good
Synonym: amazing, tremendous
Antonym: insignificant, unimportant
Sentence: We all thought his production of the play was terrific.

1228. GRUBBY - *[spell]* - G R U B B Y
Definition: dirty or grimy
Synonym: slovenly, filthy
Antonym: clean, sterile
Sentence: She refused to touch the dog because of its grubby appearance.

1229. CLUMPY - *[spell]* - C L U M P Y
Definition: full of clusters
Synonym: lumpy, knotted
Antonym: smooth
Sentence: She knew something was wrong because the cake mix came out clumpy.

1230. RUFFLE - *[spell]* - R U F F L E
Definition: destroy the smoothness of
Synonym: dishevel, rumple
Antonym: smooth, straighten
Sentence: Her dress was ruffled in the strong wind.

1231. PROMOTIONAL - *[spell]* - P R O M O T I O N A L
Definition: the act of moving someone to a higher rank or position within a business or organization
Synonym: preferment, advancement
Antonym: demotion, downgrade
Sentence: His transfer to another branch was seen as a promotional move.

1232. SCAM - *[spell]* - S C A M
Definition: a clever but dishonest trick
Synonym: fraud, deception
Antonym:
Sentence: The internet company sent out emails that contained a scam to get people's money.

1233. FORFEIT - *[spell]* - F O R F E I T
Definition: lose or have to give up by one's own act
Synonym:
Antonym:
Sentence: The team was forced to forfeit the game because too many of their players had been injured.

1234. VIBRATION - *[spell]* - V I B R A T I O N
Definition: a rapid movement to and fro
Synonym: shaking, quivering
Antonym: stillness
Sentence: The house experienced a vibration as a train crossed the tracks nearby.

1235. SLACKER - *[spell]*- S L A C K E R
Definition: person who shirks work or evades duty
Synonym: idler, loafer
Antonym:
Sentence: Because he was so behind in his work, everyone at the office thought him to be a slacker.

1236. FLEETING - *[spell]*- F L E E T I N G
Definition: passing swiftly
Synonym: ephemeral, momentary
Antonym: enduring, lasting
Sentence: For a fleeting moment, she actually thought she would win the contest.

1237. MEDITATE - *[spell]*- M E D I T A T E
Definition: engage in deep and serious thought
Synonym: contemplate, ponder
Antonym:
Sentence: He went to his room to meditate about the difficult situation.

1238. SASS - *[spell]*- S A S S
Definition: rudeness or back talk
Synonym: impudence, impertinence
Antonym:
Sentence: The mother did not appreciate her child's sass.

1239. ZIPPY - *[spell]*- Z I P P Y
Definition: lively
Synonym: sprightly, lively
Antonym: dull, lethargic
Sentence: She was always zippy after a workout.

1240. NOTHINGNESS - *[spell]*- N O T H I N G N E S S
Definition: being nonexistent
Synonym:
Antonym:
Sentence: He was disheartened by the nothingness of the night sky.

1241. INDESTRUCTIBLE - *[spell]*- I N D E S T R U C T I B L E
Definition: cannot be destroyed
Synonym: invincible, durable
Antonym: fragile, breakable
Sentence: The sturdy car seemed practically indestructible.

1242. DEFLOWER - *[spell]*- D E F L O W E R
Definition: rob of beauty

Synonym: spoil, mar
Antonym:
Sentence: Once a beauty queen, old age had quite deflowered her.

1243. TIGHTEN - *[spell]*- T I G H T E N
Definition: to become pulled or held together firmly
Synonym: constrict, narrow
Antonym: expand
Sentence: He tightened the band of the watch around his wrist.

1244. CHIDE - *[spell]*- C H I D E
Definition: to blame or scold
Synonym: admonish, castigate
Antonym: commend, approve
Sentence: He chided the puppy for chewing on his new shoes.

1245. COIN - *[spell]*- C O I N
Definition: to make up
Synonym: invent, create
Antonym:
Sentence: Without meaning to, she was able to coin a new phrase that soon spread across the country.

1246. SENSELESS - *[spell]*- S E N S E L E S S
Definition: foolish or stupid
Synonym: ludicrous, unreasonable
Antonym: wise, reasonable
Sentence: The politician called on the people to end the senseless violence.

1247. COMPLEXION - *[spell]*- C O M P L E X I ON
Definition: color and quality of the skin
Synonym: coloring, hue
Antonym:
Sentence: She had a clear, even complexion.

1248. NUMERICAL - *[spell]*- N U M E R I C AL
Definition: to put in order of number
Synonym:
Antonym:
Sentence: She put the files in numerical order.

1249. OBTAIN - *[spell]*- O B T A I N
Definition: to get something from diligence and effort
Synonym: acquire, gather

Antonym: forfeit, lose
Sentence: She was able to obtain the necessary ingredients for her recipe.

1250. JOLT - *[spell]*- J O L T
Definition: to shake up
Synonym: bump, bounce
Antonym:
Sentence: He was jolted awake by the ringing of his telephone.

1251. PRIVILEGED - *[spell]*- P R I V I L E G E D
Definition: having some special rights, advantages, or favors
Synonym:
Antonym:
Sentence: He was given a privileged position after having worked with the president closely for many years.

1252. BLEARY - *[spell]*- B L E A R Y
Definition: having an indistinct outline
Synonym: blurred, cloudy
Antonym: clear, distinct
Sentence: When she first woke up, everything looked bleary.

1253. LOCALITY - *[spell]*- L O C A L I T Y
Definition: one place and the places near it
Synonym: environment, neighborhood
Antonym:
Sentence: They began to hunt for a home in a locality close to their hometown.

1254. BROOCH - *[spell]*- B R O O C H
Definition: an ornamental pin
Synonym:
Antonym:
Sentence: She always wore a brooch on her sweaters and blouses.

1255. HIGHLIGHT - *[spell]*- H I G H L I G H T
Definition: emphasize with lighting, certain colors, etc.
Synonym: accentuate, feature
Antonym:
Sentence: The guest speaker highlighted the importance of equality for all.

1256. VICTORIOUS - *[spell]*- V I C T O R I O U S
Definition: having won a defeat against an enemy
Synonym: triumphant
Antonym: defeated

Sentence: After winning the final game of the playoffs, the team was victorious.

1257. THRUM - *[spell]*- T H R U M
Definition: play on a stringed instrument by plucking the strings
Synonym: hum, drone
Antonym:
Sentence: She could hear a thrum of music from the distance.

1258. ABUSIVENESS - *[spell]*- A B U S I V E N E S S
Definition: the state of using harsh language or actions
Synonym: cruelty, brutality
Antonym: kindness, courtesy
Sentence: He has earned a bad reputation due to his abusiveness towards his employees.

1259. HANDY - *[spell]*- H A N D Y
Definition: easy to reach or use
Synonym: convenient, useful
Antonym: impractical, useless
Sentence: Having the toolset in his home proved to be quite handy.

1260. CHUTE - *[spell]*- C H U T E
Definition: a steep sloping tube
Synonym: gutter, channel
Antonym:
Sentence: She dropped the garbage down a chute to the incinerator.

1261. RANSOM - *[spell]*- R A N S O M
Definition: price paid or demanded before a captive is set free
Synonym: payoff, payment
Antonym:
Sentence: The kidnapper wanted a ransom before he would agree to set the child free.

1262. UNGENEROUS - *[spell]*- U N G E N E R O U S
Definition: not giving or kind
Synonym: stingy, selfish
Antonym: generous, giving
Sentence: It was uncharacteristic of the ungenerous man to donate to charity.

1263. UNDISCIPLINED - *[spell]*- U N D I S C I P L I N E D
Definition: without proper control
Synonym: headstrong, unruly
Antonym: submissive, obedient

Sentence: Because he was undisciplined when it came to deadlines, the writer often fell behind in his work.

1264. TATTLE - *[spell]*- T A T T L E
Definition: tell tales or secrets
Synonym: gossip, babble
Antonym:
Sentence: The boy tattled on his sister when she broke the glass.

1265. TATTERED - *[spell]*- T A T T E R E D
Definition: torn or ragged
Synonym: shredded, shabby
Antonym:
Sentence: The child insisted on carrying her tattered stuffed bear everywhere she went.

1266. NAYSAY - *[spell]*- N A Y S A Y
Definition: oppose
Synonym:
Antonym:
Sentence: He was known to naysay all of her ideas.

1267. SHOPLIFT - *[spell]*- S H O P L I F T
Definition: to steal goods from a store while pretending to be a customer
Synonym: pilfer, steal
Antonym:
Sentence: The man was caught shoplifting several hundred dollars of merchandise.

1268. COURTEOUS - *[spell]*- C O U R T E O U S
Definition: thought of others
Synonym: polite, civil
Antonym: impolite, rude
Sentence: His mother raised him to be courteous to others.

1269. HEMLINE - *[spell]*- H E M L I N E
Definition: border of a garment
Synonym:
Antonym:
Sentence: The hemline of her dress came to her knees.

1270. PROVOKING - *[spell]*- P R O V O K I N G
Definition: something that makes angry
Synonym: instigating, annoying
Antonym: non inflammatory
Sentence: The boy was intentionally provoking of his little sister.

1271. REBIRTH - *[spell]*- R E B I R T H
Definition: to be born again
Synonym: revival, resurrection
Antonym: death, destruction
Sentence: There was a rebirth in art and culture in Italy in the sixteenth century.

1272. MISTREAT - *[spell]*- M I S T R E A T
Definition: treat badly or wrongly
Synonym: harm, abuse
Antonym: nurture, foster
Sentence: He was known to mistreat his employees.

1273. POSITIONAL - *[spell]*- P O S I T I O N A L
Definition: of, having to do with, or depending on rank or standing
Synonym:
Antonym:
Sentence: In the company, he was the positional leader while his boss took a sabbatical.

1274. SHORTFALL - *[spell]*- S H O R T F A L L
Definition: a shortage or deficit
Synonym: deficiency, lack
Antonym: abundance, plenty
Sentence: The company faced shortfall in profits that quarter.

1275. INDENTATION - *[spell]*- I N D E N T A T I ON
Definition: a being marked with a dent
Synonym: dent, depression
Antonym:
Sentence: His hand left an indentation in the soft snow.

1276. ENCIRCLE - *[spell]*- E N C I R C L E
Definition: form a circle around
Synonym: encompass, envelop
Antonym:
Sentence: The fence encircled the yard.

1277. ANTICIPATION - *[spell]*- A N T I C I P A T I O N
Definition: the act of looking forward to something
Synonym: expectancy
Antonym: dread
Sentence: Waiting for the day of the concert to arrive, the girl experienced great anticipation.

1278. ROTATION - *[spell]*- R O T A T I O N
       Definition: act or process of moving around a center or axis
       Synonym: orbit, circle
       Antonym:
       Sentence: The rotation of the ride at the amusement park made him dizzy.

1279. POSSESSIVE - *[spell]*- P O S S E S S I V E
       Definition: showing ownership
       Synonym: jealous, protective
       Antonym:
       Sentence: The child was very possessive of her toys.

1280. PROTOTYPE - *[spell]*- P R O T O T Y P E
       Definition: the first or primary type of anything
       Synonym: original, blueprint
       Antonym:
       Sentence: The inventor created a prototype of his invention.

1281. REALIZATION - *[spell]*- R E A L I Z A T I O N
       Definition: a thing understood clearly
       Synonym: awareness, recognition
       Antonym:
       Sentence: After ten years as a police officer, she came to the sudden
       realization that she didn't like her career.

1282. MIDWAY - *[spell]*- M I D W A Y
       Definition: in the middle
       Synonym: halfway, middle
       Antonym: whole, complete
       Sentence: She had to take a break midway through her exercise routine.

1283. PARTNERSHIP - *[spell]*- P A R T N E R S H I P
       Definition: having a joint interest
       Synonym: association, alliance
       Antonym: division, separation
       Sentence: They formed a partnership when they went into business
       together.

1284. ANCHOR - *[spell]*- A N C H O R
       Definition: to hold in place
       Synonym: hold
       Antonym: release
       Sentence: The poster was anchored to the telephone pole with several
       staples.

1285. ANCIENT - *[spell]*- A N C I E N T
Definition: very old
Synonym: antique, archaic
Antonym: current, modern
Sentence: The ancient book was several hundred years old.

1286. GINGERLY - *[spell]*- G I N G E R L Y
Definition: with extreme care or caution
Synonym: careful, cautious
Antonym: carelessly, recklessly
Sentence: He gingerly opened the door, not wanting to wake his sleeping daughter.

1287. SIDELONG - *[spell]*- S I D E L O N G
Definition: to one side
Synonym: askance, indirect
Antonym:
Sentence: Surprised by her remarks, the father gave his daughter a sidelong glance.

1288. REUNITE - *[spell]*- R E U N I T E
Definition: to bring or come together again
Synonym: reconcile, reconvene
Antonym: estrange, separate
Sentence: The family was reunited after being separated during the earthquake.

1289. SPITFIRE - *[spell]*- S P I T F I R E
Definition: person who has a quick and fiery temper
Synonym:
Antonym:
Sentence: She was a spitfire when it came to the well being of her children.

1290. CLINCH - *[spell]*- C L I N C H
Definition: to grasp tightly as in wrestling or boxing
Synonym: grapple, snatch
Antonym: release, loosen
Sentence: He clinched the arm of the attacker.

1291. INFURIATE - *[spell]*- I N F U R I A T E
Definition: fill with wild, fierce anger
Synonym: incense, enrage
Antonym: appease, please
Sentence: She was infuriated by her boyfriend's behavior at the concert.

1292. RECKONING - *[spell]*- R E C K O N I N G
Definition: method of computing
Synonym: calculation, estimation
Antonym:
Sentence: By her reckoning, the road trip would take nearly eight hours.

1293. FOREIGNER - *[spell]*- F O R E I G N E R
Definition: a person from another country
Synonym: alien, immigrant
Antonym: national, native
Sentence: Her neighbor seemed to be a foreigner because he didn't speak much English.

1294. BREATHTAKING - *[spell]*- B R E A T H T A K I N G
Definition: exciting
Synonym: astonishing, stunning
Antonym: boring, dull
Sentence: His view of the Grand Canyon was simply breathtaking.

1295. IMPLIED - *[spell]*- I M P L I E D
Definition: expressed indirectly
Synonym: suggested, insinuated
Antonym: expressed, stated
Sentence: The politician's remarks implied he would be running in the next election.

1296. CLASSY - *[spell]*- C L A S S Y
Definition: first-rate
Synonym: elegant, chic
Antonym: unfashionable, inferior
Sentence: They went to a classy restaurant for dinner.

1297. MAGNIFICENCE - *[spell]*- M A G N I F I C E N C E
Definition: richness of material, color, or ornament
Synonym: greatness, grandiosity
Antonym: dullness, insignificance
Sentence: The magnificence of the cathedral struck awe into all those who entered it.

1298. SUSPICIOUS - *[spell]*- S U S P I C I O U S
Definition: causing one to suspect or question
Synonym: questionable, doubtful Antonym:
Sentence: The man's suspicious behavior at the airport caused security to approach him.

1299. RESIGN - *[spell]*- R E S I G N
Definition: to give up
Synonym: relinquish, cede
Antonym:
Sentence: He resigned from his job after he found out about the company's unethical practices.

1300. PUCKISH - *[spell]*- P U C K I S H
Definition: mischievous
Synonym: naughty, impish
Antonym:
Sentence: The child was known to be puckish.

Medium Words Exercise - 4

1301. ENDURANCE - *[spell]*- E N D U R A N C E
Definition: power to withstand hard wear
Synonym: durability, longevity
Antonym:
Sentence: She selected the particular car to purchase because of its well-known endurance.

1302. ESSENTIAL - *[spell]*- E S S E N T I AL
Definition: needed to make a thing what it is
Synonym: crucial, fundamental
Antonym: inessential, unnecessary
Sentence: Good food is essential to a healthy lifestyle.

1303. FAITHLESS - *[spell]*- F A I T H L E S S
Definition: failing in one's duty
Synonym: disloyal, unreliable
Antonym: faithful, loyal
Sentence: The manager told his employees that it would be faithless to give up now.

1304. GRIMY - *[spell]*- G R I M Y
Definition: covered with dirt
Synonym: dingy, filthy
Antonym:
Sentence: The mother cringed when the child wiped her grimy hands on her clothes.

1305. IMMEDIATELY - *[spell]*- I M M E D I A T E L Y
Definition: at once or without delay
Synonym: instantly, promptly
Antonym: later, eventually
Sentence: After he broke his arm, he was immediately taken to the emergency room.

1306. MORALISTIC - *[spell]*- M O R A L I S T I C
Definition: teaching the difference between right and wrong
Synonym: virtuous, honorable

Antonym: corrupt, unethical
Sentence: She was moralistic in all things.

1307. INFUSE - *[spell]*- I N F U S E
Definition: introduce as by pouring or soaking
Synonym: imbue, impart
Antonym:
Sentence: The tea was infused with various herbs.

1308. STUNNING - *[spell]*- S T U N N I N G
Definition: having striking excellence, beauty, etc.
Synonym: attractive, sensational
Antonym: unremarkable, ordinary
Sentence: The girl was stunning in her ball gown.

1309. MERCILESS - *[spell]*- M E R C I L E S S
Definition: without showing any more kindness than justice requires
Synonym: heartless, cruel
Antonym: compassionate, gentle
Sentence: The king was merciless when it came to his enemies.

1310. CHIEFTAIN - *[spell]*- C H I E F T A I N
Definition: the leader of a clan or tribe
Synonym: boss, head
Antonym:
Sentence: The chieftain gave his followers strict orders.

1311. MAGNETIC - *[spell]*- M A G N E T I C
Definition: having the properties of a magnet
Synonym: irresistible, hypnotic
Antonym: repellent, repulsive
Sentence: She had a magnetic personalityâ€"everyone seemed attracted to her.

1312. MADDENING - *[spell]*- M A D D E N I N G
Definition: very annoying
Synonym: irritating, aggravating
Antonym: soothing, calming
Sentence: His continual chatter was maddening to her.

1313. ACADEMICâ€"[spell]â€"A C A D E M I C
Definition: having to do with schools, colleges, or universities
Synonym: scholastic
Antonym: unscholarly
Sentence: In order to better focus on academics, the girl decided to spend more time studying.

1314. QUALIFICATION - *[spell]*- Q U A L I F I C A T I O N
Definition: that which makes a person fit for a job, test, office etc.
Synonym: eligibility, proficiency
Antonym:
Sentence: The employer had a long list of qualifications for potential new-hires.

1315. OVERTIME - *[spell]*- O V E R T I M E
Definition: extra time beyond regular hours
Synonym: additional, extra
Antonym:
Sentence: He worked overtime to complete the project.

1316. CLICHÃ‰ - *[spell]*- C L I C H E
Definition: an overused expression or idea
Synonym: adage, commonplace
Antonym:
Sentence: His favorite clichÃ© was "Don't count your chickens until they're hatched."

1317. FOLKLORE - *[spell]*- F O L K L O R E
Definition: traditional beliefs, legends, or customs of a people or tribe
Synonym: legend, lore
Antonym:
Sentence: The anthropologist was an expert in folklore.

1318. SORROWFUL - *[spell]*- S O R R O W F U L
Definition: full of grief, sadness, or regret
Synonym: melancholy, grieving
Antonym: cheerful, joyful
Sentence: She felt quite sorrowful after the death of her beloved dog.

1319. ENSURE - *[spell]*- E N S U R E
Definition: make certain
Synonym: assure, guarantee
Antonym:
Sentence: Before going on vacation, she ensured that she locked up the house.

1320. TINGLE - *[spell]*- T I N G L E
Definition: to have a feeling of thrills or a pricking, stinging feeling
Synonym: tickly, prickle
Antonym:
Sentence: His fingers began to tingle because of the cold.

1321. PERSONALITY - *[spell]*- P E R S O N A L I T Y
Definition: the personal or individual quality that makes one person different from another
Synonym: characteristics, temperament
Antonym:
Sentence: Her personality was somewhat reserved.

1322. SHEARED - *[spell]*- S H E A R E D
Definition: cut to an even length
Synonym: trim, clip
Antonym:
Sentence: The groomer sheared the coat of the shaggy dog.

1323. CONVENIENCE - *[spell]*- C O N V E N I E N C E
Definition: the quality of saving trouble
Synonym: accommodation, advantage
Antonym: difficulty, hindrance
Sentence: For the sake of convenience, she decided to get takeout that night.

1324. SHIMMY - *[spell]*- S H I M M Y
Definition: an unusual shaking or vibration
Synonym: wobble, shake
Antonym:
Sentence: As she danced, she shimmied her shoulders.

1325. CORRUPTIVE - *[spell]*- C O R R U P T I V E
Definition: tending to be dishonest
Synonym: contaminating, demoralizing
Antonym: moral, honest
Sentence: The corruptive nature of politics has disillusioned many people.

1326. NEIGHBORHOOD - *[spell]*- N E I G H B O R H O O D
Definition: people living near one another
Synonym: district, community
Antonym:
Sentence: She had just moved into the neighborhood.

1327. FIGURINE - *[spell]*- F I G U R I N E
Definition: small, ornamental figure made of stone, pottery, metal, etc.
Synonym: statuette, model
Antonym:
Sentence: The woman collected figurines of angels and cherubs.

1328. LEAGUE - *[spell]*- L E A G U E
Definition: a union of persons, parties, or countries formed to help one

another
Synonym: federation, association
Antonym: disunion, separation
Sentence: The countries formed a league to look out for their mutual
interests.

1329. DETOUR - *[spell]*- D E T O U R
Definition: a roundabout way or course
Synonym: deviation, diversion
Antonym:
Sentence: To avoid traffic, they decided to take a detour.

1330. HEARTLESS - *[spell]*- H E A R T L E S S
Definition: without kindness or sympathy
Synonym: callous, cold
Antonym: compassionate, considerate
Sentence: When it came to helping others, he was completely heartless.

1331. BURDENSOME - *[spell]*- B U R D E N S O M E
Definition: hard to bear
Synonym: oppressive, difficult
Antonym: easy, light
Sentence: She loved her work, but sometimes found that being the head of
the company was too burdensome.

1332. SLICKER - *[spell]*- S L I C K E R
Definition: a long, loose, waterproof coat
Synonym: raincoat
Antonym:
Sentence: She wore a slicker when she left her house, anticipating the rain
to come.

1333. SACRED - *[spell]*- S A C R E D
Definition: connected with religion
Synonym: spiritual, divine
Antonym: profane, secular
Sentence: The burial ground of the saint was considered sacred ground.

1334. PREPAREDNESS - *[spell]*- P R E P A R E D N E S S
Definition: being ready
Synonym: readiness, willingness
Antonym: unpreparedness
Sentence: The teachers at the school were trained in emergency
preparedness.

1335. UNFAMILIAR - *[spell]*- U N F A M I L I A R
Definition: not well known
Synonym: unusual, exotic
Antonym: common, familiar
Sentence: After running several miles, she came to an unfamiliar part of her neighborhood.

1336. HUMANISM - *[spell]*- H U M A N I S M
Definition: any system of thought or action concerned with human interests and values
Synonym:
Antonym:
Sentence: He was dedicated to acts of humanism.

1337. MATERNITY - *[spell]*- M A T E R N I T Y
Definition: being a mother
Synonym:
Antonym:
Sentence: Since she was pregnant, she had to shop for clothes in the maternity section.

1338. COMMANDING - *[spell]*- C O M M A N D I N G
Definition: in control
Synonym: authoritative, dominant
Antonym: humble, unremarkable
Sentence: She has such a commanding presence that it's hard to ignore her.

1339. AIMLESS - *[spell]*- A I M L E S S
Definition: without purpose or direction
Synonym: pointless, random
Antonym: definite, methodical
Sentence: Her aimless chatter seemed never-ending.

1340. DIGNIFIED - *[spell]*- D I G N I F I E D
Definition: having proud and self-respecting manner
Synonym: distinguished, grand
Antonym: ignoble, silly
Sentence: She was quite dignified in all aspects of her manners.

1341. GARAGE - *[spell]*- G A R A G E
Definition: place where cars are kept
Synonym:
Antonym:
Sentence: Their new house had a two-car garage.

1342. TOURNAMENT - *[spell]*- T O U R N A M E N T
Definition: contest in any game of skill in which a number of competitors play a series of games
Synonym: competition, contest
Antonym:
Sentence: There was a tournament over the weekend for regional hockey teams.

1343. ARCHITECT - *[spell]*- A R C H I T E C T
Definition: a person whose profession is to design and supervise the construction of buildings
Synonym: builder, engineer
Antonym:
Sentence: The boy wanted to grow up to be an architect because he liked to build things.

1344. PIONEER - *[spell]*- P I O N E E R
Definition: a person who settles in a part of a country that has not been occupied before
Synonym: explorer, colonist
Antonym:
Sentence: The pioneers moved west to explore new lands.

1345. HIJACK - *[spell]*- H I J A C K
Definition: rob or take by force
Synonym:
Antonym:
Sentence: The traveler was hijacked when his car was stranded on the side of the road.

1346. SUMMONS - *[spell]*- S U M M O N S
Definition: a formal order or notice to appear before a judge or court of law
Synonym: calling, order
Antonym:
Sentence: The nobleman received a summons from the king.

1347. PEARLY - *[spell]*- P E A R L Y
Definition: having the color of a pearl (a hard, smooth, white gem having a soft shine like satin)
Synonym: pearlescent
Antonym:
Sentence: The stone on the necklace was pearly.

1348. UNTOUCHABLE - *[spell]*- U N T O U C H A B L E
Definition: out of reach

Synonym: invulnerable, impalpable

Antonym:

Sentence: Though powerful, the dictator was not untouchable.

1349. DISTORTION - *[spell]*- D I S T O R T I O N

Definition: a twisting out of shape

Synonym: exaggeration, falsification

Antonym:

Sentence: His distortion of the truth was obvious from his unbelievable story.

1350. DIRECTIONAL - *[spell]*- D I R E C T I O N A L

Definition: having to do with indicating direction

Synonym:

Antonym:

Sentence: The directional signal of the car indicated it would be turning left.

1351. IRRESPONSIBLE - *[spell]*- I R R E S P O N S I B L E

Definition: without a sense of being accountable for something

Synonym: careless, reckless

Antonym: responsible, accountable

Sentence: The father told his daughter that it was irresponsible to go out with friends without having told him where she was.

1352. TENDENCY - *[spell]*- T E N D E N C Y

Definition: a leaning or inclination

Synonym: propensity, habit

Antonym:

Sentence: He had the tendency to ramble on about things that interested him.

1353. SNAZZY - *[spell]*- S N A Z Z Y

Definition: fancy or flashy

Synonym: swanky, stylish

Antonym: plain, unstylish

Sentence: She wore a snazzy red vest to the holiday party.

1354. ARENA - *[spell]*- A R E N A

Definition: a space used for contests and shows

Synonym: stadium, theater

Antonym:

Sentence: The games were slated to take place in the well-known arena.

1355. SHIMMERY - *[spell]*- S H I M M E R Y

Definition: gleaming softly

Synonym: glittery, glimmering
Antonym: dull
Sentence: The surface of the lake was shimmery in the sunlight.

1356. CORRECTIVE - *[spell]*- C O R R E C T I V E
Definition: tending to make right
Synonym: healing, remedial
Antonym: non punitve
Sentence: His apology letter was intended as a corrective.

1357. ATTRACTION - *[spell]*- A T T R A C T I O N
Definition: ability to draw attention
Synonym: allurement, captivation
Antonym: repulsion, revulsion
Sentence: She experienced great attraction when she saw him for the first time.

1358. SIGHTLESS - *[spell]*- S I G H T L E S S
Definition: unable to see
Synonym: blind
Antonym:
Sentence: Some animals are born sightless but, over time, this changes.

1359. DESPAIRING - *[spell]*- D E S P A I R I N G
Definition: feeling or expressing hopelessness
Synonym: hopeless, despondent
Antonym: hopeful, optimistic
Sentence: After hours of looking, we were despairing of ever finding my lost ring.

1360. ORCHESTRA - *[spell]*- O R C H E S T R A
Definition: group of musicians organized to play together
Synonym: symphony, philharmonic
Antonym:
Sentence: The orchestra performed a beautiful medley of holiday songs.

1361. INFLICT - *[spell]*- I N F L I C T
Definition: cause to have or suffer
Synonym: impose, exact
Antonym:
Sentence: The suffering he inflicted upon her was totally inexcusable.

1362. GYP - *[spell]*- G Y P
Definition: to cheat or swindle
Synonym: bamboozle, bilk
Antonym:

Sentence: The man at the shop tried to gyp her by charging more for an oil change than the ad said.

1363. THOUSANDFOLD - *[spell]*- T H O U S A N D F O L D
Definition: a thousand times as many or as much
Synonym:
Antonym:
Sentence: She had such a good time at the concert, she would have done it again a thousandfold.

1364. ELECTOR - *[spell]*- E L E C T O R
Definition: a person who has the right to vote in an election
Synonym:
Antonym:
Sentence: Electors lined up at the polls for the presidential election.

1365. RESERVOIR - *[spell]*- R E S E R V O I R
Definition: place where water is collected and stored for use
Synonym:
Antonym:
Sentence: The city drew its water from the reservoir.

1366. SQUELCH - *[spell]*- S Q U E L C H
Definition: to cause to be silent
Synonym: thwart, muffle
Antonym:
Sentence: She squelched her sneeze during the performance.

1367. GLIMMER - *[spell]*- G L I M M E R
Definition: a faint idea or feeling
Synonym: flash, flicker
Antonym:
Sentence: When she heard the announcement, she had a glimmer of hope that she had won the prize.

1368. MIGHTILY - *[spell]*- M I G H T I L Y
Definition: in a powerful manner
Synonym: greatly, hugely
Antonym: little, weakly
Sentence: She was mightily angry that her husband forgot their anniversary.

1369. EXPERTISE - *[spell]*- E X P E R T I S E
Definition: expert knowledge or opinion
Synonym: competence, ability

Antonym: ignorance, incompetence
Sentence: She had great expertise in the field of physics.

1370. COINAGE - *[spell]*- C O I N A G E
Definition: system of coins
Synonym:
Antonym:
Sentence: In the United States, coinage includes quarters, dimes, nickels, and pennies.

1371. UNREASONABLE - *[spell]*- U N R E A S O N A B L E
Definition: not agreeable to reason or sound judgment
Synonym: illogical, senseless
Antonym: logical, rational
Sentence: The mother made unreasonable demands of her children.

1372. SCAFFOLD - *[spell]*- S C A F F O L D
Definition: a raised framework
Synonym: frame, stage
Antonym:
Sentence: The painters stood on a scaffold to reach the high ceiling.

1373. PREDICTABILITY - *[spell]*- P R E D I C T A B I L I T Y
Definition: quality of being something that can be announced or told beforehand
Synonym: regularity, consistency
Antonym: irregularity, variation
Sentence: The predictability of the game made it quite uninteresting.

1374. SCALPEL - *[spell]*- S C A L P E L
Definition: a small, straight knife used in surgery and dissections
Synonym:
Antonym:
Sentence: The doctor asked the nurse to hand him a scalpel.

1375. TARRY - *[spell]*- T A R R Y
Definition: to delay leaving
Synonym: lag, dally
Antonym:
Sentence: The man decided to tarry at his parent's house in order to wait for his sister's arrival.

1376. ILLUSTRATION - *[spell]*- I L L U S T R A T I O N
Definition: picture, diagram, or map used to explain or decorate something
Synonym: demonstration, representation

Antonym:
Sentence: The illustration in the textbook clearly explained the difficult concept.

1377. REHEARSAL - *[spell]*- R E H E A R S A L
Definition: performance beforehand for practice
Synonym: practice
Antonym:
Sentence: The actors held a dress rehearsal before opening night of the play.

1378. DEFUSE - *[spell]*- D E F U S E
Definition: to make something less serious or tense
Synonym: disarm, soothe
Antonym:
Sentence: He was able to defuse her temper by offering to take her to dinner.

1379. OPINIONATED - *[spell]*- O P I N I O N A T E D
Definition: obstinate or conceited with regards to one's own thoughts
Synonym: assertive, bossy
Antonym: shy, compromising
Sentence: She was very opinionated about how to raise children.

1380. SAMPLER - *[spell]*- S A M P L E R
Definition: something that contains samples (part to show what the result is like)
Synonym:
Antonym:
Sentence: He ordered a sampler of appetizers at the restaurant.

1381. PREFERABLE - *[spell]*- P R E F E R A B L E
Definition: to be liked better
Synonym: desirable, favored
Antonym: unlikeable
Sentence: The want ad stated that experience was preferable but not required.

1382. CASHMERE - *[spell]*- C A S H M E R E
Definition: a soft, costly wool
Synonym:
Antonym:
Sentence: She bought him a cashmere sweater for the holidays.

1383. GEOMETRIC - *[spell]*- G E O M E T R I C
Definition: consisting of straight lines, circles, triangles, etc.

Synonym:

Antonym:

Sentence: Her shirt had a geometric pattern on it.

1384. PHYSIQUE - *[spell]*- P H Y S I Q U E
Definition: bodily structure, organization, or development
Synonym: body, frame
Antonym:
Sentence: He had a very defined physique from so much working out.

1385. BECOMING - *[spell]*- B E C O M I NG
Definition: fitting or suitable
Synonym: appropriate, proper
Antonym: improper, unsuitable
Sentence: That dress was very becoming on her.

1386. SHALLOW - *[spell]*- S H A L L O W
Definition: not deep
Synonym: hollow, trivial
Antonym: deep, important
Sentence: She was very shallow and always overly concerned with her appearance.

1387. CONSIDERABLE - *[spell]*- C O N S I D E R A B L E
Definition: worth consideration, significant
Synonym: substantial, reasonable
Antonym: insignificant, insufficient
Sentence: He owed her a considerable sum of money.

1388. AMBITIOUS - *[spell]*- A M B I T I O U S
Definition: guided by the desire to rise in rank or position
Synonym: determined, aspiring
Antonym: lazy
Sentence: His ambitious nature led him to become the CEO of the company.

1389. SCANT - *[spell]*- S C A N T
Definition: not enough in size or quantity
Synonym: meager, poor
Antonym: ample, plentiful
Sentence: There was scant food in the family's cupboard.

1390. FOOTWORK - *[spell]*- F O O T W O R K
Definition: way of using the feet
Synonym:

Antonym:
Sentence: Footwork is very important in boxing.

1391. TAUNT - *[spell]*- T A U N T
Definition: tease
Synonym: provoke, gibe
Antonym:
Sentence: He was constantly taunted by his classmates.

1392. CAMPAIGN - *[spell]*- C A M P A I G N
Definition: a series of connected activities to do or get something
Synonym: movement, drive
Antonym:
Sentence: The politician had a very successful reelection campaign.

1393. SHOCKER - *[spell]*- S H O C K E R
Definition: a highly sensational written work
Synonym: thriller, cliffhanger
Antonym:
Sentence: The ending of the movie was a complete shocker.

1394. COUNTERFEIT - *[spell]*- C O U N T E R F E I T
Definition: copy used to deceive
Synonym: fraud, forgery
Antonym: authentic, original
Sentence: The criminals used counterfeit money to make their purchases.

1395. PRESENTABLE - *[spell]*- P R E S E N T A B L E
Definition: fit to be seen
Synonym: acceptable, decent
Antonym: unacceptable, unfit
Sentence: She felt the need to put on her makeup in order to make herself presentable.

1396. CEBREAKER - *[spell]*- I C E B R E A K E R
Definition: anything that helps overcome first difficulties in talking or getting acquainted
Synonym:
Antonym:
Sentence: The new hires of the company did several icebreakers to get to know each other.

1397. INGRATITUDE - *[spell]*- I N G R A T I T U D E
Definition: lack of thankfulness
Synonym: rudeness thoughtlessness,
Antonym: appreciation, gratitude

Sentence: She was irritated by his ingratitude after she threw him an extravagant surprise party.

1398. FORECAST - *[spell]*- F O R E C A S T
Definition: to calculate or predict, usually as a result of the study of data
Synonym: calculation, projection
Antonym:
Sentence: The weather forecast predicted a series of powerful thunderstorms.

1399. ADMISSIBLE - *[spell]*- A D M I S S I B LE
Definition: worthy of being allowed
Synonym: allowed, permissible
Antonym: inadmissible
Sentence: The evidence was admissible in court.

1400. LIKELIHOOD - *[spell]*- L I K E L I H O O D
Definition: probability
Synonym: prospect, tendency
Antonym:
Sentence: The likelihood of his coming in first place in the competition was slim.

Medium Words Exercise - 5

1401. PLENTEOUS - *[spell]*- P L E N T E O U S
Definition: present or existing in full supply
Synonym: abundant, bounteous
Antonym: scarce, few
Sentence: University libraries generally have a plenteous assortment of books on every subject.

1402. VAST - *[spell]*- V A S T
Definition: very great
Synonym: colossal, boundless
Antonym: limited, narrow
Sentence: He purchased a vast area of land on which to build a farm.

1403. IDEALIZE - *[spell]*- I D E A L I Z E
Definition: to think of or represent as perfect rather than as is actually true
Synonym: glorify, romanticize
Antonym:
Sentence: She had a tendency to idealize the company she worked for.

1404. BIWEEKLY - *[spell]*- B I W E E K L Y
Definition: occurring every two weeks
Synonym:
Antonym:
Sentence: The committee had mandatory biweekly meetings.

1405. CLUTCH - *[spell]*- C L U T C H
Definition: to grasp strongly
Synonym: clench, grip
Antonym: release, free
Sentence: She clutched the railing as if her life depended on it.

1406. GENEROSITY - *[spell]*- G E N E R O S I T Y
Definition: a being willing to share with others
Synonym: largesse, openhandedness
Antonym: stinginess, selfishness
Sentence: Her generosity caused her to be liked by everyone.

1407. HORRENDOUS - *[spell]*- H O R R E N D O U S
Definition: causing horror
Synonym: horrible, horrific
Antonym:
Sentence: The aftermath of the earthquake was horrendous.

1408. BASIN - *[spell]*- B A S I N
Definition: a shallow bowl for holding liquids
Synonym: bowl, sink
Antonym:
Sentence: She washed her hands in the basin.

1409. APIECE - *[spell]*- A P I E C E
Definition: for each one
Synonym: individually, separately
Antonym: together, collectively
Sentence: These pears cost twenty-five cents apiece.

1410. JACKPOT - *[spell]*- J A C K P O T
Definition: a big prize
Synonym: reward, winnings
Antonym:
Sentence: He hit the jackpot when he won the lottery.

1411. TRIAD - *[spell]*- T R I A D
Definition: group of three
Synonym: triumvirate, threesome
Antonym:
Sentence: She purchased a triad of candles for her dinner table.

1412. LIBERAL - *[spell]*- L I B E R A L
Definition: giving or given freely
Synonym: generous
Antonym:
Sentence: At the party, food was supplied in liberal amounts.

1413. GEEZER - *[spell]*- G E E Z E R
Definition: an odd or eccentric old man
Synonym:
Antonym:
Sentence: All of the children in the neighborhood feared the geezer who lived down the street.

1414. SEASONING - *[spell]*- S E A S O N I N G
Definition: something that gives better flavor
Synonym: condiment, flavoring

Antonym:
Sentence: The chef added many different seasonings to the dish.

1415. COMMITMENT - *[spell]*- C O M M I T M E N T
Definition: a being involved
Synonym: pledge, guarantee
Antonym: break, breach
Sentence: He made a commitment to her when he married her.

1416. BUMPKIN - *[spell]*- B U M P K I N
Definition: an awkward or naÃ¯ve person
Synonym: boor, clod
Antonym: sophisticate
Sentence: She felt like a complete bumpkin when she moved to the city
for the first time.

1417. CANINE - *[spell]*- C A N I N E
Definition: of or like a dog
Synonym:
Antonym:
Sentence: Something about her face somehow has a very canine look.

1418. TROUPE - *[spell]*- T R O U P E
Definition: a company of actors, singers, acrobats, etc.
Synonym: cast, crew
Antonym:
Sentence: The troupe traveled the country performing plays.

1419. BOTTOMLESS - *[spell]*- B O T T O M L E S S
Definition: so deep that the lowest point cannot be reached
Synonym: boundless, endless
Antonym: ending, limited
Sentence: He joked about how his stomach seemed to be a bottomless pit.

1420. CLARIFICATION - *[spell]*- C L A R I F I C A T I O N
Definition: act or process of making clearer
Synonym: explanation, simplification
Antonym: complication, confusion
Sentence: The teacher provided a clarification of the math problem.

1421. GUILTY - *[spell]*- G U I L T Y
Definition: having done wrong and deserving punishment
Synonym: culpable, responsible
Antonym: innocent, remorseless
Sentence: He felt guilty for having lied to his father.

1422. SISTERHOOD - *[spell]*- S I S T E R H O O D
Definition: bond between sisters
Synonym:
Antonym:
Sentence: The sorority was a sisterhood of young women who aspired to greatness.

1423. PLATOON - *[spell]*- P L A T O O N
Definition: military unit made up of two or more squads
Synonym: squad, patrol
Antonym:
Sentence: The platoon was sent across enemy lines.

1424. COMBINATION - *[spell]*- C O M B I N A T I O N
Definition: things made up by joining elements together
Synonym: merger, consolidation
Antonym: division, separation
Sentence: A combination of ice and snow made the roads quite dangerous.

1425. MISHMASH - *[spell]*- M I S H M A S H
Definition: a confused mixture
Synonym: hodgepodge, jumble
Antonym:
Sentence: The dinner was a mishmash of different ingredients.

1426. FORERUNNER - *[spell]*- F O R E R U N N E R
Definition: a sign or warning that something is coming
Synonym: precursor, herald
Antonym:
Sentence: The cold temperatures were the forerunner of winter.

1427. CHALLENGING - *[spell]*- C H A L L E N G I N G
Definition: call into question
Synonym: doubt, dispute
Antonym: accepting
Sentence: His challenging of the new law led to its discussion in a public forum.

1428. AFFLICT - *[spell]*- A F F L I C T
Definition: to cause to suffer
Synonym: distress, annoy
Antonym: aid, comfort
Sentence: Though she did not realize it, her irresponsible behavior began to afflict her family.

1429. TIMELY - *[spell]-* T I M E L Y
Definition: at the right time
Synonym: convenient, favorable
Antonym: unsuitable, improper
Sentence: Her comments about her boyfriend's proposal proved quite timely since he proposed the next day.

1430. SCORCH - *[spell]-* S C O R C H
Definition: to burn slightly
Synonym: sear, char
Antonym:
Sentence: She scorched the marshmallows to make s'mores.

1431. CERTIFIABLE - *[spell]-* C E R T I F I A B L E
Definition: something that can be declared as true
Synonym: verified, confirmed
Antonym: unconfirmed, refuted
Sentence: She found out that his license to be a doctor was not certifiable.

1432. CHEAPSKATE - *[spell]-* C H E A P S K A T E
Definition: a stingy person
Synonym: miser, stiff
Antonym:
Sentence: Because he was such a cheapskate, he refused to spend money on anything that wasn't an absolute necessity.

1433. STARGAZE - *[spell]-* S T A R G A Z E
Definition: to be absent-minded or daydreaming
Synonym: daydream, fancy
Antonym:
Sentence: He was prone to stargazing when he was bored.

1434. BLOODSHED - *[spell]-* B L O O D S H E D
Definition: slaughter
Synonym: carnage, massacre
Antonym: peace
Sentence: The battle was won, but only after great bloodshed.

1435. NORMALIZE - *[spell]-* N O R M A L I Z E
Definition: to make ordinary
Synonym: void
Antonym:
Sentence: After the accident she tried to normalize herself as much as possible.

1436. NOWADAYS - *[spell]*- N O W A D A Y S
Definition: the present day
Synonym:
Antonym:
Sentence: Nowadays, technology advances in a rapid rate.

1437. ASSIGNMENT - *[spell]*- A S S I G N M E N T
Definition: something that is given as a task or duty
Synonym: chore, duty
Antonym:
Sentence: The teacher gave her students an assignment for homework.

1438. SLINKY - *[spell]*- S L I N K Y
Definition: sneaky or furtive
Synonym:
Antonym:
Sentence: She had to be slinky when she threw her brother's surprise party.

1439. IMPRACTICABLE - *[spell]*- I M P R A C T I C A B L E
Definition: impossible to put into practice
Synonym: impossible, imprudent
Antonym: practicable
Sentence: His impracticable approach to the task did not make sense to his coworkers.

1440. DISENTANGLE - *[spell]*- D I S E N T A N G L E
Definition: free from tangles or complications
Synonym: extricate
Antonym: tangle, snarl
Sentence: The kitten had to disentangle herself from the yarn she was playing with.

1441. TOXIN - *[spell]*- T O X I N
Definition: any poison formed by an organism
Synonym: poison, venom
Antonym:
Sentence: Some animals in the rainforest have potent toxins.

1442. MISUNDERSTANDING - *[spell]*- M I S U N D E R S T A N D I N G
Definition: failure to comprehend
Synonym: confusion, misconception
Antonym: accuracy, understanding
Sentence: The husband and wife had a misunderstanding.

1443. ABUZZ - *[spell]*- A B U Z Z
Definition: filled with a humming sound created by talk or activity
Synonym: humming, droning
Antonym: hush, quiet
Sentence: The building was abuzz with excited voices during the convention.

1444. PARTAKE - *[spell]*- P A R T A K E
Definition: eat or drink something
Synonym: consume, devour
Antonym: abstain
Sentence: She encouraged her guests to partake of the snacks she had made.

1445. PARENTAGE - *[spell]*- P A R E N T A G E
Definition: family line
Synonym: lineage, ancestry
Antonym:
Sentence: He could trace his parentage back to King Henry VIII.

1446. DISTEND - *[spell]*- D I S T E N D
Definition: stretch out by pressure from within
Synonym: swell, expand
Antonym: shrink, compress
Sentence: His stomach was distended because of his problems in his digestive tract.

1447. CASTAWAY - *[spell]*- C A S T A W A Y
Definition: thrown away
Synonym: outcast, rejected
Antonym: cherished
Sentence: Dressed in worn, castaway clothing, you would never guess that she is actually wealthy.

1448. PARTIAL - *[spell]*- P A R T I A L
Definition: not complete or whole
Synonym: portion, incomplete
Antonym: complete, finished
Sentence: The detective found a partial fingerprint at the crime scene.

1449. TROUGH - *[spell]*- T R O U G H
Definition: narrow, open, boxlike container for holding food or water for livestock
Synonym:
Antonym:
Sentence: The horses ate oats from a trough.

1450. ELECTRIFY - *[spell]*- E L E C T R I F Y
Definition: charge with electricity
Synonym:
Antonym:
Sentence: During the storm, the cell phone tower was electrified by lightning.

1451. PITILESS - *[spell]*- P I T I L E S S
Definition: without mercy
Synonym: merciless, ruthless
Antonym: merciful, pitying
Sentence: The teacher was pitiless when it came to accepting late work from his students.

1452. DELICACY - *[spell]*- D E L I C A CY
Definition: fineness of quality or make
Synonym: elegance, daintiness
Antonym: coarseness, heaviness
Sentence: The delicacy of the fabric was greatly appreciated by the seamstress.

1453. UNDERSTATEMENT - *[spell]*- U N D E R S T A T E M E N T
Definition: statement that expresses a fact too weakly
Synonym:
Antonym:
Sentence: His saying that it was just sprinkling outside when it was clearly pouring was an understatement.

1454. REHASH - *[spell]*- R E H A S H
Definition: to express old material in a new form
Synonym:
Antonym:
Sentence: Every time they argued, she felt she had to rehash the same old explanations.

1455. RIGIDITY - *[spell]*- R I G I D I T Y
Definition: stiffness or firmness
Synonym: harshness, rigor
Antonym: malleability
Sentence: His rigidity when it came to the rules made for a strict work environment.

1456. QUENCH - *[spell]*- Q U E N C H
Definition: to put an end to
Synonym: stop, cease

Antonym: begin, start
Sentence: She quenched her thirst by drinking a tall glass of water.

1457. INDULGE - *[spell]*- I N D U L G E
Definition: give in to one's pleasure
Synonym: entertain, pamper
Antonym: deprive, disappoint
Sentence: She decided to indulge in her desire to go on a tropical vacation.

1458. FOREFRONT - *[spell]*- F O R E F R O N T
Definition: a place of great importance, activity, etc.
Synonym: prominence, limelight
Antonym:
Sentence: The politician was suddenly thrust into the forefront of the presidential election.

1459. NICHE - *[spell]*- N I C H E
Definition: recess or hollow in a wall for a statue, vase, etc.
Synonym: nook, alcove
Antonym:
Sentence: Her books were located in a niche on the wall.

1460. PROFANITY - *[spell]*- P R O F A N I T Y
Definition: use of vulgar language
Synonym: swearing, cursing
Antonym:
Sentence: The child got in trouble at school for using profanity.

1461. CHIRRUP - *[spell]*- C H I R R U P
Definition: to make a short, sharp sound again and again
Synonym: peep, twitter
Antonym:
Sentence: The bird chirruped outside the window.

1462. INVESTIGATE - *[spell]*- I N V E S T I G A T E
Definition: look into thoroughly
Synonym: consider, examine
Antonym: neglect, ignore
Sentence: She decided to further investigate the problem to find its cause.

1463. PAUNCH - *[spell]*- P A U N C H
Definition: belly
Synonym: bulge, gut
Antonym:
Sentence: Over the years, he had acquired quite a paunch.

1464. TRIBUTE - *[spell]*- T R I B U T E
Definition: a gift or compliment given as in acknowledgement of gratitude or esteem
Synonym: praise, compliment
Antonym: censure, condemnation
Sentence: The band played a tribute to several rock legends.

1465. TASSEL - *[spell]*- T A S S E L
Definition: an ornamental, hanging bunch of threads, small cords, beads, etc.
Synonym: fringe
Antonym:
Sentence: She placed her graduation tassel on the rearview mirror of her car.

1466. CHISEL - *[spell]*- C H I S E L
Definition: to cut or shape with a blade
Synonym: carve, sculpt
Antonym:
Sentence: He found the best materials and then began to chisel away to make a sculpture.

1467. PRANKSTER - *[spell]*- P R A N K S T E R
Definition: a person who plays playful tricks
Synonym: rascal, scamp
Antonym:
Sentence: The child was known by his family to be a prankster.

1468. SPAN - *[spell]*- S P A N
Definition: a space of time, often short or limited
Synonym: interval, period
Antonym:
Sentence: In the span of only a few hours, her entire life was changed forever.

1469. EMPOWER - *[spell]*- E M P O W E R
Definition: give authority to
Synonym: authorize, permit
Antonym: disqualify
Sentence: She felt empowered by her new position in management.

1470. FRILLY - *[spell]*- F R I L L Y
Definition: full of ruffles
Synonym: lacy, ornate
Antonym: simple, unadorned
Sentence: He refused to wear the frilly shirt his wife bought him.

1471. COLORATION - *[spell]*- C O L O R A T I O N
Definition: the way in which a person or thing is colored
Synonym: hue, complexion
Antonym:
Sentence: The coloration of dogs varied across the same breed.

1472. FRIGHTFUL - *[spell]*- F R I G H T F U L
Definition: causing horror
Synonym: dreadful, ghastly
Antonym:
Sentence: His Halloween costume was quite frightful.

1473. FOOLERY - *[spell]*- F O O L E R Y
Definition: a foolish action
Synonym: absurdity, indiscretion
Antonym:
Sentence: The youth's foolery at the carnival did not appeal to the wise old man.

1474. AVOIDANCE - *[spell]*- A V O I D A N CE
Definition: a keeping away from
Synonym: evasion, dodging
Antonym: meeting
Sentence: His avoidance of her was obvious when he didn't return her phone calls.

1475. SAFEKEEPING - *[spell]*- S A F E K E E P I N G
Definition: keeping or being kept free from harm
Synonym: protection, custody
Antonym:
Sentence: He gave the document to his wife for safekeeping.

1476. IRRITABILITY - *[spell]*- I R R I T A B I L I T Y
Definition: being easily made angry
Synonym: annoyance, irascibility
Antonym:
Sentence: Her irritability was due to the fact that she had had a terrible morning.

1477. VALUABLE - *[spell]*- V A L U A B L E
Definition: having a substantial worth
Synonym: costly, expensive
Antonym: cheap, inexpensive
Sentence: Her time was valuable, so she hated it when people wasted it.

1478. FAMED - *[spell]*- F A M E D
Definition: famous
Synonym: noted, renowned
Antonym: unimportant, unknown
Sentence: The scientist was famed for having won a Nobel Prize.

1479. INTELLECTUAL - *[spell]*- I N T E L L E C T U A L
Definition: needing or using the power of knowing
Synonym: cerebral, intelligent
Antonym: foolish, ignorant
Sentence: The child needed constant intellectual stimulation to avoid distraction.

1480. TREAD - *[spell]*- T R E A D
Definition: to set the foot down and walk
Synonym: walk, step
Antonym:
Sentence: She tread across the room to say hello to her friend.

1481. PLUNDER - *[spell]*- P L U N D E R
Definition: rob by force
Synonym: steal, pillage
Antonym: give, return
Sentence: Soldiers roamed the countryside, committing acts of violence and plunder.

1482. INDEFINITE - *[spell]*- I N D E F I N I T E
Definition: not clearly defined
Synonym: undetermined, ambiguous
Antonym: clear, definite
Sentence: The boundaries of the property were indefinite.

1483. IMAGERY - *[spell]*- I M A G E R Y
Definition: pictures formed in the mind by written words
Synonym:
Antonym:
Sentence: The poem was full of natural imagery.

1484. DISALLOW - *[spell]*- D I S A L L O W
Definition: to deny the truth or value of
Synonym: reject, disavow
Antonym: confirm, acknowledge
Sentence: Despite evidence, he continued to disallow the fact that his company was losing profits.

1485. INCONSIDERATE - *[spell]*- I N C O N S I D E R A T E
Definition: not thoughtful of others and their feelings
Synonym: thoughtless, boorish
Antonym: considerate, generous
Sentence: His inconsiderate remarks hurt the feelings of many of his family members.

1486. THEORY - *[spell]*- T H E O R Y
Definition: explanation based on observation and reasoning
Synonym: argument, hypothesis
Antonym:
Sentence: The scientist had a series of theories about several issues in biology.

1487. INCORRECT - *[spell]*- I N C O R R E C T
Definition: containing errors or mistakes
Synonym: erroneous, mistaken
Antonym: accurate, correct
Sentence: His answer to the test question was incorrect.

1488. SHRINKAGE - *[spell]*- S H R I N K A G E
Definition: act or process of drawing back or recoiling
Synonym: diminution, reduction
Antonym: enlargement, expansion
Sentence: The recipe made less than she thought because she did not take into account the shrinkage of the vegetables as they cooked.

1489. QUIETUDE - *[spell]*- Q U I E T U D E
Definition: stillness or calmness
Synonym: silence, peacefulness
Antonym: chaos, clamor
Sentence: He found the quietude of the night to be relaxing.

1490. MINIATURE - *[spell]*- M I N I A T U R E
Definition: anything represented on a very small scale
Synonym: small, little
Antonym: giant, big
Sentence: The boy had a miniature action figure.

1491. BANDAGE - *[spell]*- B A N D A G E
Definition: cloth used for dressing a wound
Synonym: gauze
Antonym:
Sentence: She used a bandage to tend to the gash on her knee.

1492. DEODORIZE - *[spell]*- D E O D O R I Z E
Definition: destroy or neutralize an offensive smell
Synonym: freshen
Antonym: pollute
Sentence: After having pets for so long, he had to deodorize the carpet.

1493. TRANSFORM - *[spell]*- T R A N S F O R M
Definition: to change in form or appearance
Synonym: mutate, change
Antonym: remain, preserve
Sentence: Her new haircut seemed to completely transform her.

1494. DIMPLE - *[spell]*- D I M P L E
Definition: small hollow indentation
Synonym: divot, cleft
Antonym:
Sentence: When she smiled, she had a dimple on each of her cheeks.

1495. COLLECTIVE - *[spell]*- C O L L E C T I V E
Definition: of a group
Synonym: aggregate, cumulative
Antonym: exclusive, unilateral
Sentence: Using their collective intellect, they came up with a solution.

1496. SCREENPLAY - *[spell]*- S C R E E N P L A Y
Definition: a motion-picture story in manuscript form
Synonym:
Antonym:
Sentence: The writer sold a screenplay which, later on, became a major motion picture.

1497. PORTABLE - *[spell]*- P O R T A B L E
Definition: capable of being carried
Synonym: movable, cartable
Antonym: stationary, stagnant
Sentence: She purchased a laptop over a PC because it was more portable.

1498. FACTUAL - *[spell]*- F A C T U A L
Definition: considered as real
Synonym: credible, legitimate
Antonym: fictional
Sentence: She gave a factual account of the events that had occurred that day.

1499. CLOMP - *[spell]*- C L O M P
Definition: to walk heavily

Synonym: clunk, thump
Antonym:
Sentence: She could hear him clomp down the hallway.

1500. VERTICAL - *[spell]*- V E R T I C A L
Definition: straight up and down
Synonym: upright, erect
Antonym: horizontal, level
Sentence: The artists carved a vertical statue.

Medium Words Exercise - 6

1501. ACCESS - *[spell]*- A C C E S S
Definition: the right or ability to approach or enter
Synonym: admittance, entry
Antonym: exit
Sentence: In order to access the concert, you must have your tickets with you.

1502. NEIGH - *[spell]*- N E I G H
Definition: prolonged, loud, quavering sound
Synonym:
Antonym:
Sentence: The horse neighed loudly when it saw its master.

1503. OVERRIDE - *[spell]*- O V E R R I D E
Definition: act in spite of
Synonym: supersede, quash
Antonym: allow, approve
Sentence: Only his boss could override the access code.

1504. ENSLAVE - *[spell]*- E N S L A V E
Definition: to take away the freedom from
Synonym: imprison, oppress
Antonym: liberate, emancipate
Sentence: After the war, the country enslaved a large number of enemy civilians.

1505. SNOOP - *[spell]*- S N O O P
Definition: to go about in a sneaking, prying way
Synonym: pry
Antonym:
Sentence: The jealous girlfriend snooped through her boyfriend's phone.

1506. SHABBY - *[spell]*- S H A B B Y
Definition: worn much
Synonym: dilapidated, threadbare
Antonym: classy, new
Sentence: She decided not to wear the dress because she was concerned it looked too shabby.

1507. CONFRONT - *[spell]*- C O N F R O N T
Definition: meet face to face
Synonym: oppose, accost
Antonym: avoid, evade
Sentence: He was determined to confront her about her lies.

1508. INJECTION - *[spell]*- I N J E C T I O N
Definition: act or process of forcing liquid into a passage, cavity, or tissue
Synonym:
Antonym:
Sentence: As a diabetic, he learned to give himself injections of insulin.

1509. NEGOTIABLE - *[spell]*- N E G O T I A B L E
Definition: capable of being talked over in order to come to mutual agreement
Synonym: debatable, transferable
Antonym:
Sentence: The man went to talk to the store clerk, hoping the price of the item was negotiable.

1510. PRODUCTION - *[spell]*- P R O D U C T I O N
Definition: act of creating
Synonym: creation, manufacture
Antonym:
Sentence: The theater group put on a production of a well-known play.

1511. ANDROID - *[spell]*- A N D R O I D
Definition: a machine that resembles a human
Synonym: automaton, cyborg
Antonym:
Sentence: The science fiction novel featured several different androids.

1512. NEW - *[spell]*- A N E W
Definition: once more
Synonym: again, repeat
Antonym: sole
Sentence: Because she messed up her project, she had to begin anew.

1513. MERRIMENT - *[spell]*- M E R R I M E N T
Definition: laughter and happiness
Synonym: amusement, revelry
Antonym: depression, gloom
Sentence: The family's merriment was due to the birth of their new son.

1514. PARENTHESIZE - *[spell]*- P A R E N T H E S I Z E
Definition: insert as in a parentheses

Synonym: interject, add
Antonym:
Sentence: The author decided to parenthesize the explanation.

1515. BILINGUAL - *[spell]*- B I L I N G U A L
Definition: speaking two different languages
Synonym:
Antonym:
Sentence: He grew up bilingual, speaking both Spanish and English.

1516. SECRECY - *[spell]*- S E C R E C Y
Definition: condition of being kept from the knowledge of others
Synonym: mystery, concealment
Antonym: openness, illumination
Sentence: The CIA agent was sworn to secrecy about his mission.

1517. COMMUNAL - *[spell]*- C O M M U N A L
Definition: of or relating to a community
Synonym: conjoint, shared
Antonym: individual, personal
Sentence: The park was a communal space.

1518. OMISSION - *[spell]*- O M I S S I O N
Definition: a leaving out
Synonym: exclusion, oversight
Antonym: inclusion, insertion
Sentence: The author's omission of the event in his biography caused the scandal.

1519. EXTINCTION - *[spell]*- E X T I N C T I O N
Definition: an extinguishing
Synonym: annihilation, destruction
Antonym:
Sentence: The exact reason for the extinction of dinosaurs is unclear.

1520. POWERHOUSE - *[spell]*- P O W E R H O U S E
Definition: a powerful, energetic, or highly effective person or group
Synonym: go-getter, hustler
Antonym:
Sentence: He was a powerhouse when it came to motivating his employees.

1521. FACTOR - *[spell]*- F A C T O R
Definition: circumstance, fact, or influence that produces a result
Synonym: determinant, component

Antonym:
Sentence: One factor in their breakup was his inability to commit.

1522. BLESSED - *[spell]*- B L E S S E D
Definition: sanctified
Synonym: consecrated, exalted
Antonym: cursed, damned
Sentence: He felt blessed to have such wonderful friends and family.

1523. SCRIBBLE - *[spell]*- S C R I B B L E
Definition: write carelessly or hastily
Synonym: scrawl, jot
Antonym:
Sentence: The student scribbled a few notes down on his paper.

1524. ENCOURAGEMENT - *[spell]*- E N C O U R A G E M E N T
Definition: condition of feeling as if one has been given courage or confidence
Synonym: reassurance, inspiration
Antonym: discouragement, dishearten
Sentence: She felt great encouragement when, after weeks of practice, she mastered playing the song on piano.

1525. KINDGERGARTEN - *[spell]*- K I N D E R G A R T E N
Definition: a school or class for children from four to six year old
Synonym:
Antonym:
Sentence: The child was excited for his first day of kindergarten.

1526. GUIDELINE - *[spell]*- G U I D E L I N E
Definition: a principle or policy for determining the future
Synonym: direction, protocol
Antonym:
Sentence: The teacher's guidelines for the project were very specific.

1527. BEFOREHAND - *[spell]*- B E F O R E H A N D
Definition: ahead of time
Synonym: earlier, sooner
Antonym: later, ensuing
Sentence: He knew about the test beforehand, so he was sure to study.

1528. SHUFFLE - *[spell]*- S H U F F L E
Definition: to walk without lifting the feet
Synonym:
Antonym:
Sentence: The student shuffled down the hallway to class.

1529. PODGY - *[spell]*- P O D G Y
    Definition: short and fat
    Synonym: chubby, portly
    Antonym: thin, skinny
    Sentence: The podgy pig bathed himself in the mud.

1530. NARROW - *[spell]*- N A R R O W
    Definition: not wide
    Synonym: slim, slender
    Antonym: fat, wide
    Sentence: He had a very narrow perception of the world.

1531. TREACHEROUS - *[spell]*- T R E A C H E R O US
    Definition: not to be trusted
    Synonym: dishonest, disloyal
    Antonym: honest, reliable
    Sentence: Benedict Arnold is remembered in history for his treacherous behavior.

1532. HONORABLE - *[spell]*- H O N O R A B L E
    Definition: having or showing a sense of what is right and proper
    Synonym: noble, upright
    Antonym: dishonest, dishonorable
    Sentence: Though he had honorable intentions, things ultimately turned out badly for him.

1533. ASTONISHMENT - *[spell]*- A S T O N I S H M E N T
    Definition: great surprise
    Synonym: amazement, wonder
    Antonym:
    Sentence: She could hardly conceal her astonishment that he had actually come home.

1534. RECOLLECTION - *[spell]*- R E C O L L E C T I O N
    Definition: act or power of recalling to mind
    Synonym: reminiscence, remembrance
    Antonym:
    Sentence: To her recollection, she had never met him before.

1535. UNWORTHY - *[spell]*- U N W O R T H Y
    Definition: not deserving
    Synonym: ineligible, undeserving
    Antonym: appropriate, qualified
    Sentence: She felt unworthy of so prestigious an honor.

1536. NOMINALLY - *[spell]*- N O M I N AL L Y
Definition: in name only
Synonym: marginally
Antonym:
Sentence: Although she loved to tell people about her faith, in truth, she is only nominally a religious person.

1537. ANIMALISTIC - *[spell]*- A N I M A L I S T I C
Definition: related to the idea that humans act like animals
Synonym: sensual, carnal
Antonym:
Sentence: His animalistic behavior ultimately got him in great trouble.

1538. NUMERABLE - *[spell]*- N U M E R A B L E
Definition: able to be counted
Synonym: numerous
Antonym: innumerable
Sentence: She received numerable votes for the position.

1539. FLUTTERY - *[spell]*- F L U T T E R Y
Definition: apt to move back and forth restlessly
Synonym: jittery, nervous
Antonym:
Sentence: She moved about the room in a fluttery commotion.

1540. INFERIOR - *[spell]*- I N F E R I O R
Definition: below most others
Synonym: lesser, secondary
Antonym: superior, first-rate
Sentence: The second car is of inferior quality compared to the first.

1541. MINGLE - *[spell]*- M I N G L E
Definition: combine in a mixture
Synonym: blend, socialize
Antonym: divide, separate
Sentence: He tried to mingle with his guests at the party.

1542. BELLOW - *[spell]*- B E L L O W
Definition: to make a loud roaring sound
Synonym: howl, bay
Antonym: whimper, whisper
Sentence: The lion could be heard bellowing from across the plain.

1543. SNUB - *[spell]*- S N U B
Definition: to treat coldly, scornfully or with contempt
Synonym: ostracize, disregard

Antonym: praise, regard
Sentence: He snubbed his childhood friend by not inviting her to the wedding.

1544. APPLICABLE - *[spell]*- A P P L I C A B L E
Definition: capable of being put to practical use
Synonym: relevant, pertinent
Antonym: irrelevant,
Sentence: The coupon was not applicable to her purchase.

1545. LOOT - *[spell]*- L O O T
Definition: goods taken away from an enemy, a captured city, etc.
Synonym: booty, haul
Antonym:
Sentence: The soldiers looted the enemy camp.

1546. GILDING - *[spell]*- G I L D I N G
Definition: a thin layer of gold with which something is decorated
Synonym: embellishment, decoration
Antonym:
Sentence: The gilding on the cover of the book was beautiful.

1547. CHARIOT - *[spell]*- C H A R I O T
Definition: a carriage pulled by horses
Synonym: carriage, buggy
Antonym:
Sentence: The emperor was driven through the streets by a horse-drawn chariot.

1548. ELAPSE - *[spell]*- E L A P S E
Definition: slip away
Synonym: expire, transpire
Antonym:
Sentence: She did not realize how much time had elapsed until she looked at the clock.

1549. NOMAD - *[spell]*- N O M A D
Definition: a member of a tribe that moves from place to place
Synonym: vagabond, migrant
Antonym:
Sentence: He considered himself a nomad, never living in any place more than a few weeks.

1550. RECEIPT - *[spell]*- R E C E I P T
Definition: a written statement that money, a package, or letter etc., has been received

Synonym:
Antonym:
Sentence: She received a receipt for the items she purchased at the store.

1551. JITTERY - *[spell]*- J I T T E R Y
Definition: nervous
Synonym: anxious, apprehensive
Antonym: calm, collected
Sentence: Because her husband had just left for the airport, she felt jittery when she saw the plane crash on TV.

1552. RAPTOR - *[spell]*- R A P T O R
Definition: a bird of prey
Synonym:
Antonym:
Sentence: The zoo had a collection of raptors from around the world.

1553. CARTRIDGE - *[spell]*- CARTRIDGE
Definition: case used to hold gunpowder, bullets or other material for use in a mechanical device
Synonym: capsule, case
Antonym:
Sentence: The cartridge held several spare bullets.

1554. DESIROUS - *[spell]*- D E S I R O U S
Definition: showing a wanting or longing
Synonym: wishful, aspiring
Antonym: apathetic, indifferent
Sentence: After working so many long hours, she was desirous of a vacation.

1555. COLLABORATE - *[spell]*- C O L L A B O R A T E
Definition: to work together
Synonym: collude, cooperate
Antonym: disagree, divorce
Sentence: The students decided to collaborate on their project.

1556. BARBED - *[spell]*- B A R B E D
Definition: having something that wounds or stings
Synonym: stinging, piercing
Antonym: dull
Sentence: The barbed tail of the creature was a dangerous weapon.

1557. WOOZY - *[spell]*- W O O Z Y
Definition: confused or muddled
Synonym: dizzy, puzzled

Antonym: certain, clear
Sentence: She felt woozy after hearing the terrible news.

1558. NESTLE - *[spell]*- N E S T L E
Definition: settle oneself comfortably or cozily
Synonym: cuddle, burrow
Antonym:
Sentence: The puppy nestled up to its owner on the couch.

1559. PRIMARILY - *[spell]*- P R I M A R I L Y
Definition: chiefly or principally
Synonym: mainly, generally
Antonym:
Sentence: She volunteered primarily because it made her feel good about herself.

1560. ANTIDOTE - *[spell]*- A N T I D O T E
Definition: medicine that counteracts poison
Synonym: remedy, cure
Antonym:
Sentence: The antidote she received at the hospital saved her life.

1561. HOMEWARD - *[spell]*- H O M E W A R D
Definition: toward home
Synonym:
Antonym:
Sentence: He was happy to at last make the homeward journey.

1562. CLIMATE - *[spell]*- C L I M A T E
Definition: the kind of weather a place has
Synonym: temperature, weather
Antonym:
Sentence: The island was known for its tropical climate.

1563. PROVERB - *[spell]*- P R O V E R B
Definition: a short, wise saying
Synonym: maxim, axiom
Antonym:
Sentence: "Don't count your chickens before they hatch" is a well-known proverb.

1564. ZESTY - *[spell]*- Z E S T Y
Definition: full of agreeable flavor
Synonym: peppy, poignant
Antonym:
Sentence: The zesty dressing was the perfect complement to the salad.

1565. INACTION - *[spell]*- I N A C T I O N
Definition: idleness
Synonym: passivity, stagnation
Antonym: action
Sentence: Her inaction in response to her daughter's attitude was appalling.

1566. ACCENT - *[spell]*- A C C E N T
Definition: a change in pitch or stress when pronouncing a word or syllable
Synonym: stress, significance
Antonym: unimportance
Sentence: In some languages, the accent on a certain syllable can change the meaning of the word.

1567. HEARTBROKEN - *[spell]*- H E A R T B R O K E N
Definition: crushed by sorrow or grief
Synonym: melancholy, doleful
Antonym: joyful, happy
Sentence: He felt heartbroken after the death of his mother.

1568. VISIBILITY - *[spell]*- V I S I B I L I T Y
Definition: condition or quality of being seeable
Synonym: clarity, perceptibility
Antonym:
Sentence: Because of the fog, visibility was low.

1569. PRACTITIONER - *[spell]*- P R A C T I T I O N E R
Definition: person engaged in a certain profession
Synonym: exponent, expounder
Antonym:
Sentence: She had been a practitioner of law for nearly a decade.

1570. SIMPLIFY - *[spell]*- S I M P L I F Y
Definition: to make easy to do or understand
Synonym: facilitate, elucidate
Antonym: confuse, obscure
Sentence: The teacher tried to simplify the concept for her students.

1571. WARINESS - *[spell]*- W A R I N E S S
Definition: the state of being watchful
Synonym: caution, alertness
Antonym: carelessness, inattention
Sentence: Her wariness of her boyfriend was due to several hurtful past relationships.

1572. HERITAGE - *[spell]* - H E R I T A G E
Definition: what is handed down from one generation to the next
Synonym: inheritance, legacy
Antonym:
Sentence: An important part of her heritage was her religious beliefs.

1573. PERFECTIBILITY - *[spell]* - P E R F E C T I B I L I T Y
Definition: capable of becoming or being made perfect
Synonym: improveability
Antonym:
Sentence: We often had long debates about the perfectibility of human nature.

1574. STINGY - *[spell]* - S T I N G Y
Definition: unwilling to spend or give money
Synonym: frugal, miserly
Antonym: extravagant, generous
Sentence: The father was always stingy when it came to buying clothes for his kids.

1575. MONUMENTAL - *[spell]* - M O N U M E N T A L
Definition: having to do with a structure set up to commemorate a person or event, etc.
Synonym: historic, significant
Antonym: common, insignificant
Sentence: The passing of the legislation was monumental.

1576. GARBAGE - *[spell]* - G A R B A G E
Definition: scraps of food to be thrown away
Synonym: rubbish, trash
Antonym:
Sentence: The leftovers were considered garbage and were thrown away.

1577. FEY - *[spell]* - F E Y
Definition: giving an impression of vague otherworldliness
Synonym: enchanted
Antonym:
Sentence: Irish folklore is full of fairies and other fey creatures.

1578. ORDINARILY - *[spell]* - O R D I N A R I L Y
Definition: usually, regularly
Synonym: commonly, customarily
Antonym: rarely, infrequently
Sentence: She ordinarily did not go on dates with coworkers, but she made an exception for him.

1579. TOTALITY - *[spell]*- T O T A L I T Y
Definition: the complete amount
Synonym: entirety, completeness
Antonym: partial, component
Sentence: The totality of the destruction by the earthquake was yet uncertain.

1580. EXISTENCE - *[spell]*- E X I S T E N C E
Definition: being
Synonym: presence, reality
Antonym:
Sentence: She was relieved when she learned of the existence of a doctor who could treat her rare condition.

1581. INTERCHANGEABLE - *[spell]*- I N T E R C H A N G E A B L E
Definition: capable of being used or put in place of each other
Synonym: identical, transposable
Antonym: different, dissimilar
Sentence: The two parts on the car are essentially interchangeable.

1582. TWITTERY - *[spell]*- T W I T T E R Y
Definition: shaky
Synonym: tremulous, quivery
Antonym: steady, solid
Sentence: She was twittery after receiving her first kiss.

1583. UNDERGARMENT - *[spell]*- U N D E R G A R M E N T
Definition: clothes worn under an outer layer of clothing
Synonym: underwear
Antonym:
Sentence: After running home in the rainstorm, even her undergarments were soaked.

1584. FORBIDDEN - *[spell]*- F O R B I D D E N
Definition: not allowed
Synonym: banned, taboo
Antonym: allowed, approved
Sentence: Criticism of the government was strictly forbidden.

1585. LEAFLET - *[spell]*- L E A F L E T
Definition: small, flat booklet of papers folded together
Synonym: booklet, flyer
Antonym:
Sentence: The members of the church passed out leaflets to passersby on the street.

1586. INTRODUCTION - *[spell]*- I N T R O D U C T I O N
Definition: a bringing into acquaintance with
Synonym: debut, launch
Antonym:
Sentence: He was eager for the introduction of his girlfriend to his parents.

1587. INEXPRESSIBLE - *[spell]*- I N E X P R E S S I B L E
Definition: beyond being put into words
Synonym: unspeakable, inconceivable
Antonym:
Sentence: Her grief over the death of her loved one was inexpressible.

1588. GENUINE - *[spell]*- G E N U I N E
Definition: actually being what it seems or is claimed to be true
Synonym: authentic, real
Antonym: phony, bogus
Sentence: She bought what she thought was a genuine leather bag from the street vendor.

1589. HARDEN - *[spell]*- H A R D E N
Definition: solidify
Synonym: cement, calcify
Antonym: soften
Sentence: The melted chocolate hardened as it cooled

1590. REPRISE - *[spell]*- R E P R I S E
Definition: a renewal or resumption of an action
Synonym: repetition, reiterate
Antonym:
Sentence: Their relationship was given an unexpected reprise when they met again years later.

1591. SCATHE - *[spell]*- S C A T H E
Definition: blast or sear with abuse
Synonym: blister, attack
Antonym: mend, praise
Sentence: The newspaper scathed the politician for his actions.

1592. VISUALIZE - *[spell]*- V I S U A L I Z E
Definition: to form a mental picture of
Synonym: picture, dream
Antonym:
Sentence: He had a hard time visualizing what his renovated kitchen would look like.

1593. MEDALLION - *[spell]*- M E D A L L I O N
Definition: a large medal
Synonym: emblem, ornament
Antonym:
Sentence: He was given a medallion for winning the competition.

1594. SPRINKLING - *[spell]*- S P R I N K L I N G
Definition: a small quantity scattered here and there
Synonym: scattering, hint
Antonym:
Sentence: She added just a sprinkling of seasoning to the recipe.

1595. VOUCH - *[spell]*- V O U C H
Definition: to be responsible for or give a guarantee for
Synonym: corroborate, assert
Antonym:
Sentence: The man vouched for his friend whom he recommended to his boss.

1596. ARCHENEMY - *[spell]*- A R C H E N E M Y
Definition: a primary enemy
Synonym: nemesis, antagonist
Antonym: ally, partner
Sentence: The comic often featured a battle between the superhero and his archenemy.

1597. SECURITY - *[spell]*- S E C U R I T Y
Definition: freedom from danger
Synonym: safety, protection
Antonym: danger, peril
Sentence: She married solely for financial security.

1598. COMMUTE - *[spell]*- C O M M U T E
Definition: travel regularly over a distance
Synonym: travel, drive
Antonym:
Sentence: He had to commute an hour to work each way.

1599. AROUSAL - *[spell]*- A R O U S AL
Definition: being stirred to action or excited
Synonym: awaken, inflame
Antonym: sleep, sleeping
Sentence: His arousal from sleep was caused by the crash outside his window.

1600. ORGANIZE - *[spell]*- O R G A N I Z E
Definition: to put into working order
Synonym: arrange
Antonym:
Sentence: She decided to organize all the shoes in her closet

Medium Words Exercise - 7

1601. SETBACK - *[spell]*- S E T B A C K
Definition: a check to progress
Synonym: reversal
Antonym:
Sentence: They experienced a minor setback in their travel plans when they got a flat tire.

1602. CONFERENCE - *[spell]*- C O N F E R E N C E
Definition: meeting of people to discuss a particular subject
Synonym: consultation, discussion
Antonym:
Sentence: They attended a conference for accountants.

1603. UNFORGETTABLE - *[spell]*- U N F O R G E T T A B L E
Definition: always remembered
Synonym: extraordinary, memorable
Antonym: forgettable
Sentence: Her goal was to make the event unforgettable.

1604. DISAGREEABLE - *[spell]*- D I S A G R E E A B L E
Definition: not to one's liking
Synonym: distasteful, objectionable
Antonym: agreeable, welcome
Sentence: She found the menu at the restaurant disagreeable.

1605. BODILY - *[spell]*- B O D I L Y
Definition: of or relating to the body
Synonym: physical
Antonym: nonphysical
Sentence: In moments of extreme fear, people may lose control of their bodily functions.

1606. INTEGRITY - *[spell]*- I N T E G R I T Y
Definition: honesty or sincerity
Synonym: principles, morality
Antonym: dishonesty, disgrace
Sentence: Amid the scandal, he was the only person in the office with clear integrity.

1607. VIGIL - *[spell]*- V I G I L
Definition: watch
Synonym: patrol, observance
Antonym:
Sentence: The mother kept a vigil for her son late into the night.

1608. FORGIVENESS - *[spell]*- F O R G I V E N E S S
Definition: the act of giving up a wish for punishment
Synonym: pardon, absolution
Antonym: blame, censure
Sentence: She was overcome with guilt and begged for forgiveness.

1609. BIRTHMARK - *[spell]*- B I R T H MA R K
Definition: a spot or mark on the skin that has been present since birth
Synonym:
Antonym:
Sentence: She had a birthmark on her right shoulder in the shape of a heart.

1610. HINDMOST - *[spell]*- H I N D M O S T
Definition: farthest back
Synonym: concluding, rear
Antonym: first, leading
Sentence: The hindmost student in line closed the door to the classroom.

1611. SIGNIFY - *[spell]*- S I G N I F Y
Definition: to be a sign of
Synonym: indicate, convey
Antonym: conceal, withhold
Sentence: The fact that his boss gave him the assignment signified her trust in him.

1612. WHEEZE - *[spell]*- W H E E Z E
Definition: to breathe with difficulty, especially with a whistling sound
Synonym: rasp, gasp
Antonym:
Sentence: After running several miles, he began to wheeze.

1613. INSIGNIFICANCE - *[spell]*- I N S I G N I F I C A N C E
Definition: unimportance
Synonym: inconsequence, nothingness
Antonym: importance, significance
Sentence: He couldn't help feeling his own insignificance when in the crowded city.

1614. TERRACE - *[spell]*- T E R R A C E
Definition: a paved outdoor space adjoining a house
Synonym: porch, deck
Antonym:
Sentence: They decided to have dinner out on the terrace.

1615. DISCOURAGEMENT - *[spell]*- D I S C O U R A G E M E NT
Definition: lack of spirit or confidence
Synonym: demoralization, disheartenment
Antonym: encouragement
Sentence: Feeling discouragement, he gave up on learning to play guitar.

1616. PARTICULAR- *[spell]*- P A R T I C U L A R
Definition: considered by itself or apart from others
Synonym: notable, uncommon
Antonym: common, general
Sentence: He was given that particular job because of his unique qualifications.

1617. HATCHET - *[spell]*- H A T C H E T
Definition: a small ax with a short handle
Synonym:
Antonym:
Sentence: His attempt to cut firewood with only a hatchet was unsuccessful.

1618. ADHESIVE- *[spell]*- A D H E S I V E
Definition: a substance used to make two things stick together
Synonym: glue, tape
Antonym:
Sentence: He used the adhesive to hang the pictures on the wall of his office.

1619. SLOSH - *[spell]*- S L O S H
Definition: to splash in or through slush, mud, or water
Synonym: splash, wade
Antonym:
Sentence: She sloshed through the snow to get to her car.

1620. SHAMEFUL - *[spell]*- S H A M E F U L
Definition: causing a painful feeling of having done something wrong or improper
Synonym: disgraceful, disreputable
Antonym: honorable, reputable
Sentence: His actions were shameful to his entire family.

1621. CONSUMABLE - *[spell]*- C O N S U M A B L E
Definition: something that may be used up
Synonym:
Antonym:
Sentence: Consumable goods sold out quickly in the wake of the storm.

1622. PREOCCUPATION- *[spell]*- P R E O C C U P A T I O N
Definition: condition of having all of one's attention taken up
Synonym: absorption, engrossment
Antonym: apathy, disinterestedness
Sentence: Her preoccupation with her appearance was due to low self-esteem.

1623. BUSHEL - *[spell]*- B U S H E L
Definition: a large quantity
Synonym: heaps, loads
Antonym: minimum, trace
Sentence: In the summer, we often buy bushels of vegetables from the farmers' market.

1624. STUTTER - *[spell]*- S T U T T E R
Definition: repeat the same sound in an effort to speak
Synonym: stammer, sputter
Antonym:
Sentence: He was so nervous about giving the speech that he began to stutter when he got up on stage.

1625. GOODWILL - *[spell]*- G O O D W I L L
Definition: kindly or friendly feeling
Synonym: generosity, kindness
Antonym: malevolence
Sentence: She taught her children to feel goodwill toward all people.

1626. REGIMENT- *[spell]*- R E G I M E N T
Definition: a military unit consisting of several battalions or squadrons
Synonym:
Antonym:
Sentence: The regiment was stationed on the edge of town.

1627. COAUTHOR - *[spell]*- C O A U T H O R
Definition: a person who works together with another writer
Synonym:
Antonym:
Sentence: The coauthor of the novel unfortunately received less recognition than his partner.

1628. IMPOSSIBILITY - *[spell]*- I M P O S S I B I L I T Y
Definition: quality or condition of being something that cannot be or happen
Synonym: hopelessness, futility
Antonym: feasibility, practicality
Sentence: The reconciliation of the couple seemed an impossibility to their friends.

1629. EXAMINATION - *[spell]*- E X A M I N A T I O N
Definition: a looking closely at
Synonym: inspection, investigation
Antonym:
Sentence: Her examination of the diary revealed it had belonged to her mother.

1630. TRICKSTER - *[spell]*- T R I C K S T E R
Definition: a person who cheats or deceives
Synonym: prankster, deceiver
Antonym:
Sentence: Because he was known as a trickster, people were always waiting for his next prank.

1631. MIDRIFF - *[spell]*- M I D R I F F
Definition: the area separating the chest from the abdomen
Synonym:
Antonym:
Sentence: The short shirt exposed some of her midriff.

1632. FEEBLE - *[spell]*- F E E B L E
Definition: lacking strength
Synonym: weak, fragile
Antonym: strong, hearty
Sentence: She made a feeble effort to complete her chores that weekend.

1633. NIFTY - *[spell]*- N I F T Y
Definition: attractive or stylish
Synonym: dandy, neat
Antonym: inferior, poor
Sentence: He found the new tool set to be pretty nifty.

1634. TRANSITIONAL - *[spell]*- T R A N S I T I O N A L
Definition: changing or passing from one condition, place, thing, etc. to another
Synonym: changeable, mercurial
Antonym: steadfast, constant

Sentence: The company was in a transitional state as a new leadership team took over.

1635. INTENSITY - *[spell]*- I N T E N S I T Y
Definition: the quality of being very great or strong
Synonym: passion, force
Antonym: calmness, weakness
Sentence: The intensity of his presence caught everyone's attention.

1636. IMPOVERISH - *[spell]*- I M P O V E R I S H
Definition: make very poor
Synonym: bankrupt, deplete
Antonym: enrich
Sentence: He was impoverished after he lost his job.

1637. RIDICULOUS - *[spell]*- R I D I C U L O U S
Definition: deserving to be made fun of or laughed at
Synonym: absurd, bizarre
Antonym: credible, serious
Sentence: Her mismatched outfit looked simply ridiculous.

1638. LOOM - *[spell]*- L O O M
Definition: appear dimly or vaguely, especially as a large, threatening shape
Synonym: hover, tower
Antonym:
Sentence: He seemed to loom in the corner of the room, watching everyone.

1639. CLOWNISH - *[spell]*- C L O W N I S H
Definition: like a silly person
Synonym: churlish, loutish
Antonym: sophisticated
Sentence: His clownish attitude made him seem younger than he really was.

1640. REVISION- *[spell]*- R E V I S I O N
Definition: act or work of changing or altering
Synonym: modification, reworking
Antonym:
Sentence: The student did several revisions of her paper before turning it in.

1641. AFLOAT- *[spell]*- A F L O A T
Definition: floating in the water or in the air
Synonym: adrift, drifting

Antonym: sinking, anchored
Sentence: They found the lost swimsuit afloat near the dock.

1642. REPUTATION- *[spell]*- R E P U T A T I O N
Definition: what people think and say about the character of a person or thing
Synonym: character, repute
Antonym:
Sentence: Over the years, he had acquired a reputation as a generous and kind individual.

1643. TOKEN - *[spell]*- T O K E N
Definition: mark or sign
Synonym: symbol, expression
Antonym:
Sentence: He gave his girlfriend a necklace as a token of his affection.

1644. PREMEDITATION- *[spell]*- P R E M E D I T A T I O N
Definition: previous deliberation or planning
Synonym:
Antonym:
Sentence: The trial revealed that he acted with premeditation, which made it a more serious offense.

1645. BACKLASH - *[spell]*- B A C K L A S H
Definition: a sudden adverse reaction caused by strong emotion
Synonym: recoil, counteraction
Antonym:
Sentence: Her ideas were controversial and there was widespread backlash.

1646. COMFORTABLE - *[spell]*- C O M F O R T A B L E
Definition: allowing a person to be relaxed
Synonym: comfy, cozy
Antonym: uncomfortable
Sentence: When she got home, she took off her shoes and put on her pajamas so she could be more comfortable.

1647. RECREATE- *[spell]*- R E C R E A T E
Definition: refresh with games, pastimes, exercises, etc.
Synonym: divert, entertain
Antonym:
Sentence: The children were given time to recreate in the afternoon.

1648. WORRISOME - *[spell]*- W O R R I S O M E
Definition: causing to suffer from disturbing thoughts

Synonym: alarming, bothersome

Antonym:

Sentence: The mother had a tendency to feel worrisome about her children.

1649. OBSERVATION- *[spell]*- O B S E R V A T I O N

Definition: act, habit, or power of seeing and noting

Synonym: scrutiny, surveillance

Antonym: ignorance, neglect

Sentence: He made the observation that she was acting strange.

1650. SPINELESS- *[spell]*- S P I N E L E S S

Definition: having no backbone or courage

Synonym: fearful, cowardly

Antonym:

Sentence: He earned a reputation as being spineless when he was unable to discipline his teenage children.

1651. MEDIUM - *[spell]*- M E D I U M

Definition: person through whom messages from spirits of the dead are supposedly sent to the living

Synonym:

Antonym:

Sentence: The medium claimed to be able to communicate with the spirits of the dead.

1652. PERSONALIZE- *[spell]*- P E R S O N A L I Z E

Definition: to make individualized

Synonym: individualize, externalize

Antonym: conform, follow

Sentence: The student tried to personalize her dormitory by adding decorations.

1653. SCATTER - *[spell]*- S C A T T ER

Definition: throw here and there

Synonym: disperse, distribute

Antonym:

Sentence: The wind scattered the petals of the flower throughout the yard.

1654. DEFORMITY - *[spell]*- D E F O R M I T Y

Definition: part that is not properly formed

Synonym: abnormality, defect

Antonym: perfection, shapeliness

Sentence: The puppy was born with an obvious deformity because it was missing one eye.

1655. TWADDLE - *[spell]*- T W A D D L E
Definition: silly, feeble, tiresome talking or writing
Synonym: nonsense, balderdash
Antonym: sense, truth
Sentence: The girl was tired of listening to her friend's mindless twaddle.

1656. SAVORY - *[spell]*- S A V O R Y
Definition: pleasing in taste or smell
Synonym: delicious, appetizing
Antonym: bland, flavorless
Sentence: The savory smells coming from the kitchen suggested a delicious dinner was in the works.

1657. MERIT - *[spell]*- M E R I T
Definition: worth or value
Synonym: dignities, excellence
Antonym: disadvantage, dishonor
Sentence: He was hired based on his many merits.

1658. EXPLOSIVE - *[spell]*- E X P L O S I V E
Definition: of or for blowing up
Synonym:
Antonym:
Sentence: She had to be careful, as the chemicals were explosive.

1659. RECORDING- *[spell]*- R E C O R D I N G
Definition: the original transcription of any sound or combination of sounds
Synonym:
Antonym:
Sentence: The police officer made a recording of his interview with the suspect.

1660. PRACTICABILITY- *[spell]*- P R A C T I C A B I L I T Y
Definition: quality of being something that can be put into practice
Synonym: usefulness, convenience
Antonym: useless, disadvantage
Sentence: The teaching methodology was known for its practicability.

1661. IMMORTAL - *[spell]*- I M M O R T A L
Definition: living forever
Synonym: imperishable, eternal
Antonym: ephemeral, temporal
Sentence: The witch cast a spell that would make her immortal.

1662. FACET - *[spell]*- F A C E T
Definition: one of many aspects of something
Synonym: feature, part
Antonym:
Sentence: An important facet of her troubles was her lack of funding.

1663. PROBABILITY- *[spell]*- P R O B A B I L I T Y
Definition: quality or fact of being likely to happen
Synonym: possibility, feasibility
Antonym: certainty
Sentence: There was a high probability of a snowstorm during the week.

1664. SKIM - *[spell]*- S K I M
Definition: remove from the top of a liquid
Synonym: separate, scoop
Antonym:
Sentence: After making the broth, she skimmed the fat off the top.

1665. SAVOR - *[spell]*- S A V O R
Definition: a taste or smell
Synonym: scent, taste
Antonym:
Sentence: The savor of the dish was unlike anything he had experienced before.

1666. FLUNK - *[spell]*- F L U N K
Definition: fail
Synonym: flop, bomb
Antonym: success, achievement
Sentence: She flunked her exam even though she spent hours studying.

1667. GEOLOGY - *[spell]*- G E O L O G Y
Definition: science that deals with the composition of the earth's crust
Synonym:
Antonym:
Sentence: Because he loved learning about rocks and the earth's makeup, he decided to study geology.

1668. REBUFF- *[spell]*- R E B U F F
Definition: blunt or sudden check to a person who makes advances
Synonym: rebuke, rejection
Antonym: praise, compliment
Sentence: Feeling confident as he approached her, he was surprised when she rebuffed him.

1669. KNURL - *[spell]*- K N U R L
Definition: small projection or protuberance
Synonym: hump, lump
Antonym: depression
Sentence: The knurl on his finger was a wart.

1670. PROVINCIAL- *[spell]*- P R O V I N C I A L
Definition: a person who lives in or comes from a place far from a big city
Synonym: rustic, yokel
Antonym: cosmopolitan, sophisticate
Sentence: Since moving to New York, she has become self-conscious about her provincial views.

1671. FIXATION - *[spell]*- F I X A T I O N
Definition: an abnormal attachment or preoccupation
Synonym: obsession, preoccupation
Antonym: disinterestedness
Sentence: Her fixation with her appearance was abnormal.

1672. INCOMPLETION - *[spell]*- I N C O M P L E T I O N
Definition: unfinished condition
Synonym:
Antonym:
Sentence: The student received a zero because of her incompletion of the work.

1673. MISCONCEPTION - *[spell]*- M I S C O N C E P T I O N
Definition: a mistaken idea or behavior
Synonym: misunderstanding, misinterpretation
Antonym: certainty, surety
Sentence: There are many misconceptions about different cultures.

1674. MORSEL - *[spell]*- M O R S E L
Definition: a small portion of food
Synonym: crumb, piece
Antonym:
Sentence: The beggar asked for just a morsel of food.

1675. SHACKLE - *[spell]*- S H A C K L E
Definition: a metal band fastened around the ankle or wrists of a prisoner, slave, etc.
Synonym: handcuff, restraint
Antonym:
Sentence: The prisoner was kept in a cell with shackles around his wrists.

1676. CONFUSION - *[spell]*- C O N F U S I O N
Definition: act of throwing into disorder
Synonym: bewilderment, disorientation
Antonym: order, clarity
Sentence: In her confusion, she completely failed to follow directions.

1677. NAMELESS - *[spell]*- N A M E L E S S
Definition: having no name
Synonym: unknown, anonymous
Antonym: designated, distinguished
Sentence: The soldier, though nameless, was recognized for his bravery.

1678. LOUSY - *[spell]*- L O U S Y
Definition: of low quality
Synonym: poor, shoddy
Antonym: superior, excellent
Sentence: He soon found the cheap car was a lousy one.

1679. ASCEND - *[spell]*- A S C E N D
Definition: to go up
Synonym: escalate, climb
Antonym: descend, drop
Sentence: After ascending the stairs to the top level, she went out onto the balcony.

1680. THOROUGHBRED - *[spell]*- T H O R O U G H B R E D
Definition: of a pure breed or stock
Synonym: pure, unmixed
Antonym: mutt, impure
Sentence: The farm was known for its thoroughbred horses.

1681. PIPSQUEAK- *[spell]*- P I P S Q U E A K
Definition: person who is small or unimportant
Synonym: twerp, shrimp
Antonym:
Sentence: The children in class called him a pipsqueak because of his small stature.

1682. REORGANIZATION- *[spell]*- R E O R G A N I Z A T I O N
Definition: act or process of putting in order again
Synonym: restructuring, rearrangement
Antonym:
Sentence: The reorganization of the leadership of the company proved to be beneficial.

1683. IMPENDING - *[spell]*- I M P E N D I N G
Definition: likely to soon happen
Synonym: forthcoming, approaching
Antonym:
Sentence: The couple began making plans for their impending engagement.

1684. DAZZLING - *[spell]*- D A Z Z L I N G
Definition: splendid
Synonym: sensational, stunning
Antonym: underwhelming, ordinary
Sentence: The intricate sculpture in the gallery was dazzling.

1685. FAIN - *[spell]*- F A I N
Definition: gladly
Synonym: willingly, eagerly
Antonym: disinclined, unwilling
Sentence: She would fain have helped him move into his new home, if only he had asked.

1686. GRUDGE - *[spell]*- G R U D G E
Definition: feeling of anger or dislike because of a real or imagined wrong
Synonym: resentment, grievance
Antonym:
Sentence: He had held a grudge against her for ten years.

1687. SHRUNKEN - *[spell]*- S H R U N K E N
Definition: grown smaller or shriveled
Synonym: contracted, diminished
Antonym: enlarged
Sentence: Over time, the woman seemed to have become shrunken with age.

1688. SAUCY - *[spell]*- S A U C Y
Definition: showing lack of respect
Synonym: impertinent, cheeky
Antonym: respectful, polite
Sentence: The child's saucy comments earned her punishment.

1689. FLAVORFUL - *[spell]*- F L A V O R F U L
Definition: having a good taste
Synonym: savory
Antonym: bland
Sentence: She found the meal at the restaurant to be quite flavorful.

1690. UNFORTUNATE - *[spell]*- U N F O R T U N A T E
Definition: not lucky
Synonym: adverse, deplorable
Antonym: lucky, fortuitous
Sentence: An unfortunate accident caused her to be paralyzed.

1691. CLEANLINESS - *[spell]*- C L E A N L I N E S S
Definition: habitually being free from dirt or filth
Synonym: freshness, sanitation
Antonym: filthy, soiled
Sentence: Cleanliness was one of his best habits.

1692. DEMOCRACY - *[spell]*- D E M O C R A C Y
Definition: government run by the people who live under it
Synonym: republic
Antonym:
Sentence: After being a dictatorship for decades, the country made the move toward democracy.

1693. EXCLAMATORY - *[spell]*- E X C L A M A T O R Y
Definition: expressing something with surprise or strong feeling
Synonym:
Antonym:
Sentence: Her exclamatory remark revealed her surprise.

1694. PERSONA- *[spell]*- P E R S O N A
Definition: the social front a person presents to others
Synonym:
Antonym:
Sentence: People saw her as an extrovert, but that was simply her on-screen persona.

1695. ORIGINALITY- *[spell]*- O R I G I N A L I T Y
Definition: ability to do, make, or think of something new
Synonym: inventiveness, creativeness
Antonym: unoriginality, banality
Sentence: The artist was recognized for her originality.

1696. DIALOGUE - *[spell]*- D I A L O G U E
Definition: a conversation between two or more people
Synonym: discussion, conference
Antonym:
Sentence: The two men struck up an interesting dialogue at the social gathering.

1697. NOURISHMENT - *[spell]*- N O U R I S H M E N T
Definition: food
Synonym: nutrient, sustenance
Antonym:
Sentence: He was exhausted because he had not had sleep and proper nourishment.

1698. BEWARE - *[spell]*- B E W A R E
Definition: to be wary
Synonym: caution, heed
Antonym: invite, risk
Sentence: He was warned to beware of his coworker.

1699. SHIVERY - *[spell]*- S H I V E R Y
Definition: quivering from cold, fear, etc.
Synonym: tremulous, quivering
Antonym:
Sentence: She felt shivery from the cold.

1700. COSMETIC - *[spell]*- C O S M E T I C
Definition: meant to improve superficially
Synonym: corrective, restorative
Antonym:
Sentence: After purchasing the home, he made several cosmetic improvements.

Medium Words Exercise - 8

1701. PNEUMONIA - *[spell]* - P N E U M O N I A
Definition: disease in which the lungs become inflamed
Synonym:
Antonym:
Sentence: She caught pneumonia and had to go to the hospital.

1702. CANDIDATE - *[spell]* - C A N D I D A T E
Definition: a person who seeks an office
Synonym: applicant, aspirant
Antonym:
Sentence: There were several very qualified candidates for the job.

1703. MELODIOUS - *[spell]* - M E L O D I O U S
Definition: harmonious
Synonym: melodic, musical
Antonym: discordant, inharmonious
Sentence: Her melodious singing was soothing to him.

1704. ATHLETIC - *[spell]* - A T H L E T I C
Definition: relating to a person who is trained to do physical exercises
Synonym: active, vigorous
Antonym:
Sentence: Being so athletic, he was good at almost all sports.

1705. K E T T L E - *[spell]* - K E T T L E
Definition: a metal container for boiling liquids or cooking other food
Synonym: pot
Antonym:
Sentence: She cooked a large quantity of soup in the kettle.

1706. UTILITY - *[spell]* - U T I L I T Y
Definition: the state of being useful
Synonym: serviceable, advantageous
Antonym: useless, hindrance
Sentence: He valued the utility of his pocketknife.

1707. ALCOVE - *[spell]* - A L C O V E
Definition: a hollow space in a wall

Synonym: compartment, niche
Antonym:
Sentence: The children used the alcove in their room to create a fort.

1708. INSIGNIA - *[spell]*- I N S I G N I A
Definition: medal, badge or other distinguishing mark
Synonym: badge, symbol
Antonym:
Sentence: The insignia on the soldier's uniform showed he was a lieutenant.

1709. VARIATION - *[spell]*- V A R I A T I O N
Definition: a differing in condition, degree, etc.
Synonym: difference, deviation
Antonym: agreement, harmony
Sentence: There were many variations within the one species of flower.

1710. ANALYTICAL - *[spell]*- A N A L Y T I C A L
Definition: relating to the act of studying something complex by breaking it into elements
Synonym: interpretive, diagnostic
Antonym: illogical
Sentence: Because he had such an analytical mind, he was very successful in math and science.

1711. INTERNAL - *[spell]*- I N T E R N A L
Definition: on the inside
Synonym: interior
Antonym: external, outer
Sentence: There was an internal investigation into the fraud within the company.

1712. SCAPEGRACE - *[spell]*- S C A P E G R A C E
Definition: a reckless, good-for-nothing person
Synonym: scamp, rascal
Antonym:
Sentence: She regarded her irresponsible father as a scapegrace.

1713. DEPOPULATE - *[spell]*- D E P O P U L A T E
Definition: reduce the inhabitants of
Synonym: desolate, abandon
Antonym:
Sentence: The lack of workable land caused the people to depopulate the area.

1714. PENOLOGY - *[spell]*- P E N O L O G Y
Definition: science of punishment for crimes and management of prisons
Synonym:
Antonym:
Sentence: The lawyer studied penology to better understand the legal system.

1715. TEMPERANCE - *[spell]*- T E M P E R A N C E
Definition: a being moderate in action, speech, habits, etc.
Synonym: moderation
Antonym: excessiveness, immoderation
Sentence: His temperance in eating at the party was due to his recent decision to diet.

1716. CENSURE - *[spell]*- C E N S U R E
Definition: expression of disapproval
Synonym: condemn, rebuke
Antonym: praise, approve
Sentence: His actions caused him to be censured by Congress.

1717. MIRACULOUS - *[spell]*- M I R A C U L O U S
Definition: constituting of a miracle
Synonym: spectacular, incredible
Antonym: ordinary, mending
Sentence: It seemed miraculous that he had survived the accident.

1718. SERIALIZE - *[spell]*- S E R I A L I Z E
Definition: to publish, broadcast, or televise in a series of installments
Synonym:
Antonym:
Sentence: The producers decided to serialize what was supposed to be a TV movie.

1719. FLOTATION - *[spell]*- F L O T A T I O N
Definition: act or process of floating
Synonym:
Antonym:
Sentence: Passengers on the ship were directed toward the flotation devices in case of emergency.

1720. BESIEGE - *[spell]*- B E S I E G E
Definition: to surround by armed forces
Synonym: blockage, beleaguer
Antonym:
Sentence: The army was able to besiege their enemies and, as a result, won the battle.

1721. LINGO - *[spell]*- L I N G O
Definition: language, especially foreign speech or language
Synonym:
Antonym:
Sentence: She did not speak the lingo of that area of the country.

1722. SUMPTUOUS - *[spell]*- S U M P T U O U S
Definition: lavish and costly
Synonym: luxurious, extravagant
Antonym: simple, inferior
Sentence: He considered his wife's weekly manicure to be a sumptuous expense.

1723. RAPSCALLION - *[spell]*- R A P S C A L L I O N
Definition: a rascal or rogue
Synonym: knave, miscreant
Antonym:
Sentence: The village rapscallion delighted in making mischief.

1724. SLAPSTICK - *[spell]*- S L A P S T I C K
Definition: comedy full of rough play
Synonym: absurd, comical
Antonym:
Sentence: She found the slapstick humor of the play to be hilarious

1725. INCOGNITO - *[spell]*- I N C O G N I T O
Definition: with one's real name, rank, character, etc. concealed.
Synonym: disguised, hidden
Antonym:
Sentence: The politician preferred to travel incognito.

1726. CONJECTURAL - *[spell]*- C O N J E C T U R A L
Definition: inclined to make an opinion without evidence
Synonym: assumed, hypothetical
Antonym: factual, proven
Sentence: His conjectural story about her absence was based on mere speculation.

1727. GAPE - *[spell]*- G A P E
Definition: open wide
Synonym: gawk, stare
Antonym:
Sentence: The woman gaped at the strange garb of the woman on the subway.

1728. EMBELLISH - *[spell]*- E M B E L L I S H
Definition: make more interesting by adding imaginary details
Synonym: elaborate
Antonym:
Sentence: The child embellished his story about why he broke his mother's vase.

1729. GARNER - *[spell]*- G A R N E R
Definition: gather and store away
Synonym: collect, accumulate
Antonym: disperse, distribute
Sentence: Squirrels garner acorns for the winter.

1730. BUFFER - *[spell]*- B U F F E R
Definition: a person or thing that softens the shock of a blow
Synonym: cushion, bumper
Antonym:
Sentence: When the boy fell off the sofa, the pillows below him acted as a buffer.

1731. MASCULINE - *[spell]*- M A S C U L I N E
Definition: of men or boys
Synonym: manly, macho
Antonym:
Sentence: Football is often considered a masculine sport.

1732. ORACLE - *[spell]*- O R A C L E
Definition: a divine revelation or person who gives these revelations
Synonym: prophecy, augury
Antonym:
Sentence: She consulted the oracle for advice.

1733. FEAT - *[spell]*- F E A T
Definition: a great or unusual deed
Synonym: achievement, accomplishment
Antonym: defeat, failure
Sentence: It was quite a feat for the knight to slay the dragon.

1734. SACRAMENT - *[spell]*- S A C R A M E N T
Definition: of certain religious ceremonies of the Christian church
Synonym:
Antonym:
Sentence: Communion is a sacrament in the Catholic church.

1735. DENUDE - *[spell]*- D E N U D E
Definition: make bare

Synonym: disrobe, expose
Antonym: clothe, cover
Sentence: A wildfire left the forest completely denuded.

1736. GABBLE - *[spell]*- G A B B L E
Definition: talk rapidly with little or no meaning
Synonym: jabber, babble
Antonym: silence, quiet
Sentence: She began to zone out of her friend's mindless gabble.

1737. EMBEZZLE - *[spell]*- E M B E Z Z L E
Definition: steal
Synonym: filch, pilfer
Antonym:
Sentence: Over several years, the CEO embezzled thousands of dollars from his company.

1738. HYPOTHESIZE - *[spell]*- H Y P O T H E S I Z E
Definition: make an assumption or guess
Synonym: speculate, theorize
Antonym:
Sentence: He began to hypothesize about why she was late for the party.

1739. SUBTLETY - *[spell]*- S U B T L E T Y
Definition: quality of being faint or mysterious
Synonym: nuance, delicacy
Antonym:
Sentence: The author's subtlety when it came to her opinions made them easy to miss.

1740. DISSOCIATION - *[spell]*- D I S S O C I A T I O N
Definition: the act of separating
Synonym: disconnection, disjunction
Antonym: attachment
Sentence: The dissociation of those two organizations was followed by a scandal.

1741. TORRENT - *[spell]*- T O R R E N T
Definition: a violent, rushing stream of water
Synonym: downpour, cascade
Antonym:
Sentence: After all of the snow and ice melted, a torrent of water raced down the river.

1742. AFFRONT - *[spell]*- A F F R O N T
Definition: words or action that intentionally express disrespect

Synonym: slight, provocation
Antonym: flattery, praise
Sentence: His obvious decision to ignore her message was an affront which greatly hurt her
feelings.

1743. INHOSPITABLE - *[spell]*- I N H O S P I T A B L E
Definition: not making visitors comfortable
Synonym: unfriendly, unwelcoming
Antonym: friendly, welcoming
Sentence: His inhospitable attitude communicated that the visitors were unwelcome.

1744. UNACCUSTOMED - *[spell]*- U N A C C U S T O M E D
Definition: not familiar or usual
Synonym: strange, unfamiliar
Antonym: accustomed, prepared
Sentence: She was unaccustomed to the relaxed environment at her new job.

1745. GAUNTLET - *[spell]*- G A U N T L E T
Definition: a heavy glove worn as part of armor
Synonym:
Antonym:
Sentence: The knight put on his gauntlets to complete his armor and rode to battle.

1746. STAGGERING - *[spell]*- S T A G G E R I N G
Definition: enormous or immense
Synonym: astounding, overwhelming
Antonym: underwhelming, insignificant
Sentence: The jury found the number of crimes the man had committed was simply staggering.

1747. BUZZWORD - *[spell]*- B U Z Z W O R D
Definition: a familiar word used to impress an audience
Synonym:
Antonym:
Sentence: There are always buzzwords in practically every profession.

1748. MATURATION - *[spell]*- M A T U R A T I O N
Definition: a ripening or maturing
Synonym: development, advancement
Antonym: undeveloped
Sentence: The puppy had not yet reached full maturation.

1749. HUCKSTER - *[spell]*- H U C K S T E R
Definition: person who sells small items
Synonym: hawker, peddler
Antonym:
Sentence: The huckster stood on the corner selling artwork.

1750. ALLEGEDLY - *[spell]*- A L L E G E D L Y
Definition: according to what has been stated positively but without proof
Synonym: supposedly, purportedly
Antonym:
Sentence: Allegedly, the meeting will take place tomorrow, but no one has told us officially.

1751. INSTABILITY - *[spell]*- I N S T A B I L I T Y
Definition: lack of firmness or steadiness
Synonym: imbalance, inconstancy
Antonym:
Sentence: The gymnast's instability was obvious as she stood on the balancing beam.

1752. EMIGRATE - *[spell]*- E M I G R A T E
Definition: leave one's own country to settle in another
Synonym: depart, migrate
Antonym:
Sentence: Because of tough economic conditions, he emigrated with his entire family to the United States.

1753. OPERABLE - *[spell]*- O P E R A B L E
Definition: fit for admitting to a surgical operation
Synonym:
Antonym:
Sentence: Because the patient was not operable, the surgery had to be delayed.

1754. PERIODIC - *[spell]*- P E R I O D I C
Definition: occurring, appearing, or done again and again at regular intervals
Synonym: occasional, intermittent
Antonym: constant, infrequent
Sentence: The sounding of the bell was periodic throughout the day.

1755. STARDOM - *[spell]*- S T A R D O M
Definition: being a star actor or performer
Synonym: acclaim, fame
Antonym: obscurity, unimportance
Sentence: Her quick rise to stardom had disastrous effects on her.

1756. TRANSFIX - *[spell]*- T R A N S F I X
Definition: to cause someone to sit or stand without moving because of surprise, shock, interest, etc.
Synonym: captivate, enchant
Antonym:
Sentence: Her gaze transfixed him.

1757. PRESTIGIOUS - *[spell]*- P R E S T I G I O U S
Definition: having, showing, or bringing great reputation or influence
Synonym: distinguished, illustrious
Antonym: obscure, ordinary
Sentence: Being a government official is a very prestigious career.

1758. ADLIB - *[spell]*- A D L I B
Definition: to make up words or music as you go along
Synonym: improvise
Antonym: planned, rehearsed
Sentence: Even though his audition was an adlib, he still managed to get the part.

1759. INFAMOUS - *[spell]*- I N F A M O U S
Definition: deserving or causing a very bad reputation
Synonym: shameful, notorious
Antonym: principled, respectable
Sentence: The child was infamous for cheating at board games.

1760. ARRESTING - *[spell]*- A R R E S T I N G
Definition: catching and holding attention
Synonym: striking, remarkable
Antonym: ordinary, unimportant
Sentence: He found the premise of the movie to be quite arresting.

1761. ITERATE - *[spell]*- I T E R A T E
Definition: say again or repeatedly
Synonym: repeat
Antonym:
Sentence: The teacher had to iterate the directions many times.

1762. BACCALAUREATE - *[spell]*- B A C C A L A U R E A T E
Definition: a degree given by a college or university
Synonym:
Antonym:
Sentence: She worked hard to earn her baccalaureate from a prestigious college.

1763. LABORIOUS - *[spell]*- L A B O R I O U S
Definition: requiring much hard work
Synonym: arduous, difficult
Antonym: easy, facile
Sentence: Running a marathon can be quite laborious.

1764. DESIGNATION - *[spell]*- D E S I G N A T I O N
Definition: act of marking out
Synonym: classification, description
Antonym:
Sentence: The designation of restaurants on the map was clear.

1765. HARDY - *[spell]*- H A R D Y
Definition: able to bear hard treatment, fatigue, etc.
Synonym: strong, tough
Antonym: weak, unhealthy
Sentence: The plant was hardy and could survive in practically any conditions.

1766. STOWAGE - *[spell]*- S T O W A G E
Definition: act of storing or packing things away
Synonym:
Antonym:
Sentence: The child's stowage of her toys under her bed was clever until her mother discovered them.

1767. ELEVATED - *[spell]*- E L E V A T E D
Definition: lifting up
Synonym: raised, high
Antonym:
Sentence: The vase of flowers sat on an elevated pedestal.

1768. DECONTAMINATE - *[spell]*- D E C O N T A M I N A T E
Definition: make free from harm by removing or destroying a harmful substance
Synonym: cleanse, disinfect
Antonym:
Sentence: After the oil spill, the gulf had to be decontaminated.

1769. FLAGON - *[spell]*- F L A G O N
Definition: container for liquids
Synonym: bottle, vessel
Antonym:
Sentence: She poured the tea into a flagon.

1770. OPACITY - *[spell]*- O P A C I T Y
Definition: being able to let a little light through; not transparent
Synonym: cloudy, murky
Antonym: clear, transparent
Sentence: The opacity of the colored glass created an interesting effect in the sunlight.

1771. POLITIC - *[spell]*- P O L I T I C
Definition: looking out for one's own interests
Synonym: prudent, shrewd
Antonym: indiscreet, unwise
Sentence: The candidate was very politic in his pursuit of his reelection.

1772. AMPUTATE - *[spell]*- A M P U T A T E
Definition: cut off from the body
Synonym: sever, dismember
Antonym: join
Sentence: Because of the terrible car accident, the doctor had to amputate the patient's arm.

1773. INTERMISSION - *[spell]*- I N T E R M I S S I O N
Definition: a time between periods of activity
Synonym: break, recess
Antonym: continuation, persistence
Sentence: She went to the concession stand during the intermission of the play.

1774. DESPITEFUL - *[spell]*- D E S P I T E F U L
Definition: malicious
Synonym: malevolent, disdainful
Antonym:
Sentence: Feeling despiteful, the child cut up her sister's most precious doll.

1775. VINCIBLE - *[spell]*- V I N C I B L E
Definition: capable of being conquered
Synonym: vulnerable, defenseless
Antonym: invincible, unconquerable
Sentence: It soon became apparent that the nation was vincible in the war.

1776. DISCONSOLATE - *[spell]*- D I S C O N S O L A T E
Definition: without hope
Synonym: forlorn, inconsolable
Antonym: soothed, comforted
Sentence: He felt disconsolate about passing his exam.

1777. WAIVER - *[spell]*- W A I V E R
Definition: an intentional giving up of some right or interest
Synonym: abdication, relinquishment
Antonym:
Sentence: She had to sign a waiver before going skydiving.

1778. HEEDLESS - *[spell]*- H E E D L E S S
Definition: careless
Synonym: thoughtless, reckless
Antonym: attentive, careful
Sentence: Heedless of her warning about the bad weather, he went out that night anyway.

1779. BLACKEN - *[spell]*- B L A C K E N
Definition: to speak evil about
Synonym: slander, defamation
Antonym: praise, commendation
Sentence: The man attempted to blacken her name by spreading harmful rumors.

1780. LUMINESCENT - *[spell]*- L U M I N E S C E N T
Definition: giving out light without much heat
Synonym: glowing, shining
Antonym: dim, dull
Sentence: In the twilight, the koi in her pond appeared luminescent.

1781. GLAMORIZE - *[spell]*- G L A M O R I Z E
Definition: make something full of glory or romance
Synonym: enhance, embellish
Antonym:
Sentence: The city of Venice is often glamorized as romantic and beautiful.

1782. BYPASS - *[spell]*- B Y P A S S
Definition: to go around
Synonym: circumvent, sidestep
Antonym: confront
Sentence: He tried to bypass the laws by illegal means.

1783. MECHANISM - *[spell]*- M E C H A N I S M
Definition: means or way by which something is done
Synonym: instrument, structure
Antonym:
Sentence: The mechanism was used to start the gears.

1784. SOUNDING - *[spell]*- S O U N D I N G
Definition: pompous
Synonym:
Antonym:
Sentence: His sounding words greatly offended her.

1785. SALVATION - *[spell]*- S A L V A T I O N
Definition: a person or thing that is saved
Synonym: rescue, saving
Antonym: abandonment, destruction
Sentence: Her quick reflexes were her salvation from a terrible car accident.

1786. HYDRATE - *[spell]*- H Y D R A T E
Definition: to combine with water
Synonym:
Antonym:
Sentence: It is important to hydrate your body during a workout.

1787. ENRICH - *[spell]*- E N R I C H
Definition: to cause to become wealthy
Synonym: improve, enhance
Antonym: deplete, impoverish
Sentence: At university, she discovered that a good education will enrich your mind.

1788. CINEMATOGRAPHER - *[spell]*- C I N E M A T O G R A P H E R
Definition: a person who makes motion pictures
Synonym:
Antonym:
Sentence: He began his career as an actor, but soon became a cinematographer.

1789. MUTINY - *[spell]*- M U T I N Y
Definition: open rebellion against authority
Synonym: uprising, insurrection
Antonym: obedience, subservience
Sentence: The group tried to start a mutiny to overthrow the government.

1790. AEROBICS - *[spell]*- A E R O B I C S
Definition: exercise that improves the body's use of oxygen
Synonym: workout
Antonym:
Sentence: Kickboxing is a popular form of aerobics.

1791. INHALATION - *[spell]*- I N H A L A T I O N
Definition: a breathing in
Synonym:
Antonym:
Sentence: The paramedics feared the boy might suffer from smoke inhalation after he was rescued from the fire.

1792. STOPPAGE - *[spell]*- S T O P P A G E
Definition: act of halting
Synonym:
Antonym: advance
Sentence: The doctor knew the stoppage of blood flow to the patient's limb was cause for amputation.

1793. RETENTION - *[spell]*- R E T E N T I O N
Definition: ability to remember
Synonym: memory, recall
Antonym: forgetfulness
Sentence: At ninety years old, the woman had lost some of her retention.

1794. SUBCONSCIOUS - *[spell]*- S U B C O N S C I O U S
Definition: not wholly alert or fully perceived
Synonym:
Antonym: conscious
Sentence: She had a subconscious inkling that something wasn't right.

1795. TENEMENT - *[spell]*- T E N E M E N T
Definition: any house or building to live in
Synonym: rental, apartment
Antonym:
Sentence: Within the tenement, there were several apartments.

1796. SCUFFLE - *[spell]*- S C U F F L E
Definition: a struggle or fight in a rough, confused manner
Synonym: brawl, fight
Antonym: peace, calm
Sentence: A scuffle broke out in the school's hallway during lunch.

1797. AQUARIUM - *[spell]*- A Q U A R I U M
Definition: tank or glass bowl in which fish and other aquatic creatures are kept
Synonym: fishbowl
Antonym:
Sentence: Since she could not have a dog in her apartment, she kept an aquarium.

1798. INVERSION - *[spell]*- I N V E R S I O N
Definition: a being turned upside down
Synonym:
Antonym:
Sentence: Many people with back problems like to use an inversion table.

1799. PERJURE - *[spell]*- P E R J U R E
Definition: to make oneself guilty of lying while under oath
Synonym: lie, deceive
Antonym: attest, certify
Sentence: The lawyer accused him of attempting to perjure his testimony.

1800. ALBEIT - *[spell]*- A L B E I T
Definition: even though
Synonym: although
Antonym:
Sentence: He did fail the test, albeit he did study.

Medium Words Exercise - 9

1801. DEJECTED - *[spell]*- D E J E C T E D
Definition: in low spirits
Synonym: crestfallen, despondent
Antonym: elated, heartened
Sentence: After receiving a letter of rejection from the college, the young man felt dejected.

1802. **PROXIMATE - *[spell]*- P R O X I M A T E**
Definition: nearest
Synonym:
Antonym:
Sentence: He used the GPS on his phone to find the proximate gas station.

1803. COLLEAGUE - *[spell]*- C O L L E A G U E
Definition: a fellow coworker
Synonym: comrade, teammate
Antonym: foe, opponent
Sentence: Because she considered him a colleague, she went to him for advice.

1804. NOVELIST - *[spell]*- N O V E L I S T
Definition: a person who writes novels (long, fictitious stories)
Synonym:
Antonym:
Sentence: The novelist was on the New York Times bestseller list for weeks.

1805. CONFESSIONAL - *[spell]*- C O N F E S S I O N AL
Definition: having to do with admission
Synonym:
Antonym:
Sentence: The confessional poets were known for revealing much of their personal feelings.

1806. DEVOID - *[spell]*- D E V O I D
Definition: entirely without
Synonym: empty, lacking
Antonym: full, whole

Sentence: After the snowstorm was predicted, every store seemed devoid of snow shovels.

1807. VEX - *[spell]* - V E X
Definition: to irritate or annoy
Synonym: disturb, peeve
Antonym:
Sentence: The girl was vexed by her little brother's singing.

1808. PROCLAMATION - *[spell]* - P R O C L A M A T I O N
Definition: an official announcement
Synonym: declaration, announcement
Antonym:
Sentence: The Congressman made a proclamation about his decision to retire from office.

1809. UTTERANCE - *[spell]* - U T T E R AN C E
Definition: the act of saying
Synonym: pronouncement, saying
Antonym:
Sentence: His utterance was barely audible.

1810. VERSED - *[spell]* - V E R S E D
Definition: experienced or practical
Synonym: proficient, experienced
Antonym: incompetent, ignorant
Sentence: He was well-versed in all things literary.

1811. FOCALIZE - *[spell]* - F O C A L I Z E
Definition: bring into focus
Synonym:
Antonym:
Sentence: She used the camera lens to focalize on the distant football game.

1812. TENURE - *[spell]* - T E N U R E
Definition: a holding or possessing
Synonym: occupation, incumbency
Antonym:
Sentence: After many years of working for the university, the professor received tenure.

1813. C A L I C O - *[spell]* - C A L I C O
Definition: spotted in colors
Synonym: brindled

Antonym: solid

Sentence: The cat had a calico coat of browns, black, and white.

1814. MEDLEY - *[spell]*- M E D L E Y

Definition: mixture of things that ordinarily do not belong together

Synonym: assortment, miscellany

Antonym: composition, organized

Sentence: The salad was a medley of different ingredients.

1815. HOSPITABLE - *[spell]*- H O S P I T A B L E

Definition: giving or liking to give welcome, food, or shelter

Synonym: courteous, neighborly

Antonym: unwelcoming, ungracious

Sentence: The man, known for being hospitable, would often invite his neighbors over.

1816. STYLISTIC - *[spell]*- S T Y L I S T I C

Definition: of or having to do with a particular mode or fashion

Synonym:

Antonym:

Sentence: The author made some very distinct stylistic choices in his writing.

1817. SCATHELESS - *[spell]*- S C A T H E L E S S

Definition: without harm

Synonym: unhurt, unblemished

Antonym: broken, damaged

Sentence: He emerged from the battle scatheless.

1818. DIORAMA - *[spell]*- D I O R A M A

Definition: a three dimensional scene viewed through a window-like opening

Synonym:

Antonym:

Sentence: Students were asked to make a diorama for one of their projects.

1819. STUDIOUS - *[spell]*- S T U D I O U S

Definition: fond of study

Synonym: scholarly, bookish

Antonym: illiterate, ignorant

Sentence: The studious nature of the child allowed him to do very well in school.

1820. STERILIZE - *[spell]*- S T E R I L I Z E

Definition: to make free from germs

Synonym: disinfect, decontaminate
Antonym:
Sentence: The doctor had to sterilize his tools before beginning the surgery.

1821.   REDUNDANCY - *[spell]*- R E D U N D A N C Y
Definition: more than is needed
Synonym: repetition, wordiness
Antonym: terseness, conciseness
Sentence: The redundancy of information in the report made it difficult to read.

1822.   IMAGINARY - *[spell]*- I M A G I N A R Y
Definition: existing only in the mind
Synonym: invented, fictitious
Antonym: factual, real
Sentence: Growing up, the child created an imaginary friend.

1823.   DEPARTMENTALIZE - *[spell]*- D E P A R T M E N T A L I Z E
Definition: divide into divisions
Synonym: compartmentalize, classify
Antonym:
Sentence: As the store grew, it became departmentalized so customers could find products more easily.

1824.   DISILLUSION - *[spell]*- D I S I L L U S I O N
Definition: set free from belief or idealism
Synonym: disenchant, disappoint
Antonym:
Sentence: When war broke out despite her efforts for peace, the diplomat felt disillusioned.

1825.   TAWDRY - *[spell]*- T A W D R Y
Definition: showy and cheap
Synonym: flashy, tasteless
Antonym:
Sentence: His political career was ruined by a tawdry affair.

1826.   HEMISPHERE - *[spell]*- H E M I S P H E R E
Definition: one half of the globe
Synonym:
Antonym:
Sentence: America is in the northern hemisphere.

1827.   PREVENTABLE - *[spell]*- P R E V E N T A B L E
Definition: that can be stopped or kept from happening

Synonym: avoidable, escapable
Antonym: inevitable, inescapable
Sentence: The fire, caused by a lighted candle, was preventable.

1828. DENOUNCE - *[spell]*- D E N O U N C E
Definition: condemn publicly
Synonym: blame, decry
Antonym: applaud, compliment
Sentence: The organization was denounced when an investigation found internal corruption.

1829. HENCE - *[spell]*- H E N C E
Definition: as a result of this
Synonym: therefore, accordingly
Antonym:
Sentence: She did not do her homework and, hence, the teacher gave her a zero.

1830. PROMPTITUDE - *[spell]*- P R O M P T I T U D E
Definition: readiness in acting or deciding
Synonym:
Antonym:
Sentence: EMS workers must respond with promptitude.

1831. PAGINATION - *[spell]*- P A G I N AT I O N
Definition: act of numbering the pages of a book or other work
Synonym:
Antonym:
Sentence: The editor discovered an error in the author's pagination.

1832. SPASTIC - *[spell]*- S P A S T IC
Definition: awkward or clumsy
Synonym:
Antonym:
Sentence: Her social skills were often somewhat spastic.

1833. SANCTIFY - *[spell]*- S A N C T I F Y
Definition: to make holy
Synonym: consecrate, hallow
Antonym: desecrate, condemn
Sentence: The tomb of the saint was sanctified.

1834. SCARCITY - *[spell]*- S C A R C I T Y
Definition: too small a supply
Synonym: insufficiency, shortage

Antonym: abundance, plenty
Sentence: The scarcity of rain created a severe drought.

1835. POPULACE - *[spell]*- P O P U L A C E
Definition: the common people
Synonym: masses, multitude
Antonym:
Sentence: The vote of the populace determined the next president.

1836. CONCOCTION - *[spell]*- C O N C O C T I O N
Definition: something that is a mix of a variety of ingredients
Synonym: mixture, medley
Antonym:
Sentence: He drank an herbal concoction that was supposed to cure his cold.

1837. RACKETEER - *[spell]*- R A C K E T E E R
Definition: person who extorts money through bribery, threats, or some other illegal means
Synonym: thief, criminal
Antonym:
Sentence: Over the years, the stockbroker acquired a reputation as a racketeer.

1838. SHAMAN - *[spell]*- S H A M A N
Definition: a man who is believed to have close contact with the spirit world
Synonym:
Antonym:
Sentence: Everyone in the tribe consulted the shaman for advice in spiritual matters.

1839. FOPPERY - *[spell]*- F O P P E R Y
Definition: behavior or dress of a vain man
Synonym: extravagance
Antonym: plainness
Sentence: His foppery made him the laughingstock of the office.

1840. WARRANT - *[spell]*- W A R R A N T
Definition: justification or authorization
Synonym: sanction, certificate
Antonym:
Sentence: The parents decided their child's action warranted punishment.

1841. BANTER - *[spell]*- B A N T E R
Definition: to tease playfully

Synonym: joke, kid
Antonym:
Sentence: Their easy banter was a sign of their friendship.

1842. LEERY - *[spell]*- L E E R Y
Definition: suspicious
Synonym: cautious, distrustful
Antonym:
Sentence: The child was usually leery of strangers.

1843. SURETY - *[spell]*- S U R E T Y
Definition: security against loss, damage or failure
Synonym: confidence, certainty
Antonym: doubt, uncertainty
Sentence: He gave his surety that he was good for the loan.

1844. BAIT - *[spell]*- B A I T
Definition: anything used to tempt or attract
Synonym: temptation, enticement
Antonym: discouragement, repulsion
Sentence: He tried to bait his child into doing homework by offering her candy.

1845. LAPEL - *[spell]*- L A P E L
Definition: the part of the front of a coat that folds back below the collar
Synonym:
Antonym:
Sentence: The lapel of his jacket was a different color than the jacket itself.

1846. SIEGE - *[spell]*- S I E G E
Definition: the surrounding of a fortified place by enemy forces trying to capture it
Synonym: beleaguer
Antonym:
Sentence: The king had to think quickly when he found his castle under siege.

1847. ASSOCIATION - *[spell]*- A S S O C I A T I O N
Definition: a group of people joined together for a common purpose
Synonym: company, organization
Antonym:
Sentence: The homeowners association met to discuss new rules for their neighborhood.

1848. JOURNALISM - *[spell]*- J O U R N A L I S M
Definition: work of writing for, editing, or publishing a newspaper or magazine
Synonym:
Antonym:
Sentence: He decided he want to study journalism in school.

1849. DISEMBARK - *[spell]*- D I S E M B A R K
Definition: to go ashore from a ship
Synonym: exit
Antonym: enter, embark
Sentence: After finally arriving at the port, the passengers disembarked.

1850. PRECEDENCE - *[spell]*- P R E C E D E N C E
Definition: act or fact of coming before in order, place, or time
Synonym: beforehand, superiority
Antonym: afterwards, subordination
Sentence: In the ER, patients with life-threatening injuries take precedence over all others.

1851. SPIRITUALITY - *[spell]*- S P I R I T U A L I T Y
Definition: devotion to matters of the soul instead of worldly things
Synonym: immaterial, otherworldliness
Antonym:
Sentence: His spirituality was the most important thing in his life.

1852. SOVEREIGN - *[spell]*- S O V E R E I G N
Definition: supreme ruler
Synonym: king, royal
Antonym:
Sentence: The sovereign passed a series of revolutionary new laws.

1853. ANONYMOUS - *[spell]*- A N O N Y M O U S
Definition: having no name
Synonym: unidentified, unnamed
Antonym: identified, distinguishable
Sentence: The author preferred to be anonymous, and so she did not publish under her real name.

1854. INTERSPERSE - *[spell]*- I N T E R S P E R S E
Definition: scatter and place here or there among things
Synonym: bestrew, distribute
Antonym: collect, gather
Sentence: His speech was interspersed with funny accounts of his childhood.

1855. SUCCUMB - *[spell]*- S U C C U M B
Definition: to give way or yield
Synonym: buckle, capitulate
Antonym: defend, fight
Sentence: She refused to succumb to his demands.

1856. DEMERIT - *[spell]*- D E M E R I T
Definition: a mark against a person's record for unsatisfactory work
Synonym:
Antonym: merit, virtue
Sentence: The scout received a demerit for his sloppy work.

1857. TROTH - *[spell]*- T R O T H
Definition: faithfulness or fidelity
Synonym:
Antonym:
Sentence: His troth to his wife could never be shaken.

1858. ESCALATION - *[spell]*- E S C A L A T I O N
Definition: the act of increasing rapidly by stages
Synonym: intensification, acceleration
Antonym: decrease, diminishment
Sentence: Over time, the escalation of the conflict led to war.

1859. TINKER - *[spell]*- T I N K E R
Definition: to work or keep busy in a rather useless way
Synonym: dabble, fiddle
Antonym:
Sentence: Whenever he needed to relax, he went to the garage to tinker with his car.

1860. FALLIBLE - *[spell]*- F A L L I B L E
Definition: capable of making a mistake
Synonym: faulty, untrustworthy
Antonym:
Sentence: Although he seems to think he's perfect, he is fallible, just like everyone else.

1861. FORGATHER - *[spell]*- F O R G A T H E R
Definition: assemble together
Synonym: meet, congregate
Antonym: disperse, scatter
Sentence: The group had to forgather for their monthly meeting.

1862. VERMIN - *[spell]*- V E R M I N
Definition: disgusting or objectionable animals like lice, fleas, and rats.

Synonym: rodent, pest
Antonym:
Sentence: The house seemed to be infested with vermin.

1863. SEPARABLE - *[spell]*- S E P A R A B L E
Definition: that can be kept apart or divided
Synonym: breakable, detachable
Antonym:
Sentence: Though the pieces of the couch came put together, they were also separable.

1864. DEBARK - *[spell]*- D E B A R K
Definition: to go ashore from a ship
Synonym: disembark, land
Antonym: embark, enter
Sentence: After arriving at the port, the passengers were allowed to debark.

1865. PHILOSOPHIZE - *[spell]*- P H I L O S O P H I Z E
Definition: to try to understand and explain things
Synonym: think, contemplate
Antonym:
Sentence: He was fond of philosophizing about his life.

1866. BADGER - *[spell]*- B A D G E R
Definition: to torment by nagging or bullying
Synonym: tease, pester
Antonym:
Sentence: Her coworkers continually badgered her.

1867. LANCER - *[spell]*- L A N C E R
Definition: a mounted soldier armed with a lance (wooden spear with sharp iron head)
Synonym:
Antonym:
Sentence: In battle, the lancers proceeded before swordsmen because their weapon had a longer range.

1868. RENOUNCE - *[spell]*- R E N O U N C E
Definition: declare that one gives up
Synonym: relinquish, waive
Antonym: embrace
Sentence: He was forced to renounce his title as governor when the scandal erupted.

1869. FILAMENT - *[spell]*- F I L A M E N T
Definition: a very fine thread
Synonym: fiber, hair
Antonym:
Sentence: The filaments in the pillow were beginning to unravel.

1870. WHEREWITHAL - *[spell]*- W H E R E W I T H A L
Definition: means for a particular purpose or need
Synonym: ability, means
Antonym:
Sentence: She was hired because she had the wherewithal to command people.

1871. RENEWAL - *[spell]*- R E N E W A L
Definition: a making like new
Synonym: rebirth, regeneration
Antonym: destruction, exhaustion
Sentence: The couple had a renewal of their vows after fifteen years.

1872. SIGNET - *[spell]*- S I G N E T
Definition: a small seal used to stamp documents
Synonym: stamp, seal
Antonym:
Sentence: The king had a signet ring he used to sign documents.

1873. SPACIOUS - *[spell]*- S P A C I O U S
Definition: having much space or room
Synonym: vast, roomy
Antonym: narrow, cramped
Sentence: He managed to rent a spacious apartment within his budget.

1874. COMPARTMENTALIZE - *[spell]*- C O M P A R T M E N T A L I Z E
Definition: arrange into sections or categories
Synonym: categorize, classify
Antonym: disorganize, disorder
Sentence: He tried to compartmentalize the project into smaller, more manageable parts.

1875. GRIZZLED - *[spell]*- G R I Z Z L E D
Definition: grayish
Synonym: silvery
Antonym:
Sentence: His beard had become grizzled over time.

1876. SECESSION - *[spell]*- S E C E S S I ON
Definition: a formal withdrawing from an organization

Synonym: breakaway, withdrawal

Antonym:

Sentence: The state's secession from the country was expected by many.

1877. ACCLAIMâ€"[spell]â€"A C C L A I M

Definition: highly praised

Synonym: applause

Antonym: disapproval

Sentence: She received great acclaim after giving a speech at graduation.

1878. INDIGNANT - *[spell]*- I N D I G N A N T

Definition: angry at something unworthy, unjust, unfair, or mean

Synonym: outraged, incensed

Antonym: pleased, delighted

Sentence: The audience was indignant over the politician's statements.

1879. SEXTUPLET - *[spell]*- S E X T U P L E T

Definition: one of six offspring born at the same time from the same mother

Synonym:

Antonym:

Sentence: A sextuplet, he grew up in a home with many other children.

1880. ASPIRE - *[spell]*- A S P I R E

Definition: having an ambition for something

Synonym: crave, intend

Antonym: neglect, oversight

Sentence: She aspired to be a doctor after completing medical school.

1881. JIMMY - *[spell]*- J I M M Y

Definition: to force open with a short crowbar

Synonym:

Antonym:

Sentence: He had to jimmy open the door when it got stuck.

1882. SUBCONTRACT - *[spell]*- S U B C O N T R A C T

Definition: an agreement in which a party agrees to carry out part of a separate agreement

Synonym:

Antonym:

Sentence: The writer subcontracted an editor for the project.

1883. HYPNOSIS - *[spell]*- H Y P N O S I S

Definition: condition resembling sleep in which a person will act according to the suggestions of a person who brought about the condition

Synonym: hypnotism, mesmerism

Antonym:
Sentence: While in a state of hypnosis, the man was bid to do many embarrassing things by the magician.

1884. REVOCATION - *[spell]*- R E V O C A T I O N
Definition: act of taking back or repealing
Synonym: repeal, annulment
Antonym: approval, confirmation
Sentence: The revocation of the law was due to much public pressure.

1885. BISECT - *[spell]*- B I S E C T
Definition: to divide into two parts
Synonym: cleave, halve
Antonym: unite, combine
Sentence: He bisected the cake into two equal portions.

1886. LOUNGE - *[spell]*- L O U N G E
Definition: stand, stroll, sit or lie at ease and lazily
Synonym: lobby, parlor
Antonym:
Sentence: He lounged on a chair across the room.

1887. PURVEYOR - *[spell]*- P U R V E Y O R
Definition: a person who supplies something
Synonym: vendor, supplier
Antonym:
Sentence: He had the misfortune of being a purveyor of bad news.

1888. FREELOAD - *[spell]*- F R E E L O A D
Definition: get something at another's expense
Synonym: bum, mooch
Antonym:
Sentence: He was known to freeload lunch from various people in his office.

1889. PRECISION - *[spell]*- P R E C I S I O N
Definition: fact or condition of being exact
Synonym: exactness, rigor
Antonym: haphazard, carelessness
Sentence: The scientist executed the experiment with precision.

1890. PRESCRIPTIVE - *[spell]*- P R E S C R I P T I V E
Definition: established by law or custom
Synonym: dictatorial
Antonym:
Sentence: Social courtesies are often prescriptive.

1891. ARMADA - *[spell]*- A R M A D A
Definition: a fleet of ships
Synonym: navy, flotilla
Antonym:
Sentence: The Spanish armada was sent to attack England in the 1500s.

1892. IRREDEEMABLE - *[spell]*- I R R E D E E M A B L E
Definition: that cannot be bought back
Synonym: incorrigible, irreparable
Antonym: redeemable, mendable
Sentence: When he chose to join the gang, he was irredeemable in the eyes of his mother.

1893. SHINDIG - *[spell]*- S H I N D I G
Definition: a merry or noisy dance, party, etc.
Synonym: gala, raucous
Antonym:
Sentence: The party he attended turned out to be more of an informal shindig than he expected.

1894. PATHOGEN - *[spell]*- P A T H O G E N
Definition: an agent capable of producing disease
Synonym: germ, bacteria
Antonym:
Sentence: The air we breathe contains many pathogens.

1895. SEMIANNUAL - *[spell]*- S E M I A N N U A L
Definition: occurring every half year
Synonym: biannual
Antonym:
Sentence: The store had its semiannual sale over the weekend.

1896. SERRATE - *[spell]*- S E R R A T E
Definition: notched like the edge of a saw
Synonym: toothed, notched
Antonym: smooth, even
Sentence: He used a serrated knife to cut the bread.

1897. UNLETTERED - *[spell]*- U N L E T T E R E D
Definition: not educated
Synonym: illiterate, ignorant
Antonym: scholarly, educated
Sentence: Though unlettered, he was a highly intelligent man.

1898. IMBECILITY - *[spell]*- I M B E C I L I T Y
Definition: being a very stupid or foolish person

Synonym: stupidity, irrationality
Antonym: wisdom, sense
Sentence: His imbecility did not make him very popular.

1899. DETESTATION - *[spell]*- D E T E S T A T I O N
Definition: an intense dislike
Synonym: hatred, abhorrence
Antonym: love, admire
Sentence: He developed a deep detestation of his boss because of her unreasonable expectations.

1900. OPTIMISTIC - *[spell]*- O P T I M I S T I C
Definition: inclined to look on the bright side of things
Synonym: buoyant, hopeful
Antonym: pessimistic, gloomy
Sentence: Despite adversity, she tried to remain optimistic.

Medium Words Exercise - 10

1901. TRAUMATIC - *[spell]*- T R A U M A T I C
Definition: of or having to do with, or produced by a wound, injury, or shock
Synonym: nightmarish, harrowing
Antonym: calming, pleasant
Sentence: After her traumatic accident, the girl didn't even want to go outside anymore.

1902. TOIL - *[spell]*- T O I L
Definition: hard work
Synonym: exertion, drudgery
Antonym:
Sentence: After much toil, the job was finally done.

1903. COMMANDANT - *[spell]*- C O M M A N D A N T
Definition: officer in command
Synonym: commander, captain
Antonym: subordinate, worker
Sentence: The commandant issued very specific orders to his subordinates.

1904. GOBLIN - *[spell]*- G O B L I N
Definition: a mischievous, evil-natured dwarf
Synonym: gremlin
Antonym:
Sentence: The story was about a group of goblins that plagued the land.

1905. FALSIFY - *[spell]*- F A L S I F Y
Definition: misrepresent
Synonym: counterfeit, deceive
Antonym: confirm, validate
Sentence: The man was found to have falsified documents that supported his innocence.

1906. ACCLIMATE - *[spell]*- A C C L I M A T E
Definition: to become accustomed to new surroundings
Synonym: adjust, adapt
Antonym: refuse, reject

Sentence: After moving away to college, it took the girl some time to acclimate to her new environment.

1907. INDISPENSABLE - *[spell]*- I N D I S P E N S A B L E
Definition: absolutely necessary
Synonym: crucial, vital
Antonym: expendable
Sentence: She was indispensable to the company.

1908. BARBARIAN - *[spell]*- B A R B A R I A N
Definition: a person who is not civilized
Synonym: primitive, savage
Antonym: sophisticated, civilized
Sentence: He seemed like a barbarian from the way he ate his food with his hands.

1909. LEEWARD - *[spell]*- L E E W A R D
Definition: on the side away from the wind
Synonym:
Antonym:
Sentence: They stood on the leeward side of the building to escape the bitter cold wind.

1910. ALMANAC - *[spell]*- A L M A N A C
Definition: an annual book with calendars, weather predictions, hours of sunrise/sunset, etc.
Synonym:
Antonym:
Sentence: In order to get a picture of what the year's weather might look like, he consulted an almanac.

1911. INSULATION - *[spell]*- I N S U L A T I O N
Definition: material used for keeping or losing heat
Synonym:
Antonym:
Sentence: The house felt drafty because it had poor insulation in the walls.

1912. SNAFU - *[spell]*- S N A F U
Definition: a snarled or confused state of things
Synonym:
Antonym:
Sentence: There was a snafu in the office when the boss took a sick day.

1913. INCENSE - *[spell]*- I N C E N S E
Definition: make very angry

Synonym: enraged, disgusted
Antonym:
Sentence: She was incensed by the fact that he didn't come to her party.

1914. EXCEEDINGLY - *[spell]*- E X C E E D I N G L Y
Definition: very greatly
Synonym: extremely, enormously
Antonym: minimally, little
Sentence: She was exceedingly pleased with the gift from her friends.

1915. HEAVENLY - *[spell]*- H E A V E N L Y
Definition: very happy, beautiful, or excellent
Synonym: blissful, glorious
Antonym: awful, disagreeable
Sentence: He felt the meal she cooked was simply heavenly.

1916. SATURATE - *[spell]*- S A T U R A T E
Definition: soak thoroughly
Synonym: drench, soak
Antonym: dry, arid
Sentence: Her clothes were saturated after the rain.

1917. VALET - *[spell]*- V A L E T
Definition: servant who takes care of a man's clothes
Synonym: servant, attendant
Antonym:
Sentence: The wealthy man hired a valet.

1918. PRIMACY - *[spell]*- P R I M A C Y
Definition: being first in order, rank, importance, etc.
Synonym: supremacy, domination
Antonym: insignificance, unimportance
Sentence: The son's primacy to inherit the throne was changed by his sudden illness.

1919. PROPELLANT - *[spell]*- P R O P E L L A N T
Definition: driving forward
Synonym:
Antonym:
Sentence: Motivation was his propellant for getting the task accomplished.

1920. PANDER - *[spell]*- P A N D E R
Definition: person who helps other people for their own desires, passions, or vices
Synonym:

Antonym:
Sentence: She claims to treat all her students the same, but she panders to a select group from wealthy families.

1921. GRATING - *[spell]*- G R A T I N G
Definition: unpleasant, annoying
Synonym: displeasing, offensive
Antonym: pleasant, agreeable
Sentence: The printer makes a grating noise that annoys everyone in the office.

1922. ILLIMITABLE - *[spell]*- I L L I M I T A B L E
Definition: without bounds
Synonym: endless, boundless
Antonym: finite, ending
Sentence: His enthusiasm seemed to be illimitable.

1923. CARCINOGEN - *[spell]*- C A R C I N O G E N
Definition: any substance that causes cancer.
Synonym: toxin, poison
Antonym:
Sentence: Many surprising substances can be carcinogens.

1924. METAPHORIC - *[spell]*- M E T A P H O R I C
Definition: using metaphors (an implied comparison between two different things)
Synonym: figurative, allegorical
Antonym: literal, real
Sentence: He had a tendency to speak in a metaphoric manner.

1925. PAROLE - *[spell]*- P A R O L E
Definition: conditional release from prison or jail before the full-term is served
Synonym: discharge
Antonym:
Sentence: The prisoner was released on parole.

1926. DECRY - *[spell]*- D E C R Y
Definition: to express strong disapproval of
Synonym: belittle, denounce
Antonym: commend, praise
Sentence: The artist decried the use of synthetic materials in artwork.

1927. DERMATOLOGY - *[spell]*- D E R M A T O L O G Y
Definition: branch of medicine that deals with the skin
Synonym:

Antonym:
Sentence: The doctor, an expert in dermatology, prescribed the girl a medication for her acne

1928. STIPEND - *[spell]*- S T I P E N D
Definition: fixed or regular pay
Synonym: salary, wage
Antonym:
Sentence: The teacher received an extra stipend for coaching basketball.

1929. A CAPPELLA - *[spell]*- A C A P P E L L A
Definition: without the accompaniment of instruments
Synonym: solo, choral
Antonym:
Sentence: The choir sang a beautiful and impressive a cappella rendition of the song.

1930. INDIFFERENCE - *[spell]*- I N D I F F E R E N C E
Definition: lack of interest or attention
Synonym: apathy, disinterest
Antonym: attention, interest
Sentence: His indifference towards sports was obvious when he didn't watch the game.

1931. TRIVIALITY - *[spell]*- T R I V I A L I T Y
Definition: quality of not being important
Synonym: pettiness, inconsequence
Antonym: importance, meaningful
Sentence: The triviality of her husband's argument made her laugh.

1932. TINDER - *[spell]*- T I N D E R
Definition: anything that catches fire easily
Synonym: kindling
Antonym:
Sentence: The campers used tinder to start a fire.

1933. COMPLAINANT - *[spell]*- C O M P L A I N A N T
Definition: a person who finds fault
Synonym: accuser, claimant
Antonym:
Sentence: She has been a complainant in so many lawsuits that she is recognized by everyone in the courthouse.

1934. SIEVE - *[spell]*- S I E V E
Definition: utensil having holes that lets liquids and small pieces pass through but not the larger pieces

Synonym: colander, filter
Antonym:
Sentence: She used a sieve to strain the seeds out of the orange juice she made.

1935. FUNEREAL - *[spell]*- F U N E R E A L
Definition: of or suitable for a funeral
Synonym: depressing, elegiac
Antonym: joyful, happy
Sentence: The room, decorated all in black, had a funereal feeling.

1936. BIDDEN - *[spell]*- B I D D E N
Definition: invited
Synonym:
Antonym: discourage, dissuade
Sentence: To stay in his boss's favor, he always did as he was bidden.

1937. LIVABILITY - *[spell]*- L I V A B I L I T Y
Definition: condition of being fit to live in
Synonym:
Antonym:
Sentence: The family was forced to move out of their apartment until its livability was improved.

1938. TOWAGE - *[spell]*- T O W A G E
Definition: a being pulled by a rope or chain
Synonym:
Antonym:
Sentence: The towage of the truck was a smaller car.

1939. RIVULET - *[spell]*- R I V U L E T
Definition: a small stream
Synonym: creek, brook
Antonym:
Sentence: The children enjoyed playing in the rivulet behind their home.

1940. DEVALUATE - *[spell]*- D E V A L U A T E
Definition: reduce the value of
Synonym: diminish, lessen
Antonym: increase, overvalue
Sentence: When the home was appraised, the estimated worth had devaluated.

1941. SHUNT - *[spell]*- S H U N T
Definition: move out of the way or turn aside
Synonym:

Antonym:

Sentence: After the divorce, she felt she was shunted aside by her ex-husband's friends and family.

1942. AUTOMATE - *[spell]*- A U T O M A T E

Definition: convert to control by a machine that moves by itself

Synonym: robotize

Antonym:

Sentence: In order to save money, the company decided to use computers to automate many of its processes.

1943. KNAVE - *[spell]*- K N A V E

Definition: tricky, dishonest man

Synonym: rogue

Antonym:

Sentence: Because he was known as a knave, no one trusted him.

1944. AERATE - *[spell]*- A E R A T E

Definition: to mix with air

Synonym: oxygenate

Antonym:

Sentence: Sometimes farmers must aerate the soil so that crops can grow.

1945. INFLEXIBLE - *[spell]*- I N F L E X I B L E

Definition: not to be turned from a purpose by persuasion or argument

Synonym: stubborn, adamant

Antonym: amenable, cooperative

Sentence: She was completely inflexible when it came to her wedding plans.

1946. PERMEABLE - *[spell]*- P E R M E A B L E

Definition: that can be passed through pores or openings

Synonym: penetrable, absorbent

Antonym: impenetrable, impermeable

Sentence: Luckily, when it began to rain, she was wearing a jacket that was not permeable.

1947. REPOSSESS - *[spell]*- R E P O S S E S S

Definition: to take ownership of again

Synonym: retake, recapture

Antonym:

Sentence: The bank repossessed his car after he did not pay his bills.

1948. ENDEAVOR - *[spell]*- E N D E A V O R

Definition: make an effort

Synonym: strive, aim

Antonym: passivity, inactivity
Sentence: Though he had never tried before, he endeavored to run his first 10K.

1949. UNCONSCIOUS - *[spell]*- U N C O N S C I O U S
Definition: unable to think or feel
Synonym: comatose, senseless
Antonym:
Sentence: After she fell from her bike, the child was knocked unconscious.

1950. QUOTABLE - *[spell]*- Q U O T A B L E
Definition: that can be repeated in exact words
Synonym:
Antonym:
Sentence: Many of the child's humorous remarks became quotable in his household.

1951. DILUTION - *[spell]*- D I L U T I O N
Definition: act of making something weaker
Synonym:
Antonym:
Sentence: The dilution of the drink was due to the melting ice.

1952. VOLUNTARY - *[spell]*- V O L U N T A R Y
Definition: done, made, or given of one's own free will
Synonym: independent, freely
Antonym: forced, involuntary
Sentence: In the wake of the hurricane, a voluntary evacuation order was issued.

1953. ABRIDGE - *[spell]*- A B R I D G E
Definition: to make shorter by using fewer words
Synonym: shorten, abbreviate
Antonym: elongate, expand
Sentence: The students read an abridged version of the book, since the original was thousands of pages long.

1954. INDEX - *[spell]*- I N D E X
Definition: list of what is in a book, indicating on what pages to find topics, names, etc.
Synonym:
Antonym:
Sentence: She searched through the index of the book to find information relevant to her research paper.

1955. DEMOGRAPHY - *[spell]*- D E M O G R A P H Y
Definition: science dealing with statistics of the human population
Synonym:
Antonym:
Sentence: The demography of the area revealed new trends in population density.

1956. SLUMBEROUS - *[spell]*- S L U M B E R O U S
Definition: sleepy or heavy with drowsiness
Synonym: comatose, inactive
Antonym: active, energetic
Sentence: The mother could tell her child was slumberous from the way his head bobbed.

1957. EJECTION - *[spell]*- E J E C T I O N
Definition: being thrown out from within
Synonym: banishment, eviction
Antonym: admittance
Sentence: Her ejection from the restaurant was due to her belligerent behavior.

1958. SNIPPET - *[spell]*- S N I P P E T
Definition: s small piece cut off
Synonym: particle, fragment
Antonym: whole, complete
Sentence: The girl cut off a snippet of hair to place in the locket for her boyfriend.

1959. HEADROOM - *[spell]*- H E A D R O O M
Definition: a clear space overhead
Synonym: clearance, opening
Antonym:
Sentence: Although the car is small, it has a surprising amount of headroom.

1960. GNOME - *[spell]*- G N O M E
Definition: a dwarf supposed to live in the earth
Synonym:
Antonym:
Sentence: She had several statutes of gnomes in her yard.

1961. SHAKEDOWN - *[spell]*- S H A K E D O W N
Definition: a thorough search
Synonym: investigation, examination
Antonym:

Sentence: After the shakedown of the prison cells, the guards found several illegal items.

1962. PORTRAITURE - *[spell]*- P O R T R A I T U R E
Definition: act of making a likeness in drawing or painting
Synonym: illustration, representation
Antonym:
Sentence: The portraiture in the hallway showed several generations of the family.

1963. SYSTEMATIC - *[spell]*- S Y S T E M A T I C
Definition: according to a system
Synonym: methodical, orderly
Antonym: chaotic, unorganized
Sentence: Using a systematic approach, she reorganized her closet.

1964. VANQUISH - *[spell]*- V A N Q U I S H
Definition: to conquer, defeat, or overcome in battle or conflict
Synonym: overpower, overcome
Antonym:
Sentence: He was vanquished by his opponents.

1965. ALUMNUS - *[spell]*- A L U M N U S
Definition: a former student of a certain school or university
Synonym:
Antonym: undergraduate
Sentence: He had a graduation party to celebrate his becoming an alumnus.

1966. INTERFAITH - *[spell]*- I N T E R F A I T H
Definition: of or for different religions
Synonym:
Antonym:
Sentence: An interfaith organization was formed to address some of the problems about tolerance at the university.

1967. DUPLEX - *[spell]*- D U P L E X
Definition: having two parts
Synonym:
Antonym:
Sentence: The house was a duplex, divided into two separate apartments.

1968. ROILY - *[spell]*- R O I L Y
Definition: muddy
Synonym: dirty, unclean

Antonym: clean
Sentence: The dog came in from outside roily and dirty.

1969. CLEANSING - *[spell]*- C L E A N S I N G
Definition: making free of dirt
Synonym: purging, restoring
Antonym: polluting, soiling
Sentence: She used a cleansing facial scrub to wash her face.

1970. NICKELODEON - *[spell]*- N I C K E L O D E O N
Definition: place of amusement with movies, etc.
Synonym:
Antonym:
Sentence: They went to a nickelodeon on Saturday.

1971. OASIS - *[spell]*- O A S I S
Definition: a fertile spot in the desert where there is some water and vegetation
Synonym: paradise, refuge
Antonym:
Sentence: After roaming the desert for hours, he thought he found an oasis.

1972. VISIONARY - *[spell]*- V I S I O N A R Y
Definition: characterized by unpractical ideas or views
Synonym: daydreamer, idealist
Antonym: practical, realist
Sentence: He was considered a visionary by those he worked with.

1973. EXTENUATE - *[spell]*- E X T E N U A T E
Definition: make the seriousness of something seem less
Synonym: whitewash, excuse
Antonym:
Sentence: Before you judge him, remember that there were extenuating circumstances.

1974. CONSOLIDATE - *[spell]*- C O N S O L I D A T E
Definition: combine into one
Synonym: unite, solidify
Antonym: diverge, disperse
Sentence: When she moved into a smaller home, she had to consolidate all her possessions.

1975. RESOUNDING - *[spell]*- R E S O U N D I N G
Definition: sounding loudly
Synonym: emphatic, forceful

Antonym: quiet, unheard
Sentence: When asked if he would vote for the bill, the politician gave a resounding no.

1976. UNDERNOURISHED - *[spell]*- U N D E R N O U R I S H E D
Definition: not sufficiently sustained with nutrition
Synonym: scrawny, skinny
Antonym:
Sentence: The child was taken to social services because he seemed undernourished.

1977. REVISAL - *[spell]*- R E V I S A L
Definition: a reading carefully and correcting
Synonym: alteration, amendment
Antonym:
Sentence: The editor's revisal of the manuscript made it much stronger.

1978. SPRUCE - *[spell]*- S P R U C E
Definition: to make or become smart or neat in appearance
Synonym: prim, clean
Antonym:
Sentence: She tried to spruce up her home by painting the walls a different color.

1979. PEDIGREE - *[spell]*- P E D I G R E E
Definition: list of ancestors of a person or animal
Synonym: ancestry, heritage
Antonym: descendants, posterity
Sentence: The dog's pedigree was quite impressive.

1980. REBUTTAL - *[spell]*- R E B U T T A L
Definition: a trying to disapprove
Synonym: reply, counterclaim
Antonym:
Sentence: The lawyer gave a rebuttal during his closing statements.

1981. UNSEASONABLE - *[spell]*- U N S E A S O N A B L E
Definition: not suitable to the characteristics of a particular season
Synonym: untimely
Antonym:
Sentence: The recipe called for several unseasonable ingredients.

1982. BACKLOG - *[spell]*- B A C K L O G
Definition: a reserve of duties or commitments that have not been carried out
Synonym:

Antonym:
Sentence: Since they had a backlog of paperwork, the employees had to work overtime.

1983. LAGGARD - *[spell]-* L A G G A R D
Definition: a person who moves too slowly or falls behind
Synonym: dawdler, lingerer
Antonym:
Sentence: She was a laggard in the 10k race.

1984. UNSAVORY - *[spell]-* U N S A V O RY
Definition: tasteless
Synonym: distasteful, bland
Antonym: tasty, delicious
Sentence: She threw the unsavory meal in the trash.

1985. PRINCIPLED - *[spell]-* P R I N C I P L E D
Definition: having a good sense of uprightness and honor
Synonym: ethical, honest
Antonym: unethical, corrupt
Sentence: He was known to be a very principled person.

1986. SUCCULENCE - *[spell]-* S U C C U L E N C E
Definition: juiciness
Synonym: luscious, moist
Antonym:
Sentence: The succulence of the apple made it delicious.

1987. IMMEDICABLE - *[spell]-* I M M E D I C A B L E
Definition: that cannot be healed
Synonym: incurable, deadly
Antonym: healthful, wholesome
Sentence: She was diagnosed with a rare immedicable condition.

1988. SERENITY - *[spell]-* S E R E N I T Y
Definition: peace and quiet
Synonym: calm, stillness
Antonym: turbulence, agitation
Sentence: She was surprised by the serenity of her home once her children went to summer camp.

1989. RIGOROUS - *[spell]-* R I G O R O U S
Definition: severe or strict
Synonym: exact, brutal
Antonym: easy, flexible
Sentence: To become a firefighter, he had to undergo rigorous training.

1990. EXPEDITION - *[spell]*- E X P E D I T I O N
Definition: journey for some special purpose
Synonym: excursion, jaunt
Antonym:
Sentence: The expedition headed south in search of new resources for
their camp.

1991. POLTERGEIST - *[spell]*- P O L T E R G E I S T
Definition: spirit or ghost
Synonym: phantom, apparition
Antonym:
Sentence: The poltergeist haunts the old house.

1992. EVERMORE - *[spell]*- E V E R M O R E
Definition: for always
Synonym: eternally, forever
Antonym:
Sentence: She promised that she would evermore pursue her dreams.

1993. HYPOCHONDRIAC - *[spell]*- H Y P O C H O N D R I A C
Definition: person who has abnormal anxiety about their health
Synonym:
Antonym:
Sentence: Ever a hypochondriac, he visited the doctor several times a
year.

1994. SCANDALIZE - *[spell]*- S C A N D A L I Z E
Definition: to offend by doing something thought to be wrong or
improper
Synonym: shock
Antonym:
Sentence: Their behavior at the party scandalized the older ladies.

1995. INCOMPATIBILITY - *[spell]*- I N C O M P A T I B I L I T Y
Definition: quality of being not compatible or harmonious
Synonym:
Antonym: compatibility
Sentence: Because of their incompatibility, they really couldn't work with
each other.

1996. TACTLESS - *[spell]*- T A C T L E S S
Definition: without the ability to say or do the right things
Synonym: unthinking, careless
Antonym: tactful, careful
Sentence: Her comments were completely tactless.

1997. DISCOMPOSE - *[spell]*- D I S C O M P O S E
Definition: disturb the self-possession of
Synonym: bewilder, discombobulate
Antonym:
Sentence: When she ran into her ex-boyfriend at the store, she felt quite discomposed.

1998. REPROACHFUL - *[spell]*- R E P R O A C H F U L
Definition: full of blame or censure
Synonym: offensive, insulting
Antonym: respectful, kind
Sentence: His reproachful tone made his displeasure with her quite obvious.

1999. ENCHANTMENT - *[spell]*- E N C H A N T M E N T
Definition: delight
Synonym: rapture, fascination
Antonym:
Sentence: His enchantment with her was due, in part, to her kind personality.

2000. UNGAINLY - *[spell]*- U N G A I N L Y
Definition: awkward or clumsy
Synonym: lumbering, cumbersome
Antonym: graceful, elegant
Sentence: The ungainly puppy ran through the house.

Hard Words Exercise - 1

2001. PLUMAGE - *[spell]*- P L U M A G E
Definition: feathers of a bird
Synonym:
Antonym:
Sentence: The bird had brightly colored plumage.

2002. STRUCTURAL - *[spell]*- S T R U C T U R A L
Definition: used in building
Synonym: fundamental, architectural
Antonym:
Sentence: After inspection, the building was found to have some structural problems.

2003. OCULAR - *[spell]*- O C U L A R
Definition: having to do with the eye
Synonym: visual, optic
Antonym:
Sentence: A rare ocular disorder caused him to lose his sight.

2004. PHANTASMAL - *[spell]*- P H A N T A S M A L
Definition: relating to things seen only in one's mind
Synonym: illusory, delusory
Antonym: real, apparent
Sentence: The hallucination was purely phantasmal.

2005. FURBISH - *[spell]*- F U R B I S H
Definition: to make lustrous
Synonym: polish, burnish
Antonym: scuff
Sentence: Collectors were dazzled by the newly-furbished antique pieces.

2006. BELLYACHE - *[spell]*- B E L L Y A C H E
Definition: to complain or grumble, especially over something insignificant
Synonym: fuss, gripe
Antonym: rejoice, praise
Sentence: He seemed to constantly bellyache over trivial things.

2007. LIEGE - *[spell]*- L I E G E
Definition: lord having the right to homage and loyal service from his followers
Synonym:
Antonym:
Sentence: The liege lord was demanding of his followers.

2008. PACIFY - *[spell]*- P A C I F Y
Definition: to make peaceful
Synonym: assuage, allay
Antonym: incite, aggravate
Sentence: After hours of effort, he was able to pacify the child.

2009. PLATEAU - *[spell]*- P L A T E A U
Definition: plain in the mountains where the height is considerably above sea level
Synonym:
Antonym:
Sentence: A cottage sat atop the plateau.

2010. CHAUFFEUR - *[spell]*- C H A U F F E U R
Definition: a person who drives a car and is an employee of another person
Synonym: driver
Antonym:
Sentence: He decided to hire a chauffeur so he could get easily from meeting to meeting.

2011. MONARCHAL - *[spell]*- M O N A R C H A L
Definition: having to do with a king
Synonym:
Antonym:
Sentence: He was an expert in monarchal history.

2012. HIRELING - *[spell]*- H I R E L I N G
Definition: person who works only for money, without interest or pride in the work
Synonym:
Antonym:
Sentence: It was obvious that the hireling had no interest in furthering his career.

2013. ADROIT - *[spell]*- A D R O I T
Definition: skilled at reaching one's goals
Synonym: deft, masterful
Antonym: incompetent, inept

Sentence: Because no one had noticed him before, they were surprised at how adroit he appeared
when he took a leadership position.

2014. INFERENTIAL - *[spell]*- I N F E R E N T I A L
Definition: having to do with or depending on the process of finding out something by
assuming or concluding
Synonym: inferable
Antonym:
Sentence: His inferential reasoning led him to a logical conclusion.

2015. CONDEMNATORY - *[spell]*- C O N D E M N A T O R Y
Definition: expressing strong disapproval
Synonym: accusatory, chiding
Antonym: complimentary, encouraging
Sentence: His condemnatory tone clearly conveyed exactly what he thought.

2016. SCRIMP - *[spell]*- S C R I M P
Definition: to be sparing of or use too little of
Synonym: skimp, economize
Antonym: waste, spend
Sentence: The family had to scrimp by on very little in order to go on a vacation later in the year.

2017. HEIRESS - *[spell]*- H E I R E S S
Definition: a female who receives the right to inherit property
Synonym:
Antonym:
Sentence: As heiress to the estate, she was to inherit several hundred acres of land.

2018. PILFER - *[spell]*- P I L F E R
Definition: steal in small quantity
Synonym: steal, commandeer
Antonym:
Sentence: The clerk was caught pilfering money from the store.

2019. DEBAR - *[spell]*- D E B A R
Definition: to prohibit
Synonym: deny, forbid
Antonym: allow, admit
Sentence: The council decided to debar two of its members for misconduct.

2020. STEEPLE - *[spell]*- S T E E P L E
Definition: high tower on a church or other building
Synonym: tower, belfry
Antonym:
Sentence: The steeple of the church could be seen from anywhere in the town.

2021. HARMONIC - *[spell]*- H A R M O N I C
Definition: having to do with agreement of sounds in music
Synonym: melodic, musical
Antonym: cacophonous, dissonance
Sentence: The harmonic sounds coming from the gymnasium suggested that the band was practicing.

2022. HABITAT - *[spell]*- H A B I T A T
Definition: place where an animal or plant naturally lives or grows
Synonym: environment, surroundings
Antonym:
Sentence: The habitat of a squirrel is a tree.

2023. ANNOTATION - *[spell]*- A N N O T A T I O N
Definition: a providing of explanatory notes or criticisms
Synonym: commentary, explanation
Antonym:
Sentence: Difficult literature often has annotations with helpful notes.

2024. INTERRUPTION - *[spell]*- I N T E R R U P T I O N
Definition: a breaking in upon
Synonym: interference, intrude
Antonym:
Sentence: The fire alarm went off suddenly, causing an interruption in the proceedings.

2025. CRANNIED - *[spell]*- C R A N N I E D
Definition: full of small, narrow openings
Synonym: cloven, cracked
Antonym: whole, seamless
Sentence: The ground in his back yard was crannied.

2026. PHARMACOLOGY - *[spell]*- P H A R M A C O L O G Y
Definition: science of drugs, their properties, preparation, uses, and effects
Synonym:
Antonym:
Sentence: In order to be a pharmacist, one has to study pharmacology.

2027. CANONICAL - *[spell]*- C A N O N I C A L
Definition: authorized or accepted
Synonym: approved, orthodox
Antonym: unacceptable, unauthorized
Sentence: Many works of literature are considered canonical and are accepted by all as great works.

2028. MEMORANDUM - *[spell]*- M E M O R A N D U M
Definition: note designating something that needs to be remembered
Synonym: note, reminder
Antonym:
Sentence: She wrote a memorandum to all her employees about the upcoming meeting.

2029. SCRUPLE - *[spell]*- S C R U P L E
Definition: a feeling of doubt about what one ought to do
Synonym: conscience, misgiving
Antonym: certainty, unconcern
Sentence: He has a strong sense of scruples.

2030. DISARMAMENT - *[spell]*- D I S A R M A M E N T
Definition: act of taking weapons away from
Synonym: demilitarization, pacification
Antonym:
Sentence: Once the war ends, the military will go through a process of disarmament.

2031. GRAPPLE - *[spell]*- G R A P P L E
Definition: struggle by seizing one another
Synonym: attack, seize
Antonym: liberate, release
Sentence: The two boys on the wrestling team grappled with each other.

2032. TRANSCRIPTION - *[spell]*- T R A N S C R I P T I O N
Definition: The act or process of making a written, printed, or typed copy of words that have been spoken
Synonym:
Antonym:
Sentence: The writer made a transcription of his work on a weekly basis.

2033. ASSEMBLE - *[spell]*- A S S E M B L E
Definition: to bring together
Synonym: gather, amass
Antonym: disperse, scatter
Sentence: In order to make a decision, she called for everyone to

assemble in the conference
room.

2034. JOSTLE - *[spell]*- J O S T L E
Definition: to shove, push or crowd against
Synonym: hustle, elbow
Antonym:
Sentence: He was jostled by the crowd on the subway on his way to work.

2035. AGENCY - *[spell]*- A G E N C Y
Definition: a person or company that has power to act for another
Synonym: firm, bureau
Antonym:
Sentence: She sought out the employment agency to help her find new
work.

2036. INIQUITY - *[spell]*- I N I Q U I T Y
Definition: a wicked act or thing
Synonym: abomination, misdeed
Antonym: virtue, goodness
Sentence: He committed an iniquity against his employees by not giving
them a raise.

2037. EMBOSS - *[spell]*- E M B O S S
Definition: decorate with a design that stands out from the surface
Synonym: etch, imprint
Antonym:
Sentence: The title of the book was embossed in gold lettering.

2038. HORIZON - *[spell]*- H O R I Z O N
Definition: line where the earth and sky seem to meet
Synonym: skyline
Antonym:
Sentence: He saw the sun coming up over the horizon.

2039. BLISSFUL - *[spell]*- B L I S S F U L
Definition: extremely joyful
Synonym: euphoric, happy
Antonym: joyless, miserable
Sentence: His blissful attitude was due to his recent engagement to the
woman of his dreams.

2040. LUSCIOUS - *[spell]*- L U S C I O U S
Definition: highly pleasant to the taste or smell
Synonym: succulent, exquisite

Antonym: bland, distasteful
Sentence: The smell of the baking brownies was luscious.

2041. SUPPLICATION - *[spell]*- S U P P L I C A T I O N
Definition: a begging humbly and earnestly
Synonym: appeal, entreaty
Antonym:
Sentence: The woman's supplication to the government for aid was ultimately unanswered.

2042. FARSIGHTED - *[spell]*- F A R S I G H T E D
Definition: looking ahead and planning wisely
Synonym: prudent, shrewd
Antonym: foolish, shortsighted
Sentence: Because she was farsighted, she had clear financial goals in mind.

2043. INCEPTION - *[spell]*- I N C E P T I O N
Definition: beginning or origin
Synonym: initiation, outset
Antonym: conclusion, end
Sentence: At the inception of the game, both teams shook hands.

2044. OVERCOMPENSATE - *[spell]*- O V E R C O M P E N S A T E
Definition: make unnecessary effort to make up for shortcoming
Synonym: recompense, atone
Antonym:
Sentence: He often tried to overcompensate for his mediocre looks by flaunting his money.

2045. SINEW - *[spell]*- S I N E W
Definition: strength or force
Synonym: vigor, force
Antonym: disability, impotence
Sentence: She was known to be a woman of great athletic sinew.

2046. COALITION - *[spell]*- C O A L I T I O N
Definition: a union
Synonym: combination, alliance
Antonym: disassociation
Sentence: Unhappy with their wages, the workers formed a coalition to try and bring about a change.

2047. NONENTITY - *[spell]*- N O N E N T I T Y
Definition: person or thing of little or no importance
Synonym:

Antonym:
Sentence: She was so unimportant in the company that she felt as if she were a nonentity.

2048. RATIONALE - *[spell]*- R A T I O N A L E
Definition: the fundamental reason
Synonym: excuse, explanation
Antonym:
Sentence: His rationale for leaving the company was his desire to find higher pay elsewhere.

2049. SOUVENIR - *[spell]*- S O U V E N I R
Definition: something given or kept for remembrance
Synonym: keepsake, memento
Antonym:
Sentence: He brought souvenirs home from overseas for each of his children.

2050. RISQUE - *[spell]*- R I S Q U E
Definition: suggestive of indecency
Synonym: lewd, provocative
Antonym: clean, decent
Sentence: Several parts of the movie were risquÃ©.

2051. CLASSIFIED - *[spell]*- C L A S S I F I E D
Definition: sorted or arranged into groups
Synonym: grouped, arranged
Antonym: disorganized
Sentence: The paperwork was classified according to importance.

2052. NEUROLOGY - *[spell]*- N E U R O L O G Y
Definition: study of the nervous system and its diseases
Synonym:
Antonym:
Sentence: The doctor was an expert in neurology.

2053. PIPKIN - *[spell]*- P I P K I N
Definition: a small earthen or metal pot
Synonym: pot, bowl
Antonym:
Sentence: The stew was cooked in a pipkin.

2054. OVERDRIVE - *[spell]*- O V E R D R I V E
Definition: to work too hard
Synonym:

Antonym:
Sentence: In order to meet the deadline, she put herself into overdrive.

2055. FORKED - *[spell]*- F O R K E D
Definition: divided into branches
Synonym: split
Antonym:
Sentence: The pathway forked off into two separate roads.

2056. PRIMITIVE - *[spell]*- P R I M I T I V E
Definition: of early times or long-ago
Synonym: ancient, archaic
Antonym: modern, advanced
Sentence: The archeologists discovered a primitive wheel at their dig site.

2057. INANITY - *[spell]*- I N A N I T Y
Definition: lack of sense or ideas
Synonym: stupidity, foolishness
Antonym:
Sentence: She never has anything interesting to say, and her conversations are constant inanity.

2058. FOREVERMORE - *[spell]*- F O R E V E R M O R E
Definition: without ever coming to an end
Synonym: always, eternally
Antonym: nevermore
Sentence: He promised to love her forevermore.

2059. TREASONABLE - *[spell]*- T R E A S O N A B L E
Definition: involving treason (betrayal of one's country or ruler)
Synonym: faithless, mutinous
Antonym:
Sentence: His remarks were considered treasonable by some people.

2060. FLANK - *[spell]*- F L A N K
Definition: the far right or left side of an army, fleet or fort
Synonym:
Antonym:
Sentence: Jackson's right flank was attacked as they attempted to retreat.

2061. CHIFFON - *[spell]*- C H I F F O N
Definition: thin cloth used for clothing, especially dresses
Synonym:
Antonym:
Sentence: Her bridesmaid dresses were made of chiffon.

2062. MORASS - *[spell]* - M O R A S S
Definition: piece of low, soft, wet ground
Synonym:
Antonym:
Sentence: The hikers passed over a morass.

2063. EMBOLDEN - *[spell]* - E M B O L D E N
Definition: encourage
Synonym: inspire, invigorate
Antonym: dissuade, intimidate
Sentence: The girl was emboldened by the words of her father.

2064. ZONAL - *[spell]* - Z O N A L
Definition: pertaining to a zone (tract or area that is distinguished from adjoining tracts for some reason)
Synonym:
Antonym:
Sentence: The zonal lines of the school districts were slated to be reconfigured.

2065. INCURABLE - *[spell]* - I N C U R A B L E
Definition: unable of being healed
Synonym: untreatable
Antonym: curable, treatable
Sentence: He was diagnosed as having an incurable disease.

2066. EXUDE - *[spell]* - E X U D E
Definition: give forth
Synonym: emanate, radiate
Antonym:
Sentence: The little boy exuded excitement.

2067. EAVESDROP - *[spell]* - E A V E S D R O P
Definition: listen to talk one is not supposed to hear
Synonym: overhear, listen
Antonym:
Sentence: The girl eavesdropped outside her brother's door.

2068. DEFINITIVE - *[spell]* - D E F I N I T I V E
Definition: something that settles a question
Synonym: conclusive, definite
Antonym: ambiguous, wavering
Sentence: After deliberating the matter for some time, she was able to give a definitive answer.

2069. BARRACKS - *[spell]*- B A R R A C K S
Definition: a building where soldiers live
Synonym: camp, garrison
Antonym:
Sentence: After a long day of training, the soldiers retreated to the barracks.

2070. LEGALITY - *[spell]*- L E G A L I T Y
Definition: condition or quality of being legal
Synonym: validity, lawfulness
Antonym: illegality, unlawfulness
Sentence: The legality of his recent activities was questionable.

2071. PURSUANCE - *[spell]*- P U R S U A N C E
Definition: following or carrying out
Synonym:
Antonym:
Sentence: The police officer was in pursuance of the bank robber.

2072. DISPERSE - *[spell]*- D I S P E R S E
Definition: to send off in different directions
Synonym: scatter, disseminate
Antonym: cluster, accumulate
Sentence: The children dispersed about the field to play dodge ball.

2073. GAVEL - *[spell]*- G A V E L
Definition: small mallet used by a presiding officer to signal for attention
Synonym:
Antonym:
Sentence: The judge used his gavel to call order to the courtroom.

2074. SABOTAGE - *[spell]*- S A B O T A G E
Definition: damage done to work, tools, machinery etc.
Synonym: destruction, treachery
Antonym: devotion, faithfulness
Sentence: The enemy tried to sabotage the artillery where all the weapons were kept.

2075. COLUMNAR - *[spell]*- COLUMNAR
Definition: like a pillar
Synonym: cylindrical, circular
Antonym:
Sentence: The structure was columnar in shape.

2076. NEGATIVISM - *[spell]*- N E G A T I V I S M
Definition: an attitude of mind marked by skepticism especially about

nearly everything affirmed by others
Synonym: pessimism
Antonym: optimism
Sentence: Her negativism brought everyone down.

2077. GANDER - *[spell]*- G A N D E R
Definition: a long look
Synonym: glance, glimpse
Antonym:
Sentence: He looked out his window to take a gander of the new neighbors.

2078. QUIZZICAL - *[spell]*- Q U I Z Z I C A L
Definition: questioning or baffled
Synonym: confused, incredulous
Antonym: clear, certain
Sentence: She gave him a quizzical look when he made the suggestion.

2079. SLENDERIZE - *[spell]*- S L E N D E R I Z E
Definition: to make or become long and thin
Synonym: slim, reduce
Antonym: enlarge, fatten
Sentence: The artists slenderized the piece of clay that she would later add to her sculpture.

2080. EXTRAVAGANCE - *[spell]*- E X T R A V A G A N C E
Definition: careless and lavish spending
Synonym: wastefulness, squandering
Antonym: economy, frugality
Sentence: His extravagance eventually caused him to go bankrupt.

2081. ELASTICITY - *[spell]*- E L A S T I C I T Y
Definition: having the quality of returning to its original shape or size after being stretched or squeezed
Synonym:
Antonym:
Sentence: The terms "right" and "wrong" have much elasticity in their meaning.

2082. ORNERY - *[spell]*- O R N E R Y
Definition: mean or irritable in disposition
Synonym: cranky, grouchy
Antonym: agreeable, friendly
Sentence: Her ornery attitude was just part of her nature.

2083. SNARE - *[spell]*- S N A R E
Definition: to trap or entangle
Synonym: allurement, catch
Antonym:
Sentence: Even though she tried to resist him, she felt herself snared by his charm.

2084. ENCUMBER - *[spell]*- E N C U M B E R
Definition: hold back
Synonym: hinder, hamper
Antonym: advance, aid
Sentence: Her plans for the department were encumbered by endless bureaucracy.

2085. APPOINTEE - *[spell]*- A P P O I N T E E
Definition: a person who has been named for an office or position
Synonym: delegate, representative
Antonym:
Sentence: As the new appointee for chairman, he took on many responsibilities.

2086. INVENTORY - *[spell]*- I N V E N T O R Y
Definition: a complete and detailed list of articles with their estimated value
Synonym:
Antonym:
Sentence: The store's inventory revealed that they should have had much more of the item in stock.

2087. GANGLY - *[spell]*- G A N G L Y
Definition: awkwardly tall and slender
Synonym: gawky, lanky
Antonym: graceful, dwarfish
Sentence: The gangly youth slumped awkwardly into his desk.

2088. SPRIGHTLY - *[spell]*- S P R I G H T L Y
Definition: lively
Synonym: vivacious, energetic
Antonym: dull, insipid
Sentence: Her sprightly attitude was contagious.

2089. SUBTENANT - *[spell]*- S U B T E N A N T
Definition: the tenant of a tenant (person who rents property, land, etc.)
Synonym:
Antonym:
Sentence: She decided to take a subtenant in order to save money on rent.

2090. EXPEDITE - *[spell]*- E X P E D I T E
Definition: making easy and quick
Synonym: accelerate, facilitate
Antonym: hinder, delay
Sentence: His help expedited the process of cleaning her living room.

2091. PRECLUSIVE - *[spell]*- P R E C L U S I V E
Definition: tending or serving to shut out or make impossible
Synonym: preventative, defensive
Antonym:
Sentence: He took preclusive measures to make sure he did not get sick.

2092. ENSNARE - *[spell]*- E N S N A R E
Definition: catch in a trap
Synonym: enmesh, entangle
Antonym: disentangle, liberate
Sentence: She was ensnared by his clever ploy to get her to go to the concert with him.

2093. SPHERICAL - *[spell]*- S P H E R I C A L
Definition: round in shape
Synonym: rounded, circular
Antonym:
Sentence: Because the basketball was flat, it had lost some of its spherical shape.

2094. PALTER - *[spell]*- P A L T E R
Definition: to talk or act insincerely
Synonym: babble, chatter
Antonym:
Sentence: Her actions were merely palter.

2095. RECOMMENDATION - *[spell]*- R E C O M M E N D A T I O N
Definition: act or speak in favor of
Synonym: approval, support
Antonym: disapproval, opposition
Sentence: The student asked the teacher to write a recommendation for him for college admission purposes.

2096. REGALIA - *[spell]*- R E G A L I A
Definition: the emblems of royalty
Synonym:
Antonym:
Sentence: The prince wore full regalia during his coronation ceremony.

2097.   AERIAL - *[spell]*- A E R I A L
Definition: of the air
Synonym: atmospheric, flying
Antonym: terrestrial, grounded
Sentence: Most birds are aerial creatures.

2098.   INFLUX - *[spell]*- I N F L U X
Definition: a steady flowing in
Synonym: arrival, inflow
Antonym: outflow
Sentence: The recent influx of new workers was due to a recent boom in company productivity.

2099.   REMNANT - *[spell]*- R E M N A N T
Definition: a piece left over after the rest has been used or sold
Synonym: particle, remains
Antonym: whole, core
Sentence: After making the quilt, she had several remnants of fabric.

2100.   PROBATIONARY - *[spell]*- P R O B A T I O N A R Y
Definition: of or having to do with trial or testing of conduct, character, qualifications etc.
Synonym: tentative, contingent
Antonym: certain, conclusive
Sentence: The new employee was placed on probationary status for his first year of employment.

Hard Words Exercise - 2

2101. EXEMPLIFICATION - *[spell]*- E X E M P L I F I C A T I ON
Definition: showing by example
Synonym: illustration
Antonym:
Sentence: She is the exemplification of what that charity stands for.

2102. RANSACK - *[spell]*- R A N S A C K
Definition: to search thoroughly
Synonym: pillage, loot
Antonym:
Sentence: Looking for a midnight snack, he ransacked the pantry.

2103. DISASSEMBLE - *[spell]*- D I S A S S E M B L E
Definition: to take apart
Synonym: dissect, dismantle
Antonym: assemble
Sentence: In order to find the problem, he disassembled the car's engine.

2104. UNCONDITIONAL - *[spell]*- U N C O N D I T I O N A L
Definition: absolute
Synonym: definite, total
Antonym: conditional, indefinite
Sentence: He promised to give his new wife his unconditional love.

2105. SUFFRAGE - *[spell]*- S U F F R A G E
Definition: the right to vote
Synonym: franchise
Antonym:
Sentence: She worked for many years on the issue of women's suffrage.

2106. AMATEUR - *[spell]*- A M A T E U R
Definition: a person who does something as a hobby rather than as a
professional
Synonym:
Antonym: expert, professional
Sentence: She was an amateur in sculpture.

2107. INTERLOCK - *[spell]*- I N T E R L O C K
Definition: to fit tightly together
Synonym: intertwine, mesh
Antonym:
Sentence: The couple interlocked their hands as they walked down the street.

2108. FORAGE - *[spell]*- F O R A G E
Definition: hunt or search for food
Synonym: rummage, scour
Antonym:
Sentence: Because there had been a drought, many animals in the area had to forage for food.

2109. BASSINET - *[spell]*- B A S S I N E T
Definition: a baby's cradle
Synonym: crib, pram
Antonym:
Sentence: The mother put the baby to sleep in a bassinet.

2110. LEGIBILITY - *[spell]*- L E G I B I L I T Y
Definition: condition of being easily read
Synonym: readability
Antonym:
Sentence: The legibility of her handwriting was much improved over the years.

2111. INADVERTENCE - *[spell]*- I N A D V E R T E N C E
Definition: having done something without planning or intention
Synonym: unintentional
Antonym:
Sentence: Due to his inadvertence, he missed the deadline and was disqualified.

2112. PERCUSSIVE - *[spell]*- P E R C U S S I V E
Definition: characterized by the sound resulting from striking one thing against another
Synonym:
Antonym:
Sentence: The percussive thunder woke her from sleep.

2113. EXPLETIVE - *[spell]*- E X P L E T I V E
Definition: exclamation or oath
Synonym: curse, interjection
Antonym:
Sentence: He had to bite his tongue to keep from uttering an expletive.

2114. STARVELING - *[spell]*- S T A R V E L I N G
Definition: extremely hungry
Synonym: famished, hungry
Antonym:
Sentence: The man was forced to steal food since he was starveling.

2115. HESITATION - *[spell]*- H E S I T A T I O N
Definition: a failing to act promptly or holding back
Synonym: doubt, indecision
Antonym: certainty, confidence
Sentence: She gave a thorough reply after a brief hesitation.

2116. OVERBLOWN - *[spell]*- O V E R B L O W N
Definition: between brightness and decay
Synonym:
Antonym:
Sentence: The flowers were reaching an overblown state.

2117. IMPOUND - *[spell]*- I M P O U N D
Definition: shut up in a pen or pound
Synonym: imprison, cage
Antonym: release, abandon
Sentence: His car was impounded after it was repossessed.

2118. PROGRESSIVE - *[spell]*- P R O G R E S S I V E
Definition: making an advancement or growth
Synonym: growing, revolutionary
Antonym: regression
Sentence: His progressive improvement in such a short time was quite an accomplishment.

2119. BOORISH - *[spell]*- B O O R I S H
Definition: rude
Synonym: barbaric, uncivilized
Antonym: mannerly, kind
Sentence: The child's boorish behavior was unacceptable to his parents.

2120. MANIFESTATION - *[spell]*- M A N I F E S T A T I O N
Definition: a showing
Synonym: expression, proof
Antonym:
Sentence: Her nightmare seemed to be a manifestation of fears in real life.

2121. FLOUNCE - *[spell]*- F L O U N C E
Definition: to make floundering movements
Synonym: bounce, fling

Antonym:
Sentence: She was unused to walking in heels, and flounced into the room.

2122. ENVELOP - *[spell]*- E N V E L O P
Definition: wrap or cover
Synonym: encase, enclose
Antonym:
Sentence: He enveloped his daughter in a loving embrace.

2123. BILLIONAIRE - *[spell]*- B I L L I O N A I R E
Definition: a person who has more than a billion dollars
Synonym:
Antonym:
Sentence: The billionaire made his fortune by gradually working his way up through the company.

2124. LOCOMOTION - *[spell]*- L O C O M O T I O N
Definition: act or power of moving from place to place
Synonym: movement, mobility
Antonym:
Sentence: The rapid locomotion of the jet was revolutionary.

2125. EXPOSURE - *[spell]*- E X P O S U R E
Definition: a being laid open without shelter or protection
Synonym: uncovering, vulnerability
Antonym: enclosure, concealment
Sentence: In order to avoid exposure to the sun, she sat in the shade.

2126. SEMINAR - *[spell]*- S E M I N A R
Definition: group of students engaged in discussion and research under the guidance of a professor
Synonym: conference, discussion
Antonym:
Sentence: She was nervous about registering for her first graduate seminar.

2127. TIMBERLAND - *[spell]*- T I M B E R L A N D
Definition: land with trees that are, or will be, useful for timber
Synonym: forest, woods
Antonym:
Sentence: He purchased the large tract of land because it was timberland.

2128. TAXONOMY - *[spell]*- T A X O N O M Y
Definition: classification
Synonym: arrangement, distribution

Antonym:
Sentence: The biologist was an expert in the taxonomy of birds.

2129. SIGNATORY - *[spell]*- S I G N A T O R Y
Definition: a signer of a document
Synonym: notary, endorser
Antonym:
Sentence: Each of the seven signatories of the Proclamation of the Provisional Government of Ireland was executed for treason.

2130. CHEEKY - *[spell]*- C H E E K Y
Definition: rude or disrespectful
Synonym: insolent, impudent
Antonym: respectful
Sentence: The student's cheeky attitude earned him a detention.

2131. MONASTERY - *[spell]*- M O N A S T E R Y
Definition: building where monks live
Synonym:
Antonym:
Sentence: The tourist visited an iconic monastery.

2132. BEWAIL - *[spell]*- B E W A I L
Definition: to mourn or weep for
Synonym: bemoan, rue
Antonym: laugh, cheer
Sentence: After the death of her friend, all she could do was bewail the loss.

2133. LITERACY - *[spell]*- L I T E R A C Y
Definition: ability to read and write
Synonym:
Antonym:
Sentence: The literacy of all children is important to our country.

2134. DIGRESS - *[spell]*- D I G R E S S
Definition: turn aside from the main subject in talking or writing
Synonym: stray, deviate
Antonym: focus
Sentence: During his acceptance speech, he began to digress.

2135. PERJURY - *[spell]*- P E R J U R Y
Definition: act or crime of willfully giving false testimony while under oath
Synonym: falsehood, deception

Antonym: frankness, honesty
Sentence: The man was accused of perjury.

2136. RECOUP - *[spell]*- R E C O U P
Definition: to make up for
Synonym: redeem, recover
Antonym: deprive, penalize
Sentence: After the stock market crashed, he tried the best to recoup his losses.

2137. SENTIMENTALITY - *[spell]*- S E N T I M E N T A L I T Y
Definition: tendency to be influenced by thoughts and feelings rather than reason
Synonym: melodrama
Antonym:
Sentence: She tended to have a great sentimentality about the past.

2138. CONFISCATE - *[spell]*- C O N F I S C A T E
Definition: to take and keep
Synonym: impound, commandeer
Antonym: return
Sentence: The teacher confiscated the student's cell phone when he used it in class.

2139. SITAR - *[spell]*- S I T A R
Definition: musical instrument with a long neck and round body
Synonym:
Antonym:
Sentence: The musician was an expert at playing many instruments, but he loved the sitar most of all.

2140. SENSIBILITY - *[spell]*- S E N S I B I L I T Y
Definition: ability to feel or perceive
Synonym: emotion, feeling
Antonym:
Sentence: She possessed a delicate sensibility and was easily offended.

2141. CONGENIALITY - *[spell]*- C O N G E N I A L I T Y
Definition: the quality of being agreeable
Synonym: affability, agreeability
Antonym: aloofness, coldness
Sentence: He was known and well-liked for his congeniality.

2142. SUPPLEMENTAL - *[spell]*- S U P P L E M E N T A L
Definition: additional
Synonym: auxiliary, supporting

Antonym:
Sentence: The teacher gave students supplemental material to study over the weekend.

2143. BILLOWY - *[spell]*- B I L L O W Y
Definition: rising or rolling in waves
Synonym: bouncy, rippling
Antonym: smooth, sleek
Sentence: The billowy fabric waved in the breeze.

2144. LONGITUDE - *[spell]*- L O N G I T U D E
Definition: a distance east or west on the earth's surface
Synonym:
Antonym:
Sentence: He sailed parallel to the longitude of the earth's surface.

2145. GNARL - *[spell]*- G N A R L
Definition: twisted or knotted
Synonym: contort, twist
Antonym:
Sentence: The woman's hands, though old and gnarled, quickly knitted a blanket.

2146. VULNERABLE - *[spell]*- V U L N E R A B L E
Definition: capable or susceptible to being wounded
Synonym: defenseless, susceptible
Antonym: guarded, protected
Sentence: He was especially vulnerable when it came to putting others first.

2147. SLOTHFUL - *[spell]*- S L O T H F U L
Definition: unwilling to work or exert oneself
Synonym: lazy, inert
Antonym: active, energetic
Sentence: Feeling slothful, she decided to sit on the coach and watch TV for the rest of the afternoon.

2148. PUFFERY - *[spell]*- P U F F E R Y
Definition: exaggerated praise
Synonym:
Antonym:
Sentence: He received puffery from his parents for winning the game.

2149. IMMEMORIAL - *[spell]*- I M M E M O R I A L
Definition: extended back beyond the bounds of memory
Synonym: ancient, old

Antonym: current, recent

Sentence: In days immemorial, the first colonists ventured to America.

2150. BAIL - *[spell]*- B A I L
Definition: to obtain the release of
Synonym:
Antonym:
Sentence: After he was arrested for something minor, his sister had to bail him out of jail.

2151. LANDLUBBER - *[spell]*- L A N D L U B B E R
Definition: a person not used to being on ships
Synonym:
Antonym:
Sentence: The seasoned sailor laughed at the landlubber aboard his ship.

2152. GRISLY - *[spell]*- G R I S L Y
Definition: causing horror
Synonym: appalling, dreadful
Antonym: comforting, pleasant
Sentence: Police are afraid that there is a grisly explanation behind the drops of blood on the floor.

2153. ESTRANGEMENT - *[spell]*- E S T R A N G E M E N T
Definition: to cause someone to no longer be involved with another person
Synonym: alienation, disaffection
Antonym:
Sentence: The woman attempted to reconcile with her sister after an estrangement.

2154. RECRIMINATE - *[spell]*- R E C R I M I N A T E
Definition: to accuse in return
Synonym: prosecute, indict
Antonym: exonerate, exculpate
Sentence: His claims were just a shallow attempt to recriminate his opponent.

2155. SEASONABLE - *[spell]*- S E A S O N A B L E
Definition: suitable to the season (one of the four periods of the year)
Synonym: timely
Antonym:
Sentence: She made a delicious salad using seasonable vegetables.

2156. GENERALIZATION - *[spell]*- G E N E R A L I Z A T I O N
Definition: act or process of making into one general statement

Synonym:

Antonym:

Sentence: She was prone to making generalizations about people.

2157.   BINGE - *[spell]*- B I N G E

Definition: a bout or spree of indulgence

Synonym: revelry, carousal

Antonym:

Sentence: After a weeklong binge, she decided to give up alcohol.

2158.   LOOPHOLE - *[spell]*- L O O P H O L E

Definition: means of escape or evasion

Synonym: escape, outlet

Antonym:

Sentence: She found a loophole in the contract that allowed her to get out of it.

2159.   GUARDIANSHIP - *[spell]*- G U A R D I A N S H I P

Definition: position or care of a person who protects

Synonym: custody, caretaking

Antonym:

Sentence: The orphan was placed in the guardianship of a foster family.

2160.   SENILE - *[spell]*- S E N I L E

Definition: of old age

Synonym: aged, decrepit

Antonym:

Sentence: As she aged, she worried about becoming senile.

2161.   RAMPAGE - *[spell]*- R A M P A G E

Definition: excited, reckless behavior

Synonym: storm, turmoil

Antonym: calm, placidity

Sentence: The mother went on a rampage at the school after finding out her son had been expelled.

2162.   FOLIAGE - *[spell]*- F O L I A G E

Definition: leaves of a plant

Synonym:

Antonym:

Sentence: The foliage of the Japanese maple tree is a striking red.

2163.   GROGGY - *[spell]*- G R O G G Y

Definition: not steady, shaky

Synonym: dazed, confused

Antonym: steady, clear-headed
Sentence: She woke up feeling groggy.

2164. SUCCESSOR - *[spell]*- S U C C E S S O R
Definition: person who follows or succeeds another in office, position, etc.
Synonym: heir, replacement
Antonym:
Sentence: The president met with his successor to make plans for the transition.

2165. IDEALISM - *[spell]*- I D E A L I S M
Definition: the pursuit of goals that one believes are noble
Synonym: optimism, hopefulness
Antonym: pessimism
Sentence: He had a very firm sense of idealism, which guided him in all his decisions.

2166. PENSION - *[spell]*- P E N S I O N
Definition: a fixed sum of money paid at regular intervals by the government to a person who is retired
Synonym: allowance, annuity
Antonym:
Sentence: He was given a pension for his many years of service.

2167. GABBY - *[spell]*- G A B B Y
Definition: very talkative
Synonym: chatty, garrulous
Antonym: quiet
Sentence: The child was quite gabby about her school day.

2168. FLUNKY - *[spell]*- F L U N K Y
Definition: a flattering, fawning person
Synonym: drudge, lackey
Antonym:
Sentence: The celebrity had a group of flunkies who did whatever he asked.

2169. PHRASAL - *[spell]*- P H R A S A L
Definition: consisting of or like a phrase or phrases
Synonym:
Antonym:
Sentence: The author coined a signature phrasal saying.

2170. UNIFICATION - *[spell]*- U N I F I C A T I O N
Definition: formation into a single unit

Synonym: merger, consolidation
Antonym: division, parting
Sentence: The unification of the political party happened suddenly.

2171. HIGHBROW - *[spell]*- H I G H B R O W
Definition: person who cares or who claims to care a great deal about knowledge and culture
Synonym: intellectual, geek
Antonym: lowbrow, philistine
Sentence: The scholar tended to stick to only highbrow society.

2172. SEDUCTION - *[spell]*- S E D U C T I O N
Definition: a tempting to do wrong
Synonym: persuasion, attraction
Antonym:
Sentence: He vowed to resist the seduction of fame and fortune.

2173. DECEPTION - *[spell]*- D E C E P T IO N
Definition: the act of making someone believe something that isn't true
Synonym: misleading, betrayal
Antonym: forthrightness, honest
Sentence: His deception caused her to lose all trust in him.

2174. PROJECTILE - *[spell]*- P R O J E C T I L E
Definition: any object that is thrown, hurled, or shot
Synonym:
Antonym:
Sentence: The boy was ashamed when he launched a projectile across the room and broke his mother's china.

2175. HAUGHTY - *[spell]*- H A U G H T Y
Definition: too proud and scornful of others
Synonym: arrogant, imperious
Antonym: humble, meek
Sentence: His haughty attitude caused him to be disliked by many.

2176. SIERRA - *[spell]*- S I E R R A
Definition: a chain of hills or mountains with jagged peaks
Synonym: mountain, ridge
Antonym: plain
Sentence: In his sightseeing travels, he made a stop in the sierra.

2177. BRIEFING - *[spell]*- B R I E F I N G
Definition: a short summary of details about something soon to be undertaken
Synonym: conference, meeting

Antonym:
Sentence: Before beginning the raid, the police force were given a briefing about their plans.

2178. MARBLE - *[spell]*- M A R B L E
Definition: to color or stain to look like marble stone
Synonym:
Antonym:
Sentence: The stone had a marbled texture.

2179. WAKE - *[spell]*- W A K E
Definition: following, behind
Synonym: aftermath
Antonym:
Sentence: She was remarkably cheerful in the wake of the bad news.

2180. AGORAPHOBIA - *[spell]*- A G O R A P H O B I A
Definition: a fear of open spaces
Synonym:
Antonym:
Sentence: After living her life so long in the cramped city, she experienced some agoraphobia
when she moved to the country.

2181. INITIATE - *[spell]*- I N I T I A T E
Definition: be the first one to start
Synonym: commence, trigger
Antonym: cease, block
Sentence: He was the first to initiate a conversation with the stranger.

2182. CASEMENT - *[spell]*- C A S E M E NT
Definition: a window
Synonym:
Antonym:
Sentence: She stood at the casement, watching her friend drive away.

2183. MILLENNIAL - *[spell]*- M I L L E N N I A L
Definition: of a thousand years
Synonym:
Antonym:
Sentence: The comet's passing by earth was millennial.

2184. ENHANCE - *[spell]*- E N H A N C E
Definition: make great in value or importance
Synonym: strengthen, upgrade
Antonym: diminish, lessen

Sentence: The room was enhanced by the addition of several comfortable chairs.

2185. CLANNISH - *[spell]*- C L A N N I SH
Definition: having to do with a group of related families
Synonym: associative, close
Antonym: friendly, open
Sentence: The group of friends was so close that they acted clannish.

2186. NEGATE - *[spell]*- N E G A T E
Definition: destroy, nullify, or make ineffective
Synonym: invalidate, neutralize
Antonym:
Sentence: One mistake could negate all of her hard work.

2187. STERILITY - *[spell]*- S T E R I L I T Y
Definition: condition of being free from germs
Synonym:
Antonym:
Sentence: Ensuring the sterility of her office was something of an obsession for her.

2188. COMMOTION - *[spell]*- C O M M O T I O N
Definition: violent movement
Synonym: agitation, turbulence
Antonym: calm, peace
Sentence: He went to the window to see what the commotion outside was all about.

2189. HALTING - *[spell]*- H A L T I N G
Definition: slow and uncertain
Synonym: wavering, awkward
Antonym:
Sentence: She walked in a halting manner after falling down the stairs.

2190. SAVVY - *[spell]*- S A V V Y
Definition: to know or understand
Synonym: acute, discerning
Antonym: blunt, coarse
Sentence: Everyone went to him for help because he was known to be computer savvy.

2191. TEXTILE - *[spell]*- T E X T I L E
Definition: something woven
Synonym: fabric, cloth

Antonym:
Sentence: She went to the industrial supply store to buy textiles.

2192. CADENCE - *[spell]*- C A D E N C E
Definition: a rising and falling sound
Synonym: pulse, vibration
Antonym:
Sentence: The cadence of the guest speaker's voice nearly put him to sleep.

2193. MEDIOCRITY - *[spell]*- M E D I O C R I T Y
Definition: neither good nor bad in quality
Synonym: commonness, ordinariness
Antonym:
Sentence: The mediocrity of his work did not impress his boss.

2194. FACILITY - *[spell]*- F A C I L I T Y
Definition: power to do anything easily and quickly
Synonym: ability, adroitness
Antonym:
Sentence: He had the facility to be successful in whatever he put his mind to.

2195. HYBRID - *[spell]*- H Y B R I D
Definition: offspring of two organisms of different varieties, species, races, etc.
Synonym: cross, combination
Antonym:
Sentence: A pluot is a hybrid of a plum and an apricot.

2196. BEDECK - *[spell]*- B E D E C K
Definition: to adorn
Synonym: decorate, embellish
Antonym:
Sentence: She wanted to look good for the dance, so she made sure to bedeck herself with
jewelry.

2197. LESION - *[spell]*- L E S I O N
Definition: an injury or hurt
Synonym: laceration, abrasion
Antonym:
Sentence: The child has a lesion on his knee from falling on the pavement.

2198. ACCUSTOMED - *[spell]*- A C C U S T O M E D
Definition: to be used to something
Synonym: customary, habituated
Antonym: abnormal, unaccustomed
Sentence: He was quite accustomed to her strange behaviors, so it did not bother him.

2199. INEFFICACY - *[spell]*- I N E F F I C A C Y
Definition: lack of the ability to produce the wanted effect
Synonym: feebleness, helplessness
Antonym: ability
Sentence: His inefficacy in terms of sports made his friends laugh at him.

2200. CONCENTRATED - *[spell]*- C O N C E N T R A T E D
Definition: brought together in one place
Synonym: condensed, fixed
Antonym: dispersed, diffused
Sentence: The sweetness of the dessert was much too concentrated for his liking.

Hard Words Exercise - 3

2201. INDECOROUS - *[spell]*- I N D E C O R O U S
Definition: not in accordance with proper behavior
Synonym: rude, improper
Antonym: proper, polite
Sentence: His indecorous behavior made people think little of him.

2202. RESILIENCE - *[spell]*- R E S I L I E N C E
Definition: power of springing back
Synonym: elasticity, pliancy
Antonym:
Sentence: The child's resilience after the injury was astounding.

2203. GUARANTEE - *[spell]*- G U A R A N T E E
Definition: promise to do something
Synonym: pledge, assurance
Antonym:
Sentence: The store guaranteed customers would be satisfied with their products.

2204. HOSTILITY - *[spell]*- H O S T I L I T Y
Definition: unfriendliness
Synonym: enmity, bitterness
Antonym: friendliness, kindness
Sentence: The man showed open hostility toward his relatives.

2205. TOUCHE - *[spell]*- T O U C H E
Definition: exclamation of acknowledging an effective point in an argument or a clever reply
Synonym:
Antonym:
Sentence: At her witty comeback, he shouted, "touchÃ©!"

2206. DALLIANCE - *[spell]*- D A L L I A N C E
Definition: flirtation
Synonym:
Antonym:
Sentence: Her dalliance with the man next door was obvious.

2207. RESTORATION - *[spell]*- R E S T O R A T I O N
Definition: a bringing back or establishing again
Synonym: recovery, revival
Antonym: destruction, abolition
Sentence: The restoration of the king to the throne brought peace to the country.

2208. STIMULATE - *[spell]*- S T I M U L A T E
Definition: to spur or rouse to go on
Synonym: arouse, excite
Antonym:
Sentence: She tried to stimulate her child's mind by giving him lots of books.

2209. APOLOGETIC - *[spell]*- A P O L O G E T I C
Definition: offering words of regret for an offense
Synonym: regretful, remorseful
Antonym: unrepentant, remorseless
Sentence: The little girl was apologetic about breaking her brother's toy.

2210. INTRUSION - *[spell]*- I N T R U S I O N
Definition: act of forcing oneself into somewhere without permission
Synonym: encroachment, imposition
Antonym:
Sentence: His intrusion into her office was unwelcome.

2211. UNCIVILIZED - *[spell]*- U N C I V I L I Z E D
Definition: barbarous
Synonym: boorish, wild
Antonym: civilized, sophisticated
Sentence: Her manners were most uncivilized.

2212. ARTILLERY - *[spell]*- A R T I L L E R Y
Definition: rockets or guns manned by a crew
Synonym: munitions, arms
Antonym:
Sentence: The well-manned artillery is what ultimately won the war.

2213. JAVELIN - *[spell]*- J A V E L I N
Definition: a light spear thrown by hand
Synonym: spear, lance
Antonym:
Sentence: The soldier threw a javelin at his enemy.

2214. FRINGE - *[spell]*- F R I N G E
Definition: border

Synonym: brink, edge
Antonym: center, inside
Sentence: He found himself at the fringe of his neighborhood during his run.

2215. PIAZZA - *[spell]*- P I A Z Z A
Definition: a large porch along one or more sides of the house
Synonym: veranda, patio
Antonym:
Sentence: Since it was a nice day, they decided to have dinner on the piazza.

2216. DISSECTION - *[spell]*- D I S S E C T I O N
Definition: act of cutting apart to examine the structure
Synonym:
Antonym:
Sentence: Each year in biology, students conducted a dissection of a frog.

2217. GLISTEN - *[spell]*- G L I S T E N
Definition: shine with a twinkling light
Synonym: glitter, sparkle
Antonym:
Sentence: Her eyes glistened with tears.

2218. ESSENCE - *[spell]*- E S S E N C E
Definition: that which makes a thing what it is
Synonym: aspect, characteristic
Antonym:
Sentence: The essence of the play was humor and wit.

2219. IMMATURITY - *[spell]*- I M M A T U R I T Y
Definition: an undeveloped condition or quality
Synonym: inexperience, incompleteness
Antonym: experience, maturity
Sentence: Her immaturity often posed a problem in the work place.

2220. FRUSTRATION - *[spell]*- F R U S T R A T I O N
Definition: a feeling of anger or annoyance caused by being unable to do something
Synonym: annoyance, exasperation
Antonym: contentment, satisfaction
Sentence: His frustration came largely from the fact that she wouldn't listen to him.

2221. EXCAVATE - *[spell]*- E X C A V A T E
Definition: make by digging

Synonym: uncover, unearth
Antonym:
Sentence: The archeologist began to excavate the artifacts from the ground.

2222. DECENTRALIZE - *[spell]*- D E C E N T R A L I Z E
Definition: to spread or distribute into smaller groups
Synonym: disperse, distribute
Antonym: centralize, assemble
Sentence: The government decided to decentralize, giving more powers to the states.

2223. GURNEY - *[spell]*- G U R N E Y
Definition: cart for moving patients in a hospital
Synonym:
Antonym:
Sentence: The man was placed on a gurney in the hospital and rushed to the emergency room.

2224. REPOSE - *[spell]*- R E P O S E
Definition: rest or sleep
Synonym: inactivity, stillness
Antonym: activity, action
Sentence: After a long day at work, she reposed on the sofa.

2225. PARISHIONER - *[spell]*- P A R I S H I O N E R
Definition: an inhabitant or member of a district that has its own church and clergyman
Synonym: follower, member
Antonym:
Sentence: All of the parishioners were intrigued by their new minister.

2226. VARIANT - *[spell]*- V A R I A N T
Definition: trending to alter or change
Synonym: alternative, differing
Antonym: similar, same
Sentence: Each case has to be examined individually, as there are variant circumstances for each.

2227. ILLITERATE - *[spell]*- I L L I T E R A T E
Definition: unable to read and write
Synonym: ignorant, uneducated
Antonym: literate, educated
Sentence: Though illiterate, the man was very intelligent.

2228. RENEGOTIATE - *[spell]*- R E N E G O T I A T E
Definition: to compromise again or anew, especially a contract
Synonym:
Antonym:
Sentence: The contractor had to renegotiate his contract after the company merger.

2229. UNACCOUNTABLE - *[spell]*- U N A C C O U N T A B L E
Definition: that cannot be fully explained
Synonym: arcane, inexplicable
Antonym: explicable, logical
Sentence: The girl's disappearance was unaccountable.

2230. COPIOUS - *[spell]*- C O P I O U S
Definition: more than enough
Synonym: ample, lavish
Antonym: scarce, meager
Sentence: There were copious amounts of food at Thanksgiving.

2231. ANTHEM - *[spell]*- A N T H E M
Definition: song of praise or patriotism
Synonym: hymn
Antonym:
Sentence: At assemblies, the school children sang the national anthem.

2232. INTERVAL - *[spell]*- I N T E R V A L
Definition: period of time between
Synonym: interim, interlude
Antonym: continuation
Sentence: The bell rang at regular intervals.

2233. EMPHATIC - *[spell]*- E M P H A T I C
Definition: said or done with force or stress
Synonym: forceful, vehement
Antonym: unemphatic
Sentence: Her answer to his request was an emphatic "no."

2234. ERRATIC - *[spell]*- E R R A T I C
Definition: not steady
Synonym: irregular, inconsistent
Antonym: steady, regular
Sentence: Her erratic heartbeat suggested a problem to the doctor.

2235. VEGETARIAN - *[spell]*- V E G E T A R I A N
Definition: a person who abstains from eating meat
Synonym:

Antonym:
Sentence: As a vegetarian, he did not eat meat.

2236. PALISADE - *[spell]*- P A L I S A D E
Definition: a line of high, steep cliffs
Synonym: cliff, slope
Antonym: plain, plateau
Sentence: The palisade dropped off into the ocean.

2237. BLOCKBUSTER - *[spell]*- B L O C K B U S T E R
Definition: something that is large or overwhelming
Synonym:
Antonym:
Sentence: The movie was a blockbuster hit, with shows selling out
everywhere

2238. MAGNIFY - *[spell]*- M A G N I F Y
Definition: cause to look larger than the real size
Synonym: enlarge, intensify
Antonym: shrink, reduce
Sentence: He had to magnify the text of the document in order to read it.

2239. DISPASSIONATE - *[spell]*- D I S P A S S I O N A T E
Definition: free from emotion
Synonym: impartial, indifferent
Antonym: biased, prejudiced
Sentence: His dispassionate attitude enabled him to better choose an
employee to promote.

2240. FORESIGHTED - *[spell]*- F O R E S I G H T E D
Definition: having or showing the power to know beforehand what is
likely to happen
Synonym: visionary, farsighted
Antonym:
Sentence: She was greatly foresighted in planning for her retirement.

2241. BLUSTERY - *[spell]*- B L U S T E R Y
Definition: storming noisily or violently
Synonym: gusty, turbulent
Antonym: calm, still
Sentence: She grabbed her jacket and scarf since it was a blustery day
outside.

2242. MALPRACTICE - *[spell]*- M A L P R A C T I C E
Definition: criminal neglect or wrong treatment of a patient by a doctor
Synonym: abuse, misconduct

Antonym:
Sentence: The doctor was sued for malpractice.

2243. SERF - *[spell]*- S E R F
Definition: a person, especially in medieval times, who was like a slave
Synonym: slave, laborer
Antonym:
Sentence: The nobleman made an effort to treat all of his serfs with fairness.

2244. CHOREOGRAPH - *[spell]*- C H O R E O G R A P H
Definition: to arrange movements, such as dances
Synonym: sync
Antonym:
Sentence: The dancer had to carefully choreograph her movements to sync with the music.

2245. MOUNTAINOUS - *[spell]*- M O U N T A I N O U S
Definition: covered with mountains
Synonym:
Antonym:
Sentence: The landscape on the border of the country was mountainous.

2246. TOLERATIVE - *[spell]*- T O L E R A T I V E
Definition: tending to permit or put up with beliefs or actions that one does not agree with
Synonym:
Antonym:
Sentence: The old dog was generally very tolerative of the child's antics.

2247. VEILING - *[spell]*- V E I L I N G
Definition: a covering up
Synonym: shroud, cloak
Antonym: unmask, unveil
Sentence: Her veiling of the statue was so that it would be a surprise for the public to see later on.

2248. GARNISH - *[spell]*- G A R N I S H
Definition: something laid on or around food as decoration
Synonym: adornment, decoration
Antonym:
Sentence: All of her dishes are prepared with a small flower as a garnish.

2249. GRISTLE - *[spell]*- G R I S T L E
Definition: cartilage found in meat
Synonym:

Antonym:
Sentence: She was unhappy with the quality of the meat and all the gristle in it.

2250. PERTURB - *[spell]*- P E R T U R B
Definition: to disturb greatly
Synonym: dismay, agitate
Antonym: content, comfort
Sentence: He was perturbed by her constant lies.

2251. TRANQUILIZE - *[spell]*- T R A N Q U I L I Z E
Definition: to make calm or peaceful
Synonym: sedate, subdue
Antonym: agitate, distress
Sentence: The bear at the zoo had to be tranquilized after it became agitated.

2252. PROCURE - *[spell]*- P R O C U R E
Definition: obtain by care or effort
Synonym: acquire, gain
Antonym:
Sentence: After much searching, he was able to procure the necessary items to fix the leak in his bathroom.

2253. COMPILER - *[spell]*- C OM P I L E R
Definition: one who collects and brings together into one list
Synonym:
Antonym:
Sentence: He was the unofficial compiler of their to-do list.

2254. FRATERNIZE - *[spell]*- F R A T E R N I Z E
Definition: associate with in a brotherly way
Synonym:
Antonym:
Sentence: The employee tried to get promoted by fraternizing with his superiors.

2255. PENETRATE - *[spell]*- P E N E T R A T E
Definition: enter into or pass through
Synonym: pierce, permeate
Antonym:
Sentence: Using a sharp knife, she was able to penetrate the skin of the mango.

2256. HEIRLOOM - *[spell]*- H E I R L O O M
Definition: a piece of personal property that has been handed down from

generation to generation
Synonym: heritage, birthright
Antonym:
Sentence: The jewelry was a valuable heirloom.

2257. SHREWISH - *[spell]-* S H R E W I S H
Definition: scolding or bad-tempered
Synonym: irritable, peevish
Antonym:
Sentence: The old woman's shrewish nature caused her grandchildren to not want to visit.

2258. HALLUCINATION - *[spell]-* H A L L U C I N A T I O N
Definition: seeing or hearing something that exists only in the imagination
Synonym: delusion, illusion
Antonym:
Sentence: The medication made her have strange hallucinations.

2259. OPTIMIZE - *[spell]-* O P T I M I Z E
Definition: to make the most of
Synonym: enhance, progress
Antonym: weaken, worsen
Sentence: He tried to optimize his time at work by skipping lunch.

2260. PREDOMINANCE - *[spell]-* P R E D O M I N A N C E
Definition: having more power, authority, or influence of others
Synonym: reign, power
Antonym:
Sentence: The predominance of the political party was due to resurgence in popularity.

2261. SOCIALIZE - *[spell]-* S O C I A L I Z E
Definition: to be concerned with human relations
Synonym: mingle, fraternize
Antonym: disjoin
Sentence: She went to the party to socialize, but she soon found she was too tired to do much talking.

2262. TYPECAST - *[spell]-* T Y P E C A S T
Definition: to cast an actor in a role that seems suited to the actor's appearance and personality
Synonym: stereotype
Antonym:
Sentence: To his surprise, he was typecast as the lead character in the play.

2263. ALLEGORY - *[spell]*- A L L E G O R Y
Definition: a story with an underlying or symbolic meaning
Synonym: fable, parable
Antonym:
Sentence: The novel Animal Farm, though it seems to be about animals, is an allegory of
historical events and characters.

2264. INSTITUTION - *[spell]*- I N S T I T U T I O N
Definition: organization established for some public or social purpose
Synonym: organization, association
Antonym:
Sentence: The institution was established to fund research on cancer.

2265. VICTIMIZE - *[spell]*- V I C T I M I Z E
Definition: to make a victim of
Synonym: cheat, fool
Antonym:
Sentence: She felt victimized by her boss's remarks.

2266. BARITONE - *[spell]*- B A R I T O N E
Definition: a voice that is between a tenor and a bass
Synonym:
Antonym:
Sentence: He sang with the baritones in the choir.

2267. LEEWAY - *[spell]*- L E E W A Y
Definition: extra space at the side or in time, money, etc.
Synonym:
Antonym:
Sentence: She left home early to give herself some leeway in getting to the meeting.

2268. SQUABBLE - *[spell]*- S Q U A B B L E
Definition: a petty, noisy quarrel
Synonym: feud, argument
Antonym: accord, agreement
Sentence: The mother could hear the squabble of her children from upstairs.

2269. TENTACULAR - *[spell]*- T E N T A C U L A R
Definition: of, forming, or resembling tentacles (long, slender growths on a plant or animal)
Synonym:
Antonym:
Sentence: The plant had tentacular leaves.

2270. SCALAWAG - *[spell]*- S C A L A W A G
Definition: an unprincipled person
Synonym: scoundrel, rogue
Antonym:
Sentence: No one trusted him because he was known as a scalawag.

2271. DISCOMBOBULATE - *[spell]*- D I S C O M B O B U L A T E
Definition: confuse
Synonym: befuddle, bewilder
Antonym:
Sentence: After the fire drill, the teacher felt discombobulated.

2272. RATIFICATION - *[spell]*- R A T I F I C A T I O N
Definition: a formal confirmation
Synonym: approval, confirmation
Antonym: disapproval, opposition
Sentence: The formal ratification of the law marked a new era in the country.

2273. DEFENSIBLE - *[spell]*- D E F E N S I B L E
Definition: justifiable
Synonym: logical, permissible
Antonym: unjustifiable, illogical
Sentence: Her anger at her teenage son for not calling home all night was defensible.

2274. PREDISPOSITION - *[spell]*- P R E D I S P O S I T I O N
Definition: previous inclination or tendency
Synonym: proclivity, propensity
Antonym: disinclination
Sentence: Because of genetics, he had a predisposition for high blood pressure.

2275. SUITABILITY - *[spell]*- S U I T A B I L I T Y
Definition: being right for the occasion
Synonym: appropriateness, fitness
Antonym:
Sentence: The suitability of the book for young children was questionable.

2276. CONFIRMATION - *[spell]*- C O N F I R M A T I O N
Definition: thing that proves to be true or correct
Synonym: verification, evidence
Antonym: denial, opposition
Sentence: He received a confirmation of his appointment by phone call.

2277. PEDOLOGY - *[spell]*- P E D O L O G Y
       Definition: scientific study of the nature of children
       Synonym:
       Antonym:
       Sentence: The man was a renowned expert in pedology.

2278. SYMPATHIZE - *[spell]*- S Y M P A T H I Z E
       Definition: to feel or show sympathy (a sharing of another's sorrow or
       trouble)
       Synonym: commiserate, empathize
       Antonym:
       Sentence: It was hard for him to sympathize with his friend when she
       created the trouble herself.

2279. HUSTLE - *[spell]*- H U S T L E
       Definition: carry, send, or move quickly
       Synonym: rush, hurry
       Antonym: crawl, creep
       Sentence: In order to make their flight, they had to hustle.

2280. SECRETARIAL - *[spell]*- S E C R E T A R I A L
       Definition: having to do with a secretary (person who keeps records for a
       person, company, etc.)
       Synonym:
       Antonym:
       Sentence: Her secretarial duties included: answering the phone, filing
       paperwork, and sending emails.

2281. FURROW - *[spell]*- F U R R O W
       Definition: wrinkle
       Synonym:
       Antonym:
       Sentence: She furrowed her brow, puzzled, when she heard the news.

2282. DELIRIUM - *[spell]*- D E L I R I U M
       Definition: a disordered state of mind
       Synonym: dementia, hallucination
       Antonym: sanity, rationality
       Sentence: After suffering from the stroke, he suffered some mild delirium.

2283. CLERICAL - *[spell]*- C L E R I C A L
       Definition: relating to a person who sells goods in a store
       Synonym:
       Antonym:
       Sentence: When he got home, he noticed a clerical error on his receipt.

2284. NOMADIC - *[spell]*- N O M A D I C
Definition: wandering
Synonym: erratic, wandering
Antonym: stagnant, still
Sentence: He was part of a nomadic tribe.

2285. FANTASTICAL - *[spell]*- F A N T A S T I C A L
Definition: picture existing only in the mind
Synonym: outlandish, wondrous
Antonym: realistic, reasonable
Sentence: The author's novels were set in a fantastical world.

2286. STEALTHY - *[spell]*- S T E A L T H Y
Definition: done in a secret or sneaky manner
Synonym: crafty, secretive
Antonym:
Sentence: The stealthy cat stole the meat from the counter.

2287. PROVOCATIVE - *[spell]*- P R O V O C A T I V E
Definition: tending to call forth actions such as thought, laughter, anger etc.
Synonym: stipulation, clause
Antonym:
Sentence: His provocative remarks made her quite angry.

2288. WELTER - *[spell]*- W E L T E R
Definition: to roll or toss
Synonym: turmoil, jumble
Antonym:
Sentence: The waves of the ocean weltered during the storm.

2289. PREMARITAL - *[spell]*- P R E M A R I T A L
Definition: before marriage
Synonym: prenuptial
Antonym:
Sentence: The couple filed some premarital paperwork.

2290. STIGMA - *[spell]*- S T I G M A
Definition: mark of disgrace
Synonym: stain, scar
Antonym:
Sentence: There is still something of a stigma surrounding mental illness.

2291. SOLIDIFY - *[spell]*- S O L I D I F Y
Definition: to make or become hard
Synonym: strengthen, cement

Antonym: dilute, dissolve
Sentence: He tried to solidify his plan for the future by making a list of goals.

2292. STRESSOR - *[spell]*- S T R E S S O R
Definition: anything which causes mental or physical stress
Synonym: annoyance, aggravation
Antonym:
Sentence: The intensity of her job was a major stressor.

2293. TENSITY - *[spell]*- T E N S I T Y
Definition: quality or condition of being stretched tight
Synonym: strain, stress
Antonym:
Sentence: The tensity of the elastic band caused it to break.

2294. TELETHON - *[spell]*- T E L E T H O N
Definition: a television program lasting many hours
Synonym:
Antonym:
Sentence: The telethon attempted to raise money for cancer research.

2295. QUIP - *[spell]*- Q U I P
Definition: a clever or witty saying
Synonym: gibe, pun
Antonym:
Sentence: He was always full of witty quips and comebacks.

2296. FRAUDULENCE - *[spell]*- F R A U D U L E N C E
Definition: being guilty of cheating or dishonesty
Synonym: chicanery, deceit
Antonym: honesty, fairness
Sentence: The man was fined for fraudulence on his taxes.

2297. CHIC - *[spell]*- C H I C
Definition: current style
Synonym: fashionable, stylish
Antonym: unfashionable, old-fashioned
Sentence: No matter what she wore, she always looked chic.

2298. MONTAGE - *[spell]*- M O N T A G E
Definition: the combination of several distinct pictures
Synonym: medley, jumble
Antonym:
Sentence: He made a photo montage for her birthday.

2299. DISPOSITION - *[spell]*- D I S P O S I T I O N
   Definition: one's habitual way of acting toward others
   Synonym: temperament, personality
   Antonym:
   Sentence: She usually had a very cheerful disposition.

2300. SENSUALITY - *[spell]*- S E N S U A L I T Y
   Definition: a liking for the pleasures of the senses
   Synonym: sensuousness
   Antonym:
   Sentence: Men were often drawn to her sensuality, which was evident
   even in her photographs.

Hard Words Exercise - 4

2301. TUMULTUOUS - *[spell]*- T U M U L T U O U S
Definition: characterized by noise or uproar
Synonym: boisterous, fierce
Antonym: peaceful
Sentence: The nation was in a tumultuous state after its leader passed away suddenly.

2302. ACCESSION - *[spell]*- A C C E S S I O N
Definition: the act of gaining a certain right or office
Synonym: attainment
Antonym:
Sentence: The prince's accession to the throne was a time of great happiness for the country.

2303. CONSOLATORY - *[spell]*- C O N S O L A T O R Y
Definition: comforting
Synonym: reassuring, encouraging
Antonym: aggravating, depressing
Sentence: After the death of his friend's mother, he adopted a consolatory attitude.

2304. SOUBRETTE - *[spell]*- S O U B R E T T E
Definition: a flirtatious, pert, lively young woman
Synonym:
Antonym:
Sentence: The soubrette flirted with the man at the party.

2305. IMPRECATE - *[spell]*- I M P R E C A T E
Definition: call down curses or evil
Synonym: curse, damn
Antonym:
Sentence: The evil sorcerer imprecated his enemies.

2306. CACOPHONOUS - *[spell]*- C A C O P H O N O U S
Definition: a harsh sound
Synonym: discordant, noisy
Antonym: harmonious, accordant

Sentence: He considered his work to be music, but some simply found it cacophonous.

2307. TRANSLUCENCE - *[spell]*- T R A N S L U C E N C E
Definition: quality of mostly letting light through but not completely transparent
Synonym:
Antonym:
Sentence: The translucence of her dress required she wear a slip.

2308. RESURGENCE - *[spell]*- R E S U R G E N C E
Definition: a rising again
Synonym: revival, rebirth
Antonym: death, destruction
Sentence: The president experienced a resurgence in popularity after passing the law.

2309. DISTRAIT - *[spell]*- D I S T R A I T
Definition: not paying attention
Synonym: dreamy, inattentive
Antonym: focused, concentrating
Sentence: In a state of complete distrait, he somehow managed to miss his bus.

2310. SOPHISTRY - *[spell]*- S O P H I S T R Y
Definition: unsound reasoning
Synonym: trickery, deception
Antonym:
Sentence: His co-workers quickly called him out for his sophistry on the subject.

2311. BIDDABLE - *[spell]*- B I D D A B L E
Definition: doing what is ordered
Synonym: obedient, compliant
Antonym: rebellious, recalcitrant
Sentence: Because he was so biddable by nature, it was easy to tell him what to do.

2312. AMBIANCE - *[spell]*- A M B I A N C E
Definition: atmosphere
Synonym: surroundings
Antonym:
Sentence: She listened to music that created a soothing ambiance while she worked.

2313. NOXIOUS - *[spell]*- N O X I O U S
Definition: very harmful to life or health
Synonym: putrid, toxic
Antonym: healthful, harmless
Sentence: The city dump emitted a noxious smell.

2314. RECALCITRANCE - *[spell]*- R E C A L C I T R A N C E
Definition: refusal to submit, conform, or comply
Synonym: defiance, unruliness
Antonym: obedience, following
Sentence: His recalcitrance to the rules of his new boss caused him to be fired.

2315. EXPENDITURE - *[spell]*- E X P E N D I T U R E
Definition: an expense
Synonym: spending
Antonym:
Sentence: Because of their recent expenditures on equipment, the company hoped to bring in a decent profit that month.

2316. POIGNANCY - *[spell]*- P O I G N A N C Y
Definition: a being piercing or stimulating to the mind, feelings, or passions
Synonym: intensity, emotion
Antonym:
Sentence: The poignancy of the movie made her want to cry.

2317. DRUBBING - *[spell]*- D R U B B I N G
Definition: a thorough defeat
Synonym: thrashing
Antonym:
Sentence: After a thorough drubbing at the game, the team practiced even harder.

2318. ABSTENTION - *[spell]*- A B S T E N T I O N
Definition: the act of refraining from or not doing something
Synonym: abstinence, refusal
Antonym:
Sentence: When the votes in the senate were counted, there were three abstentions.

2319. DIFFERENTIAL - *[spell]*- D I F F E R E N T I A L
Definition: showing qualities that are unalike
Synonym: contrasting, disparate
Antonym: alike, similar

Sentence: The differential costs of the same item at the two stores were puzzling.

2320. STOICISM - *[spell]*- S T O I C I S M
Definition: the quality or behavior of a person who accepts what happens without complaining or showing emotion
Synonym: impassiveness
Antonym:
Sentence: No matter what misfortune she suffered, she endured it with the same stoicism.

2321. ESCULENT - *[spell]*- E S C U L E N T
Definition: suitable for food
Synonym: comestible, consumable
Antonym:
Sentence: The apples, though not quite ripe enough, were still esculent.

2322. STRIDENCY - *[spell]*- S T R I D E N C Y
Definition: making or having a harsh sound
Synonym: bellow, clamor
Antonym: quiet, peace
Sentence: The stridency of the squealing tires was alarming.

2323. INTREPID - *[spell]*- I N T R E P I D
Definition: very brave
Synonym: fearless, dauntless
Antonym: afraid, cowardly
Sentence: The intrepid soldiers crossed the border into the hostile country.

2324. SOLSTITIAL - *[spell]*- S O L S T I T I A L
Definition: of or having to do with a solstice (time when the sun is at its greatest distance from the equator)
Synonym:
Antonym:
Sentence: Many pagan holidays were solstitial.

2325. OXYMORON - *[spell]*- O X Y M O R O N
Definition: figure of speech in which words of opposite meaning are used together
Synonym:
Antonym:
Sentence: The phrase "jumbo shrimp" is an oxymoron.

2326. VERTIGINOUS - *[spell]*- V E R T I G I N O U S
Definition: whirling or revolving
Synonym: spinning, turning

Antonym:
Sentence: The ride at the amusement park was vertiginous.

2327. AQUEOUS - *[spell]*- A Q U E O U S
Definition: made with water
Synonym:
Antonym:
Sentence: The medicine was made into an aqueous solution.

2328. EPITOMIZE - *[spell]*- E P I T O M I Z E
Definition: to be representative of
Synonym: embody, typify
Antonym:
Sentence: The man's actions epitomized the behavior of a gentleman.

2329. RETICENCE - *[spell]*- R E T I C E N C E
Definition: tendency to be silent or say little
Synonym: shyness, hesitation
Antonym: outspokenness, forthright
Sentence: Her reticence was simply a part of her personality.

2330. COMPENDIUM - *[spell]*- C O M P E N D I U M
Definition: summary that gives information
Synonym: digest, abstract
Antonym: abridgment
Sentence: Wanting to learn more about gardening, she bought a compendium of gardening tips.

2331. LEGISLATION - *[spell]*- L E G I S L A T I O N
Definition: the making of laws
Synonym: regulation, ruling
Antonym:
Sentence: Politicians could not agree on that particular piece of legislation.

2332. GASCONADE - *[spell]*- G A S C O N A D E
Definition: extravagant boasting
Synonym: brag, flaunt
Antonym:
Sentence: His gasconade about his accomplishments was hardly believable.

2333. COSMOPOLITE - *[spell]*- C O S M O P O L I T E
Definition: a person who feels at home in all parts of the world
Synonym:
Antonym:

Sentence: Having seen so much of the world, she felt herself to be a cosmopolite.

2334. RECUMBENCY - *[spell]*- R E C U M B E N C Y
Definition: a lying down or reclining position
Synonym: reclining
Antonym:
Sentence: His recumbency suggested that he was sleeping.

2335. REPARATION - *[spell]*- R E P A R A T I O N
Definition: a giving of satisfaction of compensation
Synonym: atonement, redress
Antonym:
Sentence: Germany was forced to pay billions in reparations after World War I.

2336. TANTARA - *[spell]*- T A N T A R A
Definition: a flourish or blast of a trumpet or horn
Synonym: fanfare
Antonym:
Sentence: The tantara announced the arrival of the king.

2337. NARCOLEPSY - *[spell]*- N A R C O L E P S Y
Definition: disorder characterized by attacks of drowsiness or deep sleep during normal
waking hours
Synonym:
Antonym:
Sentence: She was diagnosed with narcolepsy.

2338. POTENTATE - *[spell]*- P O T E N T A T E
Definition: person having great power
Synonym: ruler, sovereign
Antonym: follower, subject
Sentence: The potentate governed his country with justice and fairness.

2339. BIODEGRADABLE - *[spell]*- B I O D E G R A D A B L E
Definition: capable of being broken down by living organisms
Synonym:
Antonym:
Sentence: Cardboard and paper are biodegradable.

2340. PEPTIC - *[spell]*- P E P T I C
Definition: of promoting digestion
Synonym:

Antonym:
Sentence: He took a peptic medicine for his indigestion.

2341. VERACIOUS - *[spell]*- V E R A C I O U S
Definition: habitually speaking the truth
Synonym: credible, dependable
Antonym:
Sentence: Her veracious nature earned her the respect of those around her.

2342. SLAUGHTEROUS - *[spell]*- S L A U G H T E R O U S
Definition: murderous or destructive
Synonym: bloody, dangerous
Antonym: helpful, agreeable
Sentence: She had a slaughterous look in her eyes when she heard the bad news.

2343. REPUGNANT - *[spell]*- R E P U G N A N T
Definition: disagreeable or offensive
Synonym: distasteful, obnoxious
Antonym: agreeable, delightful
Sentence: His behavior towards faculty was repugnant.

2344. GALLANTRY - *[spell]*- G A L L A N T R Y
Definition: noble spirit or conduct
Synonym: bravery, civility
Antonym: cowardice, fear
Sentence: The queen rewarded the knight for his gallantry.

2345. ORBICULAR - *[spell]*- O R B I C U L A R
Definition: like a circle or sphere
Synonym: circular, round
Antonym:
Sentence: He swam orbicular laps in the pool.

2346. FOLIACEOUS - *[spell]*- F O L I A C E O U S
Definition: having to do with leaves; leafy
Synonym:
Antonym:
Sentence: This time of year, the dogwood tree is foliaceous, having no blooms and all leaves.

2347. SANATIVE - *[spell]*- S A N A T I V E
Definition: having the power to cure or heal
Synonym: healthful, invigorating
Antonym: damaging, harmful
Sentence: The herbs were said to be sanative.

2348. DEANERY - *[spell]*- D E A N E R Y
Definition: position of authority as a deanâ€" someone at a university that has authority over students
Synonym: administrator, principal
Antonym:
Sentence: The professor aspired to one day join the deanery of the college.

2349. RECESSIONAL - *[spell]*- R E C E S S I O N A L
Definition: piece of music sung or played during the exit of clergy, ceremony members, etc.
Synonym:
Antonym:
Sentence: A recessional played while the choir exited the church.

2350. EXIGENT - *[spell]*- E X I G E N T
Definition: demanding prompt action or attention
Synonym: urgent, pressing
Antonym:
Sentence: The situation was exigent.

2351. LECHEROUS - *[spell]*- L E C H E R O U S
Definition: lustful
Synonym: lewd, raunchy
Antonym: chaste, modest
Sentence: Her lecherous ways gave her a bad reputation.

2352. EXTRANEOUS - *[spell]*- E X T R A N E O U S
Definition: not belonging to something
Synonym: additional, irrelevant
Antonym: essential, important
Sentence: He included many extraneous details in his report.

2353. DEMIMONDE - *[spell]*- D E M I M O N D E
Definition: a class of women who have lost social standing because of promiscuity
Synonym:
Antonym:
Sentence: The demimonde were not condoned by society.

2354. METEORIC - *[spell]*- M E T E O R I C
Definition: having to do with meteors (rock or metal that enters earth's atmosphere from
space)
Synonym:

Antonym:
Sentence: The meteoric threat turned out to be unfounded.

2355. TILLAGE - *[spell]*- T I L L A G E
Definition: cultivation of land
Synonym:
Antonym:
Sentence: The tillage of the land would allow crops to grow plentifully.

2356. JETSAM - *[spell]*- J E T S A M
Definition: goods which are thrown overboard to lighten the load of a ship
Synonym:
Antonym:
Sentence: The boaters stumbled upon some debris in the water, apparently jetsam from a ship.

2357. DEFOLIATE - *[spell]*- DE F O L I A T E
Definition: to strip a tree of leaves
Synonym: strip
Antonym:
Sentence: In the autumn, trees become defoliated.

2358. ESTIMABLE - *[spell]*- E S T I M A B L E
Definition: worthy of a favorable opinion
Synonym: praiseworthy, admirable
Antonym: inestimable, detestable
Sentence: He thought of all his employees as estimable.

2359. ASSUREDLY - *[spell]*- A S S U R E D L Y
Definition: confidently
Synonym: undoubtedly, positively
Antonym: doubtfully, questionably
Sentence: He told her, quite assuredly, that he would soon be a published author.

2360. CUBOID - *[spell]*- C U B O I D
Definition: shaped like a cube
Synonym: cubical
Antonym:
Sentence: His workspace was cuboid.

2361. KEYNOTE - *[spell]*- K E Y N O T E
Definition: giving the beginning or key address of a conference
Synonym:
Antonym:

Sentence: The keynote speaker was inspirational to everyone at the conference.

2362. EGOMANIAC - *[spell]*- E G O M A N I A C
Definition: person who is abnormally self-centered
Synonym: narcissist
Antonym:
Sentence: Something of an egomaniac, he did not care much about the lives of his so-called friends.

2363. CAIRN - *[spell]*- C A I R N
Definition: A pile of stones set up as a tomb or landmark
Synonym: headstone, remembrance
Antonym:
Sentence: An ancient cairn to an unknown entity could be seen in the distance.

2364. PROPRIETARY - *[spell]*- P R O P R I E T A R Y
Definition: belonging to an owner
Synonym: copyrighted, owned
Antonym:
Sentence: Though the child was his niece, he took a proprietary interest in her.

2365. USURIOUS - *[spell]*- U S U R I O U S
Definition: practicing usury (the illegal charging of extremely high interest rates for lending money)
Synonym:
Antonym:
Sentence: The bank was known for being usurious.

2366. SUPERLATIVE - *[spell]*- S U P E R L A T I V E
Definition: of the highest kind
Synonym: outstanding, excellent
Antonym: inferior
Sentence: Her superlative expertise in financial matters helped her get the job.

2367. DISAPPROBATION - *[spell]*- D I S A P P R O B A T I ON
Definition: disapproval
Synonym: condemnation, objection
Antonym: acceptance, endorsement
Sentence: The father expressed disapprobation at his daughter's recent engagement.

2368. COLLOQUIALISM - *[spell]*- C O L L O Q U I A L I S M
Definition: a word used in everyday informal talk
Synonym: slang, informality
Antonym: formality
Sentence: Teenagers seem to always be creating new colloquialisms.

2369. STALACTITE - *[spell]*- S T A L A C T I T E
Definition: formation of rock, shaped like an icicle, hanging from the roof of a cave
Synonym:
Antonym:
Sentence: The stalactites seemed to dangle precariously from the ceiling of the cave.

2370. OCCULTATION - *[spell]*- O C C U L T A T I O N
Definition: disappearance from view or notice
Synonym: concealment, eclipse
Antonym: disclosure, appearance
Sentence: His occultation was easy enough because of the large crowd.

2371. CONGREGATION - *[spell]*- C O N G R E G A T I ON
Definition: coming together into a crowd
Synonym: assemblage, gathering
Antonym: division, separation
Sentence: There was a huge congregation of people on the street corner.

2372. CONSONANCE - *[spell]*- C O N S O N A N C E
Definition: harmony
Synonym: agreement, conformity
Antonym:
Sentence: The choir sang in consonance with the band.

2373. TENEBROUS - *[spell]*- T E N E B R O U S
Definition: shut off from the light
Synonym: dark, gloomy
Antonym: light, bright
Sentence: That sea creature dwells in the tenebrous depths of the ocean.

2374. PARSIMONY - *[spell]*- P A R S I M O N Y
Definition: extreme economy
Synonym: stinginess, frugality
Antonym: wastefulness
Sentence: The child resented her father's parsimony and the fact that he would not buy her newer, more fashionable clothing.

2375. OFFERTORY - *[spell]*- O F F E R T O R Y
Definition: collection of things given as an act of worship
Synonym: contribution, donation
Antonym:
Sentence: The church made a sizable offertory on Sunday.

2376. MUTINEER - *[spell]*- M U T I N E E R
Definition: person who takes part in a mutiny (open rebellion)
Synonym: insurgent
Antonym:
Sentence: The mutineer was imprisoned for several months.

2377. VALEDICTION - *[spell]*- V A L E D I C T I O N
Definition: an act of bidding farewell or taking leave
Synonym:
Antonym:
Sentence: The speech she gave last night was actually her valediction.

2378. INUNDATION - *[spell]*- I N U N D A T I O N
Definition: a flood
Synonym: deluge, torrent
Antonym:
Sentence: The inundation of questions overwhelmed the speaker at the conference.

2379. HABITABLE - *[spell]*- H A B I T A B L E
Definition: fit to live in
Synonym:
Antonym:
Sentence: After the home was repaired from the flood damage, it was habitable again.

2380. INDISCRETE - *[spell]*- I N D I S C R E T E
Definition: not separated into distinct parts
Synonym:
Antonym:
Sentence: The experiment found an indiscrete mass of material.

2381. DEGENERACY - *[spell]*- D E G E N E R A C Y
Definition: character condition that is declining
Synonym: corruption, debasement
Antonym:
Sentence: The king was resented for his degeneracy.

2382. PLACKET - *[spell]*- P L A C K E T
Definition: an opening or slip in a garment, especially at the top of the

skirt, to make it easy to put on
Synonym:
Antonym:
Sentence: The shirt had buttons up the front placket.

2383. BRACKEN - *[spell]*- B R A C K E N
Definition: a thicket of ferns
Synonym:
Antonym:
Sentence: As he trekked through the forest, he made his way through dense bracken.

2384. DEMURRER - *[spell]*- D E M U R R E R
Definition: a response in a court proceeding in which the defendant does not dispute the truth of the allegation but claims it is not sufficient grounds to justify legal action
Synonym:
Antonym:
Sentence: His attorney issued a demurrer at the next day's hearing.

2385. ACCELERANDO - *[spell]*- A C C E L E R A N D O
Definition: the gradual increasing of speed (in music)
Synonym: quicken, faster
Antonym: slow, crawl
Sentence: The composer added an accelerando in one portion of the music in order to add drama.

2386. DISCERNMENT - *[spell]*- D I S C E R N M E N T
Definition: keenness for understanding
Synonym: insight, judgment
Antonym:
Sentence: Using his powers of discernment, the detective found the criminal.

2387. SOMATIC - *[spell]*- S O M A T I C
Definition: of or having to do with the body
Synonym: fleshly, bodily
Antonym:
Sentence: Her somatic troubles seemed to improve with age.

2388. SPATIALITY - *[spell]*- S P A T I A L I T Y
Definition: quality or character of having to do with space
Synonym:
Antonym:
Sentence: The spatiality of the room in terms of layout made it difficult to decorate.

2389. SUAVITY - *[spell]*- S U A V I T Y
Definition: smoothly agreeable quality or behavior
Synonym:
Antonym:
Sentence: His suavity caused many people to be attracted to him.

2390. VERBIAGE - *[spell]*- V E R B I A G E
Definition: use of too many words
Synonym: redundancy, loquacity
Antonym: conciseness, terseness
Sentence: The verbiage of the guest speaker bored the audience.

2391. MANORIAL - *[spell]*- M A N O R I A L
Definition: relating to a large estate
Synonym:
Antonym:
Sentence: Her home was manorial in its size.

2392. PROVENANCE - *[spell]*- P R O V E N A N C E
Definition: source or origin
Synonym: birthplace, root
Antonym: end
Sentence: The provenance of the ancient artifact was still being
determined.

2393. NOCTURNE - *[spell]*- N O C T U R N E
Definition: dreamy or pensive musical piece
Synonym:
Antonym:
Sentence: The orchestra played a beautiful nocturne.

2394. CAPITULATION - *[spell]*- C A P I T U L A T I O N
Definition: surrender
Synonym: submission, yielding
Antonym: defending, fighting
Sentence: The army agreed to capitulation but only if certain terms were
met by their enemy.

2395. PLURALISM - *[spell]*- P L U R A L I S M
Definition: quality of being more than one
Synonym:
Antonym:
Sentence: With such a diverse population, the country has a great degree
of religious pluralism.

2396. PERMUTATION - *[spell]*- P E R M U T A T I O N
Definition: a change from one state or position to another
Synonym: alteration, changing
Antonym: stagnation
Sentence: The caterpillar made a permutation into a butterfly.

2397. PERIPHRASIS - *[spell]*- P E R I P H R A S I S
Definition: a roundabout way of speaking or writing
Synonym: circumlocution
Antonym:
Sentence: The author frequently used periphrasis in his writing.

2398. THANE - *[spell]*- T H A N E
Definition: a nobleman, ranked between an earl and a commoner
Synonym:
Antonym:
Sentence: The thane held a vast expanse of land.

2399. FECKLESS - *[spell]*- F E C K L E S S
Definition: spiritless
Synonym: weak, ineffective
Antonym: competent, efficient
Sentence: She never felt she could rely on her feckless husband.

2400. DOMINEERING - *[spell]*- D O M I N E E R I N G
Definition: inclined to rule in an overbearing or assertive way
Synonym: overbearing, tyrannical
Antonym:
Sentence: She spent years trying to get away from her domineering father.

Hard Words Exercise - 5

2401. TELEPATHY - *[spell]*- T E L E P A T H Y
Definition: communication of one mind with another without using speech
Synonym:
Antonym:
Sentence: The couple was so in tune, it seemed like they had telepathy.

2402. BLARNEY - *[spell]*- B L A R N E Y
Definition: flattering or coaxing talk
Synonym: blandishment, compliments
Antonym:
Sentence: He attempted to win her over with blarney.

2403. SOPORIFEROUS - *[spell]*- S O P O R I F E R O U S
Definition: bringing sleep
Synonym: calming, hypnotic
Antonym: exciting, stimulating
Sentence: The soporiferous medication helped him sleep peacefully for the first time in weeks.

2404. COGNITION - *[spell]*- C O G N I T I O N
Definition: act of knowing
Synonym: perception, awareness
Antonym: disregard, heedlessness
Sentence: He is a psychologist who has done extensive research on cognition.

2405. EMBARGO - *[spell]*- E M B A R G O
Definition: an order from the government forbidding trade by law
Synonym:
Antonym:
Sentence: In protest of their actions, the country enforced an embargo on all trade from their neighboring country.

2406. ANNULAR - *[spell]*- A N N U L A R
Definition: ring-shaped
Synonym: circular

Antonym:
Sentence: Wheels are annular in shape.

2407. ANTIPODES - *[spell]*- A N T I P O D E S
Definition: two places on the opposites side of the earth
Synonym:
Antonym:
Sentence: The North and South Pole are antipodes.

2408. RECANTATION - *[spell]*- R E C A N T A T I O N
Definition: a taking back formally or publicly
Synonym: retraction, abnegation
Antonym:
Sentence: In his latest speech, the politician gave a recantation of his bid for the position as governor.

2409. SURFEIT - *[spell]*- S U R F E I T
Definition: too much
Synonym: excess, profusion
Antonym: scarcity, need
Sentence: There was a surfeit of clothing in her closet.

2410. PARVENU - *[spell]*- P A R V E N U
Definition: person who has risen above his or her class
Synonym:
Antonym:
Sentence: Her fame eventually made her a parvenu.

2411. SAPONIFICATION - *[spell]*- S A P O N I F I C A T I O N
Definition: process of making soapy
Synonym:
Antonym:
Sentence: She learned the practice of saponification from her grandmother, who makes soap by hand.

2412. JOVIALITY - *[spell]*- J O V I A L I T Y
Definition: merriment
Synonym: gaiety, geniality
Antonym:
Sentence: Her joviality was due to her recent engagement.

2413. BANEFUL - *[spell]*- B A N E F U L
Definition: causing harm or destruction
Synonym: disastrous, poisonous
Antonym: beneficial, helpful
Sentence: His demanding career was baneful to his health.

2414. IMPERTINENCE - *[spell]*- I M P E R T I N E N C E
Definition: the act of being rudely bold
Synonym: impudence, audacity
Antonym:
Sentence: The student's impertinence got him in trouble with his teacher.

2415. EXASPERATION - *[spell]*- E X A S P E R A T I O N
Definition: extreme annoyance
Synonym: displeasure, fury
Antonym: enjoyment, delight
Sentence: Her exasperation was due largely to the fact that she had a lot of work to do.

2416. CONTERMINOUS - *[spell]*- C O N T E R M I N O U S
Definition: having a common boundary
Synonym: adjacent, bordering
Antonym: separate
Sentence: The neighbor's yard was conterminous with my own.

2417. LIGATURE - *[spell]*- L I G A T U R E
Definition: anything used to bind or tie up
Synonym: link, binding
Antonym:
Sentence: The ligature was used to temporarily bind his wound.

2418. PINNATE - *[spell]*- P I N N A T E
Definition: like a feather
Synonym:
Antonym:
Sentence: In texture, the animal's fur was pinnate.

2419. SCABROUS - *[spell]*- S C A B R O U S
Definition: rough with very small points or projections
Synonym: rough, scaly
Antonym:
Sentence: The scabrous texture of the material was unappealing.

2420. USURER - *[spell]*- U S U R E R
Definition: person who lends money and charges an unlawful interest rate
Synonym:
Antonym:
Sentence: Desperate, the man had no choice but to go to a usurer for help.

2421. COMESTIBLE - *[spell]*- C O M E S T I B L E
Definition: thing to eat
Synonym: food, edible

Antonym:
Sentence: Her favorite comestible was pizza.

2422. ENORMITY - *[spell]*- E N O R M I TY
Definition: extreme wickedness
Synonym: abomination, atrociousness
Antonym: delight, goodness
Sentence: The enormity of his lie was realized when an innocent man was sent to jail.

2423. LACKEY - *[spell]*- L A C K E Y
Definition: a male servant
Synonym: servant, attendant
Antonym:
Sentence: The mobster had several lackeys who did his dirty work.

2424. CARRION - *[spell]*- C A R R I O N
Definition: dead and decaying flesh
Synonym: corpse, remains
Antonym:
Sentence: Some birds, like vultures, feed on carrion.

2425. EFFLORESCE - *[spell]*- E F F L O R E S C E
Definition: to burst into bloom
Synonym: flower, burgeon
Antonym: shrink, shrivel
Sentence: The flowers began to effloresce in the spring.

2426. CORUSCATE - *[spell]*- C O R U S C A T E
Definition: give off flashes of light
Synonym: glitter, sparkle
Antonym: dim, fade
Sentence: The jewelry coruscated in the evening light.

2427. SEPTENNIAL - *[spell]*- S E P T E N N I A L
Definition: lasting seven years
Synonym:
Antonym:
Sentence: On their septennial anniversary, the couple took a long trip.

2428. SCHISM - *[spell]*- S C H I S M
Definition: division into hostile groups
Synonym: separation, fissure
Antonym: agreement, harmony
Sentence: A schism in the company caused difficulty in getting work accomplished.

2429. OMNISCIENCE - *[spell]*- O M N I S C I E N C E
Definition: knowledge of everything
Synonym:
Antonym:
Sentence: In the religion, god was omniscient.

2430. CHIMERA - *[spell]*- C H I M E R A
Definition: something that exists only in the imagination and is not possible in reality
Synonym: delusion, fantasy
Antonym: certainty, reality
Sentence: He was prone to following chimeras and neglecting his real work.

2431. BESOT - *[spell]*- B E S O T
Definition: to make foolish
Synonym: infatuate
Antonym:
Sentence: She felt that his actions were intended to besot her.

2432. ANTICLIMACTIC - *[spell]*- A N T I C L I M A C T I C
Definition: relating to an abrupt descent from important to unimportant
Synonym:
Antonym:
Sentence: The end of the book seemed quite anticlimactic.

2433. ARTIFICE - *[spell]*- A R T I F I C E
Definition: a clever trick
Synonym: con, ploy
Antonym: sincerity, artlessness
Sentence: Because he was prone to using artifice, no one trusted him.

2434. SANCTIMONY - *[spell]*- S A N C T I M O N Y
Definition: show of holiness
Synonym:
Antonym:
Sentence: Infidelity violates the sanctimony of marriage.

2435. DIPSOMANIA - *[spell]*- D I P S O M A N I A
Definition: an uncontrollable craving for alcohol
Synonym:
Antonym:
Sentence: After being sober for several years, the recovering alcoholic suffered a bout of dipsomania.

2436. NECROLOGIST - *[spell]*- N E C R O L O G I S T
Definition: a person who prepares obituaries
Synonym:
Antonym:
Sentence: The necrologist was known for his flattering and kind obituaries.

2437. XENOPHOBE - *[spell]*- X E N O P H O B E
Definition: a person who fears or hates foreigners or strange customs, etc.
Synonym: bigot, racist
Antonym:
Sentence: The man was recognized as a xenophobe by everyone at the office.

2438.

CLANGOROUS - *[spell]*- C L A N G O R O U S
Definition: making a loud ringing sound
Synonym: cacophonous, noisy
Antonym: silent, quiet
Sentence: The clangorous noise that came from the car suggested something was broken.

2439. SOCIALITY - *[spell]*- S O C I A L I T Y
Definition: social activity
Synonym:
Antonym:
Sentence: She was fond of engaging in sociality on the weekends.

2440. HAPPENSTANCE - *[spell]*- H A P P E N S T A N C E
Definition: a chance occurrence
Synonym: coincidence, incident
Antonym:
Sentence: He ran into an old friend completely by happenstance.

2441. BULWARK - *[spell]*- B U L W A R K
Definition: a person, idea, or thing that is used for protection
Synonym: barrier, defense
Antonym:
Sentence: Her sarcasm was really just a bulwark to hide her tender feelings.

2442. VOLATILE - *[spell]*- V O L A T I L E
Definition: tending to break out into violence
Synonym: explosive, changeable
Antonym:

Sentence: The world watched as the volatile country had rebellion after rebellion.

2443. PONDERABLE - *[spell]*- P O N D E R A B L E
Definition: significant enough to be worth considering
Synonym:
Antonym:
Sentence: The idea of branching out was ponderable to the CEO of the company.

2444. STATUARY - *[spell]*- S T A T U A R Y
Definition: act of making statues (images of people or animals carved in stone or wood)
Synonym: sculpture, carving
Antonym:
Sentence: The artist was an expert in all things statuary.

2445. CORRIGIBLE - *[spell]*- C O R R I G I B L E
Definition: that can be corrected
Synonym: corrective, amenable
Antonym: incurable, damaging
Sentence: The child's bad behavior did not seem to be corrigible.

2446. INCOMMENSURATE - *[spell]*- I N C O M M E N S U R A T E
Definition: not in proportion or adequate
Synonym: unequal, disproportionate
Antonym: equal, proportional
Sentence: He receives a salary that is incommensurate with his education.

2447. EVANESCENCE - *[spell]*- E V A N E S C E N C E
Definition: a fading away
Synonym: disappearance, evaporation
Antonym:
Sentence: Her enthusiasm experienced a brief period of evanescence.

2448. INCULPABLE - *[spell]*- I N C U L P A B L E
Definition: blameless
Synonym: clean, innocent
Antonym: guilty
Sentence: He was inculpable for the crime his brother committed.

2449. CHANCERY - *[spell]*- C H A N C E R Y
Definition: an office of public records
Synonym:
Antonym:
Sentence: Searching for information, she went to the chancery.

2450. MALEFICENCE - *[spell]*- M A L E F I C E N C E
Definition: the doing of evil or harm
Synonym: vice, evil
Antonym: good, beneficence
Sentence: His maleficence, though unintentional, harmed a great many people.

2451. GLOMERATE - *[spell]*- G L O M E R A T E
Definition: compactly clustered
Synonym:
Antonym:
Sentence: A glomerate group of students waited outside the building.

2452. ROSTRUM - *[spell]*- R O S T RU M
Definition: platform or stage for public speaking
Synonym: stage, podium
Antonym:
Sentence: A rostrum was erected for the guest speaker.

2453.
DILATATION - *[spell]*- D I L A T A T I O N
Definition: enlargement or expansion of a part of the body
Synonym: dilation, increase
Antonym:
Sentence: The dilatation of his pupils was due to the medication he took.

2454. IMPRUDENT - *[spell]*- I M P R U D E N T
Definition: rash, unwise
Synonym: foolish, reckless
Antonym: attentive, careful
Sentence: Going on the long trip with no planning was an imprudent decision.

2455. EVENTUALITY - *[spell]*- E V E N T U A L I T Y
Definition: a possible occurrence or condition
Synonym: possibility, chance
Antonym: uncertainty, improbability
Sentence: The eventuality of the snowstorm caused him to rush to the store to buy groceries.

2456. VARIEGATE - *[spell]*- V A R I E G A T E
Definition: to make varied in appearance
Synonym:
Antonym:
Sentence: My favorite shrub is a variegated camellia; each petal is in shades of pink, red, and white.

371

2457. ENIGMATICAL - *[spell]*- E N I G M A T I C A L
Definition: relating to a baffling or puzzling situation
Synonym: indecipherable, mysterious
Antonym:
Sentence: She found the writings of the philosopher enigmatical.

2458. AMPLIFICATION - *[spell]*- A M P L I F I C A T I O N
Definition: the act of making greater
Synonym:
Antonym:
Sentence: The amplification of the music in the small space was almost unbearable.

2459. INDEMNITY - *[spell]*- I N D E M N I T Y
Definition: payment for damage, loss, or hardship
Synonym: compensation, reimbursement
Antonym: penalty
Sentence: He was provided an indemnity for his injury at work.

2460. TENABLE - *[spell]*- T E N A B L E
Definition: that can be held or defended
Synonym: defensible, arguable
Antonym: unjustifiable, unreasonable
Sentence: The fortress did not seem to be tenable.

2461. CHARTER - *[spell]*- C H A R T E R
Definition: a written grant by the government to an organization or group
Synonym: contract, settlement
Antonym: prohibition, disagreement
Sentence: The organization was given a charter to run a school for special needs children.

2462. ANTITHESIS - *[spell]*- A N T I T H E S I S
Definition: the direct opposite
Synonym: contrary, inverse
Antonym:
Sentence: That television show is the exact antithesis of what I considered to be exciting.

2463. EXCLUSIVITY - *[spell]*- E X C L U S I V I T Y
Definition: the state of being not divided or shared with others
Synonym: singularity, oneness
Antonym:
Sentence: The store was given exclusivity in its ability to sell the product.

2464. LUCUBRATION - *[spell]*- L U C U B R A T I O N
Definition: laborious study
Synonym: examination, deliberation
Antonym:
Sentence: After much lucubration, he finally decided which candidate to hire.

2465. NODULOSE - *[spell]*- N O D U L O S E
Definition: having little knots or knobs
Synonym: knobby, knurled
Antonym: smooth, even
Sentence: The tree was nodulose in texture.

2466. TERATOLOGY - *[spell]*- T E R A T O L O G Y
Definition: study of abnormal, misshapen, or monstrous formations and organisms
Synonym:
Antonym:
Sentence: He was an expert in teratology.

2467. PEDATE - *[spell]*- P E D A T E
Definition: having a foot or feet
Synonym:
Antonym:
Sentence: Humans are pedate mammals.

2468. ALEATORIC - *[spell]*- A L E A T O R I C
Definition: composed of random elements
Synonym: haphazard, accidental
Antonym: composed, deliberate
Sentence: I found the style of the novel to be aleatoric, encompassing many disjointed styles.

2469. BATE - *[spell]*- B A T E
Definition: holding breath with fear, anticipation, excitement, etc.
Synonym:
Antonym:
Sentence: He waited, with bated breath, for her to get off the plane.

2470. BINARY - *[spell]*- B I N A R Y
Definition: consisting of two
Synonym: double
Antonym: single, unitary
Sentence: Binary code for computers uses two numbers: 0 and 1.

2471. DISCUSSANT - *[spell]*- D I S C U S S A N T
Definition: person participating in a discussion
Synonym:
Antonym:
Sentence: The discussants were all active in reviewing the issue.

2472. LEGATION - *[spell]*- L E G A T I O N
Definition: the diplomatic representative of a country and his/her staff
Synonym: embassy, delegation
Antonym:
Sentence: The legation met with foreign officials for a preliminary discussion on peace.

2473. TUNICATE - *[spell]*- T U N I C AT E
Definition: made up of concentric layers
Synonym:
Antonym:
Sentence: Onions are made up of tunicate layers.

2474. ETHNOCENTRISM - *[spell]*- E T H N O C E N T R I S M
Definition: the practice of regarding one's own race as superior to others
Synonym:
Antonym:
Sentence: The politician faced accusations of ethnocentrism.

2475. DENOMINATION - *[spell]*- D E N O M I N A T I O N
Definition: religious group or sect
Synonym:
Antonym:
Sentence: There are many different denominations of Christianity.

2476. HALITOSIS - *[spell]*- H A L I T O S IS
Definition: bad breath
Synonym:
Antonym:
Sentence: She was unable to think of a way to politely tell the man of his halitosis.

2477. LUCENT - *[spell]*- L U C E N T
Definition: bright or shining
Synonym: lustrous, aglow
Antonym: dim, dull
Sentence: She seemed lucent with happiness.

2478. OPHTHALMIC - *[spell]*- O P H T H A L M I C
Definition: of or having to do with the eye

Synonym: ocular, optic
Antonym:
Sentence: He had an ophthalmic disorder that caused problems with his eyes.

2479. ARTICULATE - *[spell]*- A R T I C U L A T E
Definition: to express in clear sounds and words
Synonym: coherent, eloquent
Antonym: inarticulate, unintelligible
Sentence: The boy, who had a fear of public speaking, was surprisingly articulate.

2480. DISJUNCTIVE - *[spell]*- D I S J U N C T I V E
Definition: causing separation
Synonym: detachment, disjoin
Antonym: junction, adhesion
Sentence: The United States has a disjunctive government, with three separate branches.

2481. EFFECTUALLY - *[spell]*- E F F E C T U A L L Y
Definition: in a manner that produces the desired results
Synonym: adequately, completely
Antonym: ineffectually
Sentence: She was given the responsibility for managing the new project, because we knew she could do it effectually.

2482. CAPACITATE - *[spell]*- C A P A C I T A T E
Definition: making able to learn something
Synonym: entrust, accredit
Antonym: deny, disallow
Sentence: His boss decided to capacitate him in the most prestigious of responsibilities.

2483. INSURRECTION - *[spell]*- I N S U R R E C T I O N
Definition: rebellion or revolt
Synonym: coup, insurgency
Antonym: compliance, obedience
Sentence: There was an insurrection after the new president was elected.

2484. CHASTISEMENT - *[spell]*- C H A S T I S E M E N T
Definition: punishment
Synonym: castigation, rebuke
Antonym:
Sentence: The children earned chastisement from their parents because of their behavior.

2485. SUDORIFEROUS - *[spell]*- S U D O R I F E R O U S
Definition: secreting or causing sweat
Synonym: sweaty, clammy
Antonym:
Sentence: Intense exercise is a sudoriferous activity.

2486. SABBATICAL - *[spell]*- S A B B A T I C AL
Definition: of or for a rest from work
Synonym: recess, furlough
Antonym:
Sentence: The professor took a sabbatical so that he could travel with his wife.

2487. EXTIRPATE - *[spell]*- E X T I R P AT E
Definition: remove completely or destroy totally
Synonym: abolish, demolish
Antonym: construct, create
Sentence: The man extirpated all of his ex's belongings.

2488. COMITY - *[spell]*- C O M I T Y
Definition: courtesy
Synonym: civility, amicability
Antonym: hostility
Sentence: His comity toward his guests made them feel welcome.

2489. AMBULATORY - *[spell]*- A M B U L A T O R Y
Definition: having to do with walking
Synonym: walk, step
Antonym:
Sentence: After being in a wheelchair for weeks, he was happy to be ambulatory again.

2490. TUMULUS - *[spell]*- T U M U L U S
Definition: mound of earth, especially one that marks an ancient grave
Synonym: mound, hillock
Antonym:
Sentence: The archaeologist explored a tumulus in the countryside.

2491. REFUTABLE - *[spell]*- R E F U T A B L E
Definition: that can be proven wrong
Synonym: debatable, speculative
Antonym: certain, definite
Sentence: His argument was refutable.

2492. UNREGENERATE - *[spell]*- U N R E G E N E R AT E
Definition: determined to have one's way

Synonym: remorseless, callous
Antonym: remorseful, guilty
Sentence: The child was unregenerate about the theme of her birthday party.

2493. PACIFIST - *[spell]*- P A C I F I S T
Definition: person who is opposed to war and fighting
Synonym:
Antonym:
Sentence: The pacifist tried to stop the war within the country.

2494. SCRUMPTIOUS - *[spell]*- S C R U M P T I O U S
Definition: very pleasing or satisfying, especially to taste or smell
Synonym: delicious, appetizing
Antonym: unappetizing, unappealing
Sentence: The meal she made looked scrumptious.

2495. AUTOMATON - *[spell]*- A U T O M A T O N
Definition: a person whose actions seem mechanical
Synonym: puppet
Antonym:
Sentence: He completed his job as if he were an automaton.

2496. NOUVEAU - *[spell]*- N O U V E A U
Definition: newly arrived
Synonym:
Antonym:
Sentence: She loves keeping up with the nouveau fashion.

2497. ANONYMITY - *[spell]*- A N O N Y M I T Y
Definition: the condition of being unknown
Synonym: nameless, inconspicuous
Antonym: recognition
Sentence: After growing up in a small town, she preferred the anonymity of a large city.

2498. DISCOMMODE - *[spell]*- D I S C O M M O D E
Definition: put to inconvenience
Synonym: bother, burden
Antonym:
Sentence: She felt having to babysit her little brother would discommode her plans for the weekend.

2499. USURPATION - *[spell]*- U S U R P A T I O N
Definition: the act of illegally or unrightfully seizing and holding a position

Synonym:
Antonym:
Sentence: The rebels' usurpation of the throne caused uproar in the country.

2500. PRETERMIT - *[spell]*- P R E T E R M I T
Definition: to leave out or leave undone
Synonym: neglect, ignore
Antonym: notice, heed
Sentence: The doctor was sued because she pretermitted treatment of the patient's serious condition.

Hard Words Exercise - 6

2501. PALPITATE - *[spell]*- P A L P I T A T E
Definition: beat very rapidly as from emotion or exercise (as with the heart)
Synonym: flutter, vibrate
Antonym: steady, still
Sentence: Her heart began to palpitate from all the caffeine she had consumed.

2502. REGIONALISM - *[spell]*- R E G I O N A L I S M
Definition: strong or steadfast attachment to a certain region
Synonym:
Antonym:
Sentence: Southern writers are often characterized by their regionalism.

2503. CABANA - *[spell]*- C A B A N A
Definition: a small tent-like shelter used on a beach
Synonym: bungalow
Antonym:
Sentence: He relaxed on the beach beneath the cabana.

2504. MEDICATE - *[spell]*- M E D I C A T E
Definition: treat with medicine
Synonym:
Antonym:
Sentence: She was medicated because of her recent injuries.

2505. EXHAUSTIBILITY - *[spell]*- E X H A U S T I B I L I T Y
Definition: quality of being able to be used up
Synonym:
Antonym:
Sentence: The exhaustibility of fossil fuels has raised concerns for the future of energy.

2506. HENPECK - *[spell]*- H E N P E C K
Definition: to subject (one's husband) to persistent nagging and domination
Synonym: badger, fuss

Antonym:
Sentence: The husband was always henpecked by his wife.

2507. DILAPIDATION - *[spell]*- D I L A P I D A T I O N
Definition: partial ruin
Synonym: mutilation, disrepair
Antonym:
Sentence: The dilapidation of the building was due to old age.

2508. POLLUTANT - *[spell]*- P O L L U T A N T
Definition: something that makes impure, foul, or dirty
Synonym: poison, toxin
Antonym:
Sentence: The pollutants in the air made it hard to breathe.

2509. TOXICOLOGY - *[spell]*- T O X I C O L O G Y
Definition: science that deals with poisons and their effects
Synonym:
Antonym:
Sentence: The police department hired a toxicology specialist to work a case where a victim was supposedly poisoned.

2510. DETACHMENT - *[spell]*- D E T A C H M E N T
Definition: lack of interest
Synonym: aloofness, disengagement
Antonym: attachment
Sentence: His general detachment from his work was a clear sign he would soon be looking for a new job.

2511. DISPOSSESSION - *[spell]*- D I S P O S S E S S I O N
Definition: the act of being forced to give up ownership of land, property, etc.
Synonym:
Antonym:
Sentence: After his dispossession of the home, he moved to another country.

2512. SUFFICIENCY - *[spell]*- S U F F I C I E N C Y
Definition: a large enough supply
Synonym: adequacy, plenty
Antonym: deficiency, scarcity
Sentence: The sufficiency of food at Thanksgiving was overwhelming.

2513. PERSONAGE - *[spell]*- P E R S O N A G E
Definition: person of distinction or importance
Synonym: dignitary

Antonym:
Sentence: He was a personage known worldwide.

2514. CLIENTELE - *[spell]*- C L I E N T E L E
Definition: customers as a group
Synonym: constituency, clients
Antonym: management, ownership
Sentence: The shop had a middle class clientele.

2515. NOMINEE - *[spell]*- N O M I N E E
Definition: person who is nominated
Synonym:
Antonym:
Sentence: All of the nominees for the office were present at the luncheon.

2516. COLIC - *[spell]*- C O L I C
Definition: severe pain in the intestines
Synonym: bellyache, stomachache
Antonym:
Sentence: She was rushed to the emergency room for colic.

2517. NUTRIMENT - *[spell]*- N U T R I M E N T
Definition: that which is required by an organism for life and growth
Synonym: food, nutrients
Antonym:
Sentence: The child suffered from a deficiency of basic nutriments.

2518. CONFOUNDED - *[spell]*- C O N F O U N D E D
Definition: hateful
Synonym: detestable
Antonym: likeable
Sentence: He thought the movie was one of the most confounded things he had ever seen.

2519. HARDY - *[spell]*- H A R D Y
Definition: able to bear hard treatment or difficult circumstances
Synonym: tough, strong
Antonym: weak, unfit
Sentence: The hardy plant was able to endure the harsh winter.

2520. IMMEDIACY - *[spell]*- I M M E D I A C Y
Definition: the quality that makes something seem interesting or important because it seems to be happening now
Synonym:
Antonym:

Sentence: She had a love of history, and the Elizabethan era had always had a sense of immediacy to her.

2521. SUPREMACY - *[spell]*- S U P R E M A C Y
Definition: condition or quality of being of the highest rank or authority
Synonym: dominance, sovereignty
Antonym: inferiority, subordination
Sentence: The king's supremacy was unquestionable.

2522. REPROOF - *[spell]*- R E P RO O F
Definition: words of blame or disapproval
Synonym: criticism, blame
Antonym: agreement, praise
Sentence: His reproof of her actions was completely unfounded.

2523. SALVE - *[spell]*- S A L V E
Definition: a creamy substance that you put on a wound to heal it or to make it less painful
Synonym:
Antonym:
Sentence: She has a homemade salve that she uses to treat sunburn.

2524. SECTIONAL - *[spell]*- S E C T I O N A L
Definition: of or having to do with a particular separated part
Synonym: divided
Antonym:
Sentence: The sofa was a sectional consisting of three pieces.

2525. ARTFUL - *[spell]*- A R T F U L
Definition: slyly clever
Synonym: shrewd, slick
Antonym: guileless, artless
Sentence: Because the child was so artful, his parents never suspected his plan.

2526. JANGLE - *[spell]*- J A N G L E
Definition: make a loud clashing sound
Synonym: clangor, dissonance
Antonym: harmony, calm
Sentence: The jangle in the kitchen suggested broken glass.

2527. HEARTSORE - *[spell]*- H E A R T S O R E
Definition: feeling or showing grief
Synonym: grieved, despairing
Antonym: lighthearted, happy

Sentence: After she broke up with her boyfriend, she couldn't help feeling heartsore.

2528. PERSECUTION - *[spell]*- P E R S E C U T I O N
Definition: the act of being caused to suffer repeatedly
Synonym: oppression, affliction
Antonym: support, encouragement
Sentence: The people suffered much persecution under the new leader.

2529. OVERTURE - *[spell]*- O V E R T U R E
Definition: an introductory part of a poem, instrumental, negotiation, agreement, etc.
Synonym: introduction, beginning
Antonym: conclusion, ending
Sentence: The overture of the ballet introduced the characters.

2530. RECONSTITUTED - *[spell]*- R E C O N S T I T U T E D
Definition: to form again
Synonym: reformed, reconstructed
Antonym: degenerated, deteriorated
Sentence: The dried vegetables were reconstituted with water.

2531. PRESENTMENT - *[spell]*- P R E S E N T M E N T
Definition: a bringing forward
Synonym: indictment, prosecution
Antonym:
Sentence: The evidence served as a presentment of his guilt.

2532. PREVALENCE - *[spell]*- P R E V A L E N C E
Definition: widespread occurrence
Synonym: predominance, popularity
Antonym: rarity, scarcity
Sentence: The prevalence of the disease increased every year.

2533. CAVERNOUS - *[spell]*- C A V E R N O U S
Definition: being like a large cave
Synonym: gaping, spacious
Antonym: cramped, narrow
Sentence: The living room in their new house was downright cavernous.

2534. MINISTER - *[spell]*- M I N I S T E R
Definition: member of the clergy serving the Church
Synonym: pastor, clergy
Antonym:
Sentence: The minister gave a moving sermon.

2535. TUMEFY - *[spell]*- T U M E F Y
Definition: to swell
Synonym: bloat, bulge
Antonym: shrink, reduce
Sentence: Her fractured wrist soon began to tumefy.

2536. CORONATION - *[spell]*- C O R O N A T I O N
Definition: ceremony of crowning a king, queen or other royalty
Synonym: crowning, inauguration
Antonym:
Sentence: At the coronation, the prince was officially made the new king.

2537. PERISHABLE - *[spell]*- P E R I S H A B L E
Definition: liable to spoil or decay
Synonym: decaying, destructible
Antonym: enduring, continuing
Sentence: The food items were perishable.

2538. CLAPTRAP - *[spell]*- C L A P T R A P
Definition: empty talk
Synonym: gossip, balderdash
Antonym:
Sentence: Practically everything that came out of his mouth was nothing but claptrap.

2539. NEGLIGIBLE - *[spell]*- N E G L I G I B L E
Definition: that can be disregarded
Synonym: insignificant, imperceptible
Antonym: consequential, significant
Sentence: The southern states usually only receive a negligible amount of snow each year, if any.

2540. HONORARY - *[spell]*- H O N O R A R Y
Definition: given or done only as an honor (credit for acting well)
Synonym: titular
Antonym:
Sentence: Because of his contributions to science, he was given an honorary doctorate from the university.

2541. ADVOCACY - *[spell]*- A D V O C A C Y
Definition: speaking or writing in favor of something
Synonym: support, backing
Antonym:
Sentence: The charity was well known for its advocacy on behalf of homeless children.

2542. INFLECTION - *[spell]*- I N F L E C T I O N
Definition: a change in the tone or pitch of the voice
Synonym: accent, intonation
Antonym:
Sentence: The inflection of his voice showed his disapproval.

2543. DECREPIT - *[spell]*- D E C R E P I T
Definition: weakened by old age
Synonym: run-down, dilapidated
Antonym:
Sentence: As he aged, the man became more and more decrepit.

2544. COMRADESHIP - *[spell]*- C O M R A D E S H I P
Definition: friendship
Synonym: fellowship, camaraderie
Antonym: antagonist, enemies
Sentence: After spending so much time together, they experienced a deep comradeship.

2545. OFFENDER - *[spell]*- O F F E N D E R
Definition: a person who violates a law or rule
Synonym: perpetrator, culprit
Antonym:
Sentence: He was given a tougher sentence because he is a repeat offender.

2546. BYLAW - *[spell]*- B Y L A W
Definition: law made by a company, club, city, etc. in order to control its own affairs
Synonym: rule, regulation
Antonym:
Sentence: The club held a meeting to create its bylaws.

2547. MAXIM - *[spell]*- M A X I M
Definition: a short rule of conduct expressed in a proverb
Synonym: adage, saying
Antonym:
Sentence: He was fond of reciting maxims to his children.

2548. FIGURATIVE - *[spell]*- F I G U R A T I V E
Definition: using words out of their literal meaning
Synonym: metaphoric, illustrative
Antonym:
Sentence: The poet used figurative language that was generally accessible to all audiences.

2549. BEDAUB - *[spell]*- B E D A U B
Definition: to smear with something dirty or sticky
Synonym: besmear, smudge
Antonym: clean, clear
Sentence: She used the brush to bedaub her face with makeup.

2550. LEVITATE - *[spell]*- L E V I T A T E
Definition: to rise or float in the air
Synonym: float, fly
Antonym: sink, fall
Sentence: The magician did a trick in which he levitated a car.

2551. INCLINATION - *[spell]*- I N C L I N A T I O N
Definition: a tending toward a certain character or condition
Synonym: tendency, disposition
Antonym: aversion, disinclination
Sentence: He had an inclination to just skip the meeting all together.

2552. GRUELING - *[spell]*- GRUELING
Definition: very tiring
Synonym: laborious, strenuous
Antonym: easy, effortless
Sentence: After eight hours of grueling efforts, he was exhausted.

2553. ARCANUM - *[spell]*- A R C A N U M
Definition: mysterious or specialized knowledge
Synonym:
Antonym:
Sentence: The spell was passed among the wizards through generations worth of arcanum.

2554. INVISIBLE - *[spell]*- I N V I S I B L E
Definition: not capable of being seen
Synonym: hidden, unseen
Antonym: visible
Sentence: He was all but invisible in the huge crowd of people.

2555. EVICTION - *[spell]*- E V I C T I O N
Definition: an expelling by legal process from land or a building
Synonym: ejection, expulsion
Antonym: admittance, boarding
Sentence: After he didn't pay his rent, he found an eviction notice in his mailbox.

2556. SUPERIORITY - *[spell]*- S U P E R I O R I T Y
Definition: quality of being above average

Synonym: advantage, excellent
Antonym: inferiority
Sentence: The superiority of her new cell phone was obvious when she took it out of the box.

2557. GULP - *[spell]* - G U L P
Definition: swallow eagerly or greedily
Synonym: guzzle, imbibe
Antonym:
Sentence: She gulped down her water.

2558. DEMOBILIZE - *[spell]* - D E M O B I L I Z E
Definition: remove from military service
Synonym: disband, retire
Antonym: activate, mobilize
Sentence: The platoon was demobilized after they fought hard and won the war.

2559. REDOUBLE - *[spell]* - R E D O U B L E
Definition: to increase greatly
Synonym: enhance, heighten
Antonym:
Sentence: After the birth of her son, she redoubled her efforts to get the house renovated.

2560. SLAVISH - *[spell]* - S L A V I S H
Definition: having to do with a person who is the property of another
Synonym: servile, groveling
Antonym: assertive, independent
Sentence: The man was slavish in his obedience to his wife.

2561. DIMENSIONAL - *[spell]* - D I M E N S I O N A L
Definition: having to do with a measurement of length or thickness
Synonym:
Antonym:
Sentence: When they got the dresser home, they discovered a slight dimensional error because it wouldn't fit in their living room.

2562. OPTICAL - *[spell]* - O P T I C A L
Definition: having to do with the eye or sight
Synonym: visual, seeing
Antonym:
Sentence: Some damage with his optical nerves caused vision problems.

2563. PERCEPTIBILITY - *[spell]* - P E R C E P T I B I L I T Y
Definition: a being aware of through the senses

Synonym: conceivability
Antonym: imperceptibility
Sentence: Her perceptibility of quiet sounds diminished with age.

2564. FOOLHARDY - *[spell]*- F O O L H A R D Y
Definition: foolishly bold
Synonym: audacious, reckless
Antonym: cautious, cowardly
Sentence: His foolhardy adventures almost cost him his life.

2565. UNDERUTILIZE - *[spell]*- U N D E R U T I L I Z E
Definition: to make use of insufficiently or wastefully
Synonym:
Antonym:
Sentence: She often underutilized the high tech tools in her kitchen.

2566. CIRCUMFERENCE - *[spell]*- C I R C U M F E R E N C E
Definition: the boundary of a surface
Synonym: girth, border
Antonym: interior, center
Sentence: He attempted to calculate the Earth's circumference in his head.

2567. NATIONALIST - *[spell]*- N A T I O N A L I S T
Definition: a person who has patriotic feelings
Synonym: patriot, loyalist
Antonym:
Sentence: As a nationalist, he valued protecting his country.

2568. DREDGE - *[spell]*- D R E D G E
Definition: dig up or collect
Synonym: unearth, raise
Antonym:
Sentence: He dredged up the facts about the murder.

2569. CONNIPTION - *[spell]*- C O N N I P T I O N
Definition: fit of hysterical excitement
Synonym: outburst, tantrum
Antonym:
Sentence: If the girl doesn't get her way, she's going to have a conniption.

2570. COMMANDMENT - *[spell]*- C O M M A N D M E N T
Definition: an order, direction, or law
Synonym: edict, rule
Antonym:
Sentence: The governor's commandment was that all citizens help their

community in their time
of hardship.

2571. IMPERMANENCE - *[spell]*- I M P E R M A N E N C E
Definition: being temporary
Synonym: transience, ephemerality
Antonym: longevity, permanence
Sentence: The hurricane proved the impermanence of many man-made structures.

2572. UNVEIL - *[spell]*- U N V E I L
Definition: to remove a covering from
Synonym: reveal, display
Antonym: veil, cover
Sentence: The grand unveiling of the statue was to take place at noon.

2573. TEMPORIZE - *[spell]*- T E M P O R I Z E
Definition: to evade immediate action or a decision in order to gain time
Synonym: delay, procrastinate
Antonym:
Sentence: It was clear from the way that he temporized that the candidate didn't want to answer the question.

2574. DOWNY - *[spell]*- D O W N Y
Definition: made of soft feather or hair
Synonym: fleecy, fuzzy
Antonym:
Sentence: The downy coat of the kitten was a delight to touch.

2575. GHOUL - *[spell]*- G H O U L
Definition: a demon
Synonym: fiend, monster
Antonym: angel, cherub
Sentence: The story featured a ghoul who terrorized the town.

2576. POLYTHEISM - *[spell]*- P O L Y T H E I S M
Definition: belief in more than one god
Synonym:
Antonym:
Sentence: The ancient Greeks practiced polytheism.

2577. DISQUALIFY - *[spell]*- D I S Q U A L I F Y
Definition: make unfit or unable to do something
Synonym: bar, exclude
Antonym: allow, include

Sentence: The football team was disqualified because they failed to follow the rules.

2578. CONTEMPLATIVE - *[spell]*- C O N T E M P L A T I V E
Definition: deep in thought
Synonym: meditative, introspective
Antonym: thoughtless, ignorant
Sentence: She could tell from the look on his face that he was feeling contemplative.

2579. CITIZENRY - *[spell]*- C I T I Z E N R Y
Definition: people who are members of a group
Synonym: society, federation
Antonym: individual, lone
Sentence: The citizenry of the country were typically well-informed.

2580. NAVIGABLE - *[spell]*- N A V I G A B L E
Definition: that ships can travel on or through
Synonym: passable, accessible
Antonym:
Sentence: The ocean was not navigable during the storm.

2581. COMMISSIONER - *[spell]*- C O M M I S S I O N E R
Definition: an official in charge of some government department
Synonym: officer, administrator
Antonym:
Sentence: He was appointed to be commissioner of the health department.

2582. COLLATE - *[spell]*- C O L L A T E
Definition: to gather information from different sources in order to study it carefully
Synonym:
Antonym:
Sentence: Three leading scientists will collate studies from around the country.

2583. NUTSHELL - *[spell]*- N U T S H E L L
Definition: in very brief form
Synonym:
Antonym:
Sentence: He summarized the project in a nutshell.

2584. DYNAMIC - *[spell]*- D Y N A M I C
Definition: energetic
Synonym: influential, charismatic

Antonym: static
Sentence: Her dynamic personality easily won people over.

2585. PATENT - *[spell]*- P A T E N T
        Definition: a government grant which gives a person or company sole
        rights to make, use, or sell a new invention
        Synonym: license, copyright
        Antonym:
        Sentence: The man was eager to get a patent on his revolutionary
        invention.

2586. BOOTLEG - *[spell]*- B O O T L E G
        Definition: to sell, transport or make something unlawfully
        Synonym: contraband, smuggle
        Antonym: legal
        Sentence: During the 1920s during Prohibition, some people sold bootleg
        alcohol.

2587. MANIPULATE - *[spell]*- M A N I P U L A T E
        Definition: handle or treat, especially skillfully
        Synonym: shape, manage
        Antonym:
        Sentence: He was known to manipulate people into seeing things his way.

2588. FORLORN - *[spell]*- F O R L O R N
        Definition: left alone and neglected
        Synonym: deserted, abandoned
        Antonym:
        Sentence: Feeling forlorn, he decided to call up some of his friends.

2589. TRIBUNAL - *[spell]*- T R I B U N A L
        Definition: court of justice
        Synonym:
        Antonym:
        Sentence: The charges against the man were put to a tribunal.

2590. SMARMY - *[spell]*- S M A R M Y
        Definition: flattering in an excessive or offensive way
        Synonym: smug, insincere
        Antonym:
        Sentence: Everyone in the office noticed his smarmy attitude toward his
        boss.

2591. DEVILTRY - *[spell]*- D E V I L T R Y
        Definition: evil action
        Synonym: mischief, devilment

Antonym: virtue, morality
Sentence: Whenever those boys get together, you can expect the usual deviltry.

2592. PREDATION - *[spell]*- P R E D A T I O N
Definition: act or habit of preying on another animal or animals
Synonym:
Antonym:
Sentence: Lions survive on predation of other animals.

2593. BLATHER - *[spell]*- B L A T H E R
Definition: foolish talk
Synonym: babble, chatter
Antonym:
Sentence: Her constant blather began to annoy him.

2594. LUNATE - *[spell]*- L U N A T E
Definition: crescent-shaped
Synonym:
Antonym:
Sentence: The lunate moon shone brightly in the sky.

2595. SAGE - *[spell]*- S A G E
Definition: showing wisdom or good judgment
Synonym: wise, astute
Antonym: dull, ignorant
Sentence: She was considered the sage of the family, and everyone turned to her for advice.

2596. SOMERSAULT - *[spell]*- S O M E R S A U L T
Definition: roll or jump, turning the heels over the head
Synonym: flip, jump
Antonym:
Sentence: The child did somersaults on the trampoline.

2597. DRAMATICS - *[spell]*- D R A M A T I C S
Definition: art of acting
Synonym: theater, acting
Antonym:
Sentence: She went to college to study dramatics.

2598. DAMNATION - *[spell]*- D A M N A T I O N
Definition: condemnation
Synonym: doom, torment
Antonym:
Sentence: His jail sentence seemed to him the equivalent of damnation.

2599. OPPORTUNE - *[spell]*- O P P O R T U N E
Definition: meeting the requirements of the time or occasion
Synonym: convenient, felicitous
Antonym: inappropriate, unfortunate
Sentence: The rain did not come at an opportune time and ruined their picnic.

2600. HATCHERY - *[spell]*- H A T C H E R Y
Definition: place for hatching eggs of fish, hens, etc.
Synonym:
Antonym:
Sentence: The hatchery raised and sold chickens and turkeys.

Hard Words Exercise - 7

2601. CAUTIONARY - *[spell]*- C A U T I O N A R Y
Definition: warning
Synonym: admonishing, preventative
Antonym: encouragement, instigate
Sentence: His failure served as a cautionary tale to those on the same path.

2602. MIMICRY - *[spell]*- M I M I C R Y
Definition: act or practice of making fun of by imitating
Synonym:
Antonym:
Sentence: Some parrots are known for their mimicry.

2603. DIVERSIFICATION - *[spell]*- D I V E R S I F I C A T I O N
Definition: to make something different so that it includes many different kinds of things or people
Synonym:
Antonym:
Sentence: The company made an attempt at diversification by making an intentional effort to hire many different types of people.

2604. FESTOON - *[spell]*- F E S T O O N
Definition: a string or chain of flowers, leaves, ribbons, etc.
Synonym: drape, hanging
Antonym:
Sentence: Every year, her Christmas tree is festooned with ornaments from her children.

2605. OVERBEARING - *[spell]*- O V E R B E A R I N G
Definition: forcing one's will on others
Synonym: domineering, oppressive
Antonym: democratic, humble
Sentence: Her mother had a very overbearing nature.

2606. RUCTION - *[spell]*- R U C T I O N
Definition: a disturbance or quarrel
Synonym: ruckus, altercation

Antonym: harmony, peace

Sentence: A sudden ruction broke out in the restaurant.

2607. SOCIABILITY - *[spell]*- S O C I A B I L I T Y

Definition: a social disposition or behavior

Synonym: amiability, affability

Antonym: coldness, dislike

Sentence: Because of her sociability, she was involved in the social committee at work.

2608. SYNONYMOUS - *[spell]*- S Y N O N Y M O U S

Definition: having the same or nearly the same meaning

Synonym: interchangeable, compatible

Antonym: opposite, antonym

Sentence: The actress's name is synonymous with drama.

2609. ALPHA - *[spell]*- A L P H A

Definition: the first of a series

Synonym: first, start

Antonym: end, omega

Sentence: Many of the problems in the alpha version of the program were fixed in later versions.

2610. INTEGRAL - *[spell]*- I N T E G R A L

Definition: necessary to make something complete

Synonym: essential, vital

Antonym: nonessential, accessory

Sentence: An integral part of the cupcakes was the icing.

2611. GAMBLER - *[spell]*- G A M B L E R

Definition: a person who plays games of chance for money

Synonym:

Antonym:

Sentence: The gambler lost his entire fortune in a single night.

2612. SPLEENFUL - *[spell]*- S P L E E N F U L

Definition: irritable or spiteful

Synonym: snide, hateful

Antonym:

Sentence: Her spleenful rant at her husband was heard by everyone in the restaurant.

2613. CONDOLENCE - *[spell]*- C O N D O L E N C E

Definition: expression of sympathy

Synonym: compassion, consolation

Antonym:

Sentence: He offered his condolences over the death of his friend's mother.

2614. IMPREGNATE - *[spell]*- I M P R E G N A T E
Definition: make pregnant
Synonym: fertilize
Antonym:
Sentence: The family had wondered why their dog was acting strange, only to find out she had been impregnated.

2615. SALVAGE - *[spell]*- S A L V A G E
Definition: act of rescuing property from a fire, flood, shipwreck, etc.
Synonym: rescue, regain
Antonym: abandon, forfeit
Sentence: The family was not able to salvage much from the fire-ridden home.

2616. SKEDADDLE - *[spell]*- S K E D A D D L E
Definition: run away in a hurry
Synonym: dash, move
Antonym:
Sentence: She hated to leave the party early, but she had to skedaddle to get to work on time.

2617. DISOBLIGE - *[spell]*- D I S O B L I G E
Definition: refuse to do a favor for
Synonym: bother, disturb
Antonym: appease, oblige
Sentence: Because he held a grudge against her, he disobliged her request.

2618. DEPRIVATION - *[spell]*- D E P R I V A T I O N
Definition: condition of having something taken away
Synonym: hardship, destitution
Antonym: gain, benefit
Sentence: When he had a stroke, his brain suffered a deprivation of oxygen.

2619. SCHEMING - *[spell]*- S C H E M I N G
Definition: making tricky plans
Synonym: deceitful, sly
Antonym: guileless
Sentence: The scheming child came up with a plan to surprise his mother with a gift.

2620. RETROCESSION - *[spell]*- R E T R O C E S S I O N
Definition: a going back

Synonym:

Antonym:

Sentence: The country initiated a retrocession of their territory to its original owners.

2621. WEATHERIZE - *[spell]*- W E A T H E R I Z E

Definition: to make safe against storm or cold

Synonym:

Antonym:

Sentence: The beach house needed to be weatherized in the face of the impending hurricane.

2622. A L I B I - *[spell]*- A L I B I

Definition: an excuse to avoid blame

Synonym: excuse, justification

Antonym:

Sentence: The case was dismissed because the man's alibi held up in court.

2623. INSPIRATIONAL - *[spell]*- I N S P I R A T I O N A L

Definition: a person, place, or thing that tends to make someone want to do or create something

Synonym: moving, emotional

Antonym:

Sentence: He found the biography to be inspirational.

2624. SELECTIVITY - *[spell]*- S E L E C T I V I T Y

Definition: having the power to choose or pick out

Synonym: discrimination, bias

Antonym:

Sentence: Her selectivity about the men she dated was due to her troubled past.

2625. DESTITUTION - *[spell]*- D E S T I T U T I O N

Definition: extreme poverty

Synonym: penury, privation

Antonym: wealth, affluence

Sentence: Having lived in destitution so many years, he never took his life of ease for granted.

2626. INCREDULITY - *[spell]*- I N C R E D U L I T Y

Definition: lack of belief

Synonym: disbelief

Antonym: belief

Sentence: His outlandish excuse for being absent was met with incredulity.

2627. PATERNITY - *[spell]*- P A T E R N I T Y
Definition: being a father
Synonym:
Antonym:
Sentence: The man took a paternity test to determine if the child was his.

2628. SCHOLASTIC - *[spell]*- S C H O L A S T I C
Definition: of schools, scholars, or education
Synonym: scholarly, academic
Antonym:
Sentence: The student won a prestigious scholastic scholarship.

2629. INADEQUATE - *[spell]*- I N A D E Q U A T E
Definition: not enough or as much as needed
Synonym: insufficient, faulty
Antonym: abundant, able
Sentence: She felt her skills were inadequate to cope with her new job.

2630. VOCATION - *[spell]*- V O C A T I O N
Definition: occupation, business, profession, or trade
Synonym: work, livelihood
Antonym: hobby
Sentence: The boy chose engineering as his vocation.

2631. GARLAND - *[spell]*- G A R L A N D
Definition: wreath or string of flowers
Synonym:
Antonym:
Sentence: The woman decorated her home with garland during the holidays.

2632. EQUIPAGE - *[spell]*- E Q U I P A G E
Definition: equipment
Synonym: gear
Antonym:
Sentence: After gathering her hiking equipage, she packed the car to head to her destination.

2633. SANITATION - *[spell]*- S A N I T A T I O N
Definition: the working out and practical application of health measures
Synonym: cleanliness, hygiene
Antonym: dirtiness, filth
Sentence: The department of sanitation worked to keep the city clean and healthy.

2634. WALLFLOWER - *[spell]*- W A L L F L O W E R
Definition: person who is shy and remains to the side at a party
Synonym: loner, introvert
Antonym: extrovert
Sentence: Though people gave him strange looks at the party, he was not ashamed of being a wallflower.

2635. ASTRAY - *[spell]*- A S T R A Y
Definition: off the right way
Synonym: awry, adrift
Antonym:
Sentence: Heading home, she took a path that led her astray.

2636. JUSTIFIABILITY - *[spell]*- J U S T I F I A B I L I T Y
Definition: being capable of being shown to be right or just
Synonym: defensibility
Antonym: indefensibility
Sentence: An examination of the records will show the justifiability of the choices he made.

2637. CHAFED - *[spell]*- C H A F E D
Definition: to rub in a way that wears away or scrapes
Synonym: irritate, corrode
Antonym: soothe, please
Sentence: The fabric of the shirt chafed her arms and back.

2638. MOBILIZE - *[spell]*- M O B I L I Z E
Definition: call into active military service
Synonym: assemble, marshal
Antonym:
Sentence: The troops were mobilized after a command from the general.

2639. INCISED - *[spell]*- I N C I S E D
Definition: cut into
Synonym: carved, cut
Antonym:
Sentence: His left thigh was incised to remove shrapnel.

2640. PITIABLE - *[spell]*- P I T I A B L E
Definition: moving to the heart
Synonym: heartrending, pathetic
Antonym: happy, joyful
Sentence: Her story about her difficult life was pitiable.

2641. HAWKER - *[spell]*- H A W K E R
Definition: person who carries wares around and offers them for sale by

shouting
Synonym: peddler
Antonym:
Sentence: The hawker sold food at the baseball game.

2642. PAINSTAKING - *[spell]*- P A I N S T A K I N G
Definition: very careful
Synonym: particular, scrupulous
Antonym: careless, lazy
Sentence: He was painstaking in his efforts to get her birthday party just right.

2643. A C C O M P A N Y - *[spell]*- A C C O M P A N Y
Definition: to go with
Synonym: escort, join
Antonym: abandon
Sentence: She agreed to accompany him to lunch.

2644. INDISTINCT - *[spell]*- I N D I S T I N C T
Definition: not clear to the eye, ear, or mind
Synonym: vague, obscure
Antonym: clear, apparent
Sentence: His voice was indistinct from everyone else's in the crowd.

2645. ARISTOCRACY - *[spell]*- A R I S T O C R A C Y
Definition: class of society having a high rank because of birth and/or title
Synonym: gentility, nobility
Antonym: commoners, proletariat
Sentence: The aristocracy was blamed for many of the country's problems.

2646. IRRECOVERABLE - *[spell]*- I R R E C O V E R A B L E
Definition: unable to be regained
Synonym: lost, absent
Antonym:
Sentence: The watch he misplaced seemed to be irrecoverable.

2647. DETRIMENTAL - *[spell]*- D E T R I M E N T A L
Definition: causing loss or damage
Synonym: adverse, damaging
Antonym: aiding, assisting
Sentence: Smoking can be detrimental to your health.

2648. SIMPLICITY - *[spell]*- S I M P L I C I T Y
Definition: a being free from difficulty or complication
Synonym: directness, modesty

Antonym: complexity, difficulty
Sentence: She had always appreciated the simplicity of a country life.

2649. DESENSITIZE - *[spell]*- D E S E N S I T I Z E
Definition: to make less feeling
Synonym: dull, numb
Antonym: enliven, animate
Sentence: After seeing so many movies, the children had become desensitized to violence.

2650. GUMMY - *[spell]*- G U M M Y
Definition: sticky like gum
Synonym: sticky, adhesive
Antonym:
Sentence: The gummy texture of the candy was not appealing to her.

2651. TRACEABLE - *[spell]*- T R A C E A B L E
Definition: that can be followed by means of marks, tracks, or clues
Synonym: detectable, identifiable
Antonym:
Sentence: The police concluded that the mysterious call to the woman's home was not traceable.

2652. RIOTOUS - *[spell]*- R I O T O U S
Definition: taking part in a riot (violent public disturbance)
Synonym: chaotic, wild
Antonym: calm, moderate
Sentence: The riotous crowd had to be controlled by the police.

2653. ABRASIVE - *[spell]*- A B R A S I V E
Definition: someone who is harsh in their attitude
Synonym: bitter, caustic
Antonym: pleasant, soothing
Sentence: Because of his sarcastic remarks, many of his classmates found him to be abrasive.

2654. INDENTURE - *[spell]*- I N D E N T U R E
Definition: a written agreement such as a contract
Synonym: arrangement, compact
Antonym:
Sentence: An indenture between both parties agreed he would provide service for several years.

2655. CHANCELLOR - *[spell]*- C H A N C E L L O R
Definition: a chief judge or government official
Synonym: authority

Antonym:
Sentence: The chancellor made most of the important decision with his counsel.

2656. MODERATION - *[spell]*- M O D E R AT I O N
Definition: a being kept within proper bounds
Synonym: restraint, balance
Antonym: excessiveness, indulgence
Sentence: It is best to drink alcohol in moderation.

2657. COMMUNICABLE - *[spell]*- C O M M U N I C A B L E
Definition: anything than can be communicated
Synonym: contagious, catching
Antonym:
Sentence: She has an irrational fear of communicable diseases.

2658. DISDAINFUL - *[spell]*- D I S D A I N F U L
Definition: feeling or showing contempt
Synonym: derisive, contemptuous
Antonym: respectful
Sentence: She noticed his disdainful sneer from across the room.

2659. DECEDENT - *[spell]*- D E C E D E NT
Definition: a dead person
Synonym:
Antonym:
Sentence: A funeral was held for the decedent.

2660. COMBATIVE - *[spell]*- C O M B A T I V E
Definition: ready to fight or oppose
Synonym: bellicose, belligerent
Antonym: agreeable, compromising
Sentence: The child's combative nature often got him in trouble.

2661. TRANSPORTABLE - *[spell]*- T R A N S P O R T A B L E
Definition: that can be moved from place to place
Synonym: mobile, migratory
Antonym:
Sentence: She purchased the iPod dock because it was easily transportable.

2662. DEFILE - *[spell]*- D E F I L E
Definition: to make dirty
Synonym: besmirch, violate
Antonym: clean, purify
Sentence: The organization had been defiled by corruption.

2663. CHISELED - *[spell]*- C H I S E L E D
Definition: having clear or sharp outlines
Synonym: distinct, sharp
Antonym:
Sentence: He had a very chiseled profile.

2664. MORONIC - *[spell]*- M O R O N I C
Definition: like a person who is stupid or foolish
Synonym: idiotic, foolish
Antonym:
Sentence: She chided him for his moronic actions.

2665. CIRCUIT - *[spell]*- C I R C U I T
Definition: a going around
Synonym: lap, circle
Antonym:
Sentence: She ran in a circuit around her neighborhood.

2666. NATIONAL - *[spell]*- N A T I O N A L
Definition: belonging to a whole country
Synonym: domestic, communal
Antonym:
Sentence: The soldier came home as a national hero.

2667. SPAWN - *[spell]*- S P A W N
Definition: offspring, especially in large numbers
Synonym: create, generate
Antonym: destroy, kill
Sentence: Many of the fish's spawn would die before reaching maturity.

2668. FEMININITY - *[spell]*- F E M I N I N I T Y
Definition: of women or womankind
Synonym:
Antonym: masculinity, manhood
Sentence: She did not adhere to traditional standards of femininity but she was beautiful anyway.

2669. SPRITZ - *[spell]*- S P R I T Z
Definition: to spray water or other liquid
Synonym: spit, spew
Antonym:
Sentence: She sprayed a spritz of perfume on her neck before leaving for her date.

2670. ACCREDIT - *[spell]*- A C C R E D I T
Definition: to give authority to

Synonym: authorize, entitle
Antonym:
Sentence: The state government had the power to accredit the school system.

2671. INDOMITABLE - *[spell]*- I N D O M I T A B L E
Definition: that cannot be discouraged, beaten or conquered
Synonym: steadfast, dauntless
Antonym: vulnerable
Sentence: Her indomitable spirit, despite adversity, won her the race.

2672. HAGGLE - *[spell]*- H A G G L E
Definition: dispute, especially about price
Synonym: bargain, barter
Antonym:
Sentence: In the market, she haggled with the merchant about the price of the item.

2673. SIREN - *[spell]*- S I R E N
Definition: kind of whistle that makes a loud, piercing sound
Synonym: alarm, whistle
Antonym:
Sentence: The siren on the fire station could be heard from miles around.

2674. FARCE - *[spell]*- F A R C E
Definition: a ridiculous mockery
Synonym: absurdity, parody
Antonym:
Sentence: The play was a farce about current day politics.

2675. REMORSEFUL - *[spell]*- R E M O R S E F U L
Definition: feeling or expressing deep, painful regret
Synonym: guilty, ashamed
Antonym: guiltless, unrepentant
Sentence: Though not remorseful about his lie, he didn't think he would get away with it.

2676. ELITIST - *[spell]*- E L I T I S T
Definition: having to do with the part that is or is thought to be the best, most talented, etc.
Synonym: snob
Antonym:
Sentence: She was an elitist when it came to her religious views.

2677. STAMPEDE - *[spell]*- S T A M P E D E
Definition: a sudden scattering or headlong flight of a large group

Synonym: rush, charge
Antonym: retreat, standing
Sentence: There was a stampede of people into the store as soon as it opened.

2678. VISAGE - *[spell]*- V I S A G E
Definition: appearance or aspect
Synonym: countenance, features
Antonym:
Sentence: She had an unforgettable visage.

2679. DISMISSIVE - *[spell]*- D I S M I S S I V E
Definition: relating to sending someone or something away
Synonym:
Antonym:
Sentence: Wanting her to leave, he made a dismissive gesture.

2680. COEDUCATION - *[spell]*- C O E D U C A T I O N
Definition: education of boys and girls together
Synonym:
Antonym:
Sentence: The school thought it best for physical education to be taught in coeducation.

2681. NOTATION - *[spell]*- N O T A T I O N
Definition: act of taking note of something
Synonym:
Antonym:
Sentence: The lawyer read the notations on his case file.

2682. DEBUNK - *[spell]*- D E B U N K
Definition: to prove false
Synonym: demystify, deflate
Antonym: verify, validate
Sentence: The duo made it their mission to debunk many well-known myths.

2683. ASSUMED - *[spell]*- A S S U M E D
Definition: not real
Synonym: false, counterfeit
Antonym: real, sincere
Sentence: In order to protect his secrecy, he traveled under an assumed name.

2684. JOURNEYMAN - *[spell]*- J O U R N E Y M A N
Definition: a worker who knows a trade very well

Synonym: artisan, craftsman
Antonym:
Sentence: After years of learning the craft of glassblowing, he became a journeyman.

2685. PRENUPTIAL - *[spell]*- P R E N U P T I A L
Definition: before a marriage or wedding
Synonym: premarital
Antonym:
Sentence: The couple went to prenuptial counseling before their wedding.

2686. COLLAPSIBLE - *[spell]*- C O L L A P S I B L E
Definition: made so as to be folded and pushed into a smaller space
Synonym:
Antonym:
Sentence: The large tent was easily collapsible so that it fit in a small canvas bag.

2687. NYMPH - *[spell]*- N Y M P H
Definition: a beautiful or graceful woman
Synonym:
Antonym:
Sentence: She was regarded as a nymph by all the men she knew.

2688. UNANIMOUS - *[spell]*- U N A N I M O U S
Definition: in complete agreement
Synonym: consistent, unified
Antonym:
Sentence: The board members made a unanimous decision to fire the CEO.

2689. POTENCY - *[spell]*- P O T E N C Y
Definition: the state or quality of being powerful or mighty
Synonym: vigor, capability
Antonym: weakness, impotence
Sentence: The potency of the spices in the dish made it overpowering.

2690. DISTURBANCE - *[spell]*- D I S T U R B A N C E
Definition: something that destroys the peace or quiet of
Synonym: brawl, confusion
Antonym: peace, calm
Sentence: He was awakened by a disturbance in his quiet neighborhood.

2691. COLONNADE - *[spell]*- C O L O N N A D E
Definition: a series of columns supporting a roof or ceiling
Synonym:

Antonym:
Sentence: To get to the meeting room, she had to pass through the colonnade.

2692. NOGGIN - *[spell]*- N O G G I N
Definition: head
Synonym:
Antonym:
Sentence: Be sure to use your noggin when making important decisions.

2693. DESTABILIZE - *[spell]*- D E S T A B I L I Z E
Definition: to make unstable
Synonym:
Antonym: stabilize
Sentence: The faltering economy destabilized many businesses.

2694. BIGOT - *[spell]*- B I G O T
Definition: intolerant person
Synonym: extremist, racist
Antonym:
Sentence: He considered all races except his own as inferior and, as a result, was considered a
bigot by everyone.

2695. LOAFER - *[spell]*- L O A F E R
Definition: person who does nothing
Synonym: idler, lounger
Antonym:
Sentence: He became a loafer on the weekends, hardly ever leaving his apartment.

2696. HYPERCRITICAL - *[spell]*- H Y P E R C R I T I C A L
Definition: too judgmental
Synonym: faultfinding, nit-picking
Antonym:
Sentence: She was always irritated about his hypercritical comments about her cooking.

2697. DEFICIENCY - *[spell]*- D E F I C I E N C Y
Definition: lack of something needed
Synonym: insufficiency, shortage
Antonym: abundance, excess
Sentence: Some doctors believe that migraines are caused by a magnesium deficiency.

2698. CAPSTONE - *[spell]*- C A P S T O N E
Definition: a finishing touch
Synonym: climax, culmination
Antonym: base, bottom
Sentence: The capstone project involved an extensive study of a narrow topic.

2699. MENIAL - *[spell]*- M E N I A L
Definition: suited to or belonging to a servant
Synonym: base, lowly
Antonym: high, elevated
Sentence: He was hired to do menial labor for the company.

2700. SOLUTION - *[spell]*- S O L U T I O N
Definition: the solving of a problem
Synonym: resolution, explanation
Antonym: problem, quandary
Sentence: After much deliberating, she figured out a solution to the problem.

Hard Words Exercise - 8

2701. ACCOMMODATION - *[spell]*- A C C O M M O D A T I O N
Definition: something that supplies aid
Synonym: assistance, adaptation
Antonym:
Sentence: She made accommodations for her neighbors, who had recently lost their home.

2702. INDISPOSED - *[spell]*- I N D I S P O S E D
Definition: slightly ill
Synonym: unwell, infirm
Antonym: healthy, well
Sentence: He explained to his guests that his wife was absent because she was indisposed at the moment.

2703. COLLEGIATE - *[spell]*- C O L L E G I A T E
Definition: of or like a college
Synonym: scholarly, scholastic
Antonym:
Sentence: The collegiate basketball season was full of unexpected victories this year.

2704. NOTION - *[spell]*- N O T I O N
Definition: an idea or understanding
Synonym: concept, assumption
Antonym:
Sentence: He somehow had the notion that he would soon be promoted.

2705. CHARACTERIZE - *[spell]*- C H A R A C T E R I Z E
Definition: describe the qualities or features of a person/thing
Synonym: describe, portray
Antonym:
Sentence: Most people would characterize him as a strong, honest leader.

2706. MODULAR - *[spell]*- M O D U L A R
Definition: of or having to do with standard pieces or components
Synonym: interchangeable
Antonym:
Sentence: She bought a modular shelving unit for her garage.

2707. EVACUEE - *[spell]* - E V A C U E E
Definition: person who is removed to a place of great safety
Synonym:
Antonym:
Sentence: The evacuees were welcomed into local churches.

2708. SOBER - *[spell]* - S O B E R
Definition: sensible, temperate or moderate
Synonym: serious, sedate
Antonym: agitate, excited
Sentence: She tended to have a sober view on her plans for the future.

2709. UNDERPIN - *[spell]* - U N D E R P I N
Definition: to support with props, stones, masonry, etc.
Synonym:
Antonym:
Sentence: He used many examples to underpin his argument for health care.

2710. UNTOWARD - *[spell]* - U N T O W A R D
Definition: unfavorable or unfortunate
Synonym: troublesome, disturbing
Antonym: fortunate, lucky
Sentence: An untoward turn of events caused her project to fail.

2711. GUNLOCK - *[spell]* - G U N L O C K
Definition: the part of the gun that controls the hammer and fires the charge
Synonym:
Antonym:
Sentence: He removed the gunlock and fired.

2712. HAVEN - *[spell]* - H A V E N
Definition: a place of shelter or safety
Synonym: refuge, asylum
Antonym:
Sentence: He boy found a haven in the home of his new foster parents.

2713. AUTHORITATIVE - *[spell]* - A U T H O R I T A T I V E
Definition: proceeding from recognized authority
Synonym: official, validated
Antonym: false, questionable
Sentence: Everyone listened to him because of his authoritative attitude.

2714. KIOSK - *[spell]* - K I O S K
Definition: a small building with one or more sides open, used as a

newsstand
Synonym:
Antonym:
Sentence: The man bought a newspaper and a soda from the kiosk.

2715. GLITCH - *[spell]*- G L I T C H
Definition: any sudden or unexpected malfunction
Synonym: defect, flaw
Antonym:
Sentence: A glitch in the software caused problems for thousands of customers.

2716. DISAFFECTION - *[spell]*- D I S A F F E C T I O N
Definition: unfriendliness
Synonym: animosity, antagonism
Antonym: rapport, satisfaction
Sentence: The disaffection between the two former friends was caused by a fight.

2717. PRESUPPOSITION - *[spell]*- P R E S U P P O S I T I O N
Definition: a taking for granted in advance
Synonym: assumption, expectation
Antonym: certainty
Sentence: His presupposition that he would go to the dance with her proved to be false.

2718. SKELETAL - *[spell]*- S K E L E T A L
Definition: of or like a skeleton (framework of bones)
Synonym: emaciated, bony
Antonym:
Sentence: The girl with the eating disorder looked skeletal.

2719. SUPERABLE - *[spell]*- S U P E R A B L E
Definition: capable of being overcome or vanquished
Synonym:
Antonym:
Sentence: The army proved to be superable in the battle.

2720. DISINCLINATION - *[spell]*- D I S I N C L I N A T I O N
Definition: a preference for avoiding something
Synonym: reluctance, hesitation
Antonym: inclination, leaning
Sentence: In spite of the advice of her parents, she felt disinclination towards college.

2721. GUESSWORK - *[spell]*- G U E S S W O R K
Definition: work, action or results based on guessing
Synonym: conjecture, hunch
Antonym: proof, reality
Sentence: Because of the detective's guesswork, they were able to solve the case.

2722. EMBLAZON - *[spell]*- E M B L A Z O N
Definition: adorn
Synonym: embellish
Antonym:
Sentence: The company's logo was emblazoned on the side of their headquarters.

2723. OVERSIGHT - *[spell]*- O V E R S I G H T
Definition: failure to notice or think of something
Synonym: omission, lapse
Antonym:
Sentence: The husband's failure to find a babysitter for his date with his wife was a slight oversight on his part.

2724. WINSOME - *[spell]*- W I N S O M E
Definition: innocently charming
Synonym: captivating, charismatic
Antonym:
Sentence: He found her smile to be winsome.

2725. IMPERSONALITY - *[spell]*- I M P E R S O N A L I T Y
Definition: absence of personal quality
Synonym:
Antonym:
Sentence: Her impersonality at her interview resulted in the company's decision not to hire her.

2726. DISHEVELED - *[spell]*- D I S H E V E L E D
Definition: rumpled
Synonym: mussed, slovenly
Antonym: neat, orderly
Sentence: Her disheveled appearance suggested she had had a rough day.

2727. REGULATORY - *[spell]*- R E G U L A T O R Y
Definition: a controlling by rule
Synonym: supervisory, administrative
Antonym:
Sentence: The government enforced many regulatory laws on trade between nations.

2728. SCAFFOLDING - *[spell]*- S C A F F O L D I N G
Definition: materials for a raised framework
Synonym:
Antonym:
Sentence: The window washers began to piece together their scaffolding.

2729. POPULOUS - *[spell]*- P O P U L O U S
Definition: full of people
Synonym: numerous, crowded
Antonym: deserted
Sentence: The city became more populous in the last ten years.

2730. INANIMATE - *[spell]*- I N A N I M A T E
Definition: not living or alive
Synonym: lifeless, inactive
Antonym: animated, living
Sentence: She tries to use her thoughts to control inanimate objects.

2731. PRESSURIZE - *[spell]*- P R E S S U R I Z E
Definition: to keep the atmospheric pressure inside at normal levels in spite of high altitude
Synonym:
Antonym:
Sentence: It is important for the cabins of airplanes to remain pressurized at all times.

2732. PHENOMENON - *[spell]*- P H E N O M E N O N
Definition: fact, event, or circumstances that can be observed and that is typically unusual
Synonym: rarity, anomaly
Antonym: normality, regularity
Sentence: The tornado was a rare phenomenon for that region.

2733. GRADATION - *[spell]*- G R A D A T I O N
Definition: a small difference that can be seen between two parts in something that changes gradually
Synonym:
Antonym:
Sentence: Her artwork is characterized by subtle gradations in color.

2734. SCRUNCH - *[spell]*- S C R U N C H
Definition: to crunch or crush
Synonym: rumple, crumple
Antonym: smooth, flatten
Sentence: The scrunched up paper could hardly be read.

2735. TRANSPARENCY - *[spell]*- T R A N S P A R E N C Y
Definition: quality of being able to see completely through
Synonym:
Antonym:
Sentence: The transparency of the windows made the room bright.

2736. ANTIQUITY - *[spell]*- A N T I Q U I TY
Definition: great age
Synonym: antique, relic
Antonym: modernity, newness
Sentence: The machine was an item of great antiquity.

2737. INTOLERABLE - *[spell]*- I N T O L E R A B L E
Definition: too much to be endured
Synonym: unacceptable, impossible
Antonym: tolerable, acceptable
Sentence: The sound of the garbage truck outside her window at 5 AM was intolerable.

2738. APATHY - *[spell]*- A P A T H Y
Definition: lack of interest
Synonym: indifference, disinterest
Antonym: enthusiasm, interest
Sentence: He felt apathy in regards to doing well in school.

2739. INTRICACY - *[spell]*- I N T R I C A C Y
Definition: complicated in nature or condition
Synonym: complexity, elaborateness
Antonym: simplicity
Sentence: The intricacy of the delicate embroidery was beautiful.

2740. OPINE - *[spell]*- O P I N E
Definition: holding or expressing opinions
Synonym: conceive, think
Antonym:
Sentence: I could opine for hours on contemporary politics, but my views are too controversial.

2741. CROTCHETY - *[spell]*- C R O T C H E T Y
Definition: full of odd notions
Synonym: cantankerous, grouchy
Antonym:
Sentence: The crotchety man irritated everyone with his opinions.

2742. ODOMETER - *[spell]*- O D O M E T E R
Definition: device for measuring distance traveled by a vehicle

Synonym:
Antonym:
Sentence: The new car had a digital odometer.

2743. ADVERSITY - *[spell]*- A D V E R S I T Y
Definition: condition of being faced with unfavorable circumstances
Synonym: difficulty, misfortune
Antonym: fortune, luck
Sentence: She never gave up, even though she was faced with great adversity.

2744. INFILTRATION - *[spell]*- I N F I L T R A T I O N
Definition: to secretly enter or join in order to get information or do harm
Synonym: invasion, intrusion
Antonym:
Sentence: The Vietcong excelled at infiltration of the civilian population.

2745. DISSIPATION - *[spell]*- D I S S I P A T I ON
Definition: the act of slowly disappearing or becoming less
Synonym: dissolution
Antonym:
Sentence: There has been a steady dissipation of the rainforest over the years.

2746. PERVERSE - *[spell]*- P E R V E R S E
Definition: morally bad
Synonym: corrupt, immoral
Antonym: innocent, pure
Sentence: He was perverse in his concept of right and wrong.

2747. THEORETICAL - *[spell]*- T H E O R E T I C A L
Definition: planned or worked out in the mind, not from experience
Synonym: hypothetical, abstract
Antonym: concrete, objective
Sentence: Some sciences are very theoretical in nature.

2748. REJUVENATE - *[spell]*- R E J U V E N A T E
Definition: to make young or vigorous again
Synonym: revivify, refresh
Antonym: damage, deplete
Sentence: He felt rejuvenated by the presence of his grandchildren.

2749. EJACULATE - *[spell]*- E J A C U L A T E
Definition: say suddenly and briefly
Synonym: exclaim, proclaim
Antonym:

Sentence: She ejaculated an answer to the teacher's question without thought.

2750. FETCHING - *[spell]*- F E T C H I N G
Definition: attractive, charming
Synonym: enchanting, captivating
Antonym: repulsive, unattractive
Sentence: She looked quite fetching in her prom dress.

2751. SAGACIOUS - *[spell]*- S A G A C I O U S
Definition: wise in a practical way
Synonym: astute, judicious
Antonym: careless, foolish
Sentence: He always went to her when he had problems so he could hear her sagacious advice.

2752. PROHIBITIVE - *[spell]*- P R O H I B I T I V E
Definition: enough to prevent something
Synonym: restrictive, limiting
Antonym: unlimited, unrestricted
Sentence: As much as I would enjoy it, I find traveling overseas is often cost prohibitive.

2753. DELICATESSEN - *[spell]*- D E L I C A T E S S E N
Definition: store that sells foods such as meat, cheese, and sandwiches
Synonym: cafÃ©
Antonym:
Sentence: The men walked to the delicatessen for lunch.

2754. OBLIVIOUS - *[spell]*- O B L I V I O U S
Definition: not mindful
Synonym: forgetful, inattentive
Antonym: attentive, aware
Sentence: She is often oblivious to her surroundings.

2755. FLIMSY - *[spell]*- F L I M S Y
Definition: lacking material strength
Synonym: feeble, rickety
Antonym:
Sentence: She decided not to walk over the bridge because it looked somewhat flimsy.

2756. UNISEX - *[spell]*- U N I S E X
Definition: suitable for use by either gender
Synonym:

Antonym:
Sentence: The garment was unisex.

2757. SURVEILLANCE - *[spell]*- S U R V E I L L A N C E
Definition: watch kept over a person
Synonym: observation, scrutiny
Antonym: carelessness, ignorance
Sentence: Several security guards kept surveillance over the important diplomat.

2758. POLYCHROME - *[spell]*- P O L Y C H R O M E
Definition: having many various colors
Synonym: multicolored, mottled
Antonym: solid, monochromatic
Sentence: The paint on the car was polychrome.

2759. TYRANNICAL - *[spell]*- T Y R A N N I C A L
Definition: of a person who uses power cruelly or unjustly
Synonym: oppressive, despotic
Antonym:
Sentence: The king's tyrannical reign came to an end when he was assassinated.

2760. GORGE - *[spell]*- G O R G E
Definition: stuff with food
Synonym: gobble, devour
Antonym: nibble
Sentence: The mother warned her child not to gorge too much on candy.

2761. SURREAL - *[spell]*- S U R R E A L
Definition: eerie or bizarre
Synonym: dreamlike
Antonym:
Sentence: The whole experience seemed surreal to her.

2762. PARTITION - *[spell]*- P A R T I T I O N
Definition: dividing up
Synonym: apportionment, separation
Antonym: whole, attachment
Sentence: The partition divided the large room into two smaller classrooms.

2763. CAVORT - *[spell]*- C A V O R T
Definition: to prance about
Synonym: romp, caper

Antonym: trudge, slog
Sentence: The children went outside to cavort in the grass.

2764. MINSTREL - *[spell]*- M I N S T R E L
Definition: a singer, musician or poet
Synonym: troubadour, entertainer
Antonym:
Sentence: A minstrel was summoned to entertain the king.

2765. PARASITIC - *[spell]*- P A R A S I T I C
Definition: living on others
Synonym:
Antonym:
Sentence: Everyone thought his girlfriend was rather parasitic because she always made him pay for anything.

2766. HACKER - *[spell]*- H A C K E R
Definition: a person who specializes in breaking into computer systems
Synonym:
Antonym:
Sentence: Authorities searched for months before they finally found the hacker.

2767. FRANCHISE - *[spell]*- F R A N C H I S E
Definition: right to vote
Synonym: suffrage, vote
Antonym:
Sentence: A bill was passed that would give the franchise to every single adult citizen.

2768. OBJECTIONABLE - *[spell]*- O B J E C T I O N A B L E
Definition: likely to be disagreeable or offensive
Synonym: distasteful, deplorable
Antonym: acceptable, agreeable
Sentence: Her coworker's attitude was objectionable.

2769. VENTURESOME - *[spell]*- V E N T U R E S O M E
Definition: willing or eager to undertake risky activities
Synonym: adventurous, courageous
Antonym: afraid, cowardly
Sentence: Feeling venturesome, the child explored the woods behind his house.

2770. BLOCKADE - *[spell]*- B L O C K A D E
Definition: blocking a place as a military tactic
Synonym: barricade, closure

Antonym: opening, cleft
Sentence: The navy used their ships to blockade the harbor, which helped caused the enemy to surrender.

2771.   MACHETE - *[spell]*- M A C H E T E
Definition: a large, heavy knife
Synonym:
Antonym:
Sentence: The explorer cut through the underbrush with a machete.

2772.   STUPENDOUS - *[spell]*- S T U P E N D O U S
Definition: amazing or marvelous
Synonym: wonderful, astonishing
Antonym: unremarkable, unimpressive
Sentence: She made a stupendous cake for her son's fifth birthday.

2773.   GAUGE - *[spell]*- G A U G E
Definition: measure accurately
Synonym: indicator, capacity
Antonym:
Sentence: She had difficulty trying to gauge how dedicated he was to the project.

2774.   REVERENCE - *[spell]*- R E V E R E N C E
Definition: a feeling of deep respect, mixed with wonder and awe
Synonym: admiration, veneration
Antonym: disregard, disrespect
Sentence: He had much reverence for his parents and grandparents.

2775.   DISPUTABLE - *[spell]*- D I S P U T A B L E
Definition: liable to be questioned or discussed
Synonym: arguable, controversial
Antonym: indisputable
Sentence: Much of the evidence on which the scientist bases his claims is disputable.

2776.   GUIDANCE - *[spell]*- G U I D A N C E
Definition: leadership or direction
Synonym: counseling, advice
Antonym:
Sentence: With his father's guidance, he achieved his goals.

2777.   SINUS - *[spell]*- S I N U S
Definition: cavity of bones in the skull that connect with the nasal cavity
Synonym:

Antonym:
Sentence: She went to the doctor because she had a severe sinus infection.

2778. RUCKUS - *[spell]*- R U C K U S
Definition: a noisy disturbance or uproar
Synonym: upheaval, brawl
Antonym: quietude, peace
Sentence: She was alarmed at the ruckus out in the street.

2779. BRASH - *[spell]*- B R A S H
Definition: showing a lack of respect
Synonym: cheeky, rude
Antonym: polite, amiable
Sentence: The child's brash attitude earned him punishment.

2780. MANNERISM - *[spell]*- M A N N E R I S M
Definition: peculiar or unique way a person behaves
Synonym: eccentricity, idiosyncrasy
Antonym:
Sentence: Her mannerisms, though strange, were endearing to all those who knew her.

2781. HECTIC - *[spell]*- H E C T I C
Definition: characterized by great activity or confusion
Synonym: frantic, chaotic
Antonym: calm, peaceful
Sentence: The streets were quite hectic during the festival.

2782. TORTUROUS - *[spell]*- T O R T U R OU S
Definition: involving or causing an infliction of severe pain
Synonym: distressing, tormenting
Antonym:
Sentence: She was so hungry that watching her husband slowly cook dinner was almost torturous.

2783. SULLEN - *[spell]*- S U L L E N
Definition: silent because of bad humor or anger
Synonym: brooding, gloomy
Antonym: agreeable, cheerful
Sentence: The child had a sullen look when she was punished.

2784. ZILCH - *[spell]*- Z I L C H
Definition: nothing
Synonym: zero, zip
Antonym: much, plenty
Sentence: The intern earned zilch for his hard work.

2785. CUMULATIVE - *[spell]*- C U M U L A T I V E
Definition: increasing or growing in amount, force, etc.
Synonym: aggregate, increasing
Antonym: decreasing, subtracting
Sentence: The student's grades were cumulative over the year.

2786. EDITION - *[spell]*- E D I T I O N
Definition: an issue of a book, newspaper or other publication published at different times with additions
Synonym:
Antonym:
Sentence: In the second edition of the book the author corrected many of his errors.

2787. FELINE - *[spell]*- F E L I N E
Definition: of a cat
Synonym:
Antonym:
Sentence: Her eyes were somewhat feline in shape.

2788. STRENUOUS - *[spell]*- S T R E N U O U S
Definition: requiring or characterized by exertion, such as action or effort
Synonym: difficult, arduous
Antonym: easy, facile
Sentence: Because the exercise was so strenuous, she was exhausted afterwards.

2789. HELM - *[spell]*- H E L M
Definition: handle or wheel by which a ship is steered
Synonym:
Antonym:
Sentence: At the helm of the ship, the captain issued commands to his men.

2790. HEARTILY - *[spell]*- H E A R T I L Y
Definition: in an enthusiastic or energetic way
Synonym: wholeheartedly
Antonym: cheerlessly
Sentence: Thomas decided to study abroad, and I support him heartily.

2791. SUGGESTIBLE - *[spell]*- S U G G E S T I B L E
Definition: capable of being influenced by suggestion
Synonym:
Antonym:
Sentence: Her suggestible nature caused people to often feed her ideas.

2792. FORGE - *[spell]* - F O R G E
Definition: an open fireplace or hearth
Synonym:
Antonym:
Sentence: The blacksmith used his forge to craft a myriad of wares.

2793. SENTRY - *[spell]* - S E N T R Y
Definition: solider stationed as a guard
Synonym: sentinel, guard
Antonym:
Sentence: The sentry guarded the door to the king's room.

2794. AFFIX - *[spell]* - A F F I X
Definition: to make firm
Synonym: fasten, glue
Antonym: detach, unfasten
Sentence: After he made sure to affix a stamp to the letter, he dropped it in the mail.

2795. INHIBITION - *[spell]* - I N H I B I T I O N
Definition: a nervous feeling that prevents you from expressing your thoughts or feelings
Synonym: reserve, suppression
Antonym: disinhibition
Sentence: Many people find that drinking alcohol causes them to lose some of their inhibitions.

2796. HEARTY - *[spell]* - H E A R T Y
Definition: warm and friendly
Synonym: genuine, sincere
Antonym: aloof, apathetic
Sentence: He offered her hearty congratulations.

2797. EVOLVE - *[spell]* - E V O L V E
Definition: develop gradually
Synonym: mature, change
Antonym:
Sentence: Over time, their relationship evolved from friendship to romance.

2798. COMBUSTIBILITY - *[spell]* - C O M B U S T I B I L I T Y
Definition: flammability
Synonym:
Antonym:
Sentence: Because of the combustibility of the material, it had very specific storing instructions.

2799. ALTERATION - *[spell]*- A L T E R A T I O N
Definition: a change in the appearance of anything
Synonym: adjustment, amendment
Antonym:
Sentence: She had to have a slight alteration made to her wedding dress.

2800. INTERCEPT - *[spell]*- I N T E R C E P T
Definition: take away or seize on the way from one place to another
Synonym: seize, hijack
Antonym:
Sentence: The enemy was able to intercept the letter and discover their plans.

Hard Words Exercise - 9

2801. ROBUST - *[spell]*- R O B U S T
Definition: strong and healthy
Synonym: vigorous, hardy
Antonym: fragile, impotent
Sentence: It came as a surprise when the normally robust child fell suddenly ill.

2802. STEREOTYPED - *[spell]*- S T E R E O T Y P E D
Definition: to believe unfairly that all people or things with a particular characteristic are the same
Synonym: hackneyed, overused
Antonym:
Sentence: He had a stereotyped view of how people from other cultures behaved.

2803. BUCCANEER - *[spell]*- B U C C A N E E R
Definition: a pirate
Synonym:
Antonym:
Sentence: The buccaneers made their way up the coastline, terrorizing the towns there.

2804. MARRIAGEABILITY - *[spell]*- M A R R I A G E A B I L I T Y
Definition: being fit to be wed
Synonym:
Antonym:
Sentence: His marriageability made him popular with women.

2805. EQUALIZER - *[spell]*- E Q U A L I Z E R
Definition: something that makes equal
Synonym:
Antonym:
Sentence: Because death comes to everyone it is, in a sense, an equalizer.

2806. PESSIMISM - *[spell]*- P E S S I M I S M
Definition: tendency to look on the dark side of things
Synonym: gloomy, cynicism

Antonym: optimistic, cheerful
Sentence: He tended to see things through a lens of pessimism.

2807. DRUDGERY - *[spell]*- D R U D G E R Y
Definition: work that is hard or tiresome
Synonym: chore, labor
Antonym: entertainment, fun
Sentence: He was exhausted when he came home from the drudgery of work.

2808. DUALITY - *[spell]*- D U A L I T Y
Definition: a two part condition or quality
Synonym:
Antonym:
Sentence: The duality of the meaning of the poem frustrated the student.

2809. IMPERFECT - *[spell]*- I M P E R F E C T
Definition: having some defect or fault
Synonym: flawed, deficient
Antonym: flawless, perfect
Sentence: All people are imperfect in some way or another.

2810. DEMONIACAL - *[spell]*- D E M O N I A C A L
Definition: of or like demons
Synonym: demonic, devilish
Antonym: angelic, godlike
Sentence: His victorious laughter was like something demoniacal.

2811. DERIVATION - *[spell]*- D E R I V A T I O N
Definition: origin
Synonym: source, ancestry
Antonym: termination, end
Sentence: The derivation of the disease was unknown, which made it hard to control.

2812. SPINSTER - *[spell]*- S P I N S T E R
Definition: an unmarried woman, especially one who is older
Synonym:
Antonym:
Sentence: At forty, the woman felt like she was surely becoming a spinster.

2813. ROUGHHOUSE - *[spell]*- R O U G H H O U S E
Definition: to play in a way that is disorderly or riotous
Synonym: horseplay, roughness
Antonym:

Sentence: The mother yelled at her sons for roughhousing inside the home.

2814. FESTIVAL - *[spell]*- F E S T I V A L
Definition: day or time of rejoicing or feasting, often because of some great happening
Synonym: gala, holiday
Antonym:
Sentence: There was a festival in honor of the patron saint of the town.

2815. PROMENADE - *[spell]*- P R O M E N A D E
Definition: walk for pleasure or display
Synonym: amble, saunter
Antonym: run, jog
Sentence: They took a lazy promenade through the park.

2816. TRIATHLON - *[spell]*- T R I A T H L O N
Definition: an athletic contest combining swimming, biking and running
Synonym:
Antonym:
Sentence: He completed his first triathlon at forty years old.

2817. UNBEKNOWNST - *[spell]*- U N B E K N O W N S T
Definition: not known
Synonym: undiscovered, unknown
Antonym: known, realized
Sentence: Unbeknownst to her, her boyfriend was planning to propose on their vacation.

2818. ACCUMULATION - *[spell]*- A C C U M U L A T I O N
Definition: collected material
Synonym: amass, gathering
Antonym: disperse, decrease
Sentence: The collector had quite an accumulation of comic books.

2819. INEBRIATE - *[spell]*- I N E B R I A T E
Definition: make drunk
Synonym: intoxicate
Antonym:
Sentence: After having several beers, he felt inebriated.

2820. EVACUATION - *[spell]*- E V A C U A T I O N
Definition: a leaving empty
Synonym: removal, withdrawal
Antonym:

Sentence: Citizens were given a mandatory evacuation order because of the impending hurricane.

2821. SCOUNDRELLY - *[spell]*- S C O U N D R E L LY
Definition: having to do with a wicked person without honor or principles
Synonym: dishonorable, malicious
Antonym:
Sentence: His scoundrelly looks caused everyone to distrust him.

2822. FORESHADOW - *[spell]*- F O R E S H A D O W
Definition: indicate beforehand
Synonym: augur, foretell
Antonym:
Sentence: The dark clouds seemed to foreshadow a storm.

2823. CONJUROR - *[spell]*- C O N J U R O R
Definition: a person who performs tricks or sorcery
Synonym: magician, enchanter
Antonym:
Sentence: He claimed his grandmother was a conjuror who could put a hex on his enemies.

2824. RAUCOUS - *[spell]*- R A U C O U S
Definition: harsh-sounding
Synonym: discordant, loud
Antonym: soft, subdued
Sentence: She was concerned by the raucous sounds coming from her neighbor's home.

2825. EDUCATIVE - *[spell]*- E D U C A T I V E
Definition: instructive
Synonym: edifying, enlightening
Antonym:
Sentence: He found the topic of the book to be quite educative.

2826. IMMOBILIZE - *[spell]*- I M M O B I L I Z E
Definition: to make unable to move
Synonym: disable, cripple
Antonym: mobilize, animate
Sentence: After the accident, he was completely immobilized.

2827. PUNCTURE - *[spell]*- P U N C T U R E
Definition: a hole made by something pointed
Synonym: hole, rupture
Antonym: whole, intact
Sentence: A puncture in the tire caused a slow leak.

2828. GENTLEMAN - *[spell]*- G E N T L E M A N
Definition: man who shows consideration for others
Synonym:
Antonym:
Sentence: Wanting to be perceived as a gentleman, he was sure to open doors and pull out chairs for his date.

2829. BELTWAY - *[spell]*- B E L T W A Y
Definition: a highway that circles around a city or area
Synonym: highway, interstate
Antonym:
Sentence: The quickest way to avoid traffic was to take the beltway.

2830. LIEUTENANT - *[spell]*- L I E U T E N A N T
Definition: a person who acts in the place of someone higher in authority
Synonym:
Antonym:
Sentence: The lieutenant in the army ordered his troops to retreat.

2831. REGALITY - *[spell]*- R E G A L I T Y
Definition: royalty
Synonym: sovereignty, regency
Antonym:
Sentence: Even though he had been deposed, the king still bore himself with great regality.

2832. FORTHRIGHT - *[spell]*- F O R T H R I G H T
Definition: straightforward
Synonym: candid, plainspoken
Antonym: tricky, devious
Sentence: He was very forthright in his answers.

2833. HARROWING - *[spell]*- H A R R O W I N G
Definition: very painful and distressing
Synonym: agonizing, torturous
Antonym: pleasant, calming
Sentence: The news of his death was quite harrowing.

2834. TRANSECT - *[spell]*- T R A N S E C T
Definition: to cut across
Synonym: bisect, intersect
Antonym:
Sentence: She transected campus in order to get to class on time.

2835. IMPRESSIBLE - *[spell]*- I M P R E S S I B L E
Definition: sensitive to impressions (effects produced on the senses or

mind)
Synonym: sensitive, impressionable
Antonym:
Sentence: The young child was impressible to her mother's actions.

2836. BEJEWEL - *[spell]*- B E J E W E L
Definition: to adorn with jewels
Synonym: bedeck
Antonym:
Sentence: The wealthy man tried to show his love by bejeweling his wife with the most
expensive designer pieces.

2837. LIBERATE - *[spell]*- L I B E R A T E
Definition: to set free
Synonym: emancipate, free
Antonym: imprison, enslave
Sentence: The man was liberated from slavery after fifteen long years.

2838. DIRK - *[spell]*- D I R K
Definition: dagger
Synonym: knife, blade
Antonym:
Sentence: The soldier did all of his fighting with a dirk.

2839. DISROBE - *[spell]*- D I S R O B E
Definition: undress
Synonym: strip
Antonym: clothe, dress
Sentence: After she had disrobed, she slipped into her pajamas.

2840. DEMEANOR - *[spell]*- D E M E A N O R
Definition: the way a person looks or acts
Synonym: behavior, manner
Antonym:
Sentence: Because he had such a pleasant demeanor, everyone wanted to be friends with him.

2841. VALIANCY - *[spell]*- V A L I A N C Y
Definition: bravery
Synonym: courage, fearlessness
Antonym: cowardice, fear
Sentence: The knight was noted for his valiancy.

2842. INCORRUPTIBLE - *[spell]*- I N C O R R U P T I B L E
Definition: incapable of corruption

Synonym: honest, moral
Antonym: corruptible, dishonest
Sentence: He had a reputation as being completely incorruptible, no matter the temptation.

2843. HEREDITARY - *[spell]*- H E R E D I T A R Y
Definition: passed by inheritance from one generation to another
Synonym: inherited, genetic
Antonym:
Sentence: The disease she has is hereditary.

2844. SCATHING - *[spell]*- S C A T H I N G
Definition: bitterly severe
Synonym: harsh, searing
Antonym: calm, gentle
Sentence: Her scathing remarks left an impression on all of her friends.

2845. COLTISH - *[spell]*- C O L T I S H
Definition: lively
Synonym: frisky, frolicsome
Antonym: depressed, lifeless
Sentence: The dog ran about the yard in a coltish manner.

2846. NICKER - *[spell]*- N I C K E R
Definition: to laugh loudly and shrilly
Synonym: roar, squawk
Antonym:
Sentence: She could not help but nicker at his clumsiness.

2847. PSYCHOPATH - *[spell]*- P S Y C H O P A T H
Definition: a person who is mentally ill or unstable
Synonym: maniac, lunatic
Antonym:
Sentence: The man who committed the murders was found to be a psychopath.

2848. ETCETERA - *[spell]*- E T C E T E R A
Definition: and so forth (abbreviated etc.)
Synonym:
Antonym:
Sentence: His chores included: cleaning his room, dusting the mantle, vacuuming the room, etcetera.

2849. DEPORTEE - *[spell]*- D E P O R T E E
Definition: a person who has been removed from a country
Synonym:

Antonym:
Sentence: A recent deportee, she had trouble readjusting to live in her home country.

2850. ASSISTANT - *[spell]*- A S S I S T A N T
Definition: a person who helps another
Synonym: aide, attendant
Antonym:
Sentence: He hired an assistant to help him with paperwork.

2851. JOUNCE - *[spell]*- J O U N C E
Definition: shake up and down
Synonym: bounce, bump
Antonym:
Sentence: The father jounced the child on his knee.

2852. SHEATHE - *[spell]*- S H E A T H E
Definition: to enclose in a case or covering
Synonym: envelop, enclose
Antonym: unwrap, uncover
Sentence: The knight sheathed his sword when he stepped inside the building.

2853. OPPOSABLE - *[spell]*- O P P O S A B L E
Definition: capable of being against
Synonym:
Antonym:
Sentence: Humans have opposable thumbs.

2854. ONSLAUGHT - *[spell]*- O N S L A U G H T
Definition: a vigorous attack
Synonym: assault, onrush
Antonym: retreat
Sentence: The onslaught of enemy soldiers caught them off-guard.

2855. EXTRAVAGANZA - *[spell]*- E X T R A V A G A N Z A
Definition: a lavish show, assemblage, etc.
Synonym: spectacular
Antonym:
Sentence: We hope that this year's Christmas program will truly be an extravaganza.

2856. OCEANAUT - *[spell]*- O C E A N A U T
Definition: an underwater explorer of an ocean or sea
Synonym:

Antonym:
Sentence: His love of the water made him decide to be an oceanaut.

2857.   WAIF - *[spell]*- W A I F
Definition: person without home or friends
Synonym: castaway, orphan
Antonym:
Sentence: The waif of the town lived under the bridge.

2858.   TRAJECTORY - *[spell]*- T R A J E C T O R Y
Definition: the curved path of a projectile, comet, planet, etc.
Synonym: course, path
Antonym:
Sentence: The trajectory of the company was not favorable.

2859.   BEHEMOTH - *[spell]*- B E H E M O T H
Definition: something large and powerful
Synonym: beast, monster
Antonym:
Sentence: The dog, weighing over one hundred pounds, was practically a
behemoth.

2860.   LIABLE - *[spell]*- L I A B L E
Definition: likely or possible, especially unpleasantly likely
Synonym: apt, inclined
Antonym: unlikely
Sentence: The dog was liable to run away when frightened.

2861.   FANCIFUL - *[spell]*- F A N C I F U L
Definition: led by imagining
Synonym: extravagant, absurd
Antonym:
Sentence: She had the fanciful notion that she could one day be a
ballerina when she didn't know a thing about dancing.

2862.   PROSTRATE - *[spell]*- P R O S T R A T E
Definition: to lay down flat
Synonym: sprawling, recumbent
Antonym: upright, standing
Sentence: She was prostrate with grief upon hearing the news.

2863.   HUMANIZE - *[spell]*- H U M A N I Z E
Definition: make or become human
Synonym:
Antonym:
Sentence: The writer has a remarkable ability to humanize his characters.

2864. PENNANT - *[spell]*- P E N N A N T
Definition: flag indicating championship
Synonym: banner, flag
Antonym:
Sentence: He hung the pennants from his football days in the living room.

2865. DRAWL - *[spell]*- D R A W L
Definition: talk in a slow way
Synonym:
Antonym:
Sentence: When he spoke, she immediately noticed his Southern drawl.

2866. REPAYABLE - *[spell]*- R E P A Y A B L E
Definition: that can or must be paid
Synonym:
Antonym:
Sentence: He felt that his debt to her was beyond repayable.

2867. PRECOGNITION - *[spell]*- P R E C O G N I T I O N
Definition: direct awareness of the future events or circumstances
Synonym: prediction, foreseeing
Antonym: hindsight, afterthought
Sentence: The psychic claimed to have precognition about the future.

2868. RESIDENCY - *[spell]*- R E S I D E N C Y
Definition: the place where a person lives
Synonym: abode, dwelling
Antonym:
Sentence: He took up residency in his childhood neighborhood.

2869. ADOLESCENCE - *[spell]*- A D O LE S C E N C E
Definition: period of growth from childhood to adulthood
Synonym: pubescence, teenage
Antonym: adulthood, infancy
Sentence: Adolescence is an important time in a young person's life.

2870. INFANTRY - *[spell]*- I N F A N T R Y
Definition: troops trained, equipped and organized to fight on foot
Synonym:
Antonym:
Sentence: The infantry marched toward the enemy lines.

2871. TRANSFUSION - *[spell]*- T R A N S F U S I O N
Definition: act of infusing or instilling
Synonym:
Antonym:

Sentence: The teacher's transfusion of enthusiasm to her students made her a great educator.

2872. REMINISCE - *[spell]*- R E M I N I S C E
Definition: talk or think about past experiences
Synonym: recall, recollect
Antonym: forget, repress
Sentence: His grandparents like to reminisce about the "good old days".

2873. CILIA - *[spell]*- C I L I A
Definition: very small hair-like projections
Synonym:
Antonym:
Sentence: Many insects have cilia on their wings.

2874. MUTATION - *[spell]*- M U T A T I O N
Definition: a change or alteration
Synonym: variation, anomaly
Antonym:
Sentence: The scientists investigated many different genetic mutations in the lab.

2875. EQUABLE - *[spell]*- E Q U A B L E
Definition: changing little
Synonym: steady, constant
Antonym:
Sentence: Over the years, her positive attitude remained equable.

2876. RESTAURANTEUR - *[spell]*- R E S T A U R A N T E U R
Definition: a keeper or owner of a restaurant
Synonym:
Antonym:
Sentence: After being a chef for two decades, he became a prominent restaurateur.

2877. SEMIAQUATIC - *[spell]*- S E M I A Q U A T I C
Definition: often found in water but not living only there
Synonym:
Antonym:
Sentence: Penguins are semiaquatic animals.

2878. ORIFICE - *[spell]*- O R I F I C E
Definition: an opening or hole
Synonym: opening, aperture
Antonym:
Sentence: The police sometimes search bodily orifices to find contraband.

2879. SYLLABIC - *[spell]*- S Y L L A B I C
Definition: of or having to do with parts of words
Synonym:
Antonym:
Sentence: The reading teacher broke the words down into syllabic parts.

2880. RECURRENCE - *[spell]*- R E C U R R E N C E
Definition: happening again
Synonym: repetitive, frequency
Antonym:
Sentence: The recurrence of errors in his report caused his boss to question his work.

2881. RESUMPTION - *[spell]*- R E S U M P T I O N
Definition: a beginning again
Synonym: restart, resurgence
Antonym: ending, finishing
Sentence: After an interruption, the concert's resumption was flawlessly executed.

2882. UNDERWHELM - *[spell]*- U N D E R W H E L M
Definition: to fail to arouse much interest or excitement
Synonym: disappoint, baffle
Antonym:
Sentence: She was completely underwhelmed by the art display.

2883. REMOUNT - *[spell]*- R E M O U N T
Definition: to mount a horse or other animal again
Synonym:
Antonym:
Sentence: After falling off the horse, she was not brave enough to remount.

2884. RECLAMATION - *[spell]*- R E C L A M A T I O N
Definition: the act of taking back
Synonym: repossession, restoration
Antonym:
Sentence: The government's reclamation of the land allowed them to establish a national park.

2885. STATIONARY - *[spell]*- S T A T I O N A R Y
Definition: not movable
Synonym: immobile, motionless
Antonym: movable, active
Sentence: The statue outside of the building was stationary.

2886. ORGANIC - *[spell]*- O R G A N I C
Definition: derived from living organisms
Synonym: natural, biological
Antonym: processed, man-made
Sentence: He ate only organic meats without additives or anything processed.

2887. SHRAPNEL - *[spell]*- S H R A P N E L
Definition: metal fragments
Synonym:
Antonym:
Sentence: The soldier went into surgery immediately in order to remove the shrapnel in his arm that he received from gunfire.

2888. ENTANGLE - *[spell]*- E N T A N G LE
Definition: get into difficulty
Synonym: involve, enmesh
Antonym: exclude, disentangle
Sentence: He found himself entangled in her mother's plot to make amends with her estranged sister.

2889. FORAY - *[spell]*- F O R A Y
Definition: raid for plunder
Synonym: pillage, invasion
Antonym:
Sentence: The pirate's foray was cut short by the troops stationed in the town.

2890. ROUNDEL - *[spell]*- R O U N D E L
Definition: a small, round ornament
Synonym:
Antonym:
Sentence: The doorknobs were decorative roundels.

2891. PREMIER - *[spell]*- P R E M I E R
Definition: first in rank or importance
Synonym: leading, prime
Antonym:
Sentence: The woman was the premier scholar in her field.

2892. ASSURANCE - *[spell]*- A S S U R A N C E
Definition: making certain
Synonym: pledge, affirmation
Antonym: doubt, uncertainty
Sentence: With the assurance of a steady job, she felt a great burden lifted from her shoulders.

2893.   JUNCTURE - *[spell]* - J U N C T U R E
Definition: point or line where two things join
Synonym: crossroad, point
Antonym:
Sentence: At this juncture, it simply would not be practical to buy a new house.

2894.   INCONVENIENT - *[spell]* - I N C O N V E N I E N T
Definition: causing trouble, difficulty, or bother
Synonym: bothersome, troublesome
Antonym: convenient, easy
Sentence: It was inconvenient for him to do the favor for her.

2895.   OBLIQUE - *[spell]* - O B L I Q U E
Definition: not straight up and down or straight across
Synonym: slanting, bent
Antonym: direct, straight
Sentence: She made oblique references to her employer, without mentioning her by name.

2896.   PROVISIONALLY - *[spell]* - P R O V I S I O N A L L Y
Definition: for the time being
Synonym: temporarily, conditionally
Antonym:
Sentence: He was hired provisionally.

2897.   SECT - *[spell]* - S E C T
Definition: group of people having the same principles, beliefs or opinions
Synonym: faction, following
Antonym:
Sentence: A conservative sect formed within the political party.

2898.   PEDIATRIC - *[spell]* - P E D I A T R I C
Definition: of or having to do with a branch of medicine dealing with children's diseases
Synonym:
Antonym:
Sentence: She was a pediatric nurse.

2899.   GLOBAL - *[spell]* - G L O B A L
Definition: of the earth as a whole
Synonym: international, worldwide
Antonym:
Sentence: The war would have global consequences.

2900. DISPLACEMENT - *[spell]*- D I S P L A C E M E N T
Definition: being removed from a usual place or position
Synonym:
Antonym:
Sentence: The new legislation inadvertently caused the displacement of many immigrants.

Hard Words Exercise - 10

2901. CABARET - *[spell]*- C A B A R E T
Definition: restaurant with entertainment such as singing and dancing
Synonym: restaurant
Antonym:
Sentence: Hoping for an exciting night, the couple went to a cabaret.

2902. MEDICINAL - *[spell]*- M E D I C I N A L
Definition: having value as medicine
Synonym: curing, healing
Antonym:
Sentence: The herbs were said to have medicinal value.

2903. IMPART - *[spell]*- I M P A R T
Definition: give a share of
Synonym: give, offer
Antonym: keep, deny
Sentence: The professor imparted her wisdom to all of her students.

2904. DEBILITY - *[spell]*- D E B I L I T Y
Definition: being weak
Synonym: decrepitude, enfeeblement
Antonym: capability, healthfulness
Sentence: Though he experienced debility from his cancer treatment, he did not give up.

2905. TRUNDLE - *[spell]*- T R U N D L E
Definition: to roll along
Synonym: bowl, fling
Antonym:
Sentence: The ball trundled down the hallway.

2906. AVIATION - *[spell]*- A V I A T I O N
Definition: art or science of operating aircraft
Synonym:
Antonym:
Sentence: Being a pilot, he specialized in aviation.

2907. KNICKERS - *[spell]*- K N I C K E R S
Definition: short, loose-fitting trousers that gather at the knees
Synonym: pants, trousers
Antonym:
Sentence: His knickers were strangely unfashionable.

2908. TRANSPOSE - *[spell]*- T R A N S P O S E
Definition: change the position or order of
Synonym: swap, switch
Antonym: keep, hold
Sentence: The writer transposed some paragraphs on the page to make the flow better.

2909. EXECUTIVE - *[spell]*- E X E C U T I V E
Definition: a person who carries out or manages affairs
Synonym: managerial, governing
Antonym: subordinate
Sentence: As an executive of the company, he had power to make many decisions.

2910. PIFFLE - *[spell]*- P I F F L E
Definition: silly talk or behavior
Synonym: nonsense, chatter
Antonym:
Sentence: Her piffle about her experiences at work made him laugh.

2911. DEFUNCT - *[spell]*- D E F U N C T
Definition: no longer in existence
Synonym: extinct, obsolete
Antonym: operating, trendy
Sentence: Cassette tapes have become completely defunct.

2912. ARMAMENT - *[spell]*- A R M A M E N T
Definition: the weapons and equipment used by the military
Synonym: weaponry, arms
Antonym:
Sentence: The military was ill prepared for battle because they lacked the necessary armaments.

2913. IRRELEVANCE - *[spell]*- I R R E L E V A N C E
Definition: being off the subject
Synonym: inapplicability
Antonym: relevant, pertinent
Sentence: The teacher pointed out the irrelevance of the student's argument about why she hadn't done her homework.

2914. ORIGINATE - *[spell]-* O R I G I N A T E
Definition: cause to be
Synonym: invent, commence
Antonym: cease, finish
Sentence: The hurricane originated over the ocean.

2915. FEDERATION - *[spell]-* F E D E R A T I O N
Definition: union of separated states, nations, etc.
Synonym: league, alliance
Antonym: division, separation
Sentence: All of the countries in the region allied themselves in a federation.

2916. INCONSUMABLE - *[spell]-* I N C O N S U M A B L E
Definition: not capable of being used up or eaten
Synonym: inedible
Antonym:
Sentence: The leftovers in the fridge were inconsumable.

2917. BLITHESOME - *[spell]-* B L I T H E S O ME
Definition: happy and cheerful
Synonym: blissful, joyful
Antonym: depressed, troubled
Sentence: She constantly tried to maintain a blithesome attitude.

2918. LUXURIOUS - *[spell]-* L U X U R I O U S
Definition: fond of comforts and beauties of life beyond what is necessary
Synonym: lavish, extravagant
Antonym: barren, destitute
Sentence: He lived a luxurious lifestyle because of his wealth and connections.

2919. TITIAN - *[spell]-* T I T I A N
Definition: auburn or golden red
Synonym: chestnut, copper
Antonym:
Sentence: Her hair was titian in the sun.

2920. ACCELERATOR - *[spell]-* A C C E L E R A T O R
Definition: a means by which to increase speed
Synonym:
Antonym:
Sentence: You always use the accelerator on a car in order to speed up

2921. INDIGESTIBLE - *[spell]-* I N D I G E S T I B L E
Definition: that cannot be digested (to break down food so the body can

absorb it)
Synonym: inedible
Antonym:
Sentence: Because he was lactose intolerant, he found dairy products almost indigestible.

2922. TURMOIL - *[spell]*- T U R M O I L
Definition: state of agitation, confusion, or commotion
Synonym: chaos, riot
Antonym: order, organization
Sentence: The country experienced turmoil after its leader was overthrown.

2923. PERMISSIVE - *[spell]*- P E R M I S S I V E
Definition: not forbidding
Synonym: allowing, permitting
Antonym: forbidding, disallowing
Sentence: Teenagers will typically gravitate to the home with the most permissive parents.

2924. ADORATION - *[spell]*- A D O R A T I O N
Definition: devoted love
Synonym: admiration, cherish
Antonym: abhor, loathe
Sentence: The young man's adoration of his wife was obvious.

2925. INFATUATE - *[spell]*- I N F A T U A T E
Definition: inspire with a foolish or extreme passion
Synonym: captivate, bewitch
Antonym:
Sentence: He was infatuated with her innocent beauty.

2926. SLAPDASH - *[spell]*- S L A P D A S H
Definition: hastily and carelessly
Synonym:
Antonym:
Sentence: The child's slapdash job at picking up her room did not satisfy her parents.

2927. PARSONAGE - *[spell]*- P A R S O N A G E
Definition: house provided for a minister by a church
Synonym:
Antonym:
Sentence: The minister lived in a humble but quaint parsonage.

2928. INCOMPETENCE - *[spell]*- I N C O M P E T E N C E
Definition: lack of ability, power, or fitness
Synonym: inability, ineptitude
Antonym: competence
Sentence: His incompetence was obvious in his work.

2929. URGENCY - *[spell]*- U R G E N C Y
Definition: need for immediate action or attention
Synonym: importance, desperate
Antonym:
Sentence: The urgency of the situation dictated he moved quickly.

2930. BROODY - *[spell]*- B R O O D Y
Definition: inclined to think or worry a long time over something
Synonym: moody, morose
Antonym: cheerful, elated
Sentence: He was broody because of his recent breakup.

2931. MARKETABILITY - *[spell]*- M A R K E T A B I LI T Y
Definition: quality of being able to be sold
Synonym:
Antonym:
Sentence: The marketability of the product made it popular with many retailers.

2932. GHOSTLY - *[spell]*- G H O S T L Y
Definition: pale, dim and shadowy like the spirit of a dead person
Synonym: ghastly, spectral
Antonym:
Sentence: She looked ghostly after witnessing the terrible car accident.

2933. EXHILARATE - *[spell]*- E X H I L A R A TE
Definition: make lively
Synonym: animate, energize
Antonym: deaden, discourage
Sentence: When she was at the magic show, she was exhilarated by the magician's tricks.

2934. BANKRUPT - *[spell]*- B A N K R U P T
Definition: unable to pay one's debt
Synonym: broke, destitute
Antonym: wealthy, rich
Sentence: Because she had lost so much money, she had to declare herself bankrupt.

2935. LECTURE - *[spell]*- L E C T U R E
Definition: a planned speech or talk on a chosen subject given before an audience
Synonym: lesson, speech
Antonym:
Sentence: The students all attended a lecture on ethics.

2936. STRAIGHT-LACED - *[spell]*- S T R A I G H T - L A C E D
Definition: very strict in matters of conduct
Synonym: rigid, conventional
Antonym: lax, relaxed
Sentence: Her grandmother had a reputation as being very straight-laced.

2937. TERMINABLE - *[spell]*- T E R M I N A B L E
Definition: that can be ended
Synonym: fixed, limited
Antonym: indefinite, unfixed
Sentence: Her contract with the company was terminable.

2938. REMEMBRANCE - *[spell]*- R E M E M B R A N C E
Definition: power to recall
Synonym: memory, reminiscence
Antonym:
Sentence: She had a fond remembrance of her father.

2939. FOREMOST - *[spell]*- F O R E M O S T
Definition: first and most notable
Synonym: first
Antonym: last, least
Sentence: Foremost on his list of chores was mowing the lawn.

2940. SINGULARITY - *[spell]*- S I N G U L A R I T Y
Definition: condition or quality of being unusual or remarkable
Synonym: uniqueness, individuality
Antonym: conformity, regularity
Sentence: His singularity when it came to the arts could not be denied.

2941. FOXED - *[spell]*- F O X E D
Definition: discolored or stained
Synonym:
Antonym:
Sentence: The pages of the old book were foxed.

2942. FORTHCOMING - *[spell]*- F O R T H C O M I N G
Definition: about to appear
Synonym: approaching, awaited

Antonym: bygone, distant
Sentence: The forthcoming exam brought a great sense of anxiety for the student.

2943. VANDALISM - *[spell]*- V A N D A L I S M
Definition: deliberately destructive to property
Synonym: destruction, ravaging
Antonym: construction, restoring
Sentence: The teens were arrested for the vandalism of the school.

2944. EMBITTER - *[spell]*- E M B I T T E R
Definition: make hard to bear
Synonym: disillusion
Antonym:
Sentence: She felt embittered over her recent breakup.

2945. HORTICULTURE - *[spell]*- H O R T I C U L T U R E
Definition: science or art of growing flowers, fruits, vegetables and other plants
Synonym: agriculture, cultivation
Antonym:
Sentence: The man specialized in the horticulture of vegetables.

2946. EXPENDABILITY - *[spell]*- E X P E N D A B I L I T Y
Definition: easily replaced; not worth saving
Synonym:
Antonym:
Sentence: Every day, they were reminded of their expendability as employees.

2947. COMPOUND - *[spell]*- C O M P O U ND
Definition: having more than one part
Synonym: amalgam, composite
Antonym: division, separation
Sentence: The quack doctor created a compound of medicines which he claimed could cure anything.

2948. SEAFARER - *[spell]*- S E A F A R E R
Definition: a sailor
Synonym:
Antonym:
Sentence: The seafarer started the motor of his boat.

2949. REBUKE - *[spell]*- R E B U K E
Definition: to express disapproval of
Synonym: reprimand, admonition

Antonym: encouragement, endorsement
Sentence: She rebuked her daughter for her misbehavior at the park.

2950. OVATION - *[spell]*- O V A T I O N
Definition: an enthusiastic public welcome or recognition
Synonym: acclaim, applause
Antonym:
Sentence: The guest speaker received an ovation from the crowd.

2951. GABLE - *[spell]*- G A B L E
Definition: a triangular ornament or canopy over a door or window
Synonym:
Antonym:
Sentence: The house had a gable on the additional wing.

2952. PARANOIA - *[spell]*- P A R A N O I A
Definition: form of psychosis characterized by continuing, elaborate delusions of persecution or grandeur
Synonym:
Antonym:
Sentence: She was institutionalized for her extreme paranoia.

2953. DIFFUSION - *[spell]*- D I F F U S I O N
Definition: act of spreading out over a large space
Synonym: dispersion, dissipation
Antonym: concentration, consolidation
Sentence: The diffusion of the fragrance filled the room.

2954. PIZZAZZ - *[spell]*- P I Z Z A Z Z
Definition: liveliness
Synonym: energy, animation
Antonym: sluggish, slow
Sentence: She tried to add some pizzazz to the room by using bright colors.

2955. DIGNITARY - *[spell]*- D I G N I T A R Y
Definition: person who has a position of honor
Synonym: luminary, star
Antonym:
Sentence: After years of working on peace efforts with a bordering country, the man was considered a dignitary.

2956. ENGROSSING - *[spell]*- E N G R O S S I N G
Definition: occupying one's complete attention
Synonym: captivating, enthralling
Antonym: tedious, uninteresting

Sentence: The movie on TV was so engrossing that she found herself watching it in its entirety.

2957. DIAGNOSTIC - *[spell]*- D I A G N O S T I C
Definition: helping to identify a condition or illness by observation
Synonym:
Antonym:
Sentence: The doctor performed a series of diagnostic tests on the patient.

2958. DISCOURTEOUS - *[spell]*- D I S C O U R T E O U S
Definition: rude
Synonym: impolite, boorish
Antonym: civil, gracious
Sentence: The child's discourteous behavior to the family's guests earned him punishment.

2959. DISENGAGE - *[spell]*- D I S E N G A G E
Definition: free or release from something that holds
Synonym: detach, disentangle
Antonym: attach, connect
Sentence: After he managed to disengage himself from his work, he went home.

2960. TRANSFIGURE - *[spell]*- T R A N S F I G U R E
Definition: to change in form or appearance
Synonym: transmute, convert
Antonym:
Sentence: Over time, success transfigured her into an egotistical person.

2961. BOARDER - *[spell]*- B O A R D E R
Definition: a person who pays for room and/or meals at another person's house
Synonym: tenant, renter
Antonym:
Sentence: The couple took on a boarder to help pay their mortgage.

2962. MANAGERIAL - *[spell]*- M A N A G E R I A L
Definition: having to do with managing
Synonym: directorial, supervisory
Antonym:
Sentence: She was given a managerial position after serving ten years with the company.

2963. CLAUSE - *[spell]*- C L A U S E
Definition: a single provision in a law or contract
Synonym: passage, provision

Antonym:
Sentence: A clause in the contract stated that profits would be divided amongst the three owners.

2964. NEUTRALITY - *[spell]*- N E U T R A L I T Y
Definition: quality or condition of being on neither side of a quarrel or war
Synonym: impartiality
Antonym: partiality, bias
Sentence: The parent struggled to maintain neutrality in the conflict between her children.

2965. FLUTED - *[spell]*- F L U T E D
Definition: having long rounded groves
Synonym:
Antonym:
Sentence: She wanted fluted wine glasses for her wedding.

2966. DESPICABLE - *[spell]*- D E S P I C A B L E
Definition: contemptible
Synonym: disgraceful, disreputable
Antonym: honorable, respectable
Sentence: The man's kidnapping of the child was a despicable act.

2967. BERTH - *[spell]*- B E R T H
Definition: place to sleep on a plane, train or ship
Synonym:
Antonym:
Sentence: After finding her way to the berth, she settled in and quickly fell asleep.

2968. LINEAR - *[spell]*- L I N E A R
Definition: of, in, or like a line, especially a straight line
Synonym: continuous, straight
Antonym:
Sentence: The airplane moved in a linear motion.

2969. CREDIBILITY - *[spell]*- C R E D I B I L I T Y
Definition: being worthy of belief
Synonym: integrity, trustworthiness
Antonym: implausibility, improbability
Sentence: His credibility made his article believable and a worthwhile read.

2970. RECOURSE - *[spell]*- R E C O U R S E
Definition: a turning to for help or protection

Synonym: appealing
Antonym:
Sentence: The refugees went to the government for recourse.

2971. DARKSOME - *[spell]*- D A R K S O M E
Definition: gloomy
Synonym: somber, bleak
Antonym: cheerful, bright
Sentence: With its black drapes and dark walls, the room seemed darksome.

2972. SINCERITY - *[spell]*- S I N C E R I T Y
Definition: freedom from pretense or deceit
Synonym: honesty, candor
Antonym: deceitfulness, insincerity
Sentence: Her sincerity in wishing her ex-boyfriend happiness was questionable.

2973. QUIETUS - *[spell]*- Q U I E T U S
Definition: a final getting rid of something
Synonym: riddance, defeat
Antonym: commencement, beginning
Sentence: With the sale, he was finally able to establish the quietus of his car.

2974. EXPANSIBLE - *[spell]*- E X P A N S I B L E
Definition: that can be made larger
Synonym: extensible, protractible
Antonym:
Sentence: The furniture could be made expansible by attaching additional pieces.

2975. TEMPERAMENT - *[spell]*- T E M P E R A M E N T
Definition: a person's nature or disposition
Synonym: disposition, personality
Antonym:
Sentence: It was clear from a young age that the child had a stubborn temperament.

2976. RELAPSE - *[spell]*- R E L A P S E
Definition: to fall or slip back
Synonym: regression, recurrence
Antonym:
Sentence: After three years of remission, he had a relapse of cancer.

2977. ELUDE - *[spell]*- E L U D E
Definition: avoid or escape by cleverness
Synonym: evade, avoid
Antonym:
Sentence: The child eluded her mother so she wouldn't have to clean the dirty dishes.

2978. CIVIL - *[spell]*- C I V I L
Definition: polite
Synonym: courteous, obliging
Antonym: rude, impolite
Sentence: She accredited his civil manners to his upbringing.

2979. NECROSIS - *[spell]*- N E C R O S I S
Definition: death from injury or disease
Synonym: fatality, death
Antonym: life, birth
Sentence: The mysterious necrosis of the victim was being investigated.

2980. GALL - *[spell]*- G A L L
Definition: too great boldness
Synonym: impudence, arrogance
Antonym: humility, kindness
Sentence: Everyone thought he had some gall to show up to the party uninvited.

2981. CARDIOVASCULAR - *[spell]*- C A R D I O V A S C U L A R
Definition: having to do with the heart and blood vessels
Synonym:
Antonym:
Sentence: Because cardiovascular problems ran in her family, she went to the doctor often.

2982. METHODICAL - *[spell]*- M E T H O D I C A L
Definition: done according to a definite plan
Synonym: deliberate, efficient
Antonym: careless, chaotic
Sentence: She was very methodical in packing up her house to move.

2983. TIPSY - *[spell]*- T I P S Y
Definition: being made to slant or slope easily
Synonym: woozy, unsteady
Antonym: steady, firm
Sentence: She was a bit tipsy after riding the rollercoaster.

2984. DECOMMISION - *[spell]*- D E C O M M I S I O N
Definition: to take out of active service
Synonym: deactivate, retire
Antonym:
Sentence: The vessel was decommissioned after being at sea for nearly fifty years.

2985. HEARTH - *[spell]*- H E A R T H
Definition: stone or brick floor of a fireplace
Synonym: fireside
Antonym:
Sentence: The family gathered around the hearth on the cold winter night.

2986. ENLIVEN - *[spell]*- E N L I V E N
Definition: make active or cheerful
Synonym: animate, brighten
Antonym: depress, discourage
Sentence: Her presence enlivened the party.

2987. COMPLIMENTARY - *[spell]*- C O M P L I M E N T A R Y
Definition: like or pertaining to praising
Synonym: flattering, appreciative
Antonym: blaming, censuring
Sentence: His remarks about her progress were quite complimentary.

2988. SCOWL - *[spell]*- S C O W L
Definition: to look angry or sullen by lowering the eyebrows
Synonym: grimace, glower
Antonym:
Sentence: She scowled at him when he made an offensive suggestion about her work.

2989. EMBASSY - *[spell]*- E M B A S S Y
Definition: the residence of an ambassador to another country and his assistants
Synonym:
Antonym:
Sentence: The ambassador arrived at he embassy just when he was most needed.

2990. TRUNCHEON - *[spell]*- T R U N C H E O N
Definition: a stick shape object for use as a weapon
Synonym: club
Antonym:
Sentence: The law enforcement officer carried a truncheon through the crime scene.

2991. THESIS - *[spell]-* T H E S I S
Definition: proposition or statement to be proved or to be maintained against objections
Synonym: theory, hypothesis
Antonym:
Sentence: The graduate student had to write a lengthy thesis about her studies.

2992. RESURFACE - *[spell]-* R E S U R F A C E
Definition: to rise to the exterior boundary again
Synonym: reappear, reemerge
Antonym:
Sentence: After years of being hidden, the documents resurfaced.

2993. AIRLIFT - *[spell]-* A I R L I F T
Definition: transportation by air
Synonym:
Antonym:
Sentence: Many victims of the flood had to be rescued by airlift.

2994. INQUEST - *[spell]-* I N Q U E S T
Definition: legal inquiry
Synonym: investigation, inquisition
Antonym:
Sentence: The lawyer made an inquest about the man who had been arrested.

2995. BRUTALITY - *[spell]-* B R U T A L I T Y
Definition: conduct that is savagely cruel
Synonym: cruelty, inhumanity
Antonym: kindness, gentleness
Sentence: The brutality of the dictator was known far and wide.

2996. MARTYR - *[spell]-* M A R T Y R
Definition: person who chooses to die or suffer rather than renounce a belief, cause, etc.
Synonym:
Antonym:
Sentence: After his death, he was viewed as a martyr.

2997. OBEDIENCE - *[spell]-* O B E D I E N C E
Definition: a doing what one is told
Synonym: acquiescence, agreement
Antonym: disobedience, misbehavior
Sentence: The dog had to be taken to obedience class.

2998. CANCEROUS - *[spell]*- C A N C E R O U S
Definition: being an evil and harmful thing that tends to spread
Synonym: destructive, harmful
Antonym: beneficial, benign
Sentence: His actions were so cancerous that they began to corrupt everyone in the office.

2999. MELLOW - *[spell]*- M E L L O W
Definition: soft and rich
Synonym: delicate, soothing
Antonym: harsh, rough
Sentence: The mellow music was relaxing.

3000. PLUMAGE - *[spell]*- P L U M A G E
Definition: feathers of a bird
Synonym:
Antonym:
Sentence: The bird had brightly colored plumage.

Conclusion

This concludes the **GED Vocabulary 3000.** We sincerely hope you've enjoyed and gained from your experience. Be sure to go over any sets of words that you may have found difficult.

CPSIA information can be obtained
at www.ICGtesting.com
Printed in the USA
LVHW081356100922
728067LV00029B/747